Biblical Theology

Biblical Theology
Old and New Testaments

GEERHARDUS VOS

WM. B. EERDMANS PUBLISHING COMPANY

ISBN 0-8028-1209-0

Tenth Printing, September 1977

PREFACE

In the words of Thomas Aquinas, Theology *a Deo docetur, Deum docet, ad Deum ducit*.[1] After suffering much from the anti-intellectual and anti-doctrinal temper of our times, Theology is perhaps in somewhat better repute now than during the early years of the present century. This change of attitude is to be welcomed, even though it must be confessed that even in conservative Protestant circles Theology is still far from receiving the attention and respect which, as the knowledge of God, it ought to have.

The present volume is entitled *Biblical Theology – Old and New Testaments*. The term 'Biblical Theology' is really unsatisfactory because of its liability to misconstruction. All truly Christian Theology must be *Biblical* Theology – for apart from General Revelation the Scriptures constitute the sole material with which the science of Theology can deal. A more suitable name would be 'History of Special Revelation', which precisely describes the subject matter of this discipline. Names, however, become fixed by long usage, and the term 'Biblical Theology', in spite of its ambiguity, can hardly be abandoned now.

Biblical Theology occupies a position between Exegesis and Systematic Theology in the encyclopaedia of theological disciplines. It differs from Systematic Theology, not in being more Biblical, or adhering more closely to the truths of the Scriptures, but in that its principle of organizing the Biblical material is historical rather than logical. Whereas Systematic Theology takes the Bible as a completed whole and endeavours to exhibit its total teaching in an orderly, systematic form, Biblical Theology deals with the material from the historical standpoint, seeking to exhibit the organic growth or development of the truths of Special Revelation from the primitive

[1] 'Is taught by God, teaches God, leads to God.'

pre-redemptive Special Revelation given in Eden to the close of the New Testament canon.

The material presented in this volume has previously been issued at various theological institutions in mimeographed form. It is a matter of satisfaction to me that it is being made available to the public in a suitable permanent printed form by the Wm. B. Eerdmans Publishing Company. The editing of the material for the press has been done by my son, the Rev. Johannes G. Vos, who studied this work as a student at Princeton Theological Seminary and is in hearty agreement with the theological viewpoint of the book. It is my hope that this volume may help many ministers and theological students to attain a deeper appreciation of the wonders of the Special Revelation of our God.

Grand Rapids, Michigan   GEERHARDUS VOS
1 September 1948

PUBLISHER'S
NOTE

This new printing, entirely reset in 1975, differs from the original publication only in the introduction of subheadings, the division of the text into shorter paragraphs, and the use of a new scheme for transliteration of the Hebrew words. The content of the book remains entirely the same as in earlier printings.

CONTENTS

The Old Testament

PART ONE
THE MOSAIC EPOCH OF REVELATION

PART TWO
THE PROPHETIC EPOCH OF REVELATION

The New Testament

Contents

The Old Testament

PART ONE
THE MOSAIC EPOCH
OF REVELATION

ONE:

INTRODUCTION: THE NATURE
AND METHOD OF BIBLICAL
THEOLOGY

The best approach towards understanding the nature of Biblical
Theology and the place belonging to it in the circle of theological
disciplines lies through a definition of Theology in general. According
to its etymology, Theology is *the science concerning God*. Other
definitions either are misleading, or, when closely examined, are found
to lead to the same result. As a frequent instance, the definition of
Theology as 'the science of religion' may be examined. If in this
definition 'religion' be understood subjectively, as meaning the
sum-total of religious phenomena or experiences in man, then it is
already included in that part of the science of anthropology which
deals with the psychical life of man. It deals with man, not with God.
If, on the other hand, religion be understood objectively, as the
religion which is normal and of obligation for man because prescribed
by God, then the further question must arise, why God demands
precisely this and no other religion; and the answer to this can be
found only in the nature and will of God; therefore ultimately, in thus
dealing with religion, we shall find ourselves dealing with God.

From the definition of Theology as the science concerning God
follows the necessity of its being based on revelation. In scientifically
dealing with impersonal objects we ourselves take the first step; they
are passive, we are active; we handle them, examine them, experiment
with them. But in regard to a spiritual, personal being this is different.
Only in so far as such a being chooses to open up itself can we come
to know it. All spiritual life is by its very nature a hidden life, a life
shut up in itself. Such a life we can know only through revelation.
If this be true as between man and man, how much more must it be
so as between God and man. The principle involved has been strikingly
formulated by Paul: 'For who among men knoweth the things of a
man, save the spirit of the man which is in him? even so the things of
God none knoweth, save the Spirit of God' [1 *Cor.* 2.11]. The inward

3

hidden content of God's mind can become the possession of man only through a voluntary disclosure on God's part. God must come to us before we can go to Him. But God is not a personal spiritual being *in general*. He is a Being infinitely exalted above our highest conception. Suppose it were possible for one human spirit to penetrate directly into another human spirit: it would still be impossible for the spirit of man to penetrate into the Spirit of God. This emphasizes the necessity of God's opening up to us the mystery of His nature before we can acquire any knowledge concerning Him. Indeed, we can go one step farther still. In all scientific study we exist alongside of the objects which we investigate. But in Theology the relation is reversed. Originally God alone existed. He was known to Himself alone, and had first to call into being a creature before any extraneous knowledge with regard to Him became possible. Creation therefore was the first step in the production of extra-divine knowledge.

Still a further reason for the necessity of revelation preceding all satisfactory acquaintance with God is drawn from the abnormal state in which man exists through sin. Sin has deranged the original relation between God and man. It has produced a separation where previously perfect communion prevailed. From the nature of the case every step towards rectifying this abnormality must spring from God's sovereign initiative. This particular aspect, therefore, of the indispensableness of revelation stands or falls with the recognition of the fact of sin.

DIVISION OF THEOLOGY INTO FOUR GREAT DEPARTMENTS

The usual treatment of Theology distinguishes four departments, which are named Exegetical Theology, Historical Theology, Systematic Theology and Practical Theology. The point to be observed for our present purpose is the position given Exegetical Theology as the first among these four. This precedence is due to the instinctive recognition that at the beginning of all Theology lies a passive, receptive attitude on the part of the one who engages in its study. The assumption of such an attitude is characteristic of all truly exegetical pursuit. It is eminently a process in which God speaks and man listens. Exegetical Theology, however, should not be regarded as confined to Exegesis. The former is a larger whole of which the latter is indeed an important part, but after all only a part. Exegetical Theology in the wider sense comprises the following disciplines:

(*a*) the study of the actual content of Holy Scripture;

(*b*) the inquiry into the origin of the several Biblical writings, including the identity of the writers, the time and occasion of composition, dependence on possible sources, etc. This is called *Introduction*, and may be regarded as a further carrying out of the process of Exegesis proper;

(c) the putting of the question of how these several writings came to be collected into the unity of a Bible or book; this part of the process bears the technical name of *Canonics;*

(d) the study of the actual self-disclosures of God in time and space which lie back of even the first committal to writing of any Biblical document, and which for a long time continued to run alongside of the inscripturation of revealed material; this last-named procedure is called the study of *Biblical Theology.*

The order in which the four steps are here named is, of course, the order in which they present themselves successively to the investigating mind of man. When looking at the process from the point of view of the divine activity the order requires to be reversed, the sequence here being

(a) the divine self-revelation;

(b) the committal to writing of the revelation-product;

(c) the gathering of the several writings thus produced into the unity of a collection;

(d) the production and guidance of the study of the content of the Biblical writings.

DEFINITION OF BIBLICAL THEOLOGY

Biblical Theology is that branch of Exegetical Theology which deals with the process of the self-revelation of God deposited in the Bible.

In the above definition the term 'revelation' is taken as a noun of action. Biblical Theology deals with revelation as a divine activity, not as the finished product of that activity. Its nature and method of procedure will therefore naturally have to keep in close touch with, and so far as possible reproduce, the features of the divine work itself. The main features of the latter are the following:

[1] *The historic progressiveness of the revelation-process*

It has not completed itself in one exhaustive act, but unfolded itself in a long series of successive acts. In the abstract, it might conceivably have been otherwise. But as a matter of fact this could not be, because revelation does not stand alone by itself, but is (so far as Special Revelation is concerned) inseparably attached to another activity of God, which we call *Redemption.* Now redemption could not be otherwise than historically successive, because it addresses itself to

5

the generations of mankind coming into existence in the course of history. Revelation is the interpretation of redemption; it must, therefore, unfold itself in instalments as redemption does. And yet it is also obvious that the two processes are not entirely co-extensive, for revelation comes to a close at a point where redemption still continues. In order to understand this, we must take into account an important distinction within the sphere of redemption itself. Redemption is partly objective and central, partly subjective and individual. By the former we designate those redeeming acts of God, which take place on behalf of, but outside of, the human person. By the latter we designate those acts of God which enter into the human subject. We call the objective acts central, because, happening in the centre of the circle of redemption, they concern all alike, and are not in need of, or capable of, repetition. Such objective-central acts are the incarnation, the atonement, the resurrection of Christ. The acts in the subjective sphere are called individual, because they are repeated in each individual separately. Such subjective-individual acts are re-generation, justification, conversion, sanctification, glorification. Now revelation accompanies the process of objective-central redemption only, and this explains why redemption extends further than revelation. To insist upon its accompanying subjective-individual redemption would imply that it dealt with questions of private, personal concern, instead of with the common concerns of the world of redemption collectively. Still this does not mean that the believer cannot, for his subjective experience, receive enlightenment from the source of revelation in the Bible, for we must remember that continually, alongside the objective process, there was going on the work of subjective application, and that much of this is reflected in the Scriptures. Subjective-individual redemption did not first begin when objective-central redemption ceased; it existed alongside of it from the beginning.

There lies only one epoch in the future when we may expect objective-central redemption to be resumed, viz., at the Second Coming of Christ. At that time there will take place great redemptive acts concerning the world and the people of God collectively. These will add to the volume of truth which we now possess.

[2] *The actual embodiment of revelation in history*
The process of revelation is not only concomitant with history, but it becomes incarnate in history. The facts of history themselves acquire a revealing significance. The crucifixion and resurrection of Christ are examples of this. We must place act-revelation by the side of

word-revelation. This applies, of course, to the great outstanding acts of redemption. In such cases redemption and revelation coincide. Two points, however, should be remembered in this connection: first, that these two-sided acts did not take place primarily for the purpose of revelation; their revelatory character is secondary; primarily they possess a purpose that transcends revelation, having a God-ward reference in their effect, and only in dependence on this a man-ward reference for instruction. In the second place, such act-revelations are never entirely left to speak for themselves; they are preceded and followed by word-revelation. The usual order is: first word, then the fact, then again the interpretative word. The Old Testament brings the predictive preparatory word, the Gospels record the redemptive-revelatory fact, the Epistles supply the subsequent, final interpretation.

[3] *The organic nature of the historic process observable in revelation*
Every increase is progressive, but not every progressive increase bears an organic character. The organic nature of the progression of revelation explains several things. It is sometimes contended that the assumption of progress in revelation excludes its absolute perfection at all stages. This would actually be so if the progress were non-organic. The organic progress is from seed-form to the attainment of full growth; yet we do not say that in the qualitative sense the seed is less perfect than the tree. The feature in question explains further how the soteric sufficiency of the truth could belong to it in its first state of emergence: in the seed-form the minimum of indispensable knowledge was already present. Again, it explains how revelation could be so closely determined in its onward movement by the onward movement of redemption. The latter being organically progressive, the former had to partake of the same nature. Where redemption takes slow steps, or becomes quiescent, revelation proceeds accordingly. But redemption, as is well known, is eminently organic in its progress. It does not proceed with uniform motion, but rather is 'epochal' in its onward stride. We can observe that where great epoch-making redemptive acts accumulate, there the movement of revelation is correspondingly accelerated and its volume increased. Still further, from the organic character of revelation we can explain its increasing multiformity, the latter being everywhere a symptom of the development of organic life. There is more of this multiformity observable in the New Testament than in the Old, more in the period of the prophets than in the time of Moses.

Some remarks are in place here in regard to a current misconstruction of this last-mentioned feature. It is urged that the discovery of so considerable an amount of variableness and differentiation in the Bible must be fatal to the belief in its absoluteness and infallibility. If Paul has one point of view and Peter another, then each can be at best only approximately correct. This would actually follow, if the truth did not carry in itself a multiformity of aspects. But infallibility is not inseparable from dull uniformity. The truth is inherently rich and complex, because God is so Himself. The whole contention ultimately rests on a wrong view of God's nature and His relation to the world, a view at bottom Deistical. It conceives of God as standing outside of His own creation and therefore having to put up for the instrumentation of His revealing speech with such imperfect forms and organs as it offers Him. The didactic, dialectic mentality of Paul would thus become a hindrance for the ideal communication of the message, no less than the simple, practical, untutored mind of Peter. From the standpoint of Theism the matter shapes itself quite differently. The truth having inherently many sides, and God having access to and control of all intended organs of revelation, shaped each one of these for the precise purpose to be served. The Gospel having a precise, doctrinal structure, the doctrinally-gifted Paul was the fit organ for expressing this, because his gifts had been conferred and cultivated in advance with a view to it.

[4] *The fourth aspect of revelation determinative of the study of Biblical Theology consists in its practical adaptability*

God's self-revelation to us was not made for a primarily intellectual purpose. It is not to be overlooked, of course, that the truly pious mind may through an intellectual contemplation of the divine perfections glorify God. This would be just as truly religious as the intensest occupation of the will in the service of God. But it would not be the full-orbed religion at which, as a whole, revelation aims. It is true, the Gospel teaches that to know God is life eternal. But the concept of 'knowledge' here is not to be understood in its Hellenic sense, but in the Shemitic sense. According to the former, 'to know' means to mirror the reality of a thing in one's consciousness. The Shemitic and Biblical idea is to have the reality of something practically interwoven with the inner experience of life. Hence 'to know' can stand in the Biblical idiom for 'to love', 'to single out in love'. Because God desires to be *known* after this fashion, He has caused His revelation to take place in the milieu of the historical life of a people. The circle of revelation is not a school, but a 'covenant'. To speak of revelation as an 'education' of humanity is a rationalistic and utterly un-scriptural way of speaking. All that God disclosed of Himself has come in response to the practical religious needs of His people as these emerged in the course of history.

THE VARIOUS THINGS SUCCESSIVELY DESIGNATED BY THE NAME OF BIBLICAL THEOLOGY

The name was first used to designate a collection of proof-texts employed in the study of Systematic Theology. Next it was appropriated by the Pietists to voice their protest against a hyperscholastic method in the treatment of Dogmatics. Of course, neither of these two usages gave rise to a new distinct theological discipline. This did not happen until a new principle of treatment, marking it off from the disciplines already existing, was introduced. The first to do this was J. P. Gabler in his treatise *De justo discrimine theologiae biblicae et dogmaticae*. Gabler correctly perceived that the specific difference of Biblical Theology lies in its historical principle of treatment. Unfortunately both the impulse of the perception and the manner of its application were influenced by the Rationalism of the school to which he belonged. The chief characteristic of this school was its disrespect for history and tradition and the corresponding worship of Reason as the sole and sufficient source of religious knowledge. A distinction was drawn between (*a*) past beliefs and usages recorded in the Bible as a matter of history and (*b*) what proved demonstrable by Reason. The former was *a priori* rejected as unauthoritative, while the latter was received as truth – not, however, because found in the Bible, but because in agreement with the deliverances of Reason. If the question was put, what use could then possibly be served by its presentation in the Bible, the answer was given that at an earlier stage of development men were not yet sufficiently acquainted with Reason to base on it their religious convictions and practice, and consequently God accommodated Himself to the ancient method of basing belief on external authority, a method now superseded.

It is important to observe that this so-called *Rationalismus Vulgaris* was not (and, so far as it still survives, is not) a purely philosophical or epistemological principle, but has a specifically religious colouring. Rationalism has so long and so violently attacked religion that it cannot seem amiss to turn the tables and for a moment criticize rationalism from the view-point of religion. The main point to notice is its undue self-assertiveness over against God in the sphere of truth and belief. This is a defect in religious endowment. Reception of truth on the authority of God is an eminently religious act. Belief in the inspiration of Scripture can be appraised as an act of worship under given circumstances. This explains why rationalism has by preference asserted itself in the field of religion even more than in that of pure philosophy. This is because in religion the sinful mind of man comes most directly face to face with the claims of an independent, superior authority. Closely looked at, its protest against tradition is a protest against God as the source of tradition, and its whole mode of treatment of Biblical Theology aims not at honouring history as the form of tradition, but at discrediting history and tradition. Further, rationalism is defective, ethically considered, in that it shows a tendency towards glorification of its own present (that is, at bottom, *of itself*) over against the future no less than the past. It reveals a strong sense of having arrived at the acme of development. The glamour of unsurpassability in which rationalism usually sees itself is not calculated to make it expect much from God in the future. In this attitude, the religious fault of self-sufficiency stands out even more pronouncedly than in the attitude towards the past.

It was formerly considered a merit to have stressed the importance of tracing the truth historically, but when this was done with a lack of fundamental piety it lost the right of calling itself theology. The rationalistic brand of Biblical Theology, at the same time that it stresses the historical, declares its product religiously worthless.

To define the issue between ourselves and this type of treatment sharply, we should remember, that it is not a question of the apprehensive function of the reason in regard to religious truth. Man is psychically so constructed that nothing can enter into his knowledge except through the gateway of the reason. This is so true, that it applies equally to the content of Special Revelation as to the ingress of truth from any other source. Nor is it a question about the legitimate functioning of the reason in supplying the mind of man with the content of natural revelation. Still further, reason has its proper place in the thinking through and systematizing of the content of Special Revelation. But the recognition of all this is not identical with nor characteristic of what we technically call rationalism. The diagnosis of the latter lies in the atmosphere of irreligion and practical disdain of God which it carries with itself wherever appearing. The main fault to be found with people of this kind is that to the pious mind their whole outlook towards God and His world appears uncongenial because lacking in the most primary sense the sensorium of religion.

Ever since its birth in this rationalistic environment Biblical Theology has been strongly affected, not only in the way in which philosophical currents have touched Theology in general, but in a special manner to which its nature especially lays it open. This is shown in the extent to which, at the present time, the treatment of Biblical Theology is influenced by the philosophy of evolution. This influence is discernible in two directions. In the first place, the qualitative advancement found by the hypothesis of evolution in the world-process is extended to the emergence of religious truth. It becomes an advance, not only from the lower to the higher, but from the barbarous and primitive to the refined and civilized, from the false to the true, from the evil to the good. Religion, it is held, began with animism; next came polytheism, then monolatry, then monotheism. Such a view, of course, excludes revelation in every legitimate sense of the word. Making all things relative, it leaves no room for the absoluteness of the divine factor.

In the second place, the philosophy of evolution belongs to the family of positivism. It teaches that nothing can be known but phenomena, only the impressionistic side of the world, not the interior objective reality, the so-called 'things in themselves'. Such things as God, the soul, immortality, a future life, etc., cannot enter into human knowledge, which in fact is no knowledge in the old solid sense. Consequently all these objective verities come to be regarded as lying beyond the province of Theology. If the name *Theology* is still retained, it is as a misnomer for a classification and discussion of religious phenomena. The question is no longer as to what is true, but simply as to what has been believed and practised in the past. Alongside of this general camouflage of the science of religion under the name of Theology, and inseparable from it, runs the turning inside out of Biblical Theology in particular. This becomes the phenomenology of the religion recorded in the literature of the Bible.

GUIDING PRINCIPLES

Over against these perversive influences it is of importance clearly to lay down the principles by which we propose to be guided in our treatment of the matter. These are:

(a) the recognition of the infallible character of revelation as essential to every legitimate theological use made of this term. This is of the essence of Theism. If God be personal and conscious, then the in-inference is inevitable that in every mode of self-disclosure He will make a faultless expression of His nature and purpose. He will communicate His thought to the world with the stamp of divinity on it. If this were otherwise, then the reason would have to be sought in His being in some way tied up in the limitations and relativities of the world, the medium of expression obstructing His intercourse with the world. Obviously the background of such a view is not Theism but pantheism.

(b) Biblical Theology must likewise recognize the objectivity of the groundwork of revelation. This means that real communications came from God to man *ab extra*. It is unfair to pass this off with a contemptuous reference to the 'dictation' view. There is nothing undignified in dictation, certainly not as between God and man. Besides, it is unscientific, for the statements of the recipients of revelation show that such a process not seldom took place.

Our position, however, does not imply that all revelation came after this objective fashion. There is an ingredient which may properly be called 'subjective revelation'. By this is meant the inward activity of the Spirit upon the depths of human sub-consciousness causing certain God-intended thoughts to well up therefrom. The Psalms offer examples of this kind of revelation, and it also occurs in the Psalmodic pieces found here and there in the prophets. Although brought up through a subjective channel, we none the less must claim for it absolute divine authority; otherwise it could not properly be called revelation. In this subjective form revelation and inspiration coalesce. We must, however, be on our guard against the modern tendency to reduce all revelation in the Scriptures to this category of the *ab intra*. That is usually intended to deprive revelation of its infallibility. A favourite form is to confine revelation proper to the bare acts of self-disclosure performed by God, and then to derive the entire thought-content of the Bible from human reflection upon these acts. Such a theory, as a rule, is made a cover for involving the whole teaching of the Bible in the relativity of purely human reflection, whose divine provenience cannot any longer be verified, because there is nothing objective left to verify it by.

The belief in the joint-occurrence of objective and subjective revelation is not a narrow or antiquated position; it is in reality the only broad-minded view, since it is willing to take into account all the facts. The offence at 'dictation' frequently proceeds from an under-estimate of God and an over-estimate of man. If God condescends to give us a revelation, it is for Him and not for us *a priori* to determine what forms it will assume. What we owe to the dignity of God is that we shall receive His speech at full divine value.

(c) Biblical Theology is deeply concerned with the question of inspiration. All depends here on what we posit as the object with which our science deals. If its object consist in the beliefs and practices of men in the past, then obviously it is of no importance whether the subject matter be considered as true in any other or higher sense than that of a reliable record of things once prevailing, no matter whether inherently true or not. A Biblical Theology thus conceived ought to classify itself with Historical Theology, not with Exegetical Theology. It professes to be a History of Doctrine for Biblical times. It treats Isaiah as it would treat Augustine, the sole question being what was believed, not whether it was true or not. Our conception of the discipline, on the other hand, considers its subject matter from the point of view of revelation from God. Hence the factor of inspiration needs to be reckoned with as one of the elements rendering the things studied 'truth' guaranteed to us as such by the authority of God.

Nor should it be objected that in this way we can postulate inspiration for so much in the Bible only as pertains to the special occasions when God engaged in the act of revelation, so that as Biblical theologians we could profess indifference at least to the doctrine of 'plenary inspiration'. The conception of partial inspiration is a modern figment having no support in what the Bible teaches about its own make-up. Whenever the New Testament speaks about the inspiration of the Old, it is always in the most absolute, comprehensive terms. Consulting the consciousness of the Scriptures themselves in this matter, we soon learn that it is either 'plenary inspiration' or nothing at all. Further, we have found that revelation is by no means confined to isolated verbal disclosures, but embraces facts. These facts moreover are not of a subordinate character: they constitute the central joints and ligaments of the entire body of redemptive revelation. From them the whole receives its significance and colouring. Unless, therefore, the historicity of these facts is vouched for, and that in a more reliable sense than can be done by mere historical research, together with the facts the teaching content will become subject to a degree of uncertainty rendering the revelation value of the whole doubtful. The trustworthiness of the revelations proper entirely depends on that of the historical setting in which they appear.

Again it should be remembered that the Bible gives us in certain cases a philosophy of its own organism. Paul, for instance, has his views in regard to the revelation structure of the Old Testament. Here the question of full inspiration, extending also to the historical teaching of Paul, becomes of decisive importance. If we believe that Paul was inspired in these matters, then it ought greatly to facilitate our task in producing the revelation structure of the Old Testament. It were superfluous labour to construct a separate view of our own. Where that is attempted, as it is by a certain school of Old Testament criticism, the method does not rest on an innocent view about the negligibility of the factor of inspiration, but on the outright denial of it.

OBJECTIONS TO THE NAME 'BIBLICAL THEOLOGY'

We shall now consider the objections that have been made to the name *Biblical Theology*.

(a) The name is too wide, for, aside from General Revelation, all Theology is supposed to rest on the Bible. It suggests a droll degree of presumption to preempt this predicate 'Biblical' for a single discipline.

(b) If it be answered that 'Biblical' need not be understood of an exceptional claim to Biblical provenience, but only concerns a peculiar method employed, viz., that of reproducing the truth in its original Biblical form without subsequent transformation, then our reply must be that, on the one hand, this of necessity would seem to cast a reflection on other theological disciplines, as though they were guilty of manipulating the truth, and that, on the other hand, Biblical Theology claims too much for itself in professing freedom from transforming treatment of the Scriptural material. The fact is that Biblical Theology just as much as Systematic Theology makes the material undergo a transformation. The sole difference is in the principle on which the transformation is conducted. In the case of Biblical Theology this is historical, in the case of Systematic Theology it is of a logical nature. Each of these two is necessary, and there is no occasion for a sense of superiority in either.

(c) The name is incongruous because ill-adjusted to the rest of our theological nomenclature. If we first distinguish the four main branches of theology by prefixing to the noun 'Theology' an adjective ending in '-al', and then proceed to name a subdivision of one of these four on the same principle, calling it Biblical Theology, this must create confusion, because it suggests five instead of four main departments, and represents as a coordination what in reality is a subordination.

For all these reasons the name 'History of Special Revelation' is greatly to be preferred. It expresses with precision and in an uninvidious manner what our science aims to be. It is difficult, however, to change a name which has the sanction of usage.

THE RELATION OF BIBLICAL THEOLOGY TO OTHER DISCIPLINES

We must now consider the relation of Biblical Theology to other disciplines of the theological family.

(*a*) Its relation to Sacred (Biblical) History. This is very close. Nor can it fail to be so, since both disciplines include in their consideration material which they have in common with each other. In Sacred History redemption occupies a prominent place, and to deal with redemption without drawing in revelation is not feasible, for, as shown above, certain acts are both redemptive and revelatory at the same time. But the same is true *vice versa*. Revelation is so interwoven with redemption that, unless allowed to consider the latter, it would be suspended in the air. In both cases, therefore, the one must trespass upon the other. Still logically, although not practically, we are able to draw a distinction as follows: in reclaiming the world from its state of sin God has to act along two lines of procedure, corresponding to the two spheres in which the destructive influence of sin asserts itself. These two spheres are the spheres of being and of knowing. To set the world right in the former, the procedure of redemption is employed; to set it right in the sphere of knowing, the procedure of revelation is used. The one yields Biblical History, the other Biblical Theology.

(*b*) Its relation to Biblical Introduction. As a rule Introduction has to precede. Much depends in certain cases on the date of Biblical documents and the circumstances of their composition for determining the place of the truth conveyed by them in the scheme of revelation. The chronology fixed by Introduction is in such cases regulative for the chronology of Biblical Theology. This, however, does not mean that the tracing of the gradual disclosure of truth cannot reach behind the dating of a document. The Pentateuch records retrospectively what unfolding of revelation there was from the beginning, but it also contains much that belongs to the chapter of revelation to and through Moses. These two elements should be clearly distinguished. So much for the cases where Biblical Theology depends on the antecedent work of Introduction. Occasionally, however, the order between the two is reversed. Where no sufficient external evidence exists for dating a document, Biblical Theology may be able to render assistance through pointing out at which time the revelation content of such a writing would best fit in with the progress of revelation.

(*c*) Its relation to Systematic Theology. There is no difference in that one would be more closely bound to the Scriptures than the other. In this they are wholly alike. Nor does the difference lie in this, that the one transforms the Biblical material, whereas the other would leave it unmodified. Both equally make the truth deposited in the Bible undergo a transformation: but the difference arises from the fact that the principles by which the transformation is effected differ. In Biblical Theology the principle is one of historical, in Systematic Theology it is one of logical construction. Biblical Theology draws a *line* of development. Systematic Theology draws a *circle*. Still, it should be remembered that on the line of historical progress there is at several points already a beginning of correlation among elements of truth in which the beginnings of the systematizing process can be discerned.

THE METHOD OF BIBLICAL THEOLOGY

The method of Biblical Theology is in the main determined by the principle of historic progression. Hence the division of the course of revelation into certain periods. Whatever may be the modern tendency towards eliminating the principle of periodicity from historical science, it remains certain that God in the unfolding of revelation has regularly employed this principle. From this it follows that the periods should not be determined at random, or according to subjective preference, but in strict agreement with the lines of cleavage drawn by revelation itself. The Bible is, as it were, conscious of its own organism; it feels, what we cannot always say of ourselves, its own anatomy. The principle of successive *Berith*-makings (Covenant-makings), as marking the introduction of new periods, plays a large role in this, and should be carefully heeded. Alongside of this periodicity principle, the grouping and correlation of the several elements of truth within the limits of each period has to be attended to. Here again we should not proceed with arbitrary subjectivism. Our dogmatic constructions of truth based on the finished product of revelation, must not be imported into the minds of the original recipients of revelation. The endeavour should be to enter into their outlook and get the perspective of the elements of the truth as presented to them. There is a point in which the historic advance and the concentric grouping of truth are closely connected. Not seldom progress is brought about by some element of truth, which formerly stood in the periphery, taking its place in the centre. The main problem will be how to do justice to the individual peculiarities of the agents in revelation. These individual traits subserve the historical plan. Some propose that we discuss each book separately. But this leads to unnecessary repetition, because there is so much that all have in common. A better plan is to apply the collective treatment in the earlier stages of revelation, where the truth is not as yet much differentiated, and then to individualize in the later periods where greater diversity is reached.

PRACTICAL USES OF THE STUDY OF BIBLICAL THEOLOGY

It remains to say something about the practical uses of the study of Biblical Theology. These may be enumerated as follows:

(*a*) It exhibits the organic growth of the truths of Special Revelation. By doing this it enables one properly to distribute the emphasis among the several aspects of teaching and preaching. A leaf is not of the same importance as a twig, nor a twig as a branch, nor a branch as the trunk of the tree. Further, through exhibiting the organic structure of revelation, Biblical Theology furnishes a special argument from design for the reality of Supernaturalism.

(*b*) It supplies us with a useful antidote against the teachings of rationalistic criticism. This it does in the following way: The Bible exhibits an organism of its own. This organism, inborn in the Bible itself, the critical hypothesis destroys, and that not only on our view, but as freely acknowledged by the critics themselves, on the ground of its being an artificial organism in later times foisted upon the Bible, and for which a newly discovered better organism should be substituted. Now by making ourselves in the study of Biblical Theology thoroughly conversant with the Biblical consciousness of its own revelation structure, we shall be able to perceive how radically criticism destroys this, and that, so far from being a mere question of dates and composition of books, it involves a choice between two widely divergent, nay, antagonistic conceptions of the Scriptures and of religion. To have correctly diagnosed criticism in its true purpose is to possess the best prophylaxis against it.

(*c*) Biblical Theology imparts new life and freshness to the truth by showing it to us in its original historic setting. The Bible is not a dogmatic handbook but a historical book full of dramatic interest. Familiarity with the history of revelation will enable us to utilize all this dramatic interest.

(*d*) Biblical Theology can counteract the anti-doctrinal tendency of the present time. Too much stress proportionately is being laid on the voluntary and emotional sides of religion. Biblical Theology bears witness to the indispensability of the doctrinal groundwork of our religious fabric. It shows what great care God has taken to supply His people with a new world of ideas. In view of this it becomes impious to declare belief to be of subordinate importance.

(*e*) Biblical Theology relieves to some extent the unfortunate situation that even the fundamental doctrines of the faith should seem to depend mainly on the testimony of isolated proof-texts. There exists a higher ground on which conflicting religious views can measure themselves as to their Scriptural legitimacy. In the long run that system will hold the field which can be proven to have grown organically from the main stem of revelation, and to be interwoven with the very fibre of Biblical religion.

(*f*) The highest practical usefulness of the study of Biblical Theology is one belonging to it altogether apart from its usefulness for the student. Like unto all theology it finds its supreme end in the glory of God. This end it attains through giving us a new view of God as displaying a particular aspect of His nature in connection with His historical approach to and intercourse with man. The beautiful statement of Thomas Aquinas is here in point: (*Theologia*) *a Deo docetur, Deum docet, ad Deum ducit.*

TWO:
THE MAPPING OUT OF THE
FIELD OF REVELATION

In the mapping out of the field of revelation, the main distinction to be drawn is that between General and Special Revelation. General Revelation is also called Natural Revelation, and Special Revelation called Supernatural Revelation. These names explain themselves. General Revelation comes to all for the reason that it comes through nature. Special Revelation comes to a limited circle for the reason that it springs from the sphere of the supernatural through a specific self-disclosure of God. It seems best to define the relation between the two separately (*a*) as that relation existed prior to, and apart from sin, and (*b*) as it exists in a modified form under the regime of sin.

First, then, we consider the relation apart from sin. Nature from which natural revelation springs consists of two sources, nature within and nature without.

God reveals Himself to the inner sense of man through the religious consciousness and the moral conscience. He also reveals Himself in the works of nature without. It is obvious that the latter must rest on the former. If there were no antecedent innate knowledge of God, no amount of nature-observation would lead to an adequate conception of God. The presupposition of all knowledge of God is man's having been created in the image of God. On the other hand, the knowledge from inner nature is not complete in itself apart from the filling-out it receives through the discovery of God in nature. Thus first does it receive its richness and concreteness. The Bible recognizes these facts. It never assumes, even in regard to the heathen, that man must be taught the existence of God or a god. When it exhorts to know God, this simply means to become acquainted with Him through knowing what He is.

Now to this antecedent knowledge from the two sources of nature there can be added a supernatural self-disclosure. This is something we usually associate with redemption, but this is not exclusively so.

We here consider it apart from man's need of redemption. The main thing to notice is that it adds a content of knowledge which nature as such could not produce. This is the very reason why it is called supernatural.

Next we take account of the manner in which the relations described are affected and modified through the entrance of sin. It is a mistake to think that the sole result of the fall was the introduction of a supernatural revelation. As we shall presently see, supernaturalism in revelation, though its need was greatly accentuated by sin, did not first originate from the fact of sin. But, sin entering in, the structure of natural revelation itself is disturbed and put in need of correction. Nature from within no longer functions normally in sinful man. Both his religious and his moral sense of God may have become blunted and blinded. And the finding of God in nature without has also been made subject to error and distortion. The innate sense of God as lying closer to the inner being of man is more seriously affected by this than his outward observation of the writing of God in nature. Hence the exhortation addressed in Scripture to the heathen, that they shall correct their foolish pre-conceptions of the nature of God through attention to the works of creation, e.g., Isa. 40.25, 26; Psa. 94.5–11. The main correction, however, of the natural knowledge of God cannot come from within nature itself: it must be supplied by the supernaturalism of redemption. Redemption in a supernatural way restores to fallen man also the normalcy and efficiency of his cognition of God in the sphere of nature. How true this is may be seen from the fact that the best system of Theism, i.e. Natural Theology, has not been produced from the sphere of heathenism, however splendidly endowed in the cultivation of philosophy, but from Christian sources. When we produce a system of natural knowledge of God, and in doing so profess to rely exclusively on the resources of reason, this is, of course, formally correct, but it remains an open question whether we should have been able to produce such a thing with the degree of excellence we succeed in imparting to it, had not our minds in the natural exercise of their faculties stood under the correcting influence of redemptive grace.

The most important function of Special Revelation, however, under the regime of sin, does not lie in the correction and renewal of the faculty of perception of natural verities; it consists in the introduction of an altogether new world of truth, that relating to the redemption of man. The newness here, as compared with the supernatural revelation in the state of rectitude, relates to both the form and content, and, further, also affects the manner in which the supernatural approach of God to man is received. As to the form of direct intercourse, this is objectified. Previously there was the most direct spiritual fellowship; the stream of revelation flowed uninterruptedly, and there was no need of storing up the waters in any reservoir wherefrom to draw subsequently. Under the rule of redemption an external embodiment is created to which the divine intercourse with man attaches itself. The objective products of redemption in facts and institutions are a reminder of this changed manner of divine approach.

The same change is observable in the perpetuation of the divine manifestations received in the past. Where an ever-flowing stream of revelation was always accessible, there existed no need of providing for the future remembrance of past intercourse. But a necessity is created for this in the looser, more easily interrupted, only in principle restored, fellowship under the present enjoyment of redemption. Hence the essential content of the new redemptive revelation is given a permanent form, first through tradition, then through its inscripturation in sacred, inspired writings. Neither for this objectivity of the content, nor for this stability of the form will there be any further need in the perfected state of things at the end. As to the newness in the content, this is the direct result of the new reaction of the divine attitude upon the new factor of sin. A different aspect of the divine nature is turned towards man. Many new things belong to this, but they can all be subsumed under the categories of justice and grace as the two poles around which henceforth the redeeming self-disclosure of God revolves. All the new processes and experiences which the redeemed man undergoes can be brought back to the one or the other of these two.

It should be emphasized, however, that in this world of redemption the substance of things is absolutely new. It is inaccessible to the natural mind as such. To be sure, God does not create the world of redemption without regard to the antecedent world of nature, nor does He begin His redemptive revelation *de novo*, as though nothing had preceded. The knowledge from nature, even though corrupted, is presupposed. Only, this does not involve that there is a natural transition from the state of nature to the state of redemption. Nature cannot unlock the door of redemption.

Finally, sin has fundamentally changed the mood of man in which he receives the supernatural approach of God. In the state of rectitude this was not a mood of fear, but of trustful friendship; in the state of sin the approach of the supernatural causes dread, something well to be distinguished from the proper reverence with which man at all times ought to meet God, and which is inseparable from the act of religion as such.

In the foregoing it has been assumed for the sake of distinction that before the fall there existed a form of Special Revelation, transcending the natural knowledge of God. This is the point at which to explain its possibility, its necessity and its concrete purpose. Its subject matter will be afterwards discussed. The possibility and necessity flow from the nature of religion as such. Religion means personal intercourse between God and man. Hence it might be *a priori* expected that God would not be satisfied, and would not allow man to be satisfied with an acquaintance based on indirection, but would crown the process of religion with the establishment of face-to-face communion, as friend holds fellowship with friend.

The same conclusion may be drawn from the concrete purpose God had in view with this first form of supernaturalism. This is connected with the state in which man was created and the advance from this to a still higher estate. Man had been created perfectly good in a moral sense. And yet there was a sense in which he could be raised to a still higher level of perfection. On the surface this seems to involve a contradiction. It will be removed by closely marking the aspect in regard to which the advance was contemplated. The advance was meant to be from unconfirmed to confirmed goodness and blessedness; to the confirmed state in which these possessions could no longer be lost, a state in which man could no longer sin, and hence could no longer become subject to the consequences of sin. Man's original state was a state of indefinite probation: he remained in possession of what he had, so long as he did not commit sin, but it was not a state in which the continuance of his religious and moral status could be guaranteed him. In order to assure this for him, he had to be subjected to an intensified, concentrated probation, in which, if he remained standing, the status of probation would be forever left behind. The provision of this new, higher prospect for man was an act of condescension and high favour. God was in no wise bound on the principle of justice to extend it to man, and we mean this denial not merely in the general sense in which we affirm that God owes nothing to man, but in the very specific sense that there was nothing in the nature of man nor of his creation, which by manner of implication could entitle man to such a favour from God. Had the original state of man involved any title to it, then the knowledge concerning it would probably have formed part of man's original endowment. But this not being so, no innate knowledge of its possibility could be expected. Yet the nature of an intensified and concentrated probation required that man should be made acquainted with the fact of the probation and its terms. Hence the necessity of a Special Revelation providing for this.

THE DIVISION OF REDEMPTIVE SPECIAL REVELATION 'BERITH'

This is what we call in dogmatic language 'The Covenant of Grace', whilst the pre-redemptive Special Revelation is commonly given the name of 'The Covenant of Works'. Care should be taken not to identify the latter with 'The Old Testament'. The Old Testament belongs after the fall. It forms the first of the two divisions of the covenant of grace. The Old Testament is that period of the covenant of grace which precedes the coming of the Messiah, the New Testament that period of the covenant of grace which has followed His appearance and under which we still live. It will be observed that the phraseology 'Old Testament' and 'New Testament', 'Old Covenant' and 'New Covenant', is often interchangeably used. This creates confusion and misunderstanding. For this reason, as well as for the sake of the subject itself, the origin and meaning of these phrases require careful attention. The Hebrew word rendered by the above nouns is *berith*. The Greek word is *diatheke*. As to *berith*, this in the Bible never means 'testament'. In fact the idea of 'testament' was entirely unknown to the ancient Hebrews. They knew nothing of a 'last will'. From this, however, it does not follow that the rendering 'covenant' would be indicated in all places where *berith* occurs. *Berith* may be employed where as a matter of fact a covenant in the sense of agreement is referred to, which is more than can be said for 'testament'. Only the reason for its occurrence in such places is never that it relates to an agreement. That is purely incidental. The real reason lies in the fact that the agreement spoken of is concluded by some special religious sanction. This, and not its being an agreement, makes it a *berith*. And similarly in other connections. A purely one-sided promise or ordinance or law becomes a *berith*, not by reason of its inherent conceptual or etymological meaning, but by reason of the religious sanction added. From this it will be understood that the outstanding characteristic of a *berith* is its unalterableness, its certainty, its eternal validity, and not (what would in certain cases by the very opposite) its voluntary, changeable nature. The *berith* as such is a 'faithful *berith*', something not subject to abrogation. It can be broken by man, and the breach is a most serious sin, but this again is not because it is the breaking of an agreement in general; the seriousness results from the violation of the sacred ceremony by which its sanction was effected.

DIATHEKE

With the Greek word *diatheke* the matter stands somewhat differently. The rendering of *berith* by this word amounted to a translation-compromise. *Diatheke* at the time when the Septuagint and the New Testament came into existence not only could mean 'testament', but such was the current meaning of the word. It was, to be sure, not its original meaning. The original sense was quite generic, viz., 'a disposition that some one made for himself' (from the middle form of the verb *diatithemi*). The legal usage, however, referring it to a testamentary disposition had monopolized the word. Hence the difficulty with which the Greek translators found themselves confronted. In making their choice of a suitable rendering for *berith* they took a word to whose meaning of 'last will' nothing in the Hebrew Bible corresponded. And not only this, the word chosen seemed to connote the very opposite of what the Hebrew *berith* stood for. If the latter expressed unchangeableness, 'testament' seemed to call up the idea of changeableness at least till the moment when the testator dies. Moreover the very term 'testament' suggests the death of the one who makes it, and this must have appeared to render it unsuitable for designating something into which God enters. When notwithstanding all these difficulties, they chose *diatheke*, weighty reasons must have determined them.

The principal reason seems to have been that there was a far more fundamental objection to the one other word that might have been adopted, the word *syntheke*. This word suggests strongly by its very form the idea of coequality and partnership between the persons entering into the arrangement, a stress quite in harmony to the genius of Hellenic religiosity. The translators felt this to be out of keeping with the tenor of the Old Testament Scriptures, in which the supremacy and monergism of God are emphasized. So, in order to avoid the misunderstanding, they preferred to put up with the inconveniences attaching to the word *diatheke*. On closer reflection these were not insurmountable. Though *diatheke* meant currently 'last will', the original generic sense of 'disposition for oneself' cannot have been entirely forgotten even in their day. The etymology of the word was too perspicuous for that. They felt that *diatheke* suggested a sovereign disposition, not always of the nature of a last will, and restored this ancient signification. And in this way they not merely overcame an obstacle; they also registered the positive gain of being able to reproduce a most important element in the Old Testament consciousness of religion.

The difficulty arising from the fact of God's not being subject to death is a difficulty only from the standpoint of Roman law. The Roman-law testament actually is not in force except where death has taken place, cp. Heb. 9.16. There existed, however, in those times a different type of testament, that of Graeco-Syrian law. This kind of testament had no necessary association with the death of the testator. It could be made and solemnly sanctioned during his life-time, and in certain of its provisions go into immediate effect. The other objection arising from the mutability of the Roman-law testament fell away likewise under this other conception. For not only was changeability foreign to it; on the contrary, the opposite idea of unchangeableness entered in strongly [cp. *Gal.* 3.15].

From the Septuagint the word *diatheke* passed over into the New Testament. The question has long been under debate whether here it should be rendered by 'covenant' or by 'testament'. The A.V. in as many as 14 instances translates *diatheke* by 'testament', in all other cases by 'covenant'. The R.V. has greatly modified this tradition. In every passage, except Heb. 9.16, where the statement allows no escape from 'testament', it has substituted 'covenant' for the 'testament' of the A.V. In all probability an exception ought likewise to have been made for Gal. 3.15, where, if not the explicit statement of Paul, at least the connection leads us to think of 'testament'. The Revisers were obviously guided in this matter by the desire to assimilate as much as possible the modes of statement in the Old Testament to those in the New Testament. This was in itself a laudable desire, but it seems that in certain cases it prevented due consideration of the exegetical requirements. Since the R.V. was made, the tendency of scholarship has on the whole favoured 'testament' rather than 'covenant'. There are passages still under debate, for instance those recording the institution of the Lord's supper, where a further return to 'testament' may seem advisable.

The distinction between a 'former *berith*' and a 'new *berith*', or an 'old *diatheke*' and a 'new *diatheke*', is found in the Bible in the following passages: Jer. 31.31; the words of institution of the supper; and a number of times, with varying phraseology, in the Epistle to the Hebrews. It is, of course, in none of these passages a *literature* distinction, corresponding to our traditional distinction between the two parts of the canon. It could not be this, because when these passages were written no second division of the canon was yet in existence.

Sometimes 2 Cor. 3.14 is quoted as a Biblical instance of the canonical distinction, because Paul speaks of the 'reading' of the old *diatheke*. It is assumed that to the reading of the old *diatheke* a reading of a new *diatheke* must correspond. In that case we should have here a prophetic foreknowledge on Paul's part of the approaching formation of a second, a new, canon. This, while not impossible, is not likely. Vs. 15 shows why Paul speaks of a 'reading' of the old *diatheke*. It is the reading of Moses, i.e., the reading of the law. Since the law is frequently called a *berith*, a *diatheke*, Paul could call its reading a reading of the old *diatheke*, and yet not suggest that a second canon was in the making. There was an old *berith*, which existed in written form, there was likewise a new *berith*, but the latter is not yet represented as likewise destined to receive written form.

The comparison is between two equally completed things, not between two things of which the one possesses completeness, the other still awaits it. The whole distinction is between two *dispensations*, two arrangements, of which the one is far superior to the other. The designation of the two canons may later have support in this Pauline passage; nevertheless it rests on an inexact interpretation. At first, even long after Paul, other terms seem to have been used for distinguishing the two parts of Scripture. Tertullian still speaks of the Old and New 'Instrument'.

Finally, it should be noted that, when the Bible speaks of a two-fold *berith*, a twofold *diatheke*, it means by the 'old' covenant not the entire period from the fall of man to Christ, but the period from Moses to Christ. Nevertheless, what precedes the Mosaic period in the description of Genesis may be appropriately subsumed under the 'Old Covenant'. It is meant in the Pentateuch as a preface to the account of the Mosaic institutions, and the preface belongs within the cover of the book. Likewise the 'New Testament' in the soteric, periodical sense of the word goes beyond the time of the life of Christ and the Apostolic age; it not only includes us, but extends into and covers the eschatological, eternal state.

THREE:
THE CONTENT OF
PRE-REDEMPTIVE SPECIAL
REVELATION

We understand by this, as already explained, the disclosure of the principles of a process of probation by which man was to be raised to a state of religion and goodness, higher, by reason of its unchangeableness, than what he already possessed. Everything connected with this disclosure is exceedingly primitive. It is largely symbolical, that is, not expressed in words so much as in tokens; and these tokens partake of the general character of Biblical symbolism in that, besides being means of instruction, they are also typical, that is, sacramental, prefigurations conveying assurance concerning the future realization of the things symbolized. The symbolism, however, does not lie in the account as a literary form, which would involve denial of the historical reality of the transactions. It is a real symbolism embodied in the actual things. The modern mythological interpretation can at this point render us this service, that it affirms the intention of the mythopoeic mind to relate in the myths actual occurrences.

FOUR PRINCIPLES

Four great principles are contained in this primeval revelation, each of them expressed by its own appropriate symbol. These were:
[1] the principle of life in its highest potency sacramentally symbolized by the tree of life;
[2] the principle of probation symbolized in the same manner by the tree of knowledge of good and evil;
[3] the principle of temptation and sin symbolized in the serpent;
[4] the principle of death reflected in the dissolution of the body.

[1] *The principle of life and what is taught concerning it by the tree of life*
The tree of life stands in the midst of the garden. The garden is 'the garden of God', not in the first instance an abode for man as such, but specifically a place of reception of man into fellowship with God in God's own dwelling-place. The God-centred character of religion

27

finds its first, but already fundamental, expression in this arrangement. [cp. *Gen.* 2.8; *Ezek.* 28.13, 16]. The correctness of this is verified by the recurrence of this piece of symbolism in eschatological form at the end of history, where there can be no doubt concerning the principle of paradise being the habitation of God, where He dwells in order to make man dwell with Himself. But this symbolism of paradise with its God-centred implication appears in still another form in the Prophets and the Psalter, viz., connected with the streams so significantly mentioned in Genesis as belonging to the garden of God, here also in part with eschatological reference. The prophets predict that in the future age waters will flow from Jehovah's holy mountain. These are further described as waters of life, just as the tree is a tree of life. But here also the waters flow from near the dwelling-place of Jehovah (His mountain), even as the tree stood in the midst of the garden. Still in the Apocalypse we read of the streams of the water of life proceeding from the throne of God in the new Jerusalem, with trees of life on either side. It will be observed that here the two symbolisms of the tree of life and the waters of life are interwoven. For the Psalter, cp. Psa. 65.9; 46.4, 5. The truth is thus clearly set forth that life comes from God, that for man it consists in nearness to God, that it is the central concern of God's fellowship with man to impart this. In the sequel the same principle appears in negative form through the expulsion of sinful man from paradise.

From the significance of the tree in general its specific use may be distinguished. It appears from Gen. 3.22, that man before his fall had not eaten of it, while yet nothing is recorded concerning any prohibition which seems to point to the understanding that the use of the tree was reserved for the future, quite in agreement with the eschatological significance attributed to it later. The tree was associated with the higher, the unchangeable, the eternal life to be secured by obedience throughout his probation. Anticipating the result by a present enjoyment of the fruit would have been out of keeping with its sacramental character. After man should have been made sure of the attainment of the highest life, the tree would appropriately have been the sacramental means for communicating the highest life. After the fall God attributes to man the inclination of snatching the fruit against the divine purpose. But this very desire implies the understanding that it somehow was the specific life-sacrament for the time after the probation. According to Rev. 2.7 it is to 'him that overcometh' that God promises to give of the tree of life in the midst of his paradise. The effort to obtain the fruit after the fall would have meant a desperate

28

attempt to steal the fruit where the title to it had been lost [cp. *Gen.* 3.22].

[2] *The second principle: Probation and what is taught concerning it in*
the symbolism of the tree of knowledge of good and evil

This tree also stands in the midst of the garden [cp. *Gen.* 2.9 and 3.3]. There is more mystery and hence far greater difference of opinion concerning this tree than there is about the tree of life.

(*a*) First there is the mythical interpretation. It takes the tree as a piece of pagan mythology introduced into the Biblical record. The idea is a thoroughly pagan one, that of the jealousy of the gods lest man should obtain something felt by them to be a private divine privilege. This result is meant to be inherently connected with the eating of the fruit: the prohibition of eating aims at the withholding from man of what is called the 'knowledge of good and evil'. As to what this knowledge of good and evil was supposed by the myth to consist in, is not interpreted by all in the same way. According to one view it was understood by the myth as the rise of man from the purely animal state in which he existed to the plane of reasonable, human existence. The gods wanted him to remain an animal, and therefore forbade the eating of the reason-imparting fruit.

According to another view the myth puts the original state of man higher; he was endowed with reason from the first. Only, he existed in a state of barbarism below all culture. The gods wanted to keep this rise to civilization from man, considering it a privilege of their own. According to these forms, then, of the mythical interpretation, the motive ascribed to the gods by the framer of the myth was the same; the difference comes in through the varying interpretation of what the 'knowledge of good and evil' was conceived to be.

An objection that may be urged against this common feature of the two forms, viz., the ascription of jealousy to the Deity, is, so far as the Biblical account is concerned, as follows: God is represented as having Himself planted the tree in the garden. This would amount to a solicitation of the very same evil result that His jealousy sought to prevent. Moreover the actual result ill accords with the situation expected in this pagan version of the narrative. After man has actually eaten of the tree, God does not act as though He had anything to fear from the encroachment of man. He retains His absolute superiority. As a poor, helpless sinner, man stands before God.

The objections to the second form of the mythical version of the account according to which the rise to a state of 'culture' was the prohibited thing are several. First of all, this view rests on the sub-ethical, physical interpretation of the phrase 'to know good and evil'. It must on this view bear the sense of knowing what is beneficial and what is harmful in the physical sphere, otherwise the obtaining of the knowledge of good and evil could not stand for progress in civilization. Now our contention is not that the phrase in question cannot and never does have the physically oriented significance. We even grant that such seems to have been an ancient application of the phrase before it was specifically applied to the ethical sphere. Not to know good and evil describes the immaturity of childhood, and also the post-maturity, the dotage of old age, when people are said to have become childish [cp. *Deut.* 1.39; *Isa.* 7.15, 16]. But our contention is this, that the phrase does have also the specific sense of maturity in the ethical sphere [cp. 2 *Sam.* 14.17, 20]; and further that the import of the narrative here requires us to take it in that sense. The concrete symptom from which in the sequel the knowledge of good and evil is illustrated is the sense of nakedness, and nakedness not as an injurious, uncomfortable state, but as something arousing sensations of an ethical kind.

A further objection against this second form of the mythical version may be drawn from the prominent part woman is represented to have played in the transaction. Would an Oriental myth-maker have given this role to a member of what is in the Orient usually regarded as the inferior sex? Could woman be regarded in such a circle as more efficient than man in the advancement of civilization? Agriculture, one of the most powerful factors in the progress of civilization, is represented in the account as a punishment, not as something desirable from man's point of view, withheld from him by the gods. In order to escape from these difficulties, of which the force cannot be denied, some writers propose to cut up the narrative into two sections, finding in the one the representation of divine jealousy roused by the fear of man's advance in culture, and in the other an account of man's fall into sin as the traditional interpretation assumes. Into this critical phase of the question we cannot enter here.

Dismissing, then, this mythological version of the account, we proceed to examine:

(*b*) a second interpretation of the tree, and of the phrase 'knowledge of good and evil' connected with it. This view attaches itself to the linguistic observation that in Hebrew 'to know' can signify 'to choose'. The name would then really mean 'the tree of the choice of good and evil'. Some keep this in the general form of 'the tree by means of which man was to make his choice of good or evil'. This would be equivalent to 'the probation-tree'. Others give a peculiar sinister sense to the word 'knowing', making it to mean 'the independent autonomous choice over against God's direction of what was good and what was evil for man'. This makes the name of the tree one of evil omen anticipating the disastrous result. In itself this would not be impossible, although it could hardly be considered a likely view. An objection, however, lies in this, that an arbitrary twist is thus given to the verb 'to know', when it is made to mean not 'to choose' in general, with a neutral connotation, but particularly 'to choose presumptuously', for which no evidence can be quoted. The most serious obstacle to the whole view, in both of its forms, arises from this, that it takes 'knowledge' as descriptive of an act, the act of 'choosing', not as descriptive of a state, the acquaintance with good and evil. Now in the sequel the symbol of the 'knowledge of good and evil' is found in the consciousness of nakedness, and nakedness stands not for an act but for a condition.

Thus we are led to the view most commonly held in the past: (c) the tree is called the tree of 'knowledge of good and evil', because it is the God-appointed instrument to lead man through probation to that state of religious and moral maturity wherewith his highest blessedness is connected. The physical meaning of the phrase has been transferred to the spiritual sphere. On this view the name does not prejudge the result. To attain to a knowledge of good and evil is not necessarily an undesirable and culpable thing. It could happen in a good way, in case man stood in probation, no less than in an evil way, in case man fell. The name is neutral as to its import. That this is so frequently overlooked is due to the prohibitive form which the probation-test assumed. Because man was forbidden to eat of the tree associated with the knowledge of good and evil, it has been rashly assumed that the knowledge of good and evil was forbidden him. Obviously there is in this a confusion of thought. The prohibitive form of the test has quite a different cause, as will be presently shown.

If now we enquire how the maturity designated as 'knowledge of good and evil' was to be attained, either in a desirable or in an undesirable sense, regard must be had first of all to the exact form of the phrase in Hebrew. The phrase is not 'knowledge of the good and the evil'. It reads, literally translated: 'knowledge of good-and-evil', i.e., of good and evil as correlated, mutually conditioned conceptions. Man was to attain something he had not attained before. He was to learn the good in its clear opposition to the evil, and the evil in its clear opposition to the good. Thus it will become plain how he could attain to this by taking either fork of the probation-choice. Had he stood, then the contrast between good and evil would have been vividly present to his mind: the good and evil he would have known from the new illumination his mind would have received through the crisis of temptation in which the two collided. On the other hand, had he fallen, then the contrast of evil with good would have even more vividly impressed itself upon him, because the remembered experience of choosing the evil and the continuous experience of doing the evil, in contrast with his memory of the good, would have shown most sharply how different the two are. The perception of difference in which the maturity consisted related to the one pivotal point, whether man would make his choice for the sake of God and of God alone.

Of course, it is possible to go back of the *mere command* of God for finding the bottom-reason for why a thing is good and evil. This bottom-reason lies in the *nature* of God regulating His command. But in the present instance it was not a question of the ultimate theology or metaphysic of evil and good. For the simple practical purpose of this first fundamental lesson it was necessary only to stake everything upon the unreasoned will of God. And there was a still further reason why this should be done. If the inherent nature of good and evil had been drawn into the scope of the test, then it would have resulted in a choice from instinct alone rather than in a choice of a deliberate character. But it was precisely the purpose of the probation to raise man for a moment from the influence of his own ethical inclination to the point of a choosing for the sake of personal attachment to God alone.

Too much is often made of the purely autonomous movement of ethics, eliminating as unworthy the unexplained, unmotivated demand of God. To do the good and reject the evil from a reasoned insight into their respective natures is a noble thing, but it is a still nobler thing to do so out of regard for the nature of God, and the noblest thing of all is the ethical strength, which, when required, will act from personal attachment to God, without for the moment enquiring into these more abstruse reasons. The pure delight in obedience adds to the ethical value of a choice. In the present case it was made the sole determinant factor, and in order to do this an arbitrary prohibition was issued, such as from the very fact of its arbitrariness excluded every force of instinct from shaping the outcome.

From the true conception of the purpose of the tree we must distinguish the interpretation placed upon it by the tempter according to Gen. 3.5. This carries a twofold implication: first that the tree has in itself, magically, the power of conferring knowledge of good and evil. This lowers the plane of the whole transaction from the religious and moral to the pagan-magical sphere. And secondly, Satan explains the prohibition from the motive of envy. This also we have already found to be a piece of pagan-mythological interpretation. Again, the divine statement in Gen. 3.22 alludes to this deceitful representation of the tempter. It is ironical.

[3] *The principle of temptation and sin symbolized in the serpent*
There is a difference between probation and temptation, and yet they appear here as two aspects of the same transaction. The close inter-weaving reflects itself even in the use of identical words for trying and tempting both in Hebrew and Greek. We may say that what was from the point of view of God a probation was made use of by the evil power to inject into it the element of temptation. The difference consists in this, that behind the probation lies a good, behind the temptation an evil, design, but both work with the same material. It is, of course, necessary to keep God free from tempting anybody with evil intent [cp. *James* 1.13]. But it is also important to insist upon the probation as an integral part of the divine plan with regard to humanity. Even if no tempter had existed, or projected himself into the crisis, even then some form for subjecting man to probation would have been found, though it is impossible for us to surmise what form.

The problem arises, how we must conceive of the role played by the serpent in the fall, and of its traditional connection with an evil spirit. There are varying views in regard to this. Quite in keeping with the modern aversion to much Biblical realism in general, many are inclined to understand the entire account as a piece of allegorizing, which in the intent of the writer was not meant to describe a single occurrence but the ever-repeated efforts of sin to find an entrance into the human heart. The serpent then becomes a symbol or allegory with the rest. This view is contrary to the plain intent of the narrative; in Gen. 3.1, the serpent is compared with the other beasts God had made; if the others were real, then so was the serpent. In vs. 14 the punishment is expressed in terms requiring a real serpent.

Others have gone to the opposite extreme of asserting that there was nothing but a serpent. The terms used in the passages just quoted would certainly fit better into this than into the allegorical view. But it ill accords with the Scriptural teaching on the animal world in general to conceive of a simple serpent as speaking. The Bible always upholds against all pantheizing confusion the distinction between man who speaks and the animals who do not speak, Balaam's ass forming the only exception on record.

It therefore becomes necessary to adopt the old, traditional view according to which there were present both a real serpent and a demonic power, who made use of the former to carry out his plan. So far from there being anything impossible in this, it finds a close analogy in the demoniacs of the Gospels, through whose mouths demons speak. Recent archaeological scholarship has at this point vindicated the correctness of the old exegesis, for in the Babylonian representations there appears often behind the figure of the serpent the figure of a demon. Besides, there is ample Biblical testimony for the presence of an evil spirit in the temptation.

True, the Old Testament throws no light upon the subject. This is for the twofold reason that, on the one hand, the fall is seldom referred to, and, on the other hand, the whole subject of evil spirits and of 'the Satan', 'the adversary' is long kept in darkness. For reference to the fall cp. Job 31.33; Hos. 6.7; Ezek. 28.1–19. For reference or allusion to the 'Evil Spirit' cp. 'the Satan' in Job; in 1 Chron. 21.1. Evil spirits in general appear, 1 Sam. 16; 1 Ki. 22. In none of these passages, however, is the first entrance of evil into the world of men brought into connection with Satan. For the first time, so far as we know, this is done in the Apocryphal book of 'Wisdom', where in 11.24, it is stated: 'By the envy of Satan death entered into the world'. In later Jewish writings also Sammael (The Angel of Death) is called 'The Old Serpent'. In the New Testament we have the words of Jesus to the Jews, John 8.44, where in the reference to the Devil he is represented as both a liar and a murderer from the beginning. This must refer to the temptation. 'The father thereof', i.e., of lying, means the primordial liar. Further, 'your father the devil' alludes to the phrase 'your seed' addressed to the serpent [Gen. 3.15]. So does the phrase 'children of the Wicked One' in Matt. 13.38. Paul in Rom. 16.20 understands of Satan what in the curse is made the serpent's punishment, viz., his being bruised under foot. 1 John 3.8 says that the Devil sins from the beginning. In Rev. 12.9, Satan is called 'the great dragon, the old serpent'.

It is said of the serpent that it was more subtle than any other beast of the field. This finds in its subtlety the reason of its fitness for serving as the demon's instrument. If Satan had appeared bluntly and boldly, the temptation would have been much less alluring. The tempter addresses himself to the woman, probably not because she is more open to temptation and prone to sin, for that is hardly the conception of the Old Testament elsewhere. The reason may have lain in this, that the woman had not personally received the prohibition from God, as Adam had; cp. 2.16, 17.

The process of the temptation divides itself in two stages. In both the central purpose of the tempter is the injection of doubt into the woman's mind. But the doubt suggested in the first stage is of an apparently innocent kind, a doubt as to the question of fact. Yet there is already mixed with this a carefully disguised allusion to the far more serious kind of doubt consisting in the distrust of God's word recognized as such. In the second stage of the temptation this serious form of doubt casts off all disguise, because in the meanwhile the woman has in principle given entrance to the thought so skilfully put before her at the beginning. In the first stage it is at the start a mere question of fact: 'Yea, has God said?' Has the prohibition been actually issued? Still even here the suggestion of a more serious aspect of the matter lies in the words 'of every tree in the garden'. In this phrasing the Serpent hints at the possibility that, should such a prohibition have been actually issued, God has made it far too sweeping through excluding man from the use of the fruit of every tree.

Now the woman reacts to this in two distinct ways. First, as to the question of bare facts, she repudiates the intimation of no prohibition having been actually issued: 'God had said'. At the same time she rejects the suggestion, as though God had ignominiously extended the scope of the prohibition to all the trees: 'We may eat of the fruit of the trees of the garden.' And yet in the more or less indignant form of this denial there already shines through that the woman had begun to entertain the possibility of God's restricting her too severely. And by entertaining this, even for a moment, she had already begun to separate in principle between the rights of God and her own rights. In doing this she has admitted the seed of the act of sinning into her heart. And still further, in this direction goes the inexact form of her quoting the words of God: 'ye shall not eat of it, neither shall ye touch it.' In this unwarranted introduction of the denial of the privilege of 'touching' the woman betrays a feeling, as though after all God's measures may have been too harsh.

Satan does not fail to follow up the advantage thus gained. Entering boldly upon the second stage of the temptation he now seeks to awaken in the woman doubt in the pronounced form of distrust of the word of God recognized as such: 'Ye shall not surely die'. In the Hebrew of these words the placing of the negative at the opening of the sentence should be observed. Where for emphasis' sake the infinitive

35

and a finite verb are put together, and to this a negation is added, the negation usually stands between. Had this been followed here, the correct rendering would have been: 'Ye shall surely not die'. This would merely have cast doubt on the fulfilment of the threat. On the other hand the unusual construction followed makes it to mean: 'It is not so (what God has said), this: ye shall surely die'. This is intended to give the lie to God's utterance in the most pointed manner. And to the temptation to charge God with lying the reasons for the likelihood of His lying is added, viz., God is one whose motives make His word unreliable. He lies from selfishness; 'For God does know that in the day ye eat thereof, then your eyes shall be opened, and ye shall be as God, knowing good and evil'.

Thus prepared, the woman needs only the inducement of the delicious appearance of the fruit, apparently confirming the beneficial effect ascribed to its eating, for committing the overt act of sin. It is not, however, the mere sensual appetite that determines her choice, for her motive was complex; 'She saw that the tree was good for food, and that it was a delight to the eyes, and that the tree was to be desired to make one wise'. In part at least, the pivotal motive of the act was identical with the pivotal motive that gave strength to the temptation. It has been strikingly observed that the woman in yielding to this thought virtually put the tempter in the place of God. It was God who had beneficent purposes for man, the serpent had malicious designs. The woman acts on the supposition that God's intent is unfriendly, whilst Satan is animated with the desire to promote her well-being.

[4] *The principle of death symbolized by the dissolution of the body*
According to Gen. 2.17, God said: 'Of the tree of knowledge of good and evil thou shalt not eat of it: for in the day that thou eatest thereof thou shalt surely die' [cp. 3.3]. On the basis of these words the belief of all ages has been that death is the penalty of sin, that the race became first subject to death through the commission of the primordial sin. At present many writers take exception to this, largely on scientific grounds. With these as such we have here nothing to do. But, as is frequently the case, strenuous attempts are made to give such a turn to the Biblical phrases as to render them compatible with what science is believed to require, and not only this, some proceed to the assertion that the Scriptural statements compel acceptance of the findings of science.

Attempts of this kind make for poor and forced exegesis. Scripture has a right to be exegeted independently from within; and only after its natural meaning has been thus ascertained, can we properly raise the question of agreement or disagreement between Scripture and science. In the present case the 'posthumous' exegetical arguments depended upon to make the Bible teach in the account of the fall that man was created subject to death, deserve examination as examples of this type of exegesis. They are the following:

Firstly, the tree of life is represented as something from which man had not yet eaten; therefore he was not yet endowed with life and consequently was subject to death.

Secondly, in Gen. 3.19, it is, we are told, explicitly affirmed that man's return to dust is natural: 'till thou return unto the ground, for out of it wast thou taken: for dust thou art, and unto dust thou shalt return'.

Thirdly, Gen. 2.17 proves that the sense of the threatening was not, sin will cause thee to die; but simply: sin will subject thee to instantaneous, premature death: '*in the day* thou eatest thereof thou shalt surely die'.

Now each of these three arguments rests on careless exegesis. The first fails to distinguish between the life man had in virtue of creation and that higher unlosable life to be attained through probation. Of the latter the tree of life was the probable prospective sacrament. That it had not as yet been eaten of could not signify such an absence of life in general as would involve the necessity of death. Man enjoyed fellowship with God in the garden, and God is according to our Lord's statement not a God of the dead but of the living [Lk. 20.38].

The second argument, in order to prove the point, would have to be wrenched from its context. The words 'dust thou art, and unto dust thou shalt return' occur in a curse. If they expressed a mere declaration of the natural working out of man's destiny, as created mortal, there would be nothing of a curse in them. Nor is it possible to say here that premature death is the element of curse involved. The preceding words forbid this, since they speak of a slow process of exhausting labour issuing unto death. The conjunction 'till' is not simply chronological, as though the words could mean: 'thou wilt have to endure hard labour up till the moment of death.' The force is climactic: 'thy hard labour will finally slay thee'. In man's struggle with the soil, the soil will conquer and claim him. Consequently, if the second half of the statement implied the naturalness of death, it would be in contradiction with the first, where returning to dust is represented as a curse. But what then do the final words, which clearly connect creation from dust with return to it, mean? The simple explanation lies in this, that they declare not the natural lot of death, but explain particularly the form in which the curse of death had been expressed in the foregoing, viz., the form of a return to dust. And this was due to the form in which the curse had been described: hard, fatal struggle with the soil. Now the closing words explain not that death must come, but why, when it comes, it will assume that specific form of a return to dust. In other words not death as such, but the manner of death is here brought into connection with the creation. Had man been created otherwise, and through sin death supervened, then death might have assumed a different form. Death is adjusted in its form to the natural, material constitution of man, but it does not spring as a necessity from this natural, material constitution.

Finally the stressing of the phrase 'in the day' in 2.17, is not only uncalled for, but, in view of the sequel of the narrative, impossible. As a threat of immediate, premature death the words have not been fulfilled, and that God subsequently mitigated or modified the curse, there is nothing whatever to suggest. Some knowledge of Hebrew idiom is sufficient to show that the phrase in question simply means 'as surely as thou eatest thereof'. Close conjunction in time is figuratively used for inevitable eventuation. Our English idiom is not unacquainted with this form of expression [cp. 1 *Ki.* 2.37].

MORTALITY AND IMMORTALITY

It may be well to define the several senses in which man can be called 'mortal' or 'immortal' in order to clear the situation as to his natural state, in regard to which so much trouble arises from confusion of thought. 'Immortality' in philosophical language may express the persistence of the soul, which, even when the body is dissolved, retains its identity of individual being. In this sense every human being is under all circumstances 'immortal', and so were our first parents created; so were they after the fall. Next, 'immortality' is used in theological terminology for that state of man in which he has nothing in him which would cause death. It is quite possible that at the same time an abstract contingency of death may overhang man, i.e., the bare possibility may exist of death in some way, for some cause, invading him, but he has nothing of it within him. It is as if we should say of somebody that he is liable to the invasion of some disease, but we should not on that account declare him to have the disease. In this second sense it can be appropriately said that man as created was 'immortal', but not that after the fall he was so, for through the act of sinning the principle of death entered into him; whereas before he was only liable to die under certain circumstances, he now inevitably had to die. His immortality in the first sense had been lost. Again, 'immortality' can designate, in eschatological language, that state of man in which he has been made immune to death, because immune to sin. Man was not, in virtue of creation, immortal in this highest sense: this is a result of redemption accompanied by eschatological treatment. Such 'immortality' is the possession, first of all of God, who has it by nature [cp. 1 *Tim.* 6.16]; next of the glorified human nature of Christ, who has it in virtue of his resurrection; next of the regenerate, here already in principle [*John* 11.26], and, of course, in their heavenly state.

At the hand of this definition of the various senses of 'immortality', as applying to the various stages or states in the history of man, it now becomes easy to determine in which of them, and in what sense, he was 'mortal'. In the first sense he is never mortal. In the second sense or stage he was immortal and mortal both, according to the definition employed: mortal as not yet lifted above the contingency of death, but non-mortal as not carrying death as a disease within himself. Here, therefore, immortality and mortality coexisted. In the third stage he is in no sense (except the first, philosophical one) anything else but mortal: he must die; death works in him. In the fourth stage, finally, the word 'mortal' has only a qualified application to the regenerate man, viz., in so far as during his earthly state death still exists and works in his body, whilst from the centre of his renewed spirit it has been in principle excluded, and supplanted by an immortal life, which is bound in the end to overcome and extrude death. In this case the coexistence of mortality and immortality is based on the bipartite nature of man.

If, then, death is actually the punishment of sin, not merely according to later Pauline teaching [*Rom.* 5.12], whose import to that effect no one denies, but according to the account of Genesis itself, the question arises: what kind or form of death? Since in theology several aspects of death have come to be distinguished, it can but conduce to clearness to put the question, even though the answer is not easy to give. If there was a symbol here, as in the case of the three other great principles of the revelation, and the symbol is always something concretely external, the answer indicated would seem to be, the reference is to bodily death. But, it is asked, how could there be such a symbolical significance of bodily death, before death was in the world? Some have pointed to the death of animals as occurring regularly before the fall of man. This cannot be discussed here, because the account gives no suggestion to that effect. So far as the language employed goes, it seems necessary to think proximately of momentary, bodily death. The Hebrew words cannot be translated 'thou shalt become mortal or 'thou shalt begin to die'. Nevertheless a deeper conception of death seems to be hinted at. It was intimated that death carried with it separation from God, since sin issued both in death and in the exclusion from the garden. If life consisted in communion with God, then, on the principle of opposites, death may have been interpretable as separation from God. In this way preparation would be made for the working out of the idea of death in a more internal sense. An allusion to the connection of death with the separation from God is found in vs. 23: 'God sent him forth to till the ground from whence he was taken'. 'Tilling the ground from whence he was taken' contains an unmistakable reminder of vs. 19. In other words: expulsion from the garden (i.e. from God's presence) means expulsion to death. The root of death is in having been sent forth from God.

FOUR:
THE CONTENT OF THE
FIRST REDEMPTIVE
SPECIAL REVELATION

The term 'redemption' is used by anticipation. It does not occur until the Mosaic period. We employ it for convenience' sake. The characteristics of God's saving approach to, and dealing with, man immediately appear. Both justice and grace are turned towards fallen man. The justice is shown in the penal character of the three curses pronounced; the grace for mankind lies implicitly in the curse upon the Tempter. It is, however, clearly present in the whole manner of God's seeking and interrogating man after the fall. In every one of its features this breathes the spirit of One who prepared for the ultimate showing of grace. We can further observe at this point how Special Revelation attaches itself to General Revelation. The feelings of shame and fear were produced in fallen man by General Revelation. To this God attaches Himself in His interview with man, which was Special Revelation.

The shame arising from nakedness is in its sexual form the most primitive mode in which the loss of innocence reveals itself. Various theological explanations have been worked out in regard to this. According to some, the physical nakedness is the exponent of the inner nakedness of the soul, deprived of the divine image. According to others the shame of sin is localized where it is in order to bring out that sin is a race matter. According to still others, shame is the reflex in the body of the principle of corruption introduced by sin into the soul. Shame would then be the instinctive perception of the degradation and decay of human nature. But for none of these views can we claim the authority of the account itself. It should be noted, however, that the shame and fear operate with reference to God. The man and the woman hide themselves, not from each other, but from the presence of God. The divine interrogation reduces the sense of shame and fear to its ultimate root in sin. God does not permit man to treat the physical as if it were sufficient reason for his sensation, but compels man to recognize in it the reflex of the ethical.

THE THREE CURSES

The three curses are pronounced in the same sequence as that in which the sin had been committed. In the curse upon the serpent lies a promise of victory over the serpent and his seed. His being condemned to go on his belly enables the woman's seed to bruise his head, whilst the serpent can only bruise the heel of the seed of the woman. The principle of ultimate victory is further resolved into its principal elements in the formulation given to this curse. They are the following: (a) The divine initiative in the work of deliverance. The emphasis rests on the pronoun: God says 'I will put enmity'. Here is not primarily an appeal to man but a divine promise. Nor does God merely instigate or promote enmity; He sovereignly *puts* it.

(b) The essence of the deliverance consists in a reversal of the attitude assumed by man towards the serpent and God respectively. Man in sinning had sided with the serpent and placed himself in opposition to God. Now the attitude towards the serpent becomes one of hostility; this must carry with it a corresponding change in man's attitude towards God. God being the mover in the warfare against Satan, man, joining in this, becomes plainly the ally of God.

(c) The continuity of the work of deliverance is declared; the enmity extends to the *seed* of the woman and of the serpent. God's promise is to the effect that he will keep up the enmity in the line of human descent and will not allow it to die out. The phrase, 'seed of the woman' indicates that the organism of the race will be drawn within the circle of redemption, which does not, of course, mean that all individuals are to become enemies of the serpent. The point is that God saves not merely individual men, but the seed of the woman.

With reference to the seed of the serpent, there are two views. According to one, this phrase designates that part of the human race which continues on the side of the serpent. In that case, 'seed' is used metaphorically. The objection to this is that thus the seed of the serpent would at the same time be part of the seed of the woman, whereas the two appear distinctly separated. To this it has been answered that henceforth only the allies of God constitute the true humanity; that they alone deserve the name of the 'seed of the woman'. It seems more plausible to seek the seed of the serpent outside of the human race. The power of evil is a collective power, a kingdom of evil, of which Satan is the head. The evil spirits are called a seed of the serpent to assimilate the figure to that in the corresponding clause. While not descended from Satan by physical propagation, they derive from him their nature.

(*d*) The issue of the enmity is foretold. In the R.V. the text-rendering reads, 'he shall *bruise* thy head, and thou shalt *bruise* his heel'. But in the margin, as an alternative translation, is given, 'he shall *lie in wait* for thy head, thou shalt *lie in wait* for his heel'. The verb, in Hebrew, is *shuf* and the marginal rendering makes this equivalent to *sha'af*. This originally means 'to snap at' something, then 'to seek to snap at' something, i.e. 'to lie in wait' for it. The verb *shuf* occurs, outside of this passage, only twice in the Old Testament [*Job* 9.17; *Psa.* 139.11]. The text in the Psalter seems incapable of meaning either 'to bruise' or 'to lie in wait for'. But in Job the sense of bruising seems indicated. To the text-rendering it is objected that, while appropriate as from the seed of the woman to the serpent, it is not the natural verb for describing what is done by the serpent. This objection is not serious. If one were to substitute for the idea of 'bruising' that of 'lying in wait for', the same result would follow, viz., its fitting the one clause and not the other. Besides this, nothing would be said in that case concerning the issue of the struggle. Both in Greek and Aramaic the words for 'beating' and 'striking' are used of bites and stings. Perhaps also the verb in the second clause is repeated from the first in order that the same expression might be retained. In Rom. 16.20, Paul uses the word 'bruising' with evident allusion to the passage before us. Observe that the pronoun 'it' in 'It shall bruise thy head', has for its antecedent 'the seed of the woman', not, as the Vulgate would have it, the woman herself, a rendering which has led some Romanist commentators to find the Virgin Mary here.

'SEED'

As to the word 'seed' there is no reason to depart from the collective sense in either case. The seed of the serpent *must* be collective, and this determines the sense of the seed of the woman. The promise is, that somehow out of the human race a fatal blow will come which shall crush the head of the serpent. Still, indirectly the possibility is hinted at that in striking this fatal blow the seed of the woman will be concentrated in one person, for it should be noticed that it is not the seed of the serpent but the serpent itself whose head will be bruised. In the former half of the curse the two seeds are contrasted; here the woman's seed and the serpent. This suggests that as at the climax of the struggle the serpent's seed will be represented by the serpent, in the same manner the woman's seed may find representation in a single person; we are not warranted, however, in seeking an exclusively personal reference to the Messiah here, as though He alone were meant by 'the woman's seed'. Old Testament Revelation approaches the concept of a personal Messiah very gradually. It sufficed for fallen man to know that through His divine power and grace God would bring out of the human race victory over the serpent. In that faith could rest. The object of their faith was much less definite than that of ours, who know the personal Messiah. But none the less, the essence of this faith, subjectively considered, was the same, viz., trust in God's grace and power to bring deliverance from sin.

HUMAN SUFFERING

Finally, we note the revelation of justice in the curses upon the woman and the man. The woman is condemned to suffer in what constitutes her nature as woman. (For the precise construction or possible emendation of the Hebrew text, cp. Dillmann's Commentary, *in loco*.) The element of grace interwoven with this consists in the implication that, notwithstanding the penalty of death, the human race will be enabled to propagate itself. The punishment of man consists in toil unto death. Not labour as such is a penalty, for man had been placed in the garden to dress it and to keep it. But *painful* labour, death-bringing labour is referred to. This applies to labour in general, but the form in which the curse puts it is derived from the most primitive form of labour, that of tilling the soil. At the same time, this brings out the idea that man must henceforth labour for the most necessary food. His will be a veritable struggle for subsistence. In the sweat of his face shall he eat bread, and 'bread', perhaps, instead of meaning food in general, has reference specifically to food produced from the soil, in contrast to the more easily procured earlier nourishment, the fruit of the garden. Nothing is said about a subjective deterioration in man, making his labour heavy and in the end fatal. The cause assigned is objective, viz., the productivity of nature is impaired. Cursed is the ground for man's sake; it brings forth thorns and thistles; here the element of grace mingling with the curse consists in that the bread will after all be bread; it will sustain life. As the woman is enabled to bring new life into the world, so the man will be enabled to support life by his toil.

FIVE:
THE NOACHIAN REVELATION
AND THE DEVELOPMENT
LEADING UP TO IT

Two features characterize the revelation of this period. In the first place, its significance lies not in the sphere of redemption, but in the sphere of the natural development of the race, although it has ultimately an important bearing on the subsequent progress of redemption. Secondly, revelation here bears on the whole a negative rather than positive character. It contents itself with bestowing a *minimum* of grace. A minimum could not be avoided either in the sphere of nature or of redemption, because in the former sphere, without at least some degree of divine interposition, collapse of the world-fabric would have resulted, and in the latter the continuity of fulfilment of the promise would have been broken off, had special grace been entirely withdrawn. These two features find their explanation in the purpose of the period in general. It was intended to bring out the consequences of sin when left so far as possible to itself. Had God permitted grace freely to flow out into the world and to gather great strength within a short period, then the true nature and consequences of sin would have been very imperfectly disclosed. Man would have ascribed to his own relative goodness what was in reality a product of the grace of God. Hence, before the work of redemption is further carried out, the downward tendency of sin is clearly illustrated, in order that subsequently in the light of this downgrade movement the true divine cause of the upward course of redemption might be appreciated. This constitutes the indirect bearing of the period under review on redemption.

The narrative proceeds in three stages. It first describes the rapid development of sin in the line of Cain. In connection with this it describes the working of common grace in the gift of invention for the advance of civilization in the sphere of nature. It shows further that these gifts of grace were abused by the Cainites and made subservient to the progress of evil in the world. We have here a story of rapid degeneration, so guided by God as to bring out the inherent tendency of sin to lead to ruin, and its power to corrupt and debase whatever of good might still develop. So far as this circle of humanity is concerned, the facts bear out the interpretation above put upon the period. The details of the description are evidently chosen with a view to emphasize the result. The slaying of Abel by Cain illustrates a rapid development of sin, issuing into murder in the second generation. Hence the careful manner in which Cain's conduct before and after the act is described. Cain committed his sin with premeditation, having been warned beforehand. After the act he denies his sin, is defiant, repudiates every obligation to the law of love. Even after God has pronounced sentence upon him, he is exclusively concerned about the consequences of his sin, not about the sin itself. When this is compared with the act committed in paradise, it becomes evident that a rapid progress in corruption of the human heart had taken place. Sin proves powerful enough to prostitute the gifts of God's common grace in the sphere of nature for purposes of evil. The first step in natural progress is taken by Enoch, the son of Cain, who built a city. Afterwards, in the eighth generation from Cain, the inventions of cattle-raising, of music, of metal-working appear. The inventors were sons of the Cainite Lamech, from whose song it appears that the increase in power and prosperity made possible by them only caused a further estrangement from God. The song [Gen. 4.23, 24] is a sword-song. Delitzsch well observes that it is an expression of Titanic arrogance. It makes its power its god, and carries its god, i.e. its sword, in its hand. What God had ordained as a measure of protection for Cain is here scorned, and sole reliance placed upon human revenge through the sword. Even Cain still felt the need of help from God; the spirit of Lamech depends upon itself alone. No trace of the sense of sin remains. It is also recorded that Lamech changed the monogamic relation between the sexes into one of polygamy.

CAINITES AND SETHITES

The narrative next proceeds to describe the development of things in the line of the Sethites [Gen. 4.25–5.32]. In connection with this line nothing is said about natural inventions and secular progress. It is the continuity of redemption that is stressed. The two kinds of progress appear distributed over the two lines of the Cainites and the Sethites. God sometimes chooses families and nations standing outside the sphere of redemption to carry on the progress in secular culture. Examples of this are: the Greeks, who were the cultivators of art; and the Romans, who received a genius for the development of legal and political institutions. Notice that, while among the Sethites the continuity of redemption is carefully marked, nothing is said about a new influx of special grace even among them. The import of the narrative remains negative. Not that the Sethites made great progress in the knowledge and service of God, but rather that they kept themselves relatively free from the degeneration of the Cainites; this is the burden of the narrative. Its high-lights are in the contrasts drawn between certain outstanding figures in this line and corresponding prominent figures in the Cainite succession. Thus Cain and Abel are put over against each other. Similarly Enoch, the son of Cain, and Enosh, the son of Seth. But the culmination of the contrast is seen in the seventh generation. Here the Sethite Enoch and the Cainite Lamech are opposites. In distinction from the pride and arrogance of Lamech, Enoch is related to have 'walked with God'. This means more than that he led a pious life, for the customary phrases for that are 'to walk before God', and 'to walk after God'. 'To walk with God' points to supernatural intercourse with God. The phrase is after this used but twice in the Old Testament, of Noah in the immediate sequel, and in Mal. 2.6 of the priests. Obviously some connection is intended between this unique degree of closeness to God and Enoch's exemption from death. Through the patriarch's translation it is once more proclaimed, that where communion with God has been restored, there deliverance from death is bound to follow. The correctness of the view taken of 'walking with God' may be verified from the later Apocalyptic tradition of the Jews, which represents Enoch as the great prophet, initiated into all mysteries. With the description of the Cainite Lamech, it will be noticed, the further pursuit of the Cainite line is dropped. The other line is continued until it reaches Noah. In harmony with this the chronology is attached to the Sethite line, for the chronology is the frame-work on which in Scripture the progress of redemption is suspended. The only other point commemorated in the Sethite tradition concerns the utterance of Lamech, Noah's father, at the birth of his child: 'This same shall comfort us for our work and toil of our hands, because (not *out of the ground*) of the ground which Jehovah has cursed' [5.29]. This saying expresses a profound sense of the burdensomeness of the curse, and in so far of the burdensomeness of sin, the cause of the curse, and it also voices a, perhaps premature, expectation that from this burden relief, comfort, will soon be found. It contrasts vividly once more with the paganistic sentiment of the Cainites, who either did not feel the curse, or, if they felt it, expected relief from themselves and their human inventions.

Notwithstanding these isolated instances of the continuity of redemptive grace, the account as a whole tends to bring out the divine purpose above formulated. Even the good kept alive was not enabled to force back the evil. Nothing is said about any influence proceeding from the Sethites upon the Cainites. While the power of redemption remained stationary, the power of sin waxed strong, and became ready to attack the good that still existed.

The character of the period in this respect finds clearest expression in what is said, *thirdly*, about the commingling of the Cainites and Sethites through intermarriage. The latter allowed themselves to become assimilated to the wickedness of the former. This was permitted by God to go on to the point where the lesson of the inherent destructive potencies of sin had been fully taught, and where it could not go on any further, because Noah and his family only having remained faithful, the continuity of the work of God appeared in danger, and where the time had been reached to teach the finishing lesson of the judgment, without which the entire period would have failed of its purpose. In the above statement the more usual interpretation of 'the daughters of men', and 'the sons of God', is followed. The former are women of the Cainites, the latter are the Sethites. This interpretation, however, is disputed by not a few exegetes. They hold that 'the sons of God' here designates, as it elsewhere sometimes does, superhuman beings, angels. We shall not discuss all the arguments that may be used in favour of or against each of these two views. The former alone would seem to fit into the construction of the significance of the period as a whole above made. We assumed the period to serve the purpose of showing the necessary outcome of sin, when left to work itself out freely. If the angel theory be accepted, this will tend to obscure the idea aimed at. In that case we shall have no longer a development of human sin left to itself, but a development under the influence of a quite extraordinary superhuman factor *ab extra*. The illogical nature of the contrast between 'daughters of men' and 'sons of God' in case the latter also belong to the human race, is not decisive. In Hebrew idiom sometimes a genus is set over against part of the genus, as though the two were mutually exclusive. The explanation lies in the circumstance, that in such cases the whole is thought of as having only the generic characteristics and nothing more, whereas to the part a certain distinction is attributed which raises it above the genus, to which nevertheless logically it belongs.

So here: the daughters of men, that is, of those who were *men and nothing more*, are set over against those who, while being men naturally, had the distinction of being *besides this the sons of God*. Ps. 73.5 and Jer. 32.20, are cases entirely similar. It has been urged that the name 'sons of God' in a spiritual sense would be out of place at such an early stage of revelation, but this overlooks the fact that the use is not carried back into that period; it is employed from the writer's standpoint. An argument in favour of the angel theory is taken from Jude's Epistle vs. 7; here, after the description of the fall of the angels in vs. 6, the writer proceeds: 'Even as Sodom and Gomorrah and the cities about them, having in like manner as these given themselves over to fornication and gone after strange flesh, etc.' It is urged that the words 'in like manner as these' must link together the angels of vs. 6 and the cities of the plain, so that the sin of the former would have also been of a sexual kind, intercourse of angels with human beings. And confirmation for this is still further found in the term 'strange flesh' meaning that angels went after human beings. It cannot be denied that this argument from Jude has some force. Closely looked at, however, it is not conclusive, and open to certain objections. 'In like manner as these' is by some interpreters taken to link together not the angels of vs. 6, and the cities of vs. 7, but Sodom and Gomorrah and 'the cities about them'. In that case no fornication of angels is referred to. A serious objection to the theory arises from the phrase 'taking to themselves wives', which could mean nothing short of permanent intermarriage, not casual fornication, between angels and women, a difficult thing to envisage. Finally, 'strange flesh' seems hard to fit into the angel theory, for the angels according to the Old Testament are not 'flesh'. On the other hand, the word precisely fits into what was the abomination of the cities of the plain, viz., homosexuality.

It ought to be observed that critical writers often connect with the angel view the further assumption that the narrative in Gen. 6 is meant to give an account of the origin of sin, that the writer was unacquainted with the story of the fall in the earlier chapters, in other words that the two accounts belong to different documents. This is what renders the exegesis of primary importance.

Fourthly, in 6.3, 5–7, we have the divine summing up of the issue of the period, and the judgment pronounced upon the prediluvian race. In regard to vs. 3, there is considerable uncertainty of interpretation. This arises from the two words *adhon* and *beshaggam*, especially from the former. The word *dun* or *din* may be rendered 'to strive' or 'to rule'. The former meaning is adopted by the A.V., which renders:

49

'My spirit shall not always strive with man'. The R.V. in the text retains this, but in the margin offers the alternative: 'shall not always abide in man'. *Beshaggam* is a compound form resolvable in two ways: it may be taken as made up of the preposition *be*, the relative *sha* (an abbreviation of *esher*') and the adverb *gam*, 'also'. This yields 'in that also'. Or it may be resolved into the preposition *be*, the infinitive of the verb *shagag*, 'to go astray', and the suffix *am*, 'their'. This yields 'in their going astray'. Each of these resolvings may be joined to each of the two given renderings of *dun* or *din*. The difference between the latter is of great importance, for the choice in favour of one or the other will place the statement in quite a different sphere. The version with 'strive' places it in the ethical sphere. God would mean by this that He will not always continue to let His Spirit exercise the restraining influence hitherto exerted upon sin. A certain limit of time, 120 years, is fixed for the divine abstention from withdrawing this influence; after that comes the judgment. And the reason assigned is either that man also is 'flesh', 'morally and religiously corrupt', or that in their going astray they are flesh, i.e., the judgment to come suits their condition. The version of *dun* or *din* with 'to rule' puts the whole matter in the physical sphere. The Spirit of God is according to the general teaching of the Old Testament the source of natural life in man [cp. *Psa.* 104.29, 30]. God by saying that His Spirit will not indefinitely abide in man announces the purpose of putting an end to the physical existence of mankind after the limit of 120 years. The reason is either that he also is flesh, by reason of sin fallen a prey to physical corruption, or that in his going astray they are become physically subject to corruption, which will actually overtake them after 120 years. The rendering of the verb with 'rule' or 'abide' deserves the preference. The ethical notion of 'the flesh', if it occurs in the Old Testament at all, can hardly be expected to occur thus early. On the alternate view of the three things mentioned, the Spirit, the flesh, the shortening of humanity's lease of life, all lie on the same line. Some would understand the 120 years of the length henceforth allotted to the life of individual men. This does not agree with the subsequent facts. It could be accepted only on the basis of a critical view, according to which the passage originally stood in no connection with the later patriarchal narratives, and that it was written by one who knew nothing of a flood, but assumed an uninterrupted development of mankind from the earliest times.

The other part of the divine summing up, the statement of vss. 5–7, offers no difficulty. In the strongest terms the extreme wickedness reached at the end of the period is described. The points brought out are *firstly*: the intensity and extent of evil ('great in the earth'); *secondly*: its inwardness ('every imagination of the thoughts of his heart'); *thirdly*: the absoluteness of the sway of evil excluding everything good ('only evil'); *fourthly*: the habitual, continuous working of evil ('all the day'). The same judgment or irremediable wickedness is even more emphatically affirmed in the words: 'It repented Jehovah that He had made man on the earth, and it grieved Him at His heart'. In anthropomorphic fashion this expresses the idea that the development of mankind frustrated the end for which God had placed man on the earth. Hence God said: 'I will destroy man whom I have created from the face of the ground; both man and beast and creeping thing and fowl of the air, for it repenteth me that I have made them'. The inclusion of the lower orders of life shows that through humanity the entire organism of nature has become infected with evil. Still it is significantly added: 'But Noah found grace in the eyes of Jehovah'. The continuity of the race is preserved. God saves enough out of the wreck to enable Him to carry out His original purpose with the selfsame humanity He had created.

REVELATION AFTER THE FLOOD

We now come to the Noachian Revelation which took place after the flood. In this positive, constructive measures were taken for the further carrying out of the divine purpose. Here again the reminder is in place that the principles disclosed and the measures taken did not directly relate to the prosecution of redemption, although an indirect bearing upon that also must not be overlooked. That the development of natural life is proximately dealt with, follows from the following: what is ordained by God and the promise made have equal reference to the entire Noachian family. But we know that the work of redemption was carried on in the line of Shem only; the arrangement made is not even confined to the human race; it is made with every living creature, nay, with the earth herself; that the *berith* is a *berith* of nature appears from the *berith*-sign; the rainbow is a phenomenon of nature, and absolutely universal in its reference. All the signs connected with redemption are bloody, sacramentally dividing signs.

The positive Noachian revelation proceeds in three stages. The first of the three recites the purpose of God, expressed in a monologue, to institute a new order of affairs. The second describes the measures taken that give content and security to this order. The third relates how the new order was confirmed in the form of a *berith*.

The *first section* consists of Gen. 8.20–22. God declares, 'I will not again curse the ground any more for man's sake . . . neither will I smite any more everything living, as I have done. While the earth remaineth, seed-time and harvest, and cold and heat, and summer and winter, and day and night shall not cease'. The regularity of nature in its great fundamental processes will henceforth continue. There is, however, added to this a qualification—'while the earth remaineth'. This pertains to the eschatological background of the deluge [cp. 1 *Pet.* 3.20, 21; 2 *Pet.* 2.5]. In vs. 21 the motive is assigned for the divine declaration: 'for that the imagination of man's heart is evil from his youth'. Before the deluge almost identical words were spoken by God to motive the necessity of the judgment, 6.5. How can the same statement explain, first, that the judgment is unavoidable, and then that there will be no repetition of the judgment henceforth? The solution of the difficulty lies in the addition of the words 'from his youth' in the second case. What was described in Gen. 6.5, was the historical culmination of a process of degeneration; that called for judgment. What is here described is the natural state of evil in the human heart as such, altogether apart from historical issues. Because the evil is thus deep-seated, no judgment can cure it. Therefore other means must be resorted to, and these other means would become impossible of execution, if repeated, catastrophic judgments of this nature in the sequel interfered with the ordinary unfolding of history.

The *second section* [9.1–7] relates the ordinances instituted in order to make possible and safeguard this programme of forbearance. These ordinances refer to the propagation of life, the protection of life, from animals and men both, and the sustenance of life. What relates to the sustenance of life has been inserted into the promise of protection of life from animals, because the permission of animal food for better sustenance naturally attached itself to this. In order to understand these measures we must clearly visualize the reduced state of the human race in which the flood had resulted. Hence the echo of some of the original creative ordinances is heard here. The command and bene-diction of fruitfulness are anew issued. The importance of this may be inferred from its double occurrence, first in vs. 1, and then again in vs. 7. As to the protection of human life from animals, vs. 2 pro-vides for the subjection of the animals to man: 'the fear of you and the dread of you shall be upon every beast of the earth, and upon every bird of the heavens, with all wherewith the ground teemeth, and all the fishes of the sea; into your hand are they delivered'. To this is added in vs. 5: 'And surely the blood of your lives will I require; at the hand of every beast will I require it'.

Originally, there was a supremacy of man [*Gen.* 1.26, 28], but, as instituted at creation, this was of the nature of a voluntary submission. This may be seen from the eschatological pictures given of it by the prophets, on the principles of a return of paradise at the end [*Isa.* 11.6–8]. In the state of sin the result is obtained by fear and dread instilled into the animals. And God promises to avenge man where devouring animals destroy his life: 'your blood of your lives will I require'. It is not possible to tell with certainty how this law works itself out; it has been suggested that every species of carnivorous animals is doomed to ultimate extinction. Intercalated between these references to hostile animals is the permission of animal food. The permission is qualified: 'but flesh with the life thereof, the blood thereof ye shall not eat'. This being coupled with the promise of vengeance from animals reveals the point of view. Since the animals are not to devour man after a carnivorous fashion, man also is not to eat animals as wild beasts devour their living prey. He must show proper reverence for life as a sacred thing, of which God alone has the disposal, and for the use of which man is dependent on the permission of God. The Levitical law repeats this prohibition, but adds as another ground the fact that the blood comes upon the altar, which, of course, for the Old Testament makes the prohibition of blood-eating absolute. Through failure to distinguish between the simple and the complicated motive this practice of absolute abstention was continued in the church for many centuries. The so-called decree of the Apostles [*Acts* 15.20] made the restraint obligatory for Gentile Christians, yet not because the thing was wrong in itself, but for the reason that no offence should be given to Jewish-Christian brethren.

The last point relates to the protection of human life from the assault of man, and lays down the divine law for the punishment of murder: 'At the hand of man, even at the hand of every man's brother, will I require the life of man. Whoso sheddeth man's blood, by man shall his blood be shed, for in the image of God made He man'. Some, in order to evade the institution of the death penalty for murder, would understand these words as a mere prediction, that murder is apt to be followed by blood-vengeance under the *lex talionis*. This exegesis is made positively impossible by the added clause: 'for in the image of God made He man'. The image of God in man can never furnish a motivation for the likelihood of the exaction of blood-vengeance.

The question remains what the image of God in man has to do with the infliction of the death-penalty. Two answers have been given to this. According to the one this clause explains why such an extraordinary power of taking away the life of another man can be conferred upon man's fellow creature. It is in virtue of the sovereignty of God, being part of the divine image, laid upon him that man can execute justice in capital matters. Others understand the clause as furnishing the reason why assault upon the life of man should meet with this extreme penalty; in life slain it is the image of God, i.e., the divine majesty that is assaulted. The latter interpretation deserves the preference. Notice the difference that here the instrument for the execution of the divine ordinance is clearly indicated: *'by man* shall his blood be shed', whereas in the case of retribution upon the animals this aspect of the matter is left indefinite. Further, the ground for the institution of the penalty appears to be a twofold one; on the one hand, the larger context in which the ordinance occurs proves it to be a measure of protection for society. At the same time the reference to the image of God shows that something still deeper underlies. It may well be questioned, whether the former alone, and that without an explicit injunction from God, could ever justify the infliction of death from one man upon another. Purely utilitarian, social considerations would be hardly sufficient here. They can come in as a secondary reason only after the matter has been put upon the high ground of the administration of justice sanctioned by God. The argument so frequently met with, that capital punishment adds but a second murder to the first, is an argument based either on total ignorance of the facts of Scripture or on open denial of the obligatory character of what the Bible teaches. How can that be characterized as a duplicated murder that professes to rest on the most explicit command of God, and over against which men have nothing to put except sentimental objections, and an unproven theory about the meliorating efficacy of forms of discipline which from their very nature exclude the punishment of death?

The *last section* is 9.8–17. God gives His promise the form of a *berith* through adding a solemn sign to it. This serves the purpose of bringing out the absolute sureness of the order instituted. Jer. 33.25 speaks in this sense of God's *berith* of day and night, i.e., of the unfailing succession of these two. Perhaps, however, there is more here than a comparative introduction of the *berith* idea: an actual reference to the Noachian episode may be intended. This is certainly the case in Isa. 54.9, where the Noachian *berith* stands in its infallibility as a type of the even greater perpetuity of the promise of God's oath of redemption. The promise to Noah has its limit in the eschatological crisis, which shall bring the earth to an end, but, though in that final catastrophe the mountains depart and the hills are removed, yet even then God's lovingkindness shall not depart from Israel, nor the *berith* of his peace be removed [vs. 10]. The representation with regard to the sign of the rainbow is anthropomorphic, but for that very reason more impressive than it could possibly be otherwise. The idea is not, as usually assumed, that by the bow man will be reminded of the divine promise, but that God Himself, were it possible for Him to forget, will by the sign Himself be reminded of His oath: 'When I bring a cloud over the earth, it shall come to pass that the bow shall be seen in the cloud, and I will remember my *berith*'. With the rainbow it is as later on it was with circumcision; both existed before, and at a certain time, the appointed time, were consecrated by God to serve as signs of his *berith*. The sign here is connected in its character with the ominous force of nature from which it pledges protection. It is produced against the background of the very clouds that had brought destruction to the earth. But it is produced upon these by the rays of the sun which in the symbolism of Scripture represent the divine grace.

SIX:
THE PERIOD BETWEEN NOAH
AND THE GREAT PATRIARCHS

The points to be discussed here are: [1] the prophetic deliverances of Noah with regard to his descendants; [2] the table of the nations; [3] the confusion of tongues; [4] the election of the Shemites.

[1]   *The prophetic deliverances of Noah* [*Gen.* 9.20–27]

These prophecies are in the case of Canaan (Ham) a curse, in the case of Japhet and Shem a blessing. The words must be regarded throughout as words of prophecy. Even paganism ascribes to such utterances a real influence to affect the persons concerned. This influence was conceived as magical, but in Scripture this is raised to the plane of inspired prophecy. Such prophecies in this early period represent the high-water mark of the advancing tide of revelation.

It will be observed, that the basis for the distinction between cursing and blessing lay in the ethical sphere. The shameless sensuality of Ham, the modesty of Japhet and Shem, marked a difference in common morality. Nevertheless it shaped in a most far-reaching manner the whole subsequent course of redemptive history. The supernatural process of redemption remains in contact with the natural development of the race. These influential traits were typical traits. They were the source of great racial dispositions. The event took place at a critical juncture where no significant event could fail to influence history for ages to come. The Old Testament recognizes that among the Canaanites the same type of sin here cursed was the dominating trait of evil. The descriptions given in the Pentateuch leave no doubt as to this [cp. *Lev.* 18.22; *Deut.* 12.29–32]. Even among the ancients outside of Israel (Japhetites) the sensual depravity in sexual life of Phoenicians, and Carthaginians in particular, had become proverbial.

The question has been raised why, instead of Ham, who had committed the sin, Canaan his son is cursed. Some assume that Ham was the youngest son of Noah, and Canaan the youngest son of

Ham. The underlying principle would then be that Ham is punished in that son who sustains the same relation to him as he sustained to Noah. This would bring out the fact of its being a sin committed against his father. There would be nothing in this against the Old Testament law of retribution, for the Old Testament is not in such points so morbidly individualistic as we are apt to be. Especially in the earlier part of Old Testament revelation the principle of generic solidarity is stressed [cp. *Ex*. 20.5, 6, where the operation of the rule both *in malam* and *in bonam partem* is affirmed]. Later revelation, especially in Ezekiel, brought the closer working out of the problem involved.

However, the facts of the genealogical relationship above assumed are subject to doubt. The usual sequence in which the names of Noah's sons are given is Shem, Ham and Japhet, which indicates that Ham occupied the middle place. Nor is there any evidence for Canaan having been the youngest son of Ham. 'Youngest son' in the Revised Version, vs. 24, is not conclusive, because the Hebrew word can be comparative as well as superlative, which would yield 'younger son' (as in R.V. margin), assigning to Ham the middle place in the triad. Under these circumstances it is best to adopt a modified form of the view proposed, and to say: Ham was punished in one of his sons because he had sinned against his father, and he was punished in that particular son, because Canaan most strongly reproduced Ham's sensual character. It should be noticed that not all the descendants of Ham are cursed but only the Canaanites; the others receive neither curse nor blessing.

Finally we must in passing touch upon the critical solution of the problem in hand. The divisive critics say that in the original version of the story the three sons of Noah were Shem, Japhet, and Canaan, and that this was afterwards changed into the present enumeration. This, of course, requires the deletion of the words 'Ham the father of' in vs. 22, and further of the words 'Ham is the father of Canaan' in vs. 18. These words were subsequently added, according to this theory, when the family relationships of Noah were altered. The curse upon Canaan consists in his being degraded to servitude to his brethren. This recurs as a refrain in the sequel to the blessings of Japhet and Shem.

The second member of the prophecy relates to Shem. Here the use of the name Jehovah seems significant. In point of fact this name contains in itself the blessing bestowed upon Shem. It lies in this, that God in the capacity of Jehovah, the God of redemption, gives

Himself to this part of the race for religious possession and enjoyment. It is a *berith*-formula, meaning far more than that the Shemites will worship Jehovah. This is the first time in Scripture that God is called the God of some particular group of mankind. It is so extraordinary a thing as to inspire the patriarch to the utterance of a doxology: 'Blessed be Jehovah, the God of Shem'. Resolved into its explicit meaning it would read: 'Blessed be Jehovah, because He is willing to be the God of Shem.'

The third member of the prophecy is of more uncertain interpretation. It reads: 'God enlarge Japhet, and let him live in the tents of Shem'. One point of uncertainty is the meaning of the verb (*yapht*, a play on the sound of the name Japhet). Is this to be taken locally or metaphorically? The former makes it refer to extension of territory, the latter understands it of enlargement, i.e. increase of prosperity. A second point of uncertainty relates to the question, who is the subject of the clause 'let him dwell'. Is this meant of God or of Japhet? The two questions are interlinked. If the subject of the second clause be Japhet, then it is but natural to understand the first clause of enlargement of territory. To dwell in the tents of some tribe or people is a common way for describing conquest of one tribe by another. For Japhet to dwell in the tents of Shem implies conquest of Shemitic territory by Japhetites. On the other hand, if 'him' in 'let him dwell' relates to God, then we should have to paraphrase as follows: May God give large prosperity to Japhet, but let Him bestow upon Shem what far transcends all such temporal blessedness, let Him (i.e. God) dwell in the tents of Shem. In that case a contrast is drawn between the objective gifts bestowed upon the Japhetites, and the personal self-communication of God upon the Shemites. The territorial rendering of 'enlarge' carrying with it the reference of 'him' to Japhet deserves the preference. The use of the name Elohim favours it, since it is not of Elohim but of Jehovah that such a gracious indwelling is predicated. Understanding it of Japhetites overrunning Shemitic lands, we should not, however, allegorize the statement, as though a spiritual dwelling together between Shemites and Japhetites were referred to. A real political conquest is intended. But ultimately such physical conquest will have for its result the coming of a religious blessing to Japhet. Occupying the tents of Shem he will find the God of Shem, the God of redemption and of revelation, there. The prophecy, both in its proximate political import and as to its ultimate spiritual consequences, was fulfilled through the subjugating of Shemitic territory by the Greeks and Romans. For this blessing became one of the most potent factors in the spread of the true religion over the earth. Delitzsch strikingly remarks: 'We are all Japhetites dwelling in the tents of Shem'.

[2] *The table of the nations*

As a piece of word-revelation this does not properly belong to the period with which we are dealing. It is something incorporated into the Mosaic account, from whatever source derived. Nevertheless, in so far as it throws backward its light upon the procedure of God at the post-diluvian time, we are justified in using it for the elucidation of the events of the latter. The table anticipates somewhat in that it speaks of nations, families, tongues, the origin of which distinction is not described till chap. 11. The table of the Shemites comes last, although genealogically this was not the sequence to be expected, which proves that this is not a piece of secular genealogy. It is a chapter belonging to the genealogy of redemption. The idea embodied in the table is that, while for the proximate future the Shemites will constitute the race of redemption, yet the other nations are by no means permanently dismissed from the field of Sacred History. Their names are registered to express the principle that in the fulness of time the divine interposition meant to return to them again, and to re-enclose them in the sacred circle.

[3] *The division of tongues* [11.1–9]

The building of a city and tower was inspired first by the desire to obtain a centre of unity, such as would keep the human race together. But the securing of this unity was by no means the ultimate purpose of the effort. Unity was to afford the possibility for founding a gigantic empire, glorifying man in his independence of God. The latest criticism finds here two myths woven together, one describing the building of a tower for preserving unity, the other relating to the building of a city for gaining renown. But this, while resembling the explanation just given, misses the inner connection between the two projects. The tower was for the sake of the city, and there is no need of dissection. God interferes with the execution of this plan, not so much, or at least not only, from opposition to its impious spirit, but chiefly from fidelity to His promise, that the sinful development of humanity will not again issue into a repeated catastrophe on the scale of the deluge. If this were not to happen, the progress of sin had to be checked. If the whole of humanity had remained concentrated, the power of sin would likewise have remained united, and doubtless soon again have reached stupendous proportions. Hence it was next necessary to break up the unity of the race. As Delitzsch has observed: 'the immoral and irreligious products of one nation are not equally destructive as those of an undivided humanity', and 'many false religions are better than one, since they paralyse one another'.

It is true that in the abstract the unity of the race, unbroken by national distinctions, is the ideal. Had sin not entered, this would undoubtedly have been the actual state of things, as it will become so in the final eschatological dispensation [cp. *Gal.* 3.28]. But for the present intervening period this is not the will of God. Nationalism, within proper limits, has the divine sanction; an imperialism that would, in the interest of one people, obliterate all lines of distinction is everywhere condemned as contrary to the divine will. Later prophecy raises its voice against the attempt at world-power, and that not only, as is sometimes assumed, because it threatens Israel, but for the far more principal reason, that the whole idea is pagan and immoral.

Now it is through maintaining the national diversities, as these express themselves in the difference of language, and are in turn upheld by this difference, that God prevents realization of the attempted scheme. Besides this, however, a twofold positive divine purpose may be discerned in this occurrence. In the first place there was a positive intent that concerned the natural life of humanity. Under the providence of God each race or nation has a positive purpose to serve, fulfilment of which depends on relative seclusion from others. And secondly, the events at this stage were closely interwoven with the carrying out of the plan of redemption. They led to the election and separate training of one race and one people. Election from its very nature presupposes the existence of a larger number from among which the choice can be made.

[4] *The election of the Shemites to furnish the bearers of redemption and revelation*

Here the question must be raised: Was there any inherent fitness in the Shemites to serve this task? The answer is in the affirmative. Two traits come under consideration, the one belonging to the sphere of psychology, the other to the sphere of religious endowment. In connection with the former the following may be noted: The Shemites have a predominantly passive, receptive, rather than active or productive mentality. At first this temperament may have been universally human, as best suited to a primitive stage of knowledge. But at this point, where humanity separates into its great branches, and the racial dispositions become diversified, it seems to have been particularly inherited and cultivated among the Shemites. The form thus originally assumed by the truth secured the possibility of its translation into the mental world of other groups of the race. It is true, we, as non-Shemites, experience considerable difficulty in understanding the Old Testament Scriptures. But much greater would have been the difficulties of the Hebrew mind in apprehending a revelation given in Greek forms of thought. At the same time the Shemites must have possessed this mental predisposition in a moderate degree. The ease with which the Arabs and Jews have assimilated the Indo-Germanic type of civilization, and the large contribution made by them to the progress of scientific and philosophic thought, prove that they carry within them a twofold capacity, that of receiving the truth in its concrete shape, and that of translating it into other abstract forms of apprehension.

In connection with the antecedent religious endowment the following points may be noted:

(a) The French writer Renan at one time endeavoured to reduce this religious endowment to a psychological one. Observing that the three great monotheistic religions have sprung up on Shemitic soil, he set up the hypothesis of a monotheistic instinct as characteristic of this racial group. Renan did not look upon this instinct as superior, but felt inclined to connect it with a lack of imaginative power. At the present day this theory is entirely discredited. In the prevailing school of 'criticism a widely different explanation of the origin of monotheism is current. It arose at a comparatively late point in the history of Israel, viz., in the period of the prophets, from about 800 to 600 B.C. The manner of its origin was thus: these prophets had begun to perceive that Jehovah was supremely ethical in his character, which perception was a result of the prospect that the national and religious existence of Israel was about to be sacrificed to the principle of retributive righteousness. Eliminating the element of national favouritism (grace) from the conception of God, and retaining as its content only the idea of strict justice, they were led to perceive, since the core of Jehovah's Deity lay in this, that the gods of the heathen, who lacked this qualification, were not truly gods, which perception practically amounted to monotheism, although it took a considerable time for this germinal idea to assume shape and to ripen.

But, apart from these totally different constructions of the critical school, Renan's hypothesis breaks down before the fact that numerous groups of Shemites appear far from monotheistic at a time when instinct certainly should have made some approach towards the end in view. Edomites and Moabites were Shemites of as pure stock as the Hebrews, yet neither of them became monotheistic in the long time they lie open to our observation in the Old Testament. Passing on from the nearer kinsmen of Israel to the remoter Assyrians, we find them possessed of a rich civilization, but none the less given over to a most luxuriant type of polytheism. The Arabs, to be sure, became in the end fanatical monotheists, but they had borrowed their monotheism from the Jews and the Christians. Nor is this all. The children of Israel themselves continued for a long time to feel the attractions of polytheism, after they had long enough known monotheism (on the critical view) to have become thoroughly imbued with it. Jeremiah complains [2.9–11] that Israel is more inclined to change its God than the heathen nations. It is not difficult to explain this. The pagan nations had no desire to change, because their religion was the natural expression of their disposition. Israel persistently struggled to throw off the yoke of Jehovah's service, because the old pagan nature of Israel felt is as a yoke. From the standpoint that the Shemites had an instinct for monotheism all this becomes entirely unexplainable.

(b) After all this has been taken into account, it should none the less be noted, that there appears among the smaller groups a certain uniformity of religion. All the deities, however great their number, are more or less modifications of the same fundamental conception. This may be readily seen from the synonymy of the names of the deities. And these names are found with slight variations of form among all the Shemitic tribes.

(c) Significant in this connection is also the element that seems to lie uppermost in the Shemitic religious consciousness. This is the element of submission, cp. the word 'Islam', meaning this very thing. This is, of course, an idea that is essential to all religion, but it is not everywhere developed with equal strength. Without it religion can never become the supreme factor in the life of the religious subject, which it must be in order to act as a great historic force. The Shemites have become leaders in the world of religion, because religion was the leading factor in their life, no matter whether for good or for evil.

(d) Still another feature worth considering here is what has been called 'tribal particularism'. By this is meant the worship of one god by some particular tribe in tribal relations. It does not exclude belief in the existence or right to worship of other gods in other circles, or even in the same circle, in other relationships. This is not monotheism, of course, but it is a pronounced form of tribal monolatry.

(e) These peculiarities of Shemitic religion stand at the farthest remove from every pantheizing form of a tendency towards unification elsewhere observed, and on the surface seemingly like it. Great emphasis is placed upon the personal character of the relationship between the god and his worshipper. The name for the Shemitic religious subject is *ebed* (servant), and an intensely practical personal name it is. Personal devotion to the deity is the keynote of this service. Negatively the same thing reveals itself in the careful distinction upheld between God and nature. The exaltation above nature of the deity, that which is called in religious terminology the 'holiness' of the gods (well to be distinguished from ethical holiness), is an outstanding trait. Where thus the transcendent power and majesty of the deity is felt, the temptation is much lessened to confound God with the world or draw Him down into the realm of nature or matter. Ordinary pantheistic monism may easily tend in precisely the opposite direction. The unity holding the individual gods together may become nothing but the impersonal life of nature. Here monism and polytheism are not only reconcilable but mutually promotive of each other. Drawing down the deity into the processes of nature leads to the introduction of sex into the life of the divine. From this results a theogony[1] and the consequent multiplication of gods. There seems reason to believe that, wherever such traits appear in Shemitic religion, they are not an ancient Shemitic inheritance, but the result of corrupting influences introduced from without. In Arabia, where the Shemitic tribes lived most secluded, such features were even at the time of Mohammed exceedingly rare. We learn in the records of the time of three goddesses only, and these were not brought into sexual relations with the male gods. In the mind of Israel there always remained a consciousness that the grosser, sensual elements of idolatry were foreign, not only to the legitimate religion of Jehovah, but also to the ancient Shemitic inheritance.

(*f*) Finally, we must observe that such religious race-dispositions were not self-produced through evolution, on the one hand, nor sufficient of themselves, on the principle of evolution, to produce the higher religion of the Old Testament. It is plain that the traits on which we have dwelt lie rather on the line of a downward than of an upward movement. Outside of Israel we find them in historic times not on the increase, but decidedly on the decrease. Within Israel itself we can trace the downward drift of this natural Shemitic faith, not merely in the struggle with alien influences, but also in a gradual internal decline. What existed, and continued to keep alive, was the remnant of a purer knowledge of God, preserved from extinction by God Himself.

[1] The begetting and birth of gods.

As to the other point, that the higher religion of the Old Testament is not a simple evolution from low beginnings, it is sufficient to point out, that nowhere else in the Shemitic world has a similar higher type of religion made its appearance, except in Israel. The only reasonable explanation for the uniqueness of Israel in this respect is that here another factor was at work, the factor of supernatural revelation.

The connection of subsequent revelation and this ancient Shemitic religion is shown in the two oldest and most common divine names, *El* and *Elohim*. The Biblical usage in regard to the word 'name' differs considerably from ours. In the Bible the name is always more than a conventional sign. It expresses character or history. Hence a change in either respect frequently gives rise to a change of name. This applies to the names of God likewise. It explains why certain divine names belong to certain stages of revelation. They serve to sum up the significance of a period. Therefore they are not names which man gives to God, but names given by God to Himself.

There is further to be distinguished in the Bible a three-fold significance of the term 'name' in its religious connections. First it may express one divine characteristic. That which we call an attribute, the Old Testament calls a name of God. Such an adjectival designation may easily pass over into a proper name. God is holy; that is His name. But it becomes a *nomen proprium* when the prophet speaks of Him as 'The Holy One of Israel'. Next, the name of God can stand abstractly and comprehensively for all that God has revealed concerning Himself. This is 'the name of God'. In this sense it is simply equivalent to Revelation, not, of course, as an act, but as a product. This use applies to both General and Special Revelation. God's name is glorious in all the earth. The pious trust in the name of God, they make it a high tower. In the third place, the name of God comes to stand realistically for God Himself. The name is equivalent to God in Theophany. Of this we shall speak later.

The name *El* is probably derived from the root *ul* meaning 'to be strong'. So *El* first meant 'strength', then 'the strong One'. Another etymology makes *El* come from *alah*, 'to precede', which would yield 'leader' or 'commander'. According to still others *El* is from the same root as the preposition *el*. It would then signify 'the one who stretches himself out towards things'. Or, 'the One to whom others go out for help'. This, however, is rather too abstract. When explaining that it signifies power we should be careful to take power in the dynamic sense, because another name seems to express the element of authority.

Originally *El* must have been in frequent use. It still occurs as an appellative in the phrase: 'It is in the *el* (power) of my hand' [*Gen.* 31.29; cp. *Prov.* 3.27; *Mic.* 2.1]. Gradually *El* was supplanted by *Elohim*. In some of the later writings of the Old Testament it does not occur at all. In the Song of Moses [*Ex.* 15], it is used several times. The later period employed it chiefly in poetry. It also continued to be used in theophoric names, or poetic designations of God. *El* occurs in the Old Testament somewhat more than 200 times.

The derivation of *Elohim* is uncertain. It may come from a Shemitic root with the basic meaning of 'to fear, to be perplexed, and so, to seek refuge'. From that, there is but one step to the notion 'dread', and this would be objectified in the sense of 'the One to be dreaded', or 'the One to whom one comes in fear or dread'. A rather novel theory is based on the observation that *El* has no plural, and *Elohim* no singular, so that *Elohim* is considered the regular plural formation of *El*. There is, however, another singular to *Elohim*, viz., *Eloah*, which, to be sure, occurs only in poetic writings, and may, therefore, be an artificial form to supply the lacking singular. Some critics consider this plural a remnant of polytheistic usage, going back to a period in which the people knew many divinities, not only one God. Against this tells the fact that *Elohim* occurs only among the Hebrews, and such a plural form for a single deity is not found among other Shemitic tribes. Israel, being the only Shemitic nation that developed monotheism, would scarcely have, alone of all others, retained such a trace of original polytheism. *Elohim* is simply a plural expressing majesty, magnitude, fulness, richness. Probably God was named *Elohim*, because the fulness of His might extended in every direction. The plural need have no more polytheistic flavour than the Greek word *theotes* (feminine) proves all original Greek deities to have been females. *Elohim* is not used in theophoric names. The Hebrew sometimes has to use it as a true numerical plural, e.g. when speaking of pagan gods. In such a case, however, it is always construed with a plural verb, whereas in a case of reference to the true God it takes a singular verb. The name *Elohim* occurs in the Old Testament more than 2,500 times.

SEVEN:
REVELATION IN THE
PATRIARCHAL PERIOD

CRITICAL VIEWS

The first question to be raised is, whether the patriarchs Abraham, Isaac, and Jacob, are historical characters. Historians holding the evolutionary theory assert that the descent of families or nations from one man is everywhere else in the field of history a pure fiction. On this view the question becomes urgent, how did these figures arise? The problem involves two elements, one as to the rise of the incidents and characters in the narrative, the other as to the origin of the names.

Common to most explanations of the critical school is the view that the incidents and character-descriptions arose out of a self-portrayal and self-idealization of the later people of Israel, during the time of the kingdom. The Israelites had a strong consciousness of their own distinctiveness as regards other people. So in these stories they mirrored themselves.

In regard to the origin of the names there is no such unanimity of opinion. According to some the names are tribal names, and the relation of cognateness among these figures reflects tribal relationships. The movements ascribed to the patriarchs stand for tribal movements and migrations. The utmost of historicity conceded from this stand-point is that, for example, Abraham may have been the leader of a tribe named after him. While this destroys the historicity of the patriarchs in the traditional sense, it is considered by many a hyper-conservative position, because it still allows a legendary basis of facts. Dillman, who was reckoned a conservative scholar, took this position.

A second view is much more extreme. Its representatives are found mainly among the Wellhausen critics; especially Stade has worked it out. According to him, the names Abraham, Isaac, and Jacob, had nothing to do originally with Hebrew genealogical history, but are names of Canaanitish figures. They were borne by Canaanitish demigods, considered by the Canaanitish tribes as their ancestors, and worshipped as such in different places. When Israel occupied the land they began to worship at these places as the Canaanites had long worshipped there, including Abraham, Isaac, and Jacob in their own list of deities. Gradually learning to feel at home in Canaan, they soon came to feel that these sacred places belonged to them, and that therefore the gods worshipped in them must be Hebrew, not Canaanitish. In order to express this and create a sort of legal title for it from history, they framed the fiction that their own ancestors Abraham, Isaac, and Jacob, had previously been in the Holy Land and consecrated these places. Thus Abraham was assigned in the narrative of Genesis to Hebron, Isaac to Beersheba, Jacob to Bethel.

Thirdly, it has also been attempted to explain these names from Babylonian antecedents. Sarah was the goddess of Haran, Abraham a god of the same place: Laban, the moon-god. The four wives of Jacob are the four phases of the moon. The twelve sons of Jacob are the twelve months of the year; the seven sons of Leah are the seven days of the week; the number of men with which Abraham defeated the invaders, 318, constitutes the number of days in the lunar year.

THE HISTORICITY OF THE PATRIARCHS

In answer to these various constructions we must first of all emphasize that the historicity of the patriarchs can never be, to us, a matter of small importance. The religion of the Old Testament being a factual religion, it is untrue that these figures retain the same usefulness, through the lessons that can be drawn from their stories, as actual history would possess. This prejudges the answer to the fundamental question, what religion is for. If, on the Pelagian principle, it serves no other purpose than to teach religious and moral lessons from example, then the historicity is no longer of material importance. We can learn the same lessons from legendary or mythical figures. But, if according to the Bible they are real actors in the drama of redemption, the actual beginning of the people of God, the first embodiment of objective religion; if Abraham was the father of the faithful, the nucleus of the Church; then the denial of their historicity makes them useless from our point of view. The whole matter depends on how we conceive of man's need as a sinner. If this be construed on the evangelical principle we cannot without serious loss of religious values assign these given figures to the region of myth or legend. If we are ready to be satisfied with the religious and moral tenor of the stories, then the conclusion is inevitable that the historical existence of Jesus likewise has become a negligible matter. Still further: if the patriarchs were not historical and some reality might still seem desirable, it would be difficult to tell why this should begin with Moses. If there be no historicity before that, then the process of redemption loses itself in a prehistoric mist at its beginnings. The only logical position is that, *if* a history of redemption is needed, it should begin with Adam and Eve.

As to the theory of self-idealization, we observe that this in no wise accounts for all the facts. One would, of course, a priori expect some resemblance between ancestors and descendants. But the resemblance postulated on such a basis does not by any means cover the elements of the description as a whole. Resemblance between people and patriarch is greatest in the case of Jacob. It is not nearly so great in the cases of the two others. Then there are differences between the patriarchs and Israel in more than one respect. The patriarch Abraham rises far above the highest point the nation ever reached. Faith was never characteristic of Israel as a nation. On the other hand, the narrative dwells on certain weaknesses and sins of the patriarchs, not merely as regards Jacob, but also as regards Abraham. Wellhausen observes that in the documents J and E the patriarchs are represented as standing under an excessive control of their wives. These women, in his view, appear more liberally endowed with character than their husbands. But, one might ask, how could the manly, warlike Israelites of the time of the early kingdom have found their ideals expressed in such figures? Nor is there perfect agreement in customs. We are told that Abraham married his half-sister, and such action was not customary among Israel in later times.

Neither can the names be satisfactorily explained from a personification of tribes. Jacob, it is true, stands as a regular name for the people; Isaac very rarely is put to such use; but Abraham occurs nowhere as a tribal name. Wellhausen admits this, but seeks to explain it on the ground that Abraham was a creation of the poetic fancy, and as such drew to himself all the material for idealization and embellishment that existed, leaving little for the adornment of Isaac and Jacob. This, however, refutes itself, because, in case Abraham were the latest creation, he would have been the poorest and least decorated figure, Isaac and Jacob having pre-empted all the existing material.

The mythological derivation of the names from Babylon is a theory not yet ripe for serious historical discussion. Gunkel, the most brilliant advocate of Babylonian influence upon the Old Testament, admits this to be so. He grants that so far all attempts to derive the names of the patriarchs from the Babylonian pantheon have proved failures. Nowhere does the Old Testament contain a trace of worship addressed to the patriarchs; on the contrary, it emphasizes that they were not proper objects of cult-address. Cp. Isa. 43.27, 'Thy fathers sinned, and thy teachers have transgressed against me'; and Isa. 63.16, 'For thou art our Father, though Abraham know us not, nor Israel acknowledge us'.

THEOPHANIES

A distinction must be drawn between the form and the content of revelation in the patriarchal period. As to the form, we notice that it is gradually gaining in importance, as compared with the past. Formerly it used to be simply stated that God spake to man, nothing being said as to the form of this speech, nor as to whether it was accompanied by any appearance. Now for the first time more or less circumstantial description of the form appears. On the whole we may say that revelation, while increasing in frequency, at the same time becomes more restricted and guarded in its mode of communication. The sacredness and privacy of the supernatural begin to make themselves felt.

To Abraham at first revelation came after the earlier indefinite fashion. In Gen. 12.4 Jehovah 'speaks' to him, but no sooner has he entered the promised land than a change of expression is introduced. In Gen. 12.7 we read that Jehovah 'appeared' unto Abraham (literally, He 'let himself be seen by Abraham'). Here is something more than mere speech. The emergence of a new element is also recognized by the building of the altar, for the altar is a shrine or house of God. In Gen. 15.13 we have again the indefinite statement that Jehovah 'said to Abraham'. But in Gen. 15.17 a visible manifestation, a theophany, takes place. In the form of the smoking furnace and the flaming torch God passes by. The theophany here assumes the character of something fearful. In chapter 17.1 we read again that Jehovah let Himself be seen by Abraham; and that this was a theophany follows from the statement of vs. 22, 'And he left off talking with him, and God went up from Abraham'.

From the life of Isaac the theophanies all but disappear, although we read in Gen. 26.2, 24 that Jehovah let Himself be seen by Isaac. In the life of Jacob they return, but with decreasing frequency as compared with the life of Abraham. In Gen. 28.13 we read of Jehovah speaking to Jacob from the top of the ladder, but this was in a dream. Yet in Gen. 35.9 we read, 'And God appeared unto Jacob again, when he came out of Padan-aram, and blessed him' [cp. *Gen.* 48.3]. Still more marked is the absence of theophanies from the life of Joseph.

As stated above, altars were frequently built in places of theophany, indicating a consciousness that the place had in some sense become the seat of God's presence. The patriarchs returned to these places, to call there upon the name of God. [*Gen.* 13.4; 35.1–7].

We notice in the next place that most of these theophanies were confined to definite localities, all of which lay within the borders of the land of promise. There is here a beginning of the attachment of Jehovah's redemptive presence to the land of Canaan. To be sure, the critics, while recognizing the significance of the facts, explain them on the different principle that the stories of theophany were later framed to give divine sanction to ancient shrines. But this does not agree with the fact that there were some theophanies without the subsequent erection of an altar [*Gen.* 17.1]; and again, we read of the erection of an altar where there is no mention of any preceding theophany [*Gen.* 13.18; 33.20]. It is true that some of these places later became popular shrines, but this is perfectly explainable from the remembrance of the ancient theophanies remaining in the minds of the people. The patriarchal history did not grow out of the locality; on the contrary, the sacred character of the locality originated from the history.

Specialization of the time of revelation is also observable. Jehovah appeared to the patriarchs at night [*Gen.* 15.5, 12; 21.12, 14; 22.1–3; 26.24]. In the night the soul is withdrawn within itself, away from the experiences and scenes of the day. Thus the privacy of the transaction is guarded.

The same effect, to a stronger degree, is obtained where the revelation occurs in the form of a vision. The word 'vision' has both a specific and a generalized use. The original meaning is that of receiving revelation by sight instead of by hearing, although, of course, within the frame of the vision hearing of an inner kind is included. Because in ancient times the visionary form was the prevailing one, vision easily became the general term for revelation, and retained this sense, even though afterwards revelation had become more differentiated in form [cp. *Isa.* 1.1]. Sometimes the body was abnormally affected, or was detached from the inner sense by which hearing took place. The seeing in such cases was an inner sight, a seeing without the help of the bodily eye, yet none the less a real, objective seeing. In the patriarchal history the term 'vision' occurs twice [*Gen.* 15.1; 46.2]. In the latter place we read that God spake 'in the visions of the night'.

The mention of the night-time leads us to think here of visions specifically so-called. In Gen. 15, the matter is much more complicated. Here also the night-time is repeatedly spoken of [vss. 5, 12, 17]; and undoubtedly vss. 12-17 describe a real visionary experience. In vs. 1 the word 'vision' occurs: 'The word of Jehovah came unto Abram in a vision, saying. . . .' Now the question arises; how much of the following occurrences does this cover? Does it relate to vss. 1-12, or is it used by way of anticipation of vss. 12-17? The latter is difficult, because the participle 'saying' links what immediately follows it closely to the expression 'came in a vision' [vs. 1]. And a chronological difficulty also arises if vss. 2-12 are to be understood as plain unvisionary discourse. The marking of the points in time at which the several items happened is such as to be hard to conceive in ordinary waking experience. In vs. 5 it is night, for stars are shining. In vs. 12 the sun is 'just going down'. In vs. 17 'the sun went down'. In a vision the ordinary laws of the sequence of time do not hold good. Consequently to place the whole disclosure in a vision removes the chronological difficulty, and enables us to consider the whole as a continuous narrative, the discrepancies of time notwithstanding. On this view the vision does not begin with vs. 12; the seeing of the starry heavens in vs. 5 already belongs to it. And yet the 'deep sleep' and the 'horror of a great darkness' [vs. 12] so unmistakably describe the phenomena of a vision coming on, that we shall have to speak of a vision within a vision, something like the play within the play in 'Hamlet'. Still, the difficulty is not decisive. The sleep and the horror of a great darkness may perhaps stand for a heightened abnormal psychical state within the already abnormal visionary state as such. If the above, however, should appear too complicated, a simple, though drastic, remedy is afforded by understanding the word 'vision' in vs. 1 as meaning generic revelation. To be sure, this does not remove the chronological difficulty between vs. 5 and vs. 12; for this it will be further necessary to place an interval of at least one day between the two points of time mentioned.

With revelation as a night occurrence the dream-form is naturally given, for dreams belong to the night. But still another motive is obviously involved. In dreaming, the consciousness of the dreamer is more or less loosened from his personality. Hence dreams were preferably used as a vehicle of revelation where the spiritual state was ill-adapted for contact with God. In this way the unfit personality was to some extent neutralized, and the mind was a mere receptacle of the message. Heathen persons receive revelation through this medium

[*Gen.* 20.3; 31.24; 40.5; 41.1]. Within the chosen family, dreams were utilized likewise where the spirituality of the person was immature or at a low ebb [*Gen.* 28.12; 31.11; 37.5, 9]. It should be noted that the divine provenience or truthfulness of the revelation is not affected by its coming in the form of a dream. The same terms are used as in other modes of revelation: God comes in a dream, speaks in a dream [*Gen.* 20.6; 28.13; 31.24]; the same applies to visions [*Gen.* 15.1; 46.2]. God has the direct access to the dream-life and complete control over everything entering into it.

THE ANGEL OF JEHOVAH

The most important and characteristic form of revelation in the patriarchal period is that through 'the Angel of Jehovah' or 'the Angel of God'. The references are: Gen. 16.7; 22.11, 15; 24.7, 40; 31.11; 48.16 [cp. also *Hos.* 12.4, with reference to *Gen.* 32.24ff.].

The peculiarity in all these cases is that, on the one hand, the Angel distinguishes himself from Jehovah, speaking of Him in the third person, and that, on the other hand, in the same utterance he speaks of God in the first person. Of this phenomenon various explanations have been offered. To explain, two critical views come under consideration. Some have proposed to render the word *mal'akh* as an abstract noun, meaning an embassy, a mission, which Jehovah despatched from Himself after an impersonal fashion. The reason for this conception is supposed to have lain in the primitive belief that Jehovah, who had so long dwelt at Sinai, could not in person depart from this place, but that, nevertheless, desiring to accompany His people on their journey to Canaan and during their abode in the holy land, He could send an influence from Himself to do what He was unable to do by personal presence. According to this view, the conception is very ancient, dating back at least to the entrance of Israel upon the holy land.

The second attempt considers the formation of the figure of the Angel as due to the late Jewish idea of the exaltation of God. It was thought unworthy of God to come into such close contact and intercourse with the earthly creation as the naive old stories related of Him. Hence the stories were rewritten from this semi-deistical point of view, and all traits and actions of this kind were represented as having been exhibited or performed by an intermediate being of the angel-class. On this understanding the figure is of late origin, as late as the emergence of this deistical way of thinking about Jehovah.

A common objection lies against both of these theories. It is this, that if the design had been to safeguard the non-removability from Sinai or the inappropriateness of mixing with the creature, then the writers or redactors would have been apt to exercise great care not to leave any instances, where the objectionable features occurred, uncorrected. As it is, side by side with the novel mode of Angel-revelation, theophanies of the old disapproved-of type continue to happen in the narrative. Something in the nature of a subsequent correction in the production of the figure cannot have taken place. Besides, on the second theory, we should expect instead of 'the Angel of Jehovah' the other phrase, '*an* Angel of Jehovah'. The objection, that before a proper noun the preceding noun standing in the construct state becomes inevitably determinate, in other words that it would be impossible to make 'Angel of Jehovah' indeterminate, even though it may have been intended so, does not hold good. The Hebrew has a way of saying 'an Angel of Jehovah'. All that is necessary is to insert the preposition *lamed* between Angel and Jehovah: 'an Angel to Jehovah'. If the intention had been to keep God and the creature apart, those interested in this would never have allowed the Angel to speak like Jehovah, for this would have obscured the very fact desired to bring out.

Of the two views discussed, the one neglects the distinctness between the Angel and God, the other neglects the identity between both. The problem is how to do justice to both. There is but one way in which this can be done: we must assume that behind the twofold representation there lies a real manifoldness in the inner life of the Deity. If the Angel sent were Himself partaker of Godhead, then He could refer to God as his sender, and at the same time speak as God, and in both cases there would be reality behind it. Without this much of what we call the Trinity, the transaction could not but have been unreal and illusory. But it is not legitimate to infer from this that the proximate purpose of such a mode of revelation was to reveal the truth of the Trinity. A thing can be based on some reality, without which it could not possibly occur, and yet serve to inculcate another fact or truth. Only in a later period and in an indirect way were the Angel-theophanies made to render service for the disclosure of the Trinity. At the time of their first occurrence this could not have been done, because the supreme interest at that time was to engrave deeply upon the mind of Israel the consciousness of the oneness of God. Premature disclosure of the Trinity would in all probability have proved a temptation to polytheism. For a long time the Deity of the Messiah and the personality of the Holy Spirit were kept more or less in the background.

But, if not the truth of the Trinity, then what was the purpose for which this new mode of revelation was inaugurated? The purpose was twofold: the one not altogether new, the other a new departure. The former we may designate the 'sacramental', the latter the 'spiritualizing' intent. By the 'sacramental' intent we understand the desire of God to approach closely to His people, to assure them in the most manifest way of His interest in and His presence with them. This sacramental intent had underlain all the theophanies from the beginning. It was not first introduced through the appearances of the Angel of Jehovah. Only, without these appearances it could not have been realized in the old simple way without endangering another principle, that of the spiritual nature of the Deity. When God walked with men and ate and drank with them, and in bodily fashion spake with them and listened to them, the instinctive conclusion that these things were the result of His nature, lay extremely near. And yet in reality they had no necessary connection with His nature, but were sacramental condescensions on His part. As such they were indispensable. But necessary as this sacramental condescension was, it was equally necessary that the spiritual nature of God be preserved as its background. And this was accomplished by conveying the impression, that behind the Angel speaking as God, and who embodied in Himself all the condescension of God to meet the frailty and limitations of man, there existed at the same time another aspect of God, in which He could not be seen and materially received after such a fashion, the very God of whom the Angel spoke in the third person. Through this division of labour between God and His Angel the indispensable core of the theophany was saved. The spiritualizing intent was auxiliary to the sacramental one. The Angel is truly divine, for otherwise He could not have discharged the sacramental function of assuring man that God was with him. But the visible, physical form of meeting this need is not due to the nature of God. The nature of man, chiefly his sinful nature, calls for it.

In the incarnation of our Lord we have the supreme expression of this fundamental arrangement. The incarnation is not the result of any inherent necessity in God. The contrary view, though widely spread, has a pantheizing background. We need God incarnate for redemptive reasons. The whole incarnation, with all that pertains to it, is one great sacrament of redemption. And yet even here special care is taken to impress believers with the absolute spirituality of Him who has thus made Himself of our nature. The principle at stake has found classical expression in John 1.18: 'No man has seen God at any time; God only begotten,[1] who is in the bosom of the Father, He has declared Him'. Because the whole fact of the Angel's appearance stood from the beginning in the service of redemption, it is but natural that the execution of important movements of redemption should be assigned to Him. Immediately after the giving of the *berith* He appears on the scene [*Gen.* 16.7]. Delitzsch well observes: 'The end and object of these appearances is to be judged by their commence-ment'. We shall see most clearly in the Mosaic period that the divine carrying out of the *berith* is on the whole entrusted to His Angel. He guards those in particular whose lives and labours are most inti-mately connected with the *berith*. Jacob says [*Gen.* 48.15, 16]: 'The God before whom my fathers Abraham and Isaac did walk, the God who has fed me all my life long unto this day, the Angel who has redeemed me from all evil, bless the lads'. Cp. also Mal. 3.1, 'the Angel of the *berith*'. Not only in nature, but also by function, is the Angel of Jehovah distinguished from ordinary angels.

The form in which the Angel appeared was a form assumed for the moment, laid aside again as soon as the purpose of its assumption had been served. Usually, but not always, it was a human form. Some have thought that the Angel was during the Old Testament dispensation permanently posssessed of such an appearance-form. This would run contrary to the variableness of the form in which the manifestations took place. It would also anticipate the incarnation, in which the new feature is precisely that the Second Person of the Godhead assumes a form which remains permanently His own [*John* 1.14]. A still more serious error is the idea that from all eternity this Person in the Godhead possessed a material form fit to bring Him within reach of the senses. This is inconsistent with the spirituality of God, and would have made the Angel-revelation result in the very misunderstanding which it was intended to preclude.

Finally, in regard to the much-mooted question, whether the Angel was created or uncreated, a clear distinction between the Person and the form of appearance suffices for answer. If, as above suggested, the Angel-conception points back to an inner distinction within the Godhead, so as to make the Angel a prefiguration of the incarnate Christ, then plainly the Person appearing in the revelation was uncreated, because God. On the other hand, if by Angel we designate the form of manifestation of which this Person availed Himself, then

[1] On this rendering, see G. Vos, *The Self-Disclosure of Jesus* (1953 ed., revised by J. G. Vos), pp. 212–226; L. Morris, *John* [New London Commentary] (1972), p. 105.

the Angel was created. It is the same in the case of Christ: the divine Person in Christ is uncreated, for Deity and being created are mutually exclusive. Nevertheless as to His human nature Jesus was created. The only difference in this respect between Him and the Angel is that under the Old Testament the created form was ephemeral, whereas through the incarnation it has become eternal.

We deal with the elements and principles of revelation contained in the life of each of the three great patriarchs successively. What the three have in common is treated in the discussion of Abraham, so that under the head of Isaac and Jacob only the new material connected with each is examined.

THE PATRIARCH ABRAHAM

[1] *The principle of election*

The first outstanding principle of divine procedure with the patriarchs is the principle of election. Hitherto the race as a whole had been dealt with. Or, as in Noah's case, there had been election of a new race out of an old one given over to destruction. Here one family is taken out of the number of existing Shemitic families, and with it, within it, the redemptive, revelatory work of God is carried forward. This is the tremendous significance of the call of Abraham. Where, after this, revelation is sporadically addressed to those outside the limits of election, the reason is that they have entered into contact with the chosen family. Thus the whole course of the special work of God is confined within the narrow channel of one people. Deists and all sorts of Rationalists frequently argued from this to the incredibility of Scriptural super-naturalism. If, they argued, God had gone to the trouble of introducing such a process of supernaturalism, He would have certainly taken pains to make it universal. Looked at closely, this argument proves a reflex of the general spirit of cosmopolitanism abroad in those times, and which is but one of the unhistorical conceptions of Rationalism. Because the God of Rationalism was at the bottom simply the God of nature, and nature is universal, therefore His self-disclosure must be as wide as nature. No account is had of the abnormal features of a state of sin, nor of the unique exigencies of a procedure of redemption. No distinction is felt between the beginning and early stages of the divine work and its later maturing. It should have been created all-finished, incapable of further progress from the outset. And, owing to this false perspective, or rather lack of perspective, the proximate narrowing and the ultimate universalizing are not kept in mind as mutually conditioning each other.

It must be acknowledged that election has also a permanent significance, of which we shall presently speak. But first of all, its temporal, instrumental purpose comes under consideration, and this is what the Rationalists failed to observe. The election of Abraham, and in the further development of things, of Israel, was meant as a particularistic means towards a universalistic end. Nor is this merely a later theological construction, made from looking back upon the finished process; from the outset there were, accompanying the narrowing steps, indications of an ultimate service to be rendered, by the election just beginning, to the cause of universalism. The very fact of Canaan being chosen for the abode of the sacred family was an indication of this kind. For although, compared with Mesopotamia, Canaan was a place of relative seclusion, and this entered as one motive for putting the patriarchs there, nevertheless archaeological research of recent times has shown that in itself Canaan was by no means a land lying isolated, aside from the great commerce and international life of the ancient world. It was actually a land where the lines of intercourse crossed. In the fulness of time its strategic position proved of supreme importance for the spreading abroad of the Gospel unto the whole earth.

The ultimate universalistic intent is also signified in the meeting between Abraham and Melchizedek. Melchizedek stood outside the circle of election recently formed. He was a representative of the earlier, pre-Abrahamic, knowledge of God. His religion, though imperfect, was by no means to be identified with the average paganism of the tribes. Abraham recognized the *El 'Elyon*, whom Melchizedek worshipped, as identical with his own God [*Gen.* 14.18, 19]. He gives him the tithe, and receives from him the blessing bestowed in the name of *El 'Elyon*, both actions of religious significance.

And not only indirectly or typically was this principle brought out; in the most explicit form at the very beginning Abraham was told that in him should 'all the families of the earth be blessed' [*Gen.* 12.3]. There is some uncertainty as to the exact rendering of the words standing in the Hebrew for 'shall be blessed'. In some passages where later the same divine promise is repeated [*Gen.* 22.18; 26.4] the species of the verb employed is the Hithpael. This admits of no other than the reflex rendering: 'in thee the nations of the earth shall bless themselves'. In other passages the Niphal species is found [*Gen.* 12.3; 18.18; 28.14]. The Niphal can be either passive or reflexive. It has been proposed, for the sake of uniformity, to make the sense in all passages the reflexive one. The English Versions, on the other hand, have forced the two passages where the Hithpael occurs, to bear a passive meaning, which

77

is against the grammar. Both Peter and Paul, quoting the promise in the New Testament, translate passively 'shall be blessed' [Acts 3.25; Gal. 3.8]. So did the Septuagint before, without discrimination of readings in the original. The quotations by the Apostles necessitate the retaining of the passive force in the Niphal passages. Still the reflexive sense in the other places also is not void of religious import. Reflexively translated, the statement means that the nations of the earth will make proverbial use of Abraham's name in invoking upon themselves good fortune: 'Wish that we were as blessed as Abraham'. Delitzsch goes so far as to vindicate for this the full spiritual sense inhering in the passive on the following ground: If the nations of the earth make Abraham's name a formula of blessing, then they thereby express themselves desirous of participating in his destiny, and under the divine plan of salvation it is so arranged that to the desire for the blessing the inheritance of the blessing is joined. In other words the proverbial use of the patriarch's name after this fashion would be equivalent to the exercise of faith. It is doubtful, however, whether this can be maintained, since naturally in the case of the wishers the desire would relate to temporal prosperity. Besides, in Gen. 12.2, 3, where the promise appears for the first time, the context indicates that a distinction is drawn between the lower and the higher aspect of the matter. In fact here three things are distinguished; first we have 'be thou a blessing', which is actually the proverbial use; then the promise continues, 'I will bless them that bless thee, and him that curses thee will I curse', which describes a determination of the lot of out-siders according to the attitude assumed by them towards Abraham; finally the closing words read, 'and in thee shall all the families of the earth be blessed'. Here evidently the third part of the promise is climacteric and must reach beyond the first and the second.

The history of the patriarchs is more universalistic than that of the Mosaic period. When the people were organized on a national basis and hedged off from other nations by the strict, seclusive rules of the law, the universalistic design was forced somewhat into the background. Further, through the conflict between Egypt and the Hebrews the real relation to the outside world became one of conflict. In the patriarchal period the opposite to this was true. Little was done to make the life of the people of God, even in an external religious sense, different from that of their environment. No ceremonial system on a large scale was set up to stress a distinction. Circumcision was the only rite instituted, and since this was also practised by the surrounding tribes, even it did not really differentiate. And positively also the principles on which God dealt with the patriarchs were of a highly spiritual nature, such as would make them universally applicable. Paul has a profound insight into this universalistic purport of patriarchal religion. His main contention with the Judaizers was that they insisted upon interpreting the patriarchal period on the basis of the Mosaic period. The reasoning [*Gal.* 3.15ff.] is in substance as follows: through the *diatheke* with Abraham the relation between God and Israel was put on a foundation of promise and grace; this could not be subsequently changed, because the older arrangement remains regulative for later institutions [vs 15], and the law was by no less than 430 years later than the Abrahamic *berith*. The revealed religion of the Old Testament in this respect resembles a tree whose root system and whose crown spread out widely, while the trunk of the tree confines the sap for a certain distance within a narrow channel. The patriarchal period corresponds to the root growth; the freely expanding crown to the revelation of the New Testament; and the relatively constricted form of the trunk to the period from Moses to Christ.

We must not forget, however, that election forms also a permanent feature in the divine procedure, and consequently remains, although with a different application, in force at the present time, no less than in the days of the Old Testament. In regard to *individuals*, the divine saving grace is always a differentiating principle. There is a people of God, a chosen people, a people of election, as truly today as in the time of the patriarchs. Of this likewise Paul was intensely conscious. We find him in the Epistle to the Romans reasoning in what at first sight appears to be a self-contradictory manner. On the one hand, as between Jew and Gentile, he upholds the principle of universalism, and proves it from the patriarchal history [*Gal.* 4.22ff.]; on the other hand, as between Jew and Jew he insists upon discrimination; not all who are descended from Abraham are children of God and of the promise [*Rom.* 9.6ff.]. The elective principle, abolished as to nationality, continues in force as to individuals. And even with respect to national privilege, while temporarily abolished now that its purpose has been fulfilled, there still remains reserved for the future a certain fulfilment of the *national* elective promise. Israel in its *racial* capacity will again in the future be visited by the saving grace of God [Rom. 11.2, 12, 25].

[2] *The objectivity of the gifts bestowed*

The second distinctive feature of God's revelation to the patriarchs concerns the objectivity of the gifts which it bestows. We have here the beginning of a factual religion, a religion attaching itself to objective divine interpositions on behalf of man. Not that the inward,

79

subjective aspect is lacking, but only that it is developed in close dependence on the external support. God does not begin with working upon the inward psychical states of the patriarchs, as though they were subjects for reform – an unbiblical attitude which is, unfortunately, characteristic of too much of modern religion. He begins with giving them promises. The keynote is not what Abraham has to do for God, but what God will do for Abraham. Then, in response to this, the subjective frame of mind that changes the inner and outer life is cultivated.

Closely connected with this feature is another, the historical-progressive character of the religion of revelation. In it the all-important thing is that God has acted in the past, is acting in the present, and promises to act in the future. Those who live under it always look back into the past, that is to say, their piety has a solid basis of tradition. Even when desiring to make progress they do not believe in the possibility of real, healthy progress without continuity with the past; they love and revere what has gone before, and dare to criticize the present in the light of the past, as well as in the light of reason, where it is necessary. Their contentedness is not of the superficial kind, such as would interfere with profound expectation from the future. At the same time they do not depend for the progress in the future on their own acquired potencies or powers, but on the same supernatural interposition and activity of God, which have produced the present out of the past. Biblical religion is thoroughly eschatological in its outlook.

Above all it is, as it was already with the patriarchs, a religion of modesty, for modesty is in religion as elsewhere a fruit that grows on the tree of historic reverence only. The specific difference in this point between Biblical religion and pagan religions, particularly nature-religions, is easily observable. Nature-religion revolves around the thought of what the deity is for all men and under all circumstances. It presents to the worship of its devotees a face the same yesterday, today, and for ever. There is no action of the deity here, no history, no progress.

The objective action of God was for the patriarchs interlinked with the three great promises. These were first, the chosen family would be made into a great nation; secondly, that the land of Canaan would be their possession; thirdly, that they were to become a blessing for all people.

[3] *The promises are fulfilled supernaturally*

Next to the objectivity of these three things promised, we notice as the third important feature of the revelation, that it emphasizes most strongly, both in word and act, the absolute monergism of the divine power in accomplishing the things promised; otherwise expressed, the strict supernaturalism of the procedure towards fulfilling the promises. This explains why, in the life of Abraham, so many things proceed contrary to nature. Not as though contrariness-to-nature possessed any positive value for its own sake. The contrariness is simply chosen as the most convenient practical means for demonstrating that nature was transcended here. Abraham was not permitted to do anything through his own strength or resources to realize what the promise set before him. With reference to the third promise this was excluded by the nature of the case. But in regard to the other two it might have seemed as if he might have contributed something toward the end in view. In point of fact he attempted to proceed on the principle of synergism in proposing to God that Ishmael should be considered the seed of the promise. But this was not accepted for the reason of Ishmael's being the product of nature, whereas a super-natural product was required [*Gen.* 17.18, 19; *Gal.* 4.23]. Abraham was kept childless until an age when he was 'as good as dead', that the divine omnipotence might be evident as the source of Isaac's birth [*Gen.* 21.1–7; *Rom.* 4.19–21; *Heb.* 11.11; *Isa.* 51.2]. The last mentioned explains the divine philosophy of this, to the naturalistic standpoint, so strange course of action: 'Look unto Abraham your father, and unto Sarah that bare you; for when he was but one I called him, and I blessed him, and made him many'. In connection with the second promise we can observe the same thing. Abraham was not allowed to acquire any possession in the land of promise. Yet he was rich and might easily have done so. But God Himself intended to fulfil this promise also without the co-operation of the patriarch; and Abraham seems to have had some apprehension of this, for he explains his refusal to accept any of the spoils from the king of Sodom by the fear lest the latter should say, 'I have made Abram rich' [*Gen.* 14.21–23].

THE DIVINE NAME 'EL-SHADDAI'

This supernaturalism in God's dealing with the patriarchs finds expression in the characteristic divine name for the period. This is the name *El-Shaddai.* In this full form the name is found six times in the Pentateuch, and once in Ezekiel. The passages are: Gen. 17.1; 28.3; 35.11; 43.14; 48.3; Ex. 6.3; Ezek. 10.5. To the six Pentateuch references a seventh may have to be added if the reading in Gen. 49.25 be changed from *eth-Shaddai* to *El-Shaddai.* The shorter, possibly abbreviated, form (*Shaddai*) occurs more frequently in the other books of the Old Testament. In Job it occurs more than 30 times, and has there been regarded as a symptom either of the antique character of the story, or of its having been written in the style of an older period. In either case it reveals a consciousness of the high age of the name. Further, the name in this shorter form is found twice in the Psalter [68.14; 91.1]; three times in the prophets [*Isa.* 13.6; *Joel.* 1.15; *Ezek.* 1.24]; and once in Ruth [1.21].

Various etymologies have been proposed, some of them quite unworthy of the occasion of its occurrence. Nöldeke finds in the ending *ai* the possessive suffix, which would yield the meaning 'my Lord'. But the word is never used in address to God, and God uses it of Himself. Where men use it, it is of God in the third person. Others propose to connect the name with a somewhat similar word meaning 'demons' in Deut. 32.17 and Psalm 106.37, two contexts speaking of Israel's idolatry in the wilderness. But the word there is differently vocalized (*shedim*). There is also a naturalistic interpretation according to which it would mean 'the thunderer'. Our choice seems to lie between the two following etymologies: (a) the word is made up of the note of the relative *sha* and the adjective *dai*, 'sufficient', thus meaning 'He who is sufficient', either to Himself or to others. This is to be found in the later Greek versions, which render *hikanos*. (b) Or it may be derived from the verb *shadad*, meaning 'to overpower', 'to destroy'. On this derivation the name would mean 'the Over-powerer', 'the Destroyer', or 'the All-powerful One'. This is the view of some of the translators of the Septuagint. In that version it is often rendered *ho Pantokrator*, 'the All-Ruler'.

The second of these two derivations deserves the preference. It best explains the appearance of the name in patriarchal history. God is there called *El-Shaddai*, because through the supernaturalism of His procedure He, as it were, overpowers nature in the service of His grace, and compels her to further His designs. Thus the name forms a connecting link between *El* and *Elohim*, on the one hand, and *Jehovah*, the Mosaic name, on the other hand. If the former signify God's relation to nature, and *Jehovah* is His redemptive name, then *El-Shaddai* may be said to express how God uses nature for supernature. A clear connection between the verb *shadad* and *Shaddai* is observed in Isa. 13.6 and Joel 1.15. In the Psalter passages and in Ruth the omni-potence and sovereignty of God are clearly emphasized. The con-ception also fits into the general tenor of Job and Ezekiel.

FAITH AS FOUND IN PATRIARCHAL RELIGION

It is but a reflex of the supernaturalism in the objective sphere, that in the subjective field of patriarchal religion the idea of faith suddenly springs into prominence. This constitutes the fourth important aspect of the doctrinal significance of our period. Gen. 15.6 is the first explicit Biblical reference to faith. Broadly speaking, faith bears a two-fold significance in Scriptural teaching and experience: it is, firstly, dependence on the supernatural power and grace of God; and secondly, the state or act of projection into a higher, spiritual world. Of late it has been treated in the latter sense by preference, and sometimes with an obvious design to minimize its soteric importance. The psychology of faith has been studied, from the theological standpoint not always felicitously, because the Biblical data have not been carefully ascertained. It may be useful to know something about the psychology of faith, but it is of far greater importance to understand its religious function in redemption, and unless the latter is apprehended, the psychology is apt to turn out, from the Biblical point of view, sheer foolishness.

To the Biblical writers faith is not a common denominator to which after some hazy fashion every religious sentiment and aspiration can be reduced. For the reason indicated, faith was in Abraham's life the chief religious act and frame of mind. His whole life was a school of faith in which the divine training developed this grace from step to step. Even at the beginning there was a heavy demand on the patriarch's faith. He was called upon to leave his country, kindred, father's house. And God at first did not name the land of his destination. 'The land that I will show thee' was its sole description. As Heb. 11.8 tells us: 'He went out, not knowing whither he went'. The statement in Gen. 12.7, that God would give him that particular country, came as a surprise to him. From Gen. 15 we learn that there was at one and the same time in Abraham a relatively mature faith, and an intense desire to have the insufficiency of his faith relieved by further assurance. When God promised that his posterity should be numerous as the stars, he believed and it was reckoned to him for righteousness. But with reference to the promised inheritance of the land he doubted.

There is fine psychological observation here. Faith and a desire for more faith frequently go hand in hand. The reason is that through faith we lay hold upon God, and in grasping the infinite object, the utter inadequacy of each single act of appropriation immediately reveals itself in the very act. It is the same in the Gospel: 'Lord, I believe; help thou mine unbelief' [*Mark* 9.24]. The climax of the training of Abraham in faith came, when God asked him to sacrifice Isaac, his son. Here again the terms descriptive of the surrender asked are multiplied to bring out its greatness: 'Take now thy son, thine only son, whom thou lovest, even Isaac'. Correspondingly here the strongest terms of divine asseveration are used in restating the promise [*Gen.* 22.2, 16–18]. It ought to be remembered that Isaac was surrendered to God not merely as an object of paternal affection, but as the exponent and instrument and pledge of the fulfilment of all the promises, which thus appeared to perish with his death.

Abraham's faith offers a good opportunity for analysing the ingredients of faith in general. At first sight it seems to take its point of departure from belief, assent to the veracity of a statement. This then would be followed by trust, as a second act called forth by and based on the belief. In point of fact, however, this sequence is not quite in accord with the psychological process. The matter to be assented to through belief is, in religion, and was in Abraham's case particularly, not something mentally demonstrable, or axiomatically certain before all demonstration. There entered into it a personal factor, viz., the trustworthiness of God, who made the declaration of the promises. Religious belief exists not in its last analysis on what we can prove to be so, but on the fact of God having declared it to be so. Behind the belief, the assent, therefore, there lies an antecedent trust distinguishable from the subsequent trust. And this reliance upon the word of God is an eminently religious act. Hence it is inaccurate to say that belief is merely the prerequisite of faith and not an element of faith itself.

To be sure, no sooner has this antecedent trust developed into belief, than this in turn is followed by a trust of far wider reach and more practical significance. For the declarations believed are not relating to abstract, indifferent matters; they are promises relating to vital concerns of life. For this reason, they solicit a reaction from the will and the emotions no less than from the intellect. They become a basis on which the entire religious consciousness comes to rest and finds assurance for its deepest and farthest-reaching practical needs and desires. Faith, therefore, begins with and ends in the trust – rest in God.

In Gen. 15.6, this is strikingly illustrated, although the rendering in the English Bible is not for this purpose the most felicitous one: 'He believed in Jehovah'. The Hebrew word *heemin* construed with the preposition *be* literally means: 'he developed assurance in Jehovah'. The Hiphil of *amen* here has a causative-productive sense, and the preposition brings out that the personal point at which this assurance sprang up was nothing else but the personal Jehovah, and that the same divine Person, in whom it sprang up, was also the One in whom it came to rest. And this personal relatedness of his faith to God imparted a strongly God-centred character to Abraham's piety. It is emphasized in the narrative that the patriarch's supreme blessedness consisted in the possession of God Himself: 'Fear not, Abraham, I am thy shield, thy exceeding great reward' [*Gen.* 15.1]. For this treasure he could cheerfully renounce all other gifts.

But this faith attached itself not merely to God in general; it was strong enough to bear the strain of trusting in the supernatural self-communication and action of God. It related specifically to the divine omnipotence and saving grace. Salvation requires at all times more than God's general providence exerted in our behalf. It implies supernaturalism, not as a curious, marvellous self-demonstration of God, but as the very core of true religiousness. On the basis of this part, as well as of other parts of Scripture in general, it is quite proper to maintain that a belief entertained and a life conducted on the basis of a relation to God through nature alone does not yield the Biblical religion at all. It is not merely a partial, it is a *different* thing. In Abraham's case this meant negatively, for securing God and the promises, a renouncing of all his own purely human resources. He expected nothing from himself. And positively he expected everything from the supernatural interposition of God. Paul with his penetrating doctrinal genius has given us a striking description of this supernaturalism of Abraham's faith, both on its negative and on its positive side, in Rom. 4.17–23 [cp, *Heb.* 11.17–19]. In both passages his faith is represented as rising to the height of trusting the omnipotence of God for the raising of Isaac from the dead, after the divine command to surrender him should have been executed. Here the two poles of negation of self-resource and of affirmation of divine omnipotence are represented by faith and resurrection. This is the reason why the Apostle compares Abraham's faith at this point to the Christian's faith in the resurrection of Jesus Christ from the dead. This kind of faith is a faith in the creative interposition of God. It trusts in Him for calling the things that are not as though they were. This does not, of course, mean that the objective content of the patriarch's faith was doctrinally identical with that of the New Testament believer. Paul does not commit the anachronism of saying that Abraham's faith had for its object the raising of Christ from the dead. What he means is that the attitude of faith towards the raising of Isaac and the attitude of faith towards the resurrection are identical in point of faith able to confront and incorporate the supernatural.

Through this emphasis on faith-trust the original Shemitic consciousness was considerably modified. Hitherto the chief element in it had been fear and awe. Fear did not, of course, vanish from the religion of Abraham. His forms of addressing God on several occasions clearly prove its continuance as a potent element in his religion [cp. *Gen.* 18.27]. In fact 'the fear of Jehovah' remains throughout the Old Testament the generic name for religion. But henceforth it is a fear that has more of reverence than of dread in it. In this sense it continues to colour the co-ordinate element of friendship and trust with reference to God. There is a peculiar strain of submission, a specific humility mixed with the trustful intercourse [*Gen.* 17.3; 18.3]; nevertheless, the predominant note is the opposite, the feeling of friendship with God. Nor is this merely a statement of mind cultivated or cherished by Abraham; it is explicitly professed, with divine delight and satisfaction as it were, by God Himself.

The classic expression of this from the divine side is in 18.17–19. God here declares that Abraham stands too near to Him for the thought of hiding his plans from him to be tolerable, for God has 'known' him, i.e., set His affection upon him. The theophanies received by the patriarch are a witness to the same fact. They form a record quite unique. At no point of the Old Testament, the life of Moses perhaps excluded, was there such a divine condescension as during the life of Abraham. If we except Gen. 15, there was a remarkable absence of the frightful in these theophanies. There is something here somewhat resembling God's ancient walk with men in the days of paradise or the life of Enoch. In recognition of all this he was by later generations called 'the friend of God', Jas. 2.23. And even in the midst of the terror of 15.12, there was a most impressive witness to the divine condescension in the remarkable setting of the theophany itself. There is probably no case surpassing this in anthropomorphic realism within the Old Testament. The dividing of the animals and the walking of God (alone) between the pieces literally signifies that God invokes upon Himself the fate of dismemberment in case He should not keep faith with Abraham [cp. *Jer.* 34.18–19].

A further function exercised by faith in the religious life of the patriarchs was that it spiritualized their attitude towards the promises. This was brought about in the following way: God not only reserved to Himself the fulfilment, but also refrained from giving the promises their divine fulfilment during the lives of the patriarchs. Thus

Abraham learned to possess the promises of God, in the promising God alone. The promises had no chance of becoming materialized through detachment from their centre in God. They could only be had and enjoyed as a part and potential outflow of the divine heart itself. For the promises are like an ethereal garment, more precious than the body of the promised thing over which it is thrown. Had the promises been quickly fulfilled, then the danger would have immediately arisen of their acquiring importance and value apart from God. In later times, when much of them had actually gone into fulfilment, this danger proved very real. The mass of the people fell from the spiritual height of Abraham's faith. The earthly and typical obscured to them the spiritual, and alongside of this there went a fatal losing of interest in Him whose gift the earthly treasures were. In the interpretation of the patriarch's faith given by Hebrews 11, this side of the matter stands in the foreground. Here it is pictured how the patriarchs were contented to dwell in tents, and did not regret the non-possession of the promised land, and the reason for this frame of mind is carefully added: it was not that through faith they looked forward in the vista of time to a more solid and comprehensive possession of Canaan than was possible in their own days; the real reason was that from the earthly, possessed or not-yet-possessed, they had learned to look upward to a form of possession of the promise identifying it more closely with God Himself: 'They looked for the city that has the foundations, whose builder and maker is God' (i.e., because its builder and maker is God) [*Heb.* 11.10].

Lastly, Abraham's faith had an important bearing on the practical monotheism of patriarchal religion. Such a reliance upon God left no room for the cultivation of or interest in any other 'divine' numen[1] that might have been conceived as existent. It is true, monotheism is nowhere theoretically formulated in the account. But God monopolized Abraham to the extent of the exclusion of all others. One motive for calling him out of his original environment was the prevalence of polytheism there; this much we learn from later Old Testament statements, e.g., Josh. 24.2, 3; among the branch of Abraham's family that remained in Haran the worship of other gods continued, at least alongside that of Jehovah [*Gen.* 31.19]. And according to Gen. 35.2, Jacob, on arriving in Canaan, charged his household to put away the foreign gods that were among them.

---

[1] A deity (orig. a nod, as expressive of will and command).

ETHICAL ELEMENTS

This finishes the discussion of faith. Side by side with it and the three preceding main topics forming the content of patriarchal revelation (election, objectivity, supernaturalism) we must now, under the same heading of content, examine the ethical elements in the patriarchal revelation. Abraham's life was conducted on a high ethical plane. Even the modern critical school agrees with this. Only, they explain this from a later ethicizing treatment of the ancient stories by writers imbued with the prophetic spirit. The record clearly means to give the impression that Abraham's life was not perfect. Why, then, should the idealizing redactors have left so much or any of the less worthy elements uneliminated? While the record does not cover up or condone the patriarchs' defects, it places, over against these, great virtues. Apart from the specifically-religious traits already touched upon under the head of faith, the main virtues emphasized are: hospitality, magnanimity, self-sacrifice, loyalty. Abraham was taught that the religious favour of God cannot continue except accompanied by ethical living. The purpose of God's choosing him was, according to Gen. 18.17-19, that he might command his children to keep the way of Jehovah to do righteousness and justice; and on this was suspended the fulfilment of the promises: 'to the end that Jehovah may bring upon Abraham that which he has spoken of him'. Abraham admits that his prayer for the preservation of Sodom can have no effect, except there be a remnant of righteous men in the city. He recognizes that there is a difference in ethics between the pagans and his own circle, for to Abimelech he says: 'I thought, surely the fear of God is not in this place', though, curiously enough, he resorts to a half-lie to escape the danger of such inferior ethics.

Ethics are not, however, represented as independent of religion, much less as the sole content of religion; but they are the product of religion. Gen. 17.1 contains the classic expression of this: 'I am El-Shaddai; walk before me, then thou shalt be blameless'. The 'walking before Jehovah' pictures the constant presence of Jehovah to his mind as walking behind him, and supervising him. The thought of the divine approval furnishes the motive for obedience. Also the force of El-Shaddai must be noticed. What shapes his conduct is not the general thought of God as moral ruler, but specifically the thought of El-Shaddai, who fills his life with miraculous grace. Thus morality is put on a redemptive basis and inspired by the principle of faith.

Further, the ethical character of Old Testament religion is symbolized by circumcision. This, therefore, is the place for discussing this ceremony. The older theologians were inclined to explain its observance among other nations from their contact with Israel. This is no longer a tenable view. Circumcision was practised not merely by a number of Shemitic proples closely connected with Israel, such as Edom, Ammon, Moab, the Arabs, but it was also widely diffused among non-Shemitic races. It existed among the Egyptians. It has been found among the American tribes, and in islands of the Southern Pacific. It undoubtedly existed before the time of Abraham. We must, therefore, admit that it was not given to Abraham as a previously unknown thing, but introduced into his family invested with a new significance. The rite was everywhere a religious one. Herodotus thought that the Egyptians practised it as a sanitary measure, a view which later found favour among rationalists. At present this notion is well-nigh universally abandoned, although a few writers still assume that, as a secondary motive, the increase of fruitfulness came into play.

In its original conception it was a tribal badge, hence not received in infancy, but when the grown-up young man was for the first time admitted into full tribal rights. But membership in tribe or clan was closely associated with religion. Some have thought of circumcision as a sacrifice, perhaps a remnant of human sacrifice, part doing service for the whole. Others think it a relic of the barbaric custom of self-mutilation in honour of the deity. There is no evidence of this even as regards pagan circumcision. It is absolutely excluded so far as Israel is concerned. The Old Testament forbids every mutilation of the human body, and requires for every sacrifice absolute cleanness, whereas in circumcision precisely the unclean is removed. The removal of uncleanness seems to have everywhere underlain the practice among Israel and outside. It belonged to the ritual sphere, and outside of Israel no deeper ethical or spiritual meaning seems to have been attached to, or developed out of it. But it was God's intention that the ritual should subserve the teaching of ethical and spiritual truth. This was not, however, done by manner of explicit statement. The ritual was at first left to teach its own lesson. All that is enjoined upon Abraham in Gen. 17 is the external performance. In the time of Moses, according to Ex. 6.12, 30, it had begun to be metaphorically used for the removal of disqualification in speech. In Deuteronomy, however, where the prophetic strain of revelation is anticipated, the concept is transferred outright to the spiritual sphere. In Lev. 26.41, the necessity is spoken of that the uncircumcised heart of the Israelites shall be humbled. In Deut. 10.16, Moses exhorts the people to circumcise the foreskin of their hearts. In Deut. 30.6 the thought assumes the form of a promise:

'the Lord thy God will circumcise thine heart, to love the Lord thy God with all thine heart and all thy soul'.

These ideas are further developed in the prophets. Jeremiah says: 'Take away the foreskin of your hearts, ye men of Judah' [4.4]. This prophet also speaks metaphorically, but with a turn towards the ethical, of uncircumcised ears, meaning inability to hearken [6.10]. He threatens the Israelites with judgment, because, like the Egyptians, Edomites, Ammonites, and Moabites, they are 'circumcised in uncircumcision', i.e., while having the external sign, they lack the circumcision of the heart [9.25, 26]. The statement implies that, though for others circumcision might be a purely external thing, for Israel it ought to be something more. Similarly, Ezekiel represents Jehovah as complaining that the house of Israel have brought into the temple aliens uncircumcised in heart and uncircumcised in flesh [44.7]. From the law and the prophets the ethical and spiritual interpretation passed over into the New Testament, where we find it with Paul [*Rom.* 2.25–29; 4.11; *Eph.* 2.11; *Phil.* 3.3; *Col.* 2.11–13].

For the doctrinal understanding of circumcision two facts are significant; first, it was instituted before the birth of Isaac; secondly, in the accompanying revelation only the second promise, relating to numerous posterity, is referred to. These two facts together show that circumcision has something to do with the process of propagation. Not in the sense that the act is in itself sinful, for there is no trace of this anywhere in the Old Testament. It is not the act but the product, that is, *human nature*, which is unclean, and stands in need of purification and qualification. Hence circumcision is not, as among pagans, applied to grown-up young men, but to infants on the eighth day. Human nature is unclean and disqualified in its very source. Sin, consequently, is a matter of the race and not of the individual only. The need of qualification had to be specially emphasized under the Old Testament. At that time the promises of God had proximate reference to temporal, natural things. Hereby the danger was created that natural descent might be understood as entitling to the grace of God. Circumcision teaches that physical descent from Abraham is not sufficient to make true Israelites. The uncleanness and disqualification of nature must be taken away. Dogmatically speaking, therefore, circumcision stands for justification and regeneration, plus sanctification [*Rom.* 4.9–12; *Col.* 2.11–13].

THE PATRIARCH ISAAC

Isaac's life forms a sharp contrast to that of Abraham. The contrast, strange to say, arises from the similarity. Abraham's history teems with originality; in Isaac's there is repetition of these originalities on almost every page. In the protracted barrenness of his wife, in his exposure to danger in Gerar, in the treatment received from Abimelech, in the differentiation of character between his two sons – in all this the similarity is too striking to be regarded as accidental. It has not escaped the critics, many of whom think that Isaac is a mere genealogical link serving to express the unity between Edom and Israel. All the inventive genius of the legend having been squandered upon Abraham, nothing new remained that could be used to embellish Isaac. But this explains nothing if, as Wellhausen thinks, Abraham's is the latest figure in the patriarchal triad. Dillman offers the genealogical solution of the problem in a different form. According to him there were certain elements in the Abrahamitic immigration, which more faithfully preserved the original customs than the others, and the legend symbolizes this by portraying their representative, Isaac, as doing the same things over again, and repeating the acts and experiences which characterized the life of Abraham.

To this it must be rejoined that similarity in acts and experiences does not fitly symbolize similarity in customs and modes of life. It would have been more expressive in such a case to represent Isaac as dwelling in the same places where Abraham had dwelt, and this is precisely what the Biblical narrative does not do. Hengstenberg comments upon the character of Isaac, which he thinks was passive and impressionable: 'the powerful personality of Abraham made such a deep impression on the soft nature of his son, that he follows him even where imitation is reprehensible'. But this overlooks the principle that, in the history of revelation, character is not to be regarded as an ultimate datum; the revelation does not spring from the character; on the contrary, the character is predetermined by the necessities of the revelation. If, therefore, there be such a scarcity of the new, such a lack of assertive originality, in the story of Isaac, the reason for this must lie in the need of thus expressing some important revelation principle.

What this principle is we believe has been best expressed by Delitzsch in his observation that 'Isaac is the middle member of the patriarchal triad, and as such throughout a more secondary and passive than active member. The historical process usually illustrates this principle, that the middle part of it is relatively weaker than the beginning, the funda-mental figure of its rhythmical motion being the amphimacer'.[1] He

1 A short between two longs.

seems to affirm this of history in general. It is sufficient for our present purpose to apply it to the history of redemption, and to patriarchal history as a typical part of this. The redeeming work of God passes by its very nature through three stages. Its beginnings are marked by a high degree of energy and productivity; they are creative beginnings. The middle stage is a stage of suffering and self-surrender, and is therefore passive in its aspect. This in turn is followed by the resumed energy of the subjective transformation, characterizing the third stage. Now the middle one of these stages is represented by Isaac.

The principle finds expression, however, not merely in the general lack of originality, but more positively also in the account of the demanded sacrifice of Isaac. As furnishing an illustration of Abraham's faith this has been already discussed; here we are concerned with its objective significance only. Not a few critics have attempted to explain the narrative of Gen. 22 as a polemic of the later prophetic spirit against human sacrifice, which was at that time still sporadically occurring among the Israelites. But there is no trace whatsoever of polemic in the narrative. The statement that God commands Abraham to offer up Isaac distinctly implies that in the abstract the sacrifice of a human being cannot be condemned on principle. It is well to be cautious in committing oneself to that critical opinion, for it strikes at the very root of the atonement. The rejection of the 'blood theology' as a remnant of a very barbaric type of primitive religion rests on such a basis. Other writers have assumed that there is a protest here, not, to be sure, against human sacrifice, as such, but against that particular form of it which prevailed in Oriental systems of nature-worship, where the gods are believed to be subject to birth and death, and consequently it behoves their devotees to immolate themselves in fellowship with them. But not of this either is there any indication in the narrative. The transaction is not intended to throw light on the mode, but rather on the fundamental principle of sacrifice.

Sacrifice occupies an essential place in the work of redemption. Hitherto this work had been almost exclusively represented as a work of supernatural power. In the life of Abraham this had been most strongly emphasized. Hence there might have easily resulted a certain inadequacy in the expression of the work as a whole. Divine power, while absolutely necessary, covers only one aspect of the process. Sin is disturbance in the *moral* sphere, and here not power alone but passivity, suffering, atonement, obedience, are required to restore the normal status. All Biblical sacrifice rests on the idea that the gift of life to God, either in consecration or in expiation, is necessary to the action or the restoration of religion. What passes from man to God is not regarded as property but, even though it be property for a symbolic purpose, means always in the last analysis the gift of *life*. And this is, in the original conception, neither in expiation nor in consecration the gift of alien life; it is the gift of life of the offerer himself. The second principle underlying the idea is that man in the abnormal relations of sin is disqualified for offering this gift of his life in his own person. Hence the principle of vicariousness is brought into play: one life takes the place of another life.

These two principles can here be simply stated; the proof of their Biblical basis must wait till our discussion of the Mosaic system of sacrifice. All that is necessary here is to observe how clearly the two ideas mentioned find expression in the narrative. Abraham is asked by God to offer life, that which in point of life is dearest to him, his only son. At the same time it is declared by the interposition of the Angel and the pointing out of the ram in the thicket, that the substitution of one life for another life would be acceptable to God. Not the sacrifice of human life as such, but the sacrifice of average sinful human life, is deprecated by the Old Testament. In the Mosaic law these things are taught by an elaborate symbolism. Here on this primordial occasion they find expression through a simple symbolism of an even more eloquent and realistic kind. Thus there was placed side by side with the emphasis on the divine creative omnipotence the stress on the necessity of sacrifice. It is not difficult to trace the co-existence and joint-necessity of both factors in the doctrinal teaching of the New Testament. Paul speaks of the atonement by Christ in words borrowed from this occurrence, Rom. 8.32. It has been suggested that the place where the event happened, one of the mountains of the land of Moriah [*Gen.* 22.2] links this sacrifice through its locality with the sacrificial cultus in the temple at Jerusalem.

THE PATRIARCH JACOB

The main principle embodied in the history of Jacob-Israel is that of subjective transformation of life, with a renewed stress on the productive activity of the divine factor. This must be kept in mind in order to read the history aright. Of the characters of the three patriarchs, that of Jacob is least represented as an ideal one. Its reprehensible features are rather strongly brought out. This is done in order to show that divine grace is not the reward for, but the source of noble traits. Grace overcoming human sin and transforming human nature is the keynote of the revelation here.

93

[1] *Election*

In order to prove this, first of all the principle of election is placed in the foreground, and that not in its racial and transitory, but in its individual and permanent significance. That this should be done here, and not earlier, we might *a priori* expect. Election is a principle entering specifically into the *application* of redemption; therefore it should appear in the last member of the patriarchal triad. Election is intended to bring out the *gratuitous* character of grace. With regard to the objective part of the work of redemption there is scarcely any need of stressing this. That man himself has made no contribution towards accomplishing the atonement is obvious in itself. But no sooner does the redeeming work enter into the subjectivity of man than the obviousness ceases, although the reality of the principle is not, of course, in the least abated. The semblance easily results, that in receiving and working out the subjective benefits of grace for his transformation, the individual man has to some extent been the decisive factor. And to affirm this, to however small a degree, would be to detract in the same proportion from the monergism of the divine grace and from the glory of God. Hence at this point by an explicit declaration the principle is rendered for ever secure, a principle which the finest psychological observation could never have raised above all possibility of doubt.

This also explains why the declaration comes in at the very beginning of the third part of the patriarchal history, even before the birth of Jacob and Esau. For, from the subsequent lives of these two men it would have been no less difficult than from the lives of ordinary saints to prove that all human goodness is exclusively the fruit of divine grace. For although Jacob, in comparison with Esau, revealed some ethically ignoble qualities, yet in spiritual appreciation of the promise he proved himself the superior of the two. In order to guard against all misunderstandings arising from this, the principle was established at a point where no such considerations, pro or con, could possibly enter into the matter. Even at the risk of exposing the divine sovereignty to the charge of arbitrariness, the matter was decided prior to the birth of the two brothers.

It may indeed be thought that there had been in patriarchal history an earlier occasion, viz., in connection with the birth of Isaac and of Ishmael, for inculcating the lesson involved. Undoubtedly election entered as the determining factor on that occasion likewise; but the point to observe is that there the circumstances were so shaped as to stake everything on the issue of supernaturalism in producing the seed of the promise. The contrast is between the younger woman, able to bear children by nature, and the older woman, already as good as dead. For making it an exhibition of the moral aspect of election, the fact that Sarah was the free woman and Hagar the slave woman would have stood in the way; whereas for bringing out the factor of omnipotence this contrast between free and slave was negligible. On the other hand, in the case of Jacob and Esau everything is carefully arranged so as to eliminate from the outset all factors tending to obscure the moral issue of the absolute sovereignty of God. The two children are born of the same mother, and moreover at the same birth; and to exclude every thought of natural preference, the younger is preferred to the elder. No conceivable way remained of accounting for this differentiation except to attribute it to the sovereign choice of God. The statement about the elder serving the younger has its proximate reference to the racial relations between the Israelites and the Edomites. But that its import was not exhausted by this appears, apart from the general typical bearing of Old Testament history, from the use made by Paul of the event to establish the principle of individual election [*Rom.* 9.11–13].

It will be observed that Paul here adds an explanation of the end which the disclosure of this purpose served in the plan of God. The phrase 'the elective purpose of God' is explained in the following words: 'not of works but of Him that calleth'. This is equivalent to: 'not of works but of grace', the idea of 'calling' being with Paul an exponent of divine monergism. Revelation of the doctrine of election, therefore, serves the revelation of the doctrine of grace. God calls attention to His sovereign discrimination between man and man, to place the proper emphasis upon the truth, that His grace alone is the source of all spiritual good to be found in man. Election, consequently, is not according to Scripture a blind unreadable fate; it serves to the extent indicated an intelligible purpose. In this respect it differs from the fate of the pagans, which hangs, an impersonal mystery, even above the gods. The observation thus made is, of course, not capable of solving all the enigmas of the doctrine of election. There may be many other grounds of election, unknown and unknowable to us. But this one reason we *do* know, and in knowing it we at the same time know that, whatever other reasons exist, they can have nothing to do with any meritorious ethical condition of the objects of God's choice.

[2] *The Bethel dream-vision*

The next occasion on which an important revelation element was introduced into the life of Jacob was the dream-vision he received at Bethel [*Gen.* 28.10–22]. Jacob was on a journey away from the land of promise, moreover on his way to a family infected with idolatry and worldliness, for the imitation of whose sins his own nature predisposed him. There was special need, therefore, at this time, of a personal communication from God to him, whereby subjectively he should be brought under the influence of the promises. The fact of the revelation assuming the form of a dream points, as before noted, to the low ebb of the receiver's spirituality. The vision beheld in the dream is that of a ladder set up on the earth, the top of it reaching to heaven, and the angels of God ascending and descending whilst Jehovah stands at the top and repeats to him the ancient promises. The angels are the ministers of God's interposition for the sustenance, guidance, and protection of Jacob.

In connection with this the name Elohim seems to be significant, all the more because in the sequel of the statement it gives way to Jehovah, where the closer religious relationship is spoken of. The angels ascend, as it were, to carry up Jacob's wants and entreaties; they descend to bring down to him the grace and gifts of God. Dillman finds significance in the feature that the ascending of the angels is mentioned before their descending: the angels were already there ministering in Jacob's behalf before he became aware of their presence. With the tenor of the vision agrees the fact that in the subjective transformation wrought upon the patriarch various subjective experiences and instances of discipline played a large part. But this was only one side of the meaning of the vision. Besides being a reassurance for Jacob's future life, it also bore a sacramental significance with regard to the continual intimate presence of Jehovah with him. He said 'Surely Jehovah is in this place, and I knew it not' and 'this is none other than the house of God, and this is the gate of heaven'.

These words do not necessarily imply surprise at God's general presence and agency in the place, as if Jacob conceived of God as by nature bound to the land of Canaan. We have already seen that what was peculiar to the holy land were the redemptive theophanies, theophanic appearances of God. Jacob evidently wondered at this, that these appearances, if but in a dream, nevertheless remained attached to his person, and followed him in his wanderings. Although now exiled from his father's house, as Ishmael had been, he was not like the latter placed outside of the line of sacred inheritance through which the promises were to be transmitted. And the core of it all lay in the abiding of Jehovah with him wherever he went. Our Saviour Himself placed this deeper second interpretation upon Jacob's vision. When declaring to Nathanael, 'Ye shall see the heavens opened and the angels of God ascending and descending upon the Son of Man' [*John* 1.51], He implied that in His own life and ministry the idea of communion with God illustrated by Jacob's vision had received its supreme realization.

The vow pronounced by Jacob at the close of the vision combines the two elements contained in it in such a way that the ministration for which the angels stood results in binding him to the acceptance of Jehovah as his personal property and object of service. The construction adopted by the Authorized Version, which makes the main clause begin with the words, 'then shall Jehovah be my God', is to be preferred to that of the Revised Version, in which the main clause begins with 'then this stone, etc'. This is the only case in patriarchal history of the promising of a vow.

[3] *The wrestling at Peniel*

The third event in the history illustrating the specific principle involved is that described in Gen. 32; it relates Jacob's wrestling with a strange person on his return to the land of promise. The transaction is highly mysterious. Many modern interpreters consider it mythical in character. It is asserted that this particular myth was common in various forms among the Shemitic tribes, and that through this episode it obviously found entrance into the patriarchal legend. Varying answers are given to the question, Whom does the strange wrestler represent? Some say, he is the patron-deity of the land disputing Jacob's entrance into it. Or the story is believed to have been originally entirely detached from the given figure of Jacob, and to have represented the contest of the Sun with the demon of Winter. Still others think the story explains the sacredness and popularity of the shrine at Peniel. The shrine was more frequented than others, because there Jacob had wrestled with the deity and compelled the latter to bless him.

In all these modern interpretations the wrestling is interpreted after a purely physical fashion. Jacob was physically stronger than the one who wrestled with him. An over-spiritualizing view often fell into the opposite extreme, interpreting the event as a purely spiritual, internal, perhaps visionary, transaction. But there must have been an external bodily side to the experience, since it left a physical mark upon Jacob. On the other hand, it cannot have been entirely physical either; the terms are not realistic enough for that and differ widely from those in which the pagan myths adduced for comparison are clothed. The veil of mystery overhanging the account is peculiar to it and absent from pagan mythology. In harmony with the character of revelation in the early period the spiritual and physical must have gone hand in hand. Side by side with the physical struggle there must have run an inward contest of the spirit. But these two accompanied each other from beginning to end.

The view has been wrongly advocated, that the outward wrestling and the inward contest are mutually opposed elements, successive the one to the other. The former half would then be a symbolical summing up of Jacob's entire previous attitude and conduct, placing before him what he had been doing from the beginning, wrestling with God in his natural perversity, and that with such a persistence that, in spite of all His discipline, God did not prevail against him. This wrong wrestling with God symbolized the cunning and deceitful efforts by which he had striven to seize the promises. The encounter showed that these had brought upon him not merely the enmity of Esau but also the displeasure of God. This first stage of the wrestling lasted till the break of day. Then God touched the hollow of his thigh. This symbolized an act by which God forced him to change his previous course of conduct. It was the symbol of the terrifying encounter with Esau that proved the crisis of his life. After this there was no more wrestling by physical force, i.e., by human endeavour. Its place was taken by wrestling in prayer: 'I will not let thee go except thou bless me'. This second stage of the experience, then, would stand for Jacob's subsequent life, purified by divine grace.

The interpretation, while attractive in itself, runs contrary to the plain intent of the narrative. The account evidently wishes us to understand that the touching of the thigh, so far from inducing Jacob to give up the struggle, only made him all the more determined to persist. And only by virtue of this heroic persistence did he in the end obtain the blessing from the stranger. The first stage, therefore, symbolized not a reprehensible but a commendable thing. The very point of the account is that he did not let himself be overcome even by an apparently insurmountable disqualification. It cannot be said that he first had recourse to prayer after his bodily strength was taken away from him. The correctness of this criticism of the view in question is confirmed by the inspired interpretation of the event given in Hosea 12.4, 5: 'In his human strength he fought with God, and he fought with the Angel and prevailed; he wept and made supplication unto him.' Here no two stages of opposite spiritual import are put in contrast; the whole is of one and the same tenor, a glorious example of heroic conduct before God, commendable throughout. It symbolized the strenuous efforts Jacob was making through the better part of his nature to secure the divine favour and blessing.

In so far it is quite correct to find here an illustration of the persistency of faith and prayer, the Old Testament prototype, as it were, of our Lord's encounter with the Syro-Phoenician woman. Only, while true in general, this view is not specific enough. It is not merely said that Jacob wrestled with the stranger, but also, and even primarily, that the latter wrestled with Jacob. We must, therefore, take into account the element of divine displeasure Jacob had to overcome, always remembering that this entered into the whole transaction from beginning to end. And this fact coloured the frame of mind in which the patriarch prayed, and makes his experience an example for us of prayer, not so much in general, but of a specific kind. It is prayer for forgiveness of sin and the removal of divine displeasure on account of sin that we here find illustrated. And in consonance with this the blessing craved and received was the blessing of pardon and a return to normal relations with God. The event taught Jacob that inheritance of the promises can rest on forgiveness of sin and a purified conscience only.

The change wrought finds expression in the change of name from Jacob to Israel. Jacob means 'he who takes by the heel or supplants'. Israel means 'he who wrestles with God'. Yet, notwithstanding this solemn change of name, the two names Jacob and Israel continue to be used side by side in the narrative. It was different in the case of Abraham. But Abraham was a new name given to express a change in the objective sphere, a destiny assigned by God, exempt from relapse or imperfection. In a subjective transformation, on the other hand, the old is never entirely done away with. As before, side by side with Jacob's perversity, there had been an element of spirituality, so also afterwards, side by side with the now matured spirituality, there remained traces of the old nature. Hence God continued to subject the patriarch to the discipline of affliction even to his old age.

EIGHT:
REVELATION IN THE
PERIOD OF MOSES

This part of the subject can most conveniently be divided up into the following parts:

[A] The place of Moses in the organism of Old Testament revelation.
[B] The form of revelation in the Mosaic period.
[C] The content of the Mosaic revelation.

[A] THE PLACE OF MOSES IN THE ORGANISM OF OLD TESTAMENT REVELATION

Whether Moses can be said to have played a prominent part in the development of the religion of the Old Testament depends on the philosophico-literary-critical standpoint from which the matter is approached. It was difficult for the school of Wellhausen not to reduce the importance of Moses as a leader in religious progress, because they felt bound by their premises to ascribe the role traditionally assigned to him to the great prophets of the eighth century. It was held that these, and not Moses, were the creators of what is distinctive and permanently valuable in the Old Testament religion, namely ethical monotheism. Moses was said not to have been a monotheist, and to have had no conception of God as a spiritual being. This school of criticism regarded all the legal and narrative contents of the Pentateuch, even the Decalogue, as of much later origin than the Mosaic age. Moses was regarded as having united several Hebrew tribes in the worship of Jehovah as the god of their confederacy, but it was held that to this god he gave no other conception qualitatively than had been his before. The relation in which the newly adopted god stood to his people was regarded as not based on ethical principles, nor cultivated for ethical purposes.

From these statements it will be readily seen how hard it must be for the adherents of such views rationally to account for the prominence of Moses in the religious tradition of Israel. Some, in fact, realizing the impossibility of this, reach the conclusion that the whole figure of Moses is unhistorical, no less than that of the patriarchs. There may have been a Moses-clan, but no person of that name ever existed. For the exodus from Egypt, Mizraim, they substitute a migration of the Moses-clan from Mizrim, a region in Northern Arabia. So Cheyne, for the further details of whose views on this matter an article in the *Encyclopaedia Biblica* may be compared.

The majority of the Wellhausen school of critics by no means adopt this extreme view. They draw the line where the legendary period ceases and that of history begins in the time of Moses. Hence at least they cannot forego trying to answer the question, how Moses earned the credit of eminent religious leadership that is his by right of tradition. One answer frequently given is that by his political leadership he laid the foundations on which subsequently the higher spiritual religion could be built. But in that case Moses builded better than he knew. Having no intention of producing something religiously new and better, he can claim no credit for the consequences derived from his work. And after all, the very point that the later higher conditions were actually consequences of his political activity is the point standing in need of proof. No successful effort had or has been made to demonstrate in what way precisely the praiseworthy political leadership in course of time gave rise to the raising of the moral plane of life, so that a better God could be born out of them.

It is sometimes said that the great deliverances wrought by Moses in the name of Jehovah established in the consciousness of the people a claim upon their loyalty to Him who through His servant Moses had done all this for them. And this sense of loyalty became the great lever, of which availing themselves, later leading spirits succeeded in moralizing the religion of Israel. This, however, solves the problem only in words, not actually. Other tribes cannot have lived without similar experiences of deliverance wrought, nor been utterly lacking in a sense of loyalty due, and yet no ethicizing results in their case sprang from this. True, the experiences of the Israelites were extraordinary, and therefore might account for greater results than the mere average good fortunes enjoyed by average nations, and likewise derived by them from their gods. But to appeal to this would come perilously near to admitting that in the case of Israel there was a supernatural factor at work, and this is precisely the thing this class of writers wish to avoid by their construction. After all, loyalty is, considered in the light of ethics, a neutral conception. To be loyal to some god for deliverances received, while not as yet ascribing an ethical character to this god, will not lead to a higher ethical type of religion. It may tighten the hold of divine commands upon man, but it will not alter the nature of the commands from non-ethical to ethical.

The same criticism must be applied to another effort towards solving the same, from the critical standpoint fundamental, problem. It has been suggested that Moses sank the seed of ethical fruitage into the soil of Israel's religion, when through free choice he caused them to adopt Jehovah as their God. Jehovah and Israel did not originally belong together. Thus the religion instituted by Moses was not a nature-religion, but a religion of free choice. To this it should be replied that free choice as such, and not motivated by ethical considerations, is not particularly valuable from a historico-religious point of view. All depends again on the motives from which the choice is directed. Free choice is not a divinity out of whose womb righteous gods and righteous men are born together. It lacks spiritual pregnancy. Unconsciously writers who use this explanation would seem to have put behind the process their own Pelagian appraisal of free choice. Still further, these writers are not willing themselves to admit that the free choice postulated for the time of Moses created an actually free religion for Israel. Some of them doubt that such a thing as a freely-entered *berith* took place in that day between Jehovah and Israel. And practically all of them insist that the whole religious relationship remained one of necessity, Jehovah being as much bound to the people as they were bound to Him. Finally, instances are not lacking in the history of religion where other groups have adopted or coadopted new gods after the fashion of a more or less free choice. Syncretism has by no means always been an unconscious or compulsory process. And yet no ethical results have followed.

THE PROMINENCE OF MOSES

We must now show that from very early times Moses did occupy a most prominent place in the religious consciousness of Israel. This can be done without venturing out into the labyrinth of Pentateuchal criticism with all its confusing paths of authorships and dates. Without dispute, in the oldest Pentateuchal stories Moses stands out as the great religious leader of his people, and these stories are, according to the critics, even in their written form, older then the eighth-century prophets. The stories as orally circulating must have been, of course, much older still. In the oldest writing prophets, Amos and Hosea, a supreme place is given to Moses. Hosea says: 'By a prophet Jehovah brought Israel out of Egypt, and by a prophet was he preserved' [*Hos.* 12.13]. Amos, while not mentioning him by name, evidently thinks of Moses in connection with the words: 'the whole family which I brought up out of the land of Egypt'. And that an ethical purpose was connected with this act of redemption is shown in the next words: 'You only have I known of all the families of the earth: therefore I will visit upon you all your iniquities' [*Amos* 3.1, 2; cp. *Isa.* 63.11; *Jer.* 15.1].

The true, inward significance of Moses, when we place him within the unfolding scheme of revelation, can be made clear in several directions. For one thing he was, retrospectively considered, instrumental in bringing the great patriarchal promises to an incipient fulfilment, at least in their external, provisional embodiment. Israel became in truth a great nation, and this was due not exclusively to their rapid increase; the organization received through Moses enabled them to attain national coherence. Moses likewise led them to the border of the promised land. With regard to the third promise,[1] it must be admitted that Moses contributed to its fulfilment after a negative fashion only. Before a blessing could actually proceed from Israel to the nations, it was first of all necessary that the fundamental difference between Israel and the nations, that is, the principal difference between the true religion and paganism, should be clearly exhibited. And this was done through the conflict between Israel and Egypt which Moses precipitated. It will be shown afterwards, that this conflict was not superficially confined to the national-political sphere, but sprang from deeper religious principles. Therefore, after a negative fashion, credit for preparing the way for the fulfilment of the third promise also cannot be withheld from Moses.

Prospectively considered Moses also occupies a dominant place in the religious development of the Old Testament. He is placed not merely at the head of the succession of prophets, but placed over them in advance. His authority extends over subsequent ages. The later prophets do not create anything new; they only predict something new. It is true, Moses can be co-ordinated with the prophets: [*Deut.* 18.18; 'a prophet like unto thee']. Nevertheless the prophets themselves are clearly conscious of the unique position of Moses. They put his work not so much on a line with their own, as with the stupendous eschatological work of Jehovah for His people expected in the latter

[1] See pp. 78–80.

days [cp. *Isa.* 10.26; 11.11; 63.11, 12; *Jer.* 23.5–8; *Mic.* 7.15]. According to Num. 12.7, Moses was set over *all* God's house. It is entirely in keeping with this prospective import of Moses and his work, that his figure acquires typical proportions to an unusual degree. He may be fitly called *the redeemer* of the Old Testament. Nearly all the terms in use for the redemption of the New Testament can be traced back to his time. There was in his work such a close connection between revealing words and redeeming acts as can be paralleled only from the life of Christ. And the acts of Moses were to a high degree supernatural, miraculous acts. This typical relation of Moses to Christ can easily be traced in each of the three offices we are accustomed to distinguish in the soteric work of Christ. The 'prophet' of Deut. 18.15, reaching his culmination in the Messiah, is 'like unto' Moses. Moses fulfilled priestly functions at the inauguration of the Old *Berith*, before the Aaronic priesthood was instituted [*Ex.* 24.4–8]. Our Lord refers to this as a typical transaction, when inaugurating the New *Diatheke* at the institution of the supper [*Lk.* 22.20]. Moses intercedes for Israel after the commission of the sin of the golden calf, and that by offering his own person vicariously for bearing the punishment of the guilty [*Ex.* 32.30–33]. A royal figure, of course, Moses could not at that time be called, for Jehovah alone is King of Israel. None the less, through his legislative function Moses typified the royal office of Christ.

All this reflected itself in the peculiar relation the people were made to sustain toward Moses. This relation is even described as one of faith and of trust [*Ex.* 14.31; 19.9]. The resemblance of this relation of the Israelites towards Moses to the relation of the Christian towards Christ had not escaped the notice of Paul, who says that 'our fathers were all under the cloud, and all passed through the sea; and were all baptized unto Moses in the cloud and in the sea' [1 *Cor.* 10.1–3]. Just as in baptism an intimate relation is established between the believer and Christ, based on the saviourship of Christ, even so the mighty acts of divine deliverance wrought through Moses pledged Israel to faith in him. And, as during the ministry of Jesus faith and unbelief proved the two decisive factors, so during the wilderness journey a great drama of faith and unbelief was enacted, deciding the people's fate [*Heb.* 3, 4].

[B] THE FORM OF REVELATION IN THE MOSAIC PERIOD

Here we must distinguish between the revelation directly communicated to and through the person of Moses, on the one hand, and forms of revelation emerging in his time, but not directly passing through his person.

In harmony with the important role played by Moses, we find a special clearness and directness affirmed of the intercourse between him and God. There was no prophet who was honoured with the direct and continuous access to Jehovah that Moses enjoyed. In this respect also Moses seems to have prefigured Christ. As Christ reveals the Father in virtue of a most direct and an uninterrupted vision of Him, and not as a result of isolated communications, so Moses, though to a lower degree, stands nearer to God, and is more, in all that he speaks and does, the mouthpiece of God than any subsequent prophet. The distinction between Moses, on the one hand, and Aaron and Miriam on the other, is formulated in Num. 12. Here he is called 'my servant Moses', not in the menial sense of merely a servant, but in the high sense of a trusted servant, initiated into all that his master does. He is faithful in all God's house. This name 'Servant of Jehovah' is afterwards given to the Messiah, in the prophecy of Isaiah. Moses appreciated the unique distinction implied in this [*Ex.* 33.12].

Most strikingly Moses' intimate relation to God and the honour it conferred are symbolized by the reflection of divine glory on his countenance after the forty days and forty nights spent with God upon the mountain [*Ex.* 34.29ff.]. Paul, while recognizing the greatness, dwells rather on its limitations, as compared with the glory of his own ministration under the New *Diatheke*, in 2 Cor. 3. The Pentateuch itself recognizes these limitations. According to *Ex.* 33.17–23, Moses was not permitted to see the 'face' of God, but only as it is anthropomorphically called, his 'back'. It is no contradiction to this, when in Num. 12 Moses is said to behold the *temunah*, the 'form of God', for this is not identical with the 'face'. True, it is also said that God spake with him 'face to face' [*Ex.* 33.11]. 'Face to face' is an adverbial phrase synonymous with 'mouth to mouth', and by no means equivalent to a vision of the divine face [*Num.* 12.8]. Compare further, Ex. 34.5: 'stood with him there and proclaimed the name of Jehovah'. Also 33.18, 19: 'Show me thy glory'. . . . 'I will make all my goodness [probably "goodliness", "loveliness"] pass before thee and will proclaim the name of Jehovah before thee'. On the occasion of Ex. 24.10, when Moses with the others had gone up on the mountain, after the making of the *berith*, in order to 'see' the God of Israel, what they actually saw was not the divine face, but only, as it were, God's 'feet'. This is the same idea as is expressed in the figure of the 'back of God' [*Ex.* 33.23].

The forms of revelation connected with the work of Moses, though not communicated through him personally, are four in number: The pillar and the cloud, the Angel of Jehovah, the Name of Jehovah, the Face of Jehovah. These have in common that they express the permanence of the divine presence, and are distinguished in that respect from the fleeting, ephemeral forms of manifestation in the patriarchal period. The significance of this can be understood only if it be placed in the larger setting of the divine communication with mankind in general. Before the fall there was such an abiding presence of God with man in paradise. After the fall a certain remnant of this continued, though not in the old gracious form. The throne with the Cherubim still stood in the East of the garden of God. God still walked with Enoch. With the flood all this is changed. God has, as it were, with-drawn this sacramental revelation-presence into heaven. This, however, was an abnormal state of things, for the ultimate design of all God's converse with man is, that He may make His abode with His people. Consequently from now on all revelation tends towards the realization of this design. The theophanies of the patriarchal period must be regarded as incipient fulfilments of it. But the fulfilment was only partial. The presence was there only at times; it was granted to a few select persons only; it was confined to the great turning-points in their history; it was veiled in deepest mystery. With the time of Moses there came the opposite to this in all respects.

THE PILLAR OF CLOUD AND FIRE

Of the pillar of cloud and fire we read in the following passages: Ex. 13.21, 22, where it is explicitly stated that Jehovah was in the phenomenon, and that it did not depart from before the people; afterwards it moves to a position behind them so as to be between them and their Egyptian pursuers before the passage through the Red Sea [*Ex.* 14.19, 20]; through the pillar Jehovah looks forth upon the Egyptians to discomfit them [*Ex.* 14.24]; when the people mur-mured because they doubted the divine presence with them, the glory of Jehovah appeared in the cloud [*Ex.* 16.10]; next we meet with a cloud revealing Jehovah on Sinai at the giving of the law, which cloud is also called a 'fire', although nothing is said about a pillar on this occasion [*Ex.* 19.9, 16, 18]; in Ex. 24.16 this same cloud upon Sinai is mentioned again as containing the glory of Jehovah, the appearance of which is described as 'like devouring fire' [vs. 17], and Moses enters into the midst of the cloud [vs. 18]; after this we meet with the pillar again in Ex. 33.9; where it descends (from the mount or from heaven?) and stands at the door of the provisional tent pitched by Moses, while all the people worship every one at his tent door [vs. 10]; according to Ex. 34.5, Jehovah descends from heaven in the cloud upon Mount Sinai. It is altogether probable that the so-called *Shekinah*, the glory in the holy of holies of tabernacle and temple, was a continuation of all this; in fact the feature of permanence so strongly emphasized almost requires it. Of this, however, we shall speak later when dealing with the tabernacle.

THE ANGEL OF JEHOVAH

Of the Angel of Jehovah we read first in Ex. 3.2, where He appears to Moses in a flame of fire out of the midst of the bush, and His identity with God is shown by the fact of God's calling unto Moses out of the bush. Next we find Him referred to in Ex. 14.19; here He goes before the camp of Israel, and with the pillar moves from before to behind. In Ex. 23.20, 21 a formal promise is made regarding Him; He is to accompany Israel: 'Behold, I send an Angel before thee, to keep thee by the way, and to bring thee unto the place which I have prepared; take ye heed before him, and hearken unto his voice; provoke him not; for he will not pardon your transgression: for my name is in him'. The entire tenor of this passage forbids our thinking that an ordinary angel is spoken of, although the text reads 'an angel', not 'the angel'. From the Septuagint reading 'my angel' we may infer that this form (with the suffix) stood originally in the Hebrew text. We learn from the statement that the Angel's function was the comprehensive one of leading the people to Canaan. We further learn that, in respect of sinning against Him, He is identical with God. On the other hand, in Ex. 32.34 we meet with 'my angel', and in Ex. 33.2 with 'an angel'. The situation here requires this, for the sending of the angel appears as a retraction of Jehovah's original promise that He Himself would go with the people [*Ex.* 33.3–5], and the sending of 'the Angel of Jehovah' could not have been represented as anything less than Jehovah's own going. It is only after Moses' expostulation at the changed proposal that God finally is prevailed upon to abide by the original agreement: 'my Presence shall go with thee, and I will give thee rest' [*Ex.* 33.14].

The Angel of Jehovah appears in the history of Balaam, Num. 22, where he frustrates Balak's design for cursing Israel. This forms a concrete instance of His general task consisting in the guidance and defence of His people [cp. *Num.* 20.16].

THE NAME AND THE FACE OF JEHOVAH

In two of the Angel contexts discussed we have already met with the two remaining revelation forms, 'the Name' and 'the Face' of Jehovah. 'The Name' we encountered in Ex. 23.21, where it is affirmed that 'the Name' is in the Angel. Nothing short of identification can be meant by this, for it is stated as the ground why sin committed against the Name-bearing Angel will not be pardoned by Him. The other form, 'the Presence', met us in Ex. 33.14, 'My Presence shall go with thee'. This must be equivalent to Jehovah's own going [cp. vs. 17]. 'Presence' stands for the Hebrew *Panim* which also proves the identification. The *Panim* is likewise identified with the Angel. Isaiah, referring to the wilderness-journey, says that the Angel of God's *Panim* saved the people [*Isa.* 63.9].

One more identification occurs in Deuteronomy. It is that between the 'Name' and the glory in the sanctuary. Jehovah is said to have put His 'Name' in the place of the sanctuary. The place where His 'Name' is, is called His habitation. Jehovah causes His 'Name' to dwell there [*Deut.* 12.5, 11, 21; 14.23, 24; 16.2, 6, 11; 26.2]. It is plain, especially from the latter way of speaking, that the phrase is meant to be understood realistically. It is not a mere figure of speech for saying that the sanctuary is God's property, nor that His magnificent Name is in the exercise of the cultus pronounced or called upon there. Of 'dwelling' in the sanctuary God Himself is always the subject.

From the foregoing it will be noted that to the three meanings previously found for the Name of God in a religious sense a fourth one must be added. In this fourth sense the Name is not something in the apprehension of man; it is objective, equivalent to Jehovah Himself. Still there always remains a difference in point of view between Jehovah as such and His 'Name'. The 'Name' is God in revelation. And the same distinction applies to the use of the *Shekinah*, the Angel and the Presence.

[C] THE CONTENT OF THE MOSAIC REVELATION

We now come to the discussion of the content of the Mosaic Revelation. This part of the subject is complex, and hence it will be necessary clearly to place before ourselves at the outset the main divisions belonging to it. These are:

(*a*) the factual basis of the Mosaic organization given in the redemption from Egypt;

(*b*) the making of the *Berith* with Israel with which the organization entered into being;

(*c*) the general nature of the organization, the theocracy;

(*d*) the Decalogue;

(*e*) the ritual law, its symbolical and typical character, with the three strands composing it, that of divine indwelling, that of sacrifice, that of purification.

[1] The factual basis of the Mosaic organization consisting in the redemption from Egypt

The exodus from Egypt *is* the Old Testament redemption. This is not an anachronistic, allegorizing manner of speaking. It is based on the inner coherence of Old Testament and New Testament religion itself. These two, however different their forms of expression, are yet one in principle. The same purpose and method of God run through both. If, as is frequently urged nowadays, the Old Testament should be rejected and scorned as unworthy of the ideal religion, one may be sure that this attitude is due to abandonment of the entire soteric strain of the Biblical religion as such. There may be, of course, single uncongenial features telling in the opinion of some against the Old Testament, but the source of the antagonism lies deeper, and will be found, on closer examination, to relate to what Old Testament and New Testament have in common, *the realism of redemption*. The substance upon which the impression was made under the Old Testament may have been earthly clay; none the less the matrix that stamped it bore the lineaments of eternal law and truth. We can here observe again how inseparably revelation through words is united to facts, nay how for whole stretches the demarcation line between acts and words may even seem to have been lost altogether.

There is an irreconcilable difference between the religious consciousness that is at all times clearly or dimly aware of springing up and drawing nourishment from this soil of facts, and the consciousness that has emancipated itself from belief in the reality of the facts. Nor is it a difference in belief only; it is a difference in atmosphere and feeling of self. In spite of all his limitations the Old Testament believer stands nearer to us in this respect than the so-called modern idealizer or spiritualizer of the Christian religion. The closest linking together of the facts and the practice of religious life is observable at this very point now reached by us. The Decalogue opens with one of the most profound references to the soteric procedure of God in delivering the people from Egypt [Ex. 20.2]. The first offer of the *Berith* is preceded by an even more elaborate statement that seems baptized in the very warmth of divine affection [19.4]. And the long introductory discourse of Deuteronomy, semi-prophetic in spirit, partakes of the same tone and character. As late as Isaiah the people are called upon to remind themselves of the ultimate roots of their religious origin in the things Jehovah did for them in the remote past [Isa. 51.2].

What then are the outstanding principles of the exodus-deliverance that were thus made regulative of all future salvation and bind things past and things to come indissolubly together?

DELIVERANCE FROM FOREIGN BONDAGE

First of all, redemption is here portrayed as, before everything else, a deliverance from an objective realm of sin and evil. The favourite individualizing and internalizing of sin finds no support here. No people of God can spring into existence without being cut loose from a world opposed to God and to themselves in their very origin. The Egyptian power is in this respect as truly typical as the divine power that wrought the deliverance. Its attitude and activity were shaped with this in view. What held under the Hebrews was not mere political dependence, but harsh bondage. Their condition is represented as a condition of slavery. The Egyptians exploited them for selfish ends regardless of Israel's own welfare. Ever since, redemption has attached to itself this imagery of enslavement to an alien power. John 8.33–36 as well as Rom. 8.20–21, reach back into these far origins.

Further, to this enslaving power a high degree of malignity is ascribed, that it might fitly typify the mind of sin in the world. In part at least the hardening of Pharaoh's heart is explainable from the same reason. His obduracy was to reveal the true inward nature of that of which he was a figure. Of course, this hardening was by no means an arbitrary divine act; it was a judicial process: the king first hardened himself, and then, in punishment for this, he was further hardened by God. It is the well-known Scriptural law of sin being punished by irretrievable abandonment to sin, a law by no means confined to the Old Testament, but found in the New Testament as well. The ethics of the matter, however, do not concern us here. This kingdom of evil headed up in Pharaoh embraces first of all the human elements of paganism. Probably, however, the account does not mean to confine it to this. Sin is at every point more than the sum-total of purely human influences it brings to bear upon its victims. A religious, demonic background is thrown back of the human figures that move across the canvas. Not merely the Egyptians, but likewise the Egyptians' gods are involved in the conflict. The plagues come in here for notice. They are inextricably mixed up with the Egyptian idolatry. This idolatry was nature-worship, embracing the good and beneficent as well as the evil and baneful aspects of nature. Jehovah, in making these harm their own worshippers, shows His superiority to this whole realm of evil. This is stated in so many words: 'Against all the gods of Egypt I will execute judgment: I am Jehovah' [*Ex.* 12.12]. The same demonic powers that were concerned in the antitypical redemption wrought by Christ, and there displayed their intensest activity, had a hand in this opposition to the redemption from Egypt.

DELIVERANCE FROM SIN

So much for the objective side of the matter. There was, however, a subjective side to it also. The Hebrews were delivered not merely from outside foreign bondage, they were likewise rescued from inward spiritual degradation and sin. Two views have been taken as to the religious condition of the people at this time. According to one they had practically lost all knowledge of the true God, and were deeply immersed in and identified with the idolatrous practices of the Egyptians. This was the view of John Spencer, an English theologian of the Seventeenth Century, advocated in his work *De Legibus Hebraeorum Ritualibus.*

Connected with this theory was a peculiar opinion concerning the origin of the ceremonial laws imposed upon the people in the time of Moses. The purpose of these laws was to leave room for a gradual weaning away of the Hebrews from their idolatrous Egyptian customs. God, fearing lest a too sudden prohibition of these customs should cause an utter relapse into heathenism, condescended to tolerate their observance for a season. The other view falls into the opposite extreme. It assumes that the Israelites had on the whole kept themselves from contamination with the idolatry of Egypt. Both views in their extreme form must be rejected. The true religion had not entirely vanished from among Israel. They still knew enough to perceive that Jehovah was the God of their fathers, for in the name of the God of the patriarchs Moses was sent to them. Names compounded with *El* are found in the record. They must have felt themselves to some extent specifically Shemitic in their religious traditions.

On the other hand we are not warranted in passing this relatively favourable judgment upon the people as a whole. From Josh. 24.14 and Ezek. 23.8, 19, 21, we learn that Israel served idols in Egypt. The history of the wilderness journey with its repeated apostasies, such as the worship of the golden calf, becomes unintelligible, unless we may assume that the people had left Egypt in a corrupt state religiously. Perhaps also the worship of the calf-image, and the demon-worship related in Lev. 17.7, might be interpreted as of Egyptian origin. As will be later shown, however, there is no evidence that the ritual law was a mere accommodation to the corrupt tendencies of the people. But it remains true that there must have existed enough of religious decline and corruption among them to make their deliverance from Egypt more than a mere external national benefit to them without deeper spiritual significance.

It should be remembered that in the history of God's people external bondage is frequently a concomitant of spiritual unfaithfulness to Jehovah. We need not deny, of course, that the secondary causes of Israel's oppression lay in political considerations and racial antipathies. Only, political developments never furnish a sufficient explanation of what happens in Sacred History. The Egyptians were but instruments in carrying out the designs of God. That God had ordered the bondage beforehand for a specific purpose is made probable by its having been foretold to Abraham on the occasion of the making of the *Berith* [*Gen.* 15.13].

A DISPLAY OF DIVINE OMNIPOTENCE

Next we observe, in regard to the method of the deliverance, the emphasis throughout thrown on the divine omnipotence for bringing it about. Above all else Jehovah's might is celebrated in the account. This furnishes the keynote to the song of Ex. 15, a profound poetical interpretation of the exodus from this point of view [vss. 6, 7, 11]. As remarked above, there is a unique accumulation of miracles in this part of the history. The number of the plagues is ten, the Scriptural number of completeness. The dividing of the waters of the sea is the culminating act in the great drama of redemption. The sacred poetry of later times was fond of celebrating these acts of God and basing on them the assured hope of future similar deliverances. Jehovah's omnipotence and the exodus remain from this time onward associated in the tradition of Israel.

With this emphasis on the element of power, it is no wonder that everything in the history is carefully arranged to place it in the proper relief. When Moses in his own strength sought to deliver the people, the result was a failure. When, after an interval of forty years and actually commissioned by Jehovah to guide and effect the redemption, he assumes the task in the totally opposite spirit of absolute dependence upon God, thoroughly recognizing his own unfitness, God promises that He will smite Egypt with all His wonders [*Ex.* 3.20]. He puts His wonders into the hand of Moses [4.21]. He proceeds to redeem Israel with a stretched-out arm and great judgments [6.6]. The hardening of Pharaoh's heart, while intended to make him a pronounced exponent of evil, had also the further intention of prolonging the process of deliverance, thus creating room for the fullest display of miraculous power. This is said in so many words: 'I will harden Pharaoh's heart. and multiply my signs and my wonders in the land of Egypt' [7.3]. The task had to be made more difficult in order that the omnipotence effecting it might be the more apparent. Nay, Pharaoh's whole existence and personality and conduct seem to have been shaped with this in view. In Ex. 9.16, Jehovah declares: 'But in very deed for this cause have I made thee to stand, for to show thee my power, and that my name may be declared through all the earth'. Even if the words 'made thee to stand' mean 'kept thee standing longer on the stage of history, whereas under ordinary circumstances thou wouldst have fallen before', they bear out the view in question. Still more is this the case, if the stronger rendering be adopted: 'I have caused thee to stand upon the scene', i.e., have called thee into being [cp. *Rom.* 9.17]. Finally the conflict between the works wrought by Moses and the signs of the Egyptian magicians show that a transaction in the sphere of power is described.

A DEMONSTRATION OF SOVEREIGN GRACE

Again, the deliverance from Egypt was a signal demonstration of the sovereign grace of God. The Egyptians were judged with respect to their idolatry, and the Israelites were rescued and spared, in spite of having become associated with their oppressors in idolatrous practices. It is plain that the principle of sovereign grace alone will account for such facts. This is called 'putting a difference between

Israelites and Egyptians' [*Ex.* 8.23; 11.7]. In harmony with this it is repeatedly stated in the Pentateuch, that the source of Israel's privilege lies exclusively in free divine grace, not in any good qualities possessed by the people from themselves [*Deut.* 7.7; 9.4–6]. True, God's love for the Mosaic Israel is traced back to His love for the fathers. This carries the relationship of free choice one step further back, but does not in substance alter its nature, for the fathers too were chosen in the sovereign love of God.

The idea of sonship, here for the first time emerging [cp. *Gen.* 6.2], belongs to the same train of thought [*Ex.* 4.22; *Deut.* 32.6]. Sonship is from the nature of the case unmeritorious. We also meet again the peculiar affectionate use of the verb 'to know', previously met with in regard to Abraham [*Ex.* 2.24, 25]. Also the verb 'to choose' is used. This is peculiar to Deuteronomy [7.6, 7; 14.2]. Finally, the term 'redemption' enters into religious use here. Its specific meaning (different from such general terms as 'to rescue', 'to deliver') lies precisely in this, that it describes the loving reacquisition of something formerly possessed. There is not yet in the Old Testament any reflection on that element so easily associated with the conception, viz.,that a redemption-price is paid. Only by way of metaphor this thought emerges in an isolated instance [*Isa.* 43.3]. The sense is in the Pentateuchal passages simply that of attachment shown in the renewal of the ancient ownership. Hence in the later chapters of the prophecy of Isaiah, where the background is that of deliverance from exile, the term attains to great frequency. The passages in the Pentateuch are: Ex. 6.6; 15.13; Deut. 7.8; 9.26; 13.5; 21.8.

THE NAME 'JEHOVAH'

With this feature of the sovereignty shown in redemption is connected the specifically Mosaic name of God, Jehovah. This form is a pronunciation in which the vowels of *Adonai* were given to the consonants of the name in question. The writing of these vowels sprang originally from the Jewish scrupulousness refraining from the utterance of this most sacred name altogether. Because *Adonai* was always read in place of it, therefore, when vowels were added, for convenience' sake the vowels required for the reading of *Adonai* were simply attached. It was, of course, never contemplated at that time that the consonants standing in the text, and which it would have been the height of impiety to remove, should have in pronunciation joined to them these alien vowels. This was first done in Christian reading, when the old Jewish scrupulosity was no longer felt, and thus the hybrid form *Jehovah* arose. It has been in use since the sixteenth century. Unfortunately, the renderings of the Bible into the various vernaculars continued the Jewish practice of reading Adonai, and so put 'Lord' or its equivalent in the other languages, for Jehovah. Modern scholarship thinks it has discovered the original pronunciation of the name, customary up to the time when Jewish superstition abolished it, and it is now commonly found in critical books in the form 'Jahveh'. Certain, however, this sounding of the word is not. Even if certainty could be obtained in this respect, it would scarcely be advisable to introduce 'Jahveh' into the reading of Scripture, especially not for liturgical purposes. Still it is a step in the right direction that the American Revision has restored *Jehovah*. When the suspicious critical flavour of 'Jahveh' shall have somewhat evaporated, and stronger new evidence for the correctness of 'Jahveh' shall have been obtained, the latter will perhaps come to its rights again. Meanwhile, there is no excuse for continuing the total non-use of the sacred name, now that 'Jehovah' has, through the American Revision, made its reappearance in our Bible.

In Ex. 6.3 we read that the revelation of the name belongs to, and is characteristic of the Mosaic period. Proceeding on the inference that the writer of this passage could not possibly have regarded it as known in older times, the divisive criticism has laid this passage at the basis of the distinction between Elohistic and Jahvistic documents. There are, however, strong objections to this literalistic exegesis of the passage. It is *a priori* improbable that Moses should have been sent to his brethren, whom he had to recall from forgetfulness of the God of their forefathers, with a new, formerly unknown, name of this God upon his lips. Then there is the fact that Moses' mother bears a name compounded with Jehovah, in its abbreviated form *Jo*, viz., *Jokhebed*. And this name occurs in the very same document to which Ex. 6.3, belongs, so that the additional assumption, unfavoured by aught else, of an interpolation of the name *Jokhebed* in this document is required. Closely looked at, Ex. 6.3 does not require the absolute previous unknownness of the word. The statement need mean nothing more than that the patriarchs did not as yet possess the practical knowledge and experience of that side of the divine character which finds expression in the name. 'To know' in the Hebrew conception, and the same word in our everyday parlance, are two quite different things. The context of Ex. 6.3 even renders probable that a practical, experiential knowledge is referred to. In vss. 6, 7 we read: 'I will redeem you with a stretched-out arm – and I will take you to me for a people, and I will be to you a God, and ye shall know that I am Jehovah your God'.

Through the redemption they will learn, not that there is a Jehovah, but what Jehovah means to them, that Jehovah is their God, or that their God is Jehovah.

Of course, the assumption of a pre-Mosaic existence of the name does not imply that it existed as early as the narrator in Genesis, speaking for his own person, introduces it. How much older than the exodus it is we cannot tell. *A priori* the hypothesis cannot be excluded that in earlier times it may have had other associations. The name may have been current in small circles; a different etymology from that of Ex. 3 may have been ascribed to it. It may even have come from an extra-Hebrew source. The views, however, proposed in this last-named direction are some of them impossible, all of them highly problematical. An Egyptian origin has been assumed by Voltaire, Schiller, Comte, and others. This is out of the question, because the deliverance from Egypt is represented as involving a conflict between Jehovah and the gods of the Egyptians.

According to Colenso, Land, and others, the name is North-Shemitic, and designated in its former environment the god of heaven, the giver of fruitfulness, in whose honour the orgiastic worship of Syria was practised. There is what purports to be an ancient oracle, in which the name *Iao* is identified with Dionysos, so that Jehovah would be the Canaanitish Dionysos. At first a relatively high antiquity was ascribed to this piece, so as to render the explanation possible that the Syrian form *Iao* was the original, from which then the Hebrews would have borrowed their Jehovah. This, of course, became impossible when the late date became apparent, for at so late a date the Israelites had been long in possession of the name Jehovah. The likelihood on that supposition would be that the Syrian worshippers of such an *Iao* had borrowed the name of their deity from the well-known name of the God of Israel.

More recently it has been thought that the name was discovered in early Egyptian lists of Canaanitish places, such as Baitiyah, Babiyah. It has also been found in the name of a king of Hamath reading Yaubidi in Assyrian inscriptions. A hypothesis much in vogue among the Wellhausenians is that Jehovah was a god of the Kenites, a tribe in the district of Sinai, to whom the father-in-law of Moses belonged, which would explain Jehovah's association with that mountain. Then there is still the hypothesis that Jehovah is identical with the form Yahu, or Yah, occurring in Assyrio-Babylonian proper names, which the Hebrew priests would have changed into Jahveh, in order to suggest derivation from *hayah*, 'to be'.

Equally futile as most of these theories of provenience are some of the etymologies, largely naturalistic, proposed in explanation of the original sense of the word itself. It has been connected with *hawah*, 'to fall', on the view of its meaning 'he who rushes, crashes down', a storm-god, or, even more primitively, a meteoric stone fallen from heaven. Or *hawah* has been compared in the sense of 'to blow', which it has in Arabic. Wellhausen observes: 'the etymology is quite obvious; he rides through the air, he blows'. Again the sense of 'falling' has been introduced after this fashion; Jahveh is a Hiphil form, which yields 'he who causes to fall', i.e., the rain-, the storm-god. Thus Robertson Smith, Stade and others. Far less naturalistic is the derivation, likewise from the Hiphil, proposed by Kuenen, 'he who causes to be', i.e., the Creator, or, with a more historic turn, 'he who causes his promises to be', that is, fulfils them.

All these derivations are purely conjectural. It is obvious that, whatever the original meaning lying behind the Old Testament usage, if such there was, the authoritative sense for the religion of Israel has been fixed through the revelation of Ex. 3, and with this alone we have here to deal. God says to Moses: *Ehyeh asher Ehyeh*. Then this is abbreviated to *Ehyeh*, and finally turned from the first into the third person *Yehweh*. The solution of the mystery must lie in the fuller form.

What can such a sentence mean? Here again, where the inquiry is into the intent of the writer exclusively, opinions of expositors vary widely. There is at the start the issue of construction. We may read the sentence straight down from the beginning: 'I am what I am', and attach our interpretation, whatever it is, directly to this. Or, and this is syntactically just as possible in the Hebrew, we may start to read from the middle, placing the first word at the end, which would yield: 'I, who am, truly am'. Further into the question of rendering there enters the analogy of the similarly constructed sentence, Ex. 33.19, which, since it is likewise associated with the name Jehovah, must needs be regulative, at least as to construction, for the formula of Ex. 3. If there we read: 'I will be gracious to whom I will be gracious', we are bound to read here: 'I am what I am'. On the other hand, if there we construe: 'to whom I will be gracious I will be (truly) gracious', we cannot very well do otherwise here in Ex. 3.14: 'I, who am, (truly) am'.

Keeping this in mind, let us now briefly review the solutions offered. One is that the sentence expresses the inscrutability of God: 'I am what I am; what I am is not to be curiously enquired into; my being cannot be expressed by any name'. Against this weighs the fact that all the other divine names are expressive of something. A name to express namelessness, i.e., unknowableness, would be under the circumstances quite out of place. It was at this juncture of supreme importance that God should in some striking manner reveal Himself, so as to emphasize and define some aspect of His character, needful for the people to know. On this view, of course, the construction is the one straight down from the beginning.

Another solution is, that God here asseverates the reality of His being. For this the construction will have to set in at the middle: 'I, who am, (truly) am'. In its more philosophic form this may be called the ontological view. It would approach what the schoolmen have tried to express in the doctrine that God is pure being. But this is far too abstract an idea to be suitable here. It would bear no direct application to the need of the Israelites at this juncture. They, surely, had something else and more urgent to do than to lose themselves in speculations anent the mode of God's existence. Feeling this, some, while retaining the idea, have endeavoured to give it a more practical turn. Jehovah is called the Being One *par excellence*, because He attests His being by acting. To the instinct of our modern language such an association is not unfamiliar. We say a thing is 'actual', meaning it is 'real', although 'actual' etymologically means 'that which acts'. But that this was as familiar to the Hebrew instinct of language formation would be difficult to prove. It is rather an abstract idea, and no traces of it in Hebrew idiom have been discovered.

A third effort to put meaning into the phrase is that of Robertson Smith. He calls attention to Ex. 3.12, where God says to Moses: 'Certainly I shall be with thee', and considers the clause 'I shall be' an abbreviation for 'I shall be with you'. This understanding again requires the reading of the sentence to start from the middle: 'I, who will be with you, surely will be with you'. There are two objections to this. For one thing it changes the singular 'thee' addressed to Moses to the plural 'you' addressed to the Israelites. Besides this, it assumes that in such a statement the really important part of the import could be left to be supplied. The 'with you' is actually the core of the whole promise, and this would have remained unexpressed.

Less open to objection than all these offered solutions is the old view, according to which, reading the clause straight from beginning to end, it gives expression to the self-determination, the independence of God, that which, especially in soteric associations, we are accustomed to call His *sovereignty*. Considerable support this receives from the analogously-phrased sentence in Ex. 33.19, where the context seems to call rather for an affirmation of the sovereignty of God in bestowing the favour of vision of Himself than for an assurance to the effect that, promising to be gracious, He will be truly gracious. Thus taken, the name Jehovah signifies primarily that in all God does for His people, He is from-within-determined, not moved upon by outside influences.

But from this there issues immediately another thought, quite inseparable from it, viz., that being determined from within, and not subject to change within, He is not subject to change at all, particularly not subject to it in relation to His people. Thus understood, the name fits admirably into the situation of its revealing. Jehovah, the absolute God, acting with unfettered liberty, was the very God to help them in their unworthiness as regards themselves, and in their impotence as regards the Egyptians. That sovereignty underlies God's giving Himself to Israel is stated in so many words: 'I will take you to me for a people, and I will be to you a God, and ye shall know that I am Jehovah, your God' [Ex. 6.7]. But the other element, that of faithfulness, is equally much emphasized from the beginning: 'Jehovah, the God of your fathers, the God of Abraham, the God of Isaac, and the God of Jacob, hath sent me unto you: this is my name for ever, and this is my memorial unto all generations' [Ex. 3.15]. 'I have remembered my covenant. Wherefore say unto the children of Israel, I am Jehovah' [Ex. 6.5, 6, 8]. In Ex. 33.19, where God gives a disclosure of His sovereignty to Moses, this is brought into connection with the name Jehovah. In the later Scriptures the second element, that of faithfulness, is especially associated with the name [Deut. 7.9; Isa. 26.4; Hos. 2.20; Mal. 3.6].

THE PASSOVER

The last prominent feature in the Exodus redemption is the expiatory strand running through it. This consists in the Passover. Notwithstanding its sovereignty, grace could not be exercised without an accompanying atonement. In virtue of this rite the Slayer passed over the houses of the Israelites. In fact the name *Pasach* is derived from this. The verb means first 'to leap', then 'to jump over', then 'to spare'. Both Ex. 12.13 and 27 explain the etymology in this way [cp. also Isa. 31.5]. To be sure, as in the case of Jehovah, so here, other naturalistic explanations have been proposed. The word has been derived from the triumphant passage of the sun through the equinoctial point into the sign of the Ram; Passover would then originally have been the spring-festival of the Equinox. The name has also been explained from the ritual dancing performed at the spring festival.

According to the account the blood put upon the houses was not a mere signal by which the dwellings of the Hebrews could be recognized. It may have been this too, but its real efficacy was derived from its sacrificial character. This is affirmed explicitly, Ex. 12.27: 'It is the sacrifice of Jehovah's Passover, who passed over the houses of the children of Israel in Egypt' [cp. Ex. 34.25; Num. 9.7–10; 1 Cor. 5.7]. Notwithstanding these unequivocal statements most of the old Protestant theologians denied the sacrificial character of the Passover. This was from reaction to the Romish doctrine of the mass. In support of this doctrine the Romanists appealed to the Passover as the corresponding typical sacrifice of the Old Testament. It was in order to deprive them of this argument that Protestants went to the length of denying that the Passover had been a sacrifice.

Now, if it was a sacrifice, the question next arises, to what class of sacrifices it belongs. Some features it had peculiar to itself, but on the whole it will have to be classified with the peace-offerings. Notwithstanding the emphasis thrown on the expiatory element, it cannot be subsumed under the sin-offerings, for of these the offerer was not allowed to eat, whereas it was obligatory to eat the Passover. The idea prominent in every peace-offering was that of berith-fellowship with God. The meal was an exponent of the state of peace and blessedness enjoyed. But precisely because this meal followed the sacrifice proper, there must be recognized in it a reminder of the necessary dependence of such a state of privilege on antecedent expiation. It is a mistake to think that, in the sin-offerings only, expiation was afforded. Wherever there is slaying and manipulation of blood there is expiation, and both these were present in the Passover. The element of purification, closely connected with that of expiation, is separately symbolized in that the application of the blood had to be made by a bunch of hyssop. Hyssop figures everywhere as an instrument of purification. From the ordinary peace-offerings, later regulated by the law, the Passover had the following points of difference: it had and retained the historical background; through the bitter herbs eaten with it the bitterness of the Egyptian bondage was kept alive in the memory of Israel. Further, it was distinctly a national feast, whereas the ordinary peace-offerings were of a private character. Hence it was celebrated, not on a private, but on a family basis. None of the meat was to be taken out of the house. If one family was not able to consume it, two families had to join. Not a bone of the lamb was to be broken, and for this reason it was roasted in fire, not boiled in water. This close connection with the national life of Israel explains why the Passover was not instituted until the organization of Israel as a nation had come near. Circumcision dates from Abraham, the Passover from Moses.

Modern criticism on the whole denies the historical-commemorative origin of the Passover. Its connection with the exodus was an after-thought. Like the other feasts, it was in existence first as a nature-feast of nomadic or agricultural significance. It is assumed by most writers of this class, that the Passover was originally the feast of the sacrifice of the first-born; so Wellhausen, Robertson Smith and others. This first-born sacrifice is usually understood on the principle of a tribute-payment to the deity. Robertson Smith, however, would exclude this whole idea of tribute-payment from the primitive religion of Israel. He explains the surrender of the first-born from the taboo-character of every first birth. There are some critics who do not favour the connection of the rite with the gift of the first-born to the deity at all. Benzinger (see article in *Encyclopaedia Biblica*) considers the Passover an ancient blood-rite, by which in times of pestilence and other occa-sions of danger, protection was sought from the Destroyer. This comes nearer again, at least in its general conception, to the account of Exodus. There is no need of being overmuch exercised on account of these various theories. They do in no way discredit the Biblical repre-sentation. In analogy with what we know of circumcision, the observance of the Passover among Israel might have been placed on an antecedent basis, although undoubtedly it was invested with new meaning. That the Hebrews had been previously accustomed to observe a religious festival in the Spring, we know from their request to Pharaoh [*Ex.* 8.1, 27]. This may have been a feast of the sacrifice of the first-born. As to the theory of an ancient blood-rite, this likewise God may have incorporated into the historically-instituted feast.

[2] The 'Berith' made between Jehovah and Israel

The Making of the *Berith* between Jehovah and Israel is the next subject for consideration under the head of the Content of the Mosaic Revelation. This memorable event is described in Ex. 24. Some preparations for the promulgation of the Decalogue should be read together with this chapter, Ex. 19. It should be noticed, that here the *berith* appears for the first time as a two-sided arrangement, although that is by no means the reason of its being called a *berith*. This reason lies entirely in the ceremony of ratification. As to the arrangement itself, great emphasis is placed on the voluntary acceptance of the *berith* by the people. It is true, the initiative in designing the terms is strictly vindicated for Jehovah. No parleying, no co-operation between God and man in determining the nature and content are from the standpoint of the narrative conceivable. It is Jehovah's covenant exclusively in that respect. Still, the *berith* is placed before the people, and their assent required [*Ex.* 19.5, 8; 24.3].

It is precisely this emphasis thrown on the voluntariness of the union, that leads the critics to deny the historicity of the event. Previously to the great prophets the religion of Israel did not possess such a voluntary nature. If here it is represented as bearing that character, the reason can, on the critical premises, only be, that this part of the documents stands under the influence of the prophetic ideas, and does not reflect history. By the prophets the thought was first developed that Jehovah and Israel are bound together in a free and ethical relationship. But even the earliest of these prophets do not yet so represent it, as if a *berith* existed underlying the religion of Israel. First in the Deuteronomic law-book, written (according to the critical scheme) in the latter half of the seventh century, does this formula appear. Its sudden emergence at that point is supposed to be due to what 2 Kings 22 relates as having happened, viz., the entering upon a solemn league on the part of the people to observe these Deuteronomic ordinances. Now, since for greater impressiveness and effectiveness it had been thought best to derive this newly produced and newly quasi-discovered law-book from Moses, and since the intention was to bind the people to it by a *berith*, necessity arose and consistency required that the matter be represented as a procedure followed in Moses' time, all that was now required of the people being simply a reaffirmation of the earlier *berith*-acceptance of the Mosaic date. In this manner, according to these writers, the *berith* conception made its entrance into the historiography of the Old Testament religion; it was subsequently introduced, according to them, into all the older documents in which previously it had not occurred.

The weakness of this critical construction lies in two points. Altogether too much importance is ascribed by it to the presence or absence or frequency of the term *berith* to determine the essential character of the Old Testament religion. The term does not of itself denote either two-sidedness or one-sidedness, voluntariness or necessity, and is not fit to serve as an indicator of the inner nature of the religion itself. A religion might have a *berith* connected with it, into which nevertheless very little of mutual free choice entered. The critics at this point are still under the spell of the dogmatic preconception that *berith* is a synonym for 'compact' or 'agreement'. Besides, the narrative of 2 Kings 22 in no wise clears up the origin of the *berith*-religion-concept as alleged by the critics. What is described in this chapter is not a *berith* between Jehovah and the people, but between the king and the people in the presence of Jehovah.

As to the proceedings described in Ex. 24, we notice that they are made up of the same two elements that entered into the Passover transaction. In fact, the latter might properly be called an anticipation of the *berith*-making at Sinai. There was first the sacrificial expiation or purification. This was followed by the partaking of the sacrificial meal. We find the combination of these two likewise on the present occasion. That the meal upon the mountain represents the goal and consumma-tion of the *berith* may be inferred from the fact that the account opens with the injunction concerning it, although this could not be executed until all the intervening things were done.

From the circumstances of this separation by seven verses between the injunction and its fulfilment, the inference has been drawn that two different accounts of the *berith*-making are woven together here, one according to which it was made by the ceremony of eating with Jehovah upon the mount [vss. 1, 2, 9–11], and the other according to which it was made by the sacrifices [vss. 3–8]. This dissection is not only unnecessary, but impossible. The sacrifices consisted in part of peace-offerings, and no peace-offering is complete without a meal. On the other hand, the meal described in vss. 9–11 is so unmistakably a sacrificial meal as to become unintelligible without the preceding account of the sacrifice. The sacrifice includes the element of expiation. For the fundamental *berith*-making this was indispensable; every one entering upon a union of this kind would first purify himself through sacrifice or otherwise. Already before the giving of the Decalogue the people had been enjoined to sanctify themselves and wash their gar-ments, particularly the priests [*Ex.* 19.10, 22]. Yet this assumption, so natural in itself, has been rejected by recent writers in favour of a modern theory as to the significance of blood in sacrifice. According to them the function of blood is not (at least not until comparatively late times) to expiate, but to effect a sacramental union, the parties partaking in the blood of a common life. This would in itself yield a quite suitable meaning here, as the *berith* might easily be conceived of as a life-union between Jehovah and Israel. While the idea is attractive, there are scarcely points of contact in the Old Testament for such a conception of the *berith*. The *berith* lies not in the sphere of mystical life; it belongs to the sphere of conscious assurance. Besides, the division of the blood into two parts and the separated use made of each does not readily lend itself to this theory, since on the basis of it, it would have been appropriate rather to unite most closely the application of the blood to Jehovah on the altar [vs. 6] and its application to the people [vs. 8]. The natural view to take of it is, that before the blood could act for the benefit of the people it had to do its work with reference to Jehovah, and this could scarcely consist in aught else than to make the prerequisite expiation.

The book which Moses wrote, and with reference to which the *berith* was made, contained all the words of Jehovah, or as vs. 3 expresses it, 'the words and the judgments'. Some say the words are the Decalogue and the judgments all that follows, up to the close of chap. 23. This is a possible interpretation, although it might be objected to it, that the Decalogue had been addressed to the people by Jehovah's own mouth. In favour of it speaks the difficulty of understanding 'the words' of 20.22–26, in case they are not understood of the Decalogue.

The *berith* had, of course, a national reference to Israel as a whole. This is implied in the summons to ascend addressed to the representatives of the people [vs. 1], and also by the twelve pillars built together with the altar [vs. 4].

Finally, the meeting with Jehovah at the conclusion of the ceremony must be understood in closest connection with the relation that had been established. The phrase 'the God of Israel' is highly significant here. Through the *berith*-making, Jehovah had become 'the God of Israel' in this new profound sense. The vision spoken of is not an ordinary vision to impart knowledge. It is the fulfilment of sacramental approach to and unusual union with Jehovah. How different it was from the ordinary vision of the Deity is indicated by the words: 'And upon the nobles of the children of Israel, He laid not his hand'. Ordinarily it is considered dangerous or even fatal to get sight of the Deity. Through the *berith* this had now been changed. An anticipation of this we met before in the history of Jacob [*Gen.* 32.30]. That the vision had its limitations is implied in vs. 10b.

[3] The organization of Israel: the theocracy
Next we must consider the general organization of Israel that originated in this *berith*. This is usually designated as 'the theocracy'. This name for it is not found in the Scriptures, although it admirably describes what the Biblical account represents Israel's constitution to have been.

Probably the term was coined by Josephus. He observes in regard to the governments of other nations, that some of these were monarchies, others oligarchies, still others democracies; what God set up among Israel was a theocracy. Obviously Josephus finds in this something distinctive and unique. This is correct as far as the great systems of civilization of that day were concerned. But it is not quite correct, if Israel be compared with other Shemitic tribes. The theocratic principle, i.e., the principle of the deity being the supreme authority and power in national life, seems to have been not uncommon among the Shemites. We may infer as much from the observation that *Melekh*, 'King', is a frequent Shemitic name for the deity. But while under ordinary circumstances this was a mere belief, it proved among Israel an undoubted reality. The laws under which Israel lived not merely had the divine sanction behind them in the general sense in which all law and order ultimately derives from God through general revelation by way of the conscience, but in the specific sense, that Jehovah had directly revealed the law. In other words Jehovah in person performed the task usually falling to a human king. And in the sequel also, Jehovah by supernatural interposition, when necessary, continued to act the role of King of the nation. This fact was so deeply embedded in the consciousness of the leaders of Israel that still in the time of Gideon and Samuel it was felt to forbid the setting up of a purely human kingdom. The union of the religious lordship and the national kingship in the one Person of Jehovah involved that among Israel civil and religious life were inextricably interwoven. If the union had happened to exist in any other person but God, a division of the two spheres of relationship might have been conceivable. The bond to God is so one and indivisible that no separation of the one from the other can be conceived. Hence the later prophetic condemnation of politics, not merely wicked politics, but politics *per se*, as derogatory to the royal prerogative of Jehovah.

Further it ought to be noticed that between these two concentric spheres the religious one has the pre-eminence. It is that for the sake of which the other exists. For our system of political government such an interrelation would, of course, seen a serious, intolerable defect. Not so among Israel. The chief end for which Israel had been created was not to teach the world lessons in political economy, but in the midst of a world of paganism to teach true religion, even at the sacrifice of much secular propaganda and advantage.

Nor was it merely a question of teaching religion for the present world. A missionary institution the theocracy never was intended to be in its Old Testament state. The significance of the unique organization of Israel can be rightly measured only by remembering that the theocracy typified nothing short of the perfected kingdom of God, the consummate state of Heaven. In this ideal state there will be no longer any place for the distinction between church and state. The former will have absorbed the latter. In a rough way the principle involved was already apprehended by Josephus. In the passage introducing the word 'theocracy' he observes that Moses, by giving such a constitution to the Israelites, did not make religion a part of virtue, but made all other virtues to be a part of religion. The fusion between the two spheres of secular and religious life is strikingly expressed by the divine promise that Israel will be made 'a kingdom of priests and an holy nation' [Ex. 19.6]. As priests they are in, nay, constitute the kingdom.

THE FUNCTION OF LAW

From the nature of the theocracy thus defined we may learn what was the function of the law in which it received its provisional embodiment. It is of the utmost importance carefully to distinguish between the purpose for which the law was professedly given to Israel at the time, and the various purposes it actually came to serve in the subsequent course of history. These other ends lay, of course, from the outset in the mind of God. From the theistic standpoint there can be no outcome in history that is not the unfolding of the profound purpose of God. In this sense Paul has been the great teacher of the philosophy of law in the economy of redemption. Most of the Pauline formulas bear a negative character. The law chiefly operated towards bringing about and revealing the failure of certain methods and endeavours. It served as a pedagogue unto Christ, shut up the people under sin, was not given unto life, was weak through the flesh, worked condemnation, brings under a curse, is a powerless ministry of the letter. These statements of Paul were made under the stress of a totally different philosophy of the law-purpose, which he felt to be inconsistent with the principles of redemption and grace.

This Pharisaic philosophy asserted that the law was intended, on the principle of merit, to enable Israel to earn the blessedness of the world to come. It was an eschatological and therefore most comprehensive interpretation. But in its comprehensiveness it could not fail being comprehensively wrong, if it should prove wrong. Paul's philosophy, though a partial one, and worked out from a retrospective standpoint, had the advantage of being correct within the limited sphere in which he propounded it. It is true, certain of the statements of the Pentateuch and of the Old Testament in general may on the surface seem to favour the Judaistic position. That the law cannot be kept is nowhere stated in so many words. And not only this, that the keeping of the law will be rewarded is stated once and again. Israel's retention of the privileges of the *berith* is made dependent on obedience. It is promised that he who shall do the commandments shall find life through them. Consequently writers have not been lacking who declared that, from a historical point of view, their sympathies went with the Judaizers, and not with Paul.

Only a moment's reflection is necessary to prove that this in untenable, and that precisely from a broad historical standpoint Paul had far more accurately grasped the purport of the law than his opponents. The law was given after the redemption from Egypt had been accomplished, and the people had already entered upon the enjoyment of many of the blessings of the *berith*. Particularly their taking possession of the promised land could not have been made dependent on previous observance of the law, for during their journey in the wilderness many of its prescripts could not be observed. It is plain, then, that law-keeping did not figure at that juncture as the meritorious ground of life-inheritance. The latter is based on grace alone, no less emphatically than Paul himself places salvation on that ground. But, while this is so, it might still be objected, that law-observance, if not the ground for receiving, is yet made the ground for retention of the privileges inherited. Here it can not, of course, be denied that a real connection exists. But the Judaizers went wrong in inferring that the connection must be *meritorious*, that, if Israel keeps the cherished gifts of Jehovah through observance of His law, this must be so, because in strict justice they had *earned* them. The connection is of a totally different kind. It belongs not to the legal sphere of merit, but to the symbolico-typical sphere of *appropriateness of expression*.

As stated above, the abode of Israel in Canaan typified the heavenly, perfected state of God's people. Under these circumstances the ideal of absolute conformity to God's law of legal holiness had to be upheld. Even though they were not able to keep this law in the Pauline, spiritual sense, yea, even though they were unable to keep it externally and ritually, the requirement could not be lowered. When apostasy on a general scale took place, they could not remain in the promised land. When they disqualified themselves for typifying the state of holiness, they *ipso facto* disqualified themselves for typifying that of blessedness, and had to go into captivity. This did not mean that every individual

Israelite, in every detail of his life, had to be perfect, and that on this was suspended the continuance of God's favour. Jehovah dealt primarily with the nation and through the nation with the individual, as even now in the covenant of grace He deals with believers and their children in the continuity of generations. There is solidarity among the members of the people of God, but this same principle also works for the neutralizing of the effect of individual sin, so long as the nation remains faithful. The attitude observed by the nation and its representative leaders was the decisive factor. Although the demands of the law were at various times imperfectly complied with, nevertheless for a long time Israel remained in possession of the favour of God. And, even when the people as a whole become apostate, and go into exile, Jehovah does not on that account suffer the *berith* to fail. After due chastisement and repentance He takes Israel back into favour.

This is the most convincing proof that law–observance is not the meritorious ground of blessedness. God in such cases simply repeats what He did at the beginning, viz., receive Israel into favour on the principle of free grace. It is in agreement with this, when the law is represented in the Old Testament, not as the burden and yoke which it later came to be in the religious experience of the Jews, but as one of the greatest blessings and distinctions that Jehovah had conferred upon his people [*Deut.* 4.7, 8; *Psa.* 147.19, 20; cp. even Paul, *Rom.* 9.4, 5]. And in Paul's teaching the strand that corresponds to this Old Testament doctrine of holiness as the indispensable (though not meritorious) condition of receiving the inheritance is still distinctly traceable.

From the above it will be seen how distorted and misleading it would be to identify the Old Testament with law, negatively considered, and the New Testament with gospel. This would mean that there was no gospel under the old dispensation at all. The Pauline statements are sometimes apt to lead into this error. But they are not meant by the Apostle in this absolute, mutually exclusive sense. An illuminating analogy in this respect is furnished by the way in which Paul speaks of faith and its relation to the two dispensations. In Gal. 3.23, 25, he speaks of the 'coming' of faith, as though there had never been any faith before. And yet the same Paul in Rom. 4.16ff., speaks at length of the role played by faith in the life of Abraham, and how it virtually dominated the entire Old Testament system.

It is evident that there are two distinct points of view from which the content of the old dispensation can be regarded. When considered in comparison with the final unfolding and rearranged structure of the New Testament, negative judgments are in place. When, on the other hand, the Old Testament is taken as an entity by itself and as rounded off provisionally in itself, and looked at, as it were, with the eyes of the Old Testament itself, we find it necessary to take into account the positive elements by which it prefigured and anticipated typically the New Testament. And thus we find that there was real gospel under the theocracy. The people of God of those days did not live and die under an unworkable, unredemptive system of religion, that could not give real access to and spiritual contact with God. Nor was this gospel-element contained exclusively in the revelation that preceded, accompanied, and followed the law; it is found *in the law itself*. That which we call 'the legal system' is shot through with strands of gospel and grace and faith. Especially the ritual law is rich in them. Every sacrifice and every lustration proclaimed the principle of grace. Had it been otherwise, then the idea of positive, vital continuity would have to be abandoned. There would be conflict and opposition instead. Such is the Gnostic position, but it is not the view either of the Old Testament itself, or of Paul, or of the Church theology.

And yet again, we must not forget that this revelation and promulgation of the gospel in the Mosaic institutions bore, as to its form, a legal character, and differs, in this respect, from the form it exhibits at the present time. For even these gospel-carrying institutions were part of a great system of ordinances, whose observance had been made obligatory for the people. Hence there was a lack of freedom even in the presentation of and attendance to the gospel. The gospel was preached under the constraint of law and received under the same. It was not permitted to rise superior to the legal environment in which it had been placed. Only the New Testament has brought the full liberty in this respect.

[4] The Decalogue

The Decalogue strikingly illustrates the redemptive structure of the theocracy as a whole. It is introduced by the summing up of what Jehovah has done for Israel in delivering them from the house of bondage. Considering the time of its promulgation, we might even call it a brief résumé in advance of the whole system regulated subsequently in the detailed laws. But this would overlook the fact that one component element of the law, and that one much in evidence elsewhere, is absent from the Decalogue. It contains no ceremonial commandments. In a sense, therefore, it not so much anticipates as condenses, and in condensing eliminates and idealizes. It joins together the beginning and the end of the entire theocratic movement, the redeeming act of God, and the resultant state of holiness and conformity to the nature and will of God into which the theocracy is designed to issue. At the same time it gives these elements in a form that is adjusted to the practical needs and limitations of the people. Like the theocracy in general it hovers above the life of the people as an ideal never realizable, nor realizable at the then existing stage; and at the same time it descends into and condescends to the abnormalities of Israel.

This in some sense ideal and idealizing character of the Decalogue has not failed of observation by the evolutionary critics, and given rise to the opinion that it could not possibly be a product of the Mosaic age, which, as shown above, is assigned and must be assigned, from the critical premises, to a low plane of religious development. The historico-critical treatment of the Decalogue in recent times is interesting and instructive in the extreme. There was a time, when even advanced critics were inclined to make an exception for the Decalogue in the midst of their comprehensive denial of the Mosaic origin of the other Pentateuchal laws. It is true, this was conceded with certain qualifications. The second word, forbidding the making and worship of images, could not be Mosaic, because image-worship was considered inoffensive for a long time after the Mosaic age. And of the other words not the present extended form was derived from Moses, but a more simple and compact form containing the gist of the injunction.

The Wellhausen school has swept away even this modest remnant of conservatism. The main ground on which this revision of the view of the older critics is based lies in the ethical character of the Decalogue. Ethical ideas did not become central in the religion of Israel until the time of the prophets. Before their age (middle of the eighth century B.C.) the popular religion was centred in the cult, and of this the Decalogue contains nothing. Hence the present critical view that the Decalogue is the precipitate of the ethical movement of prophecy, possibly not composed earlier than the seventh century, perhaps during the reign of Manasseh.

It must be urged against this that the main burden of the prophetic preaching of ethics keeps in much closer contact with contemporary developments than the Decalogue. The prophetic message revolves round such things as the oppression of the poor by the rich, the corruptness of the administration of justice. These are things not even alluded to in the Decalogue. The situation to which the prophets address themselves, therefore, is much more concrete and complex than that contemplated in the Decalogue. And even if it were true that the Israelites of the pre-prophetic period did not look upon ethical things as the centre of their religion, it would by no means follow from this, that revelation could not have long before singled out the ethical as of supreme importance and in immediate need of attention. The Decalogue, on our view at least, was not the product of the religion of the people, but the revelation of God. The critical contention, here as in so many other points, holds good only when the philosophy of evolution is made the silent premise of the argument. More recently still, critical writers have begun to see again that the Decalogue breathes a different and more primitive spirit than the preaching of the prophets. It is proposed to return to the view of Mosaic origin, but in a modified form. Moses, it is now alleged, wrote seven of these ten commandments. The three denied him are the first, the second and the fourth. Only, it was not the lawgiver's intention to forbid the things mentioned in the other seven absolutely. He meant to forbid them within the limits of Israel. Outside of that circle the otherwise prohibited things were permitted. In answer to this it may be observed, that, while the words are primarily addressed to Israel, this was due entirely to the circumstance of the historical situation, and can never prove the existence in the mind of the legislator of a double standard, rendering a thing sinful when done to a fellow-Israelite, and condonable when done to non-Israelites.

OF WORLD-WIDE APPLICATION

The primary application to Israel in no wise interferes with a world-wide application in all ethical relationships. The pronouns and pronominal suffixes are in the feminine singular, because they are addressed to the nation of Israel. Certain features at first sight would seem applicable to Israel alone, for instance what is said of the deliverance from the Egyptian bondage. But these features are rare, especially in the text of Exodus. There are more of them in Deuteronomy; compare the motivation of the fourth word. Deuteronomy repeats the Decalogue for a hortatory purpose, which brings it into closer contact with the momentary situation of Israel. And, apart from this, we must remember that the history of Israel was shaped by God intentionally so as to mirror all important situations befalling the people of God in all subsequent ages. When Jehovah appeals to the redemption from Egypt as a motive for obedience, He appeals to something that has its spiritual analogy in the life of all believers. The historical adjustment does not detract from the universal application, but subserves it.

RELIGIOUS IN CHARACTER

The most striking feature of the Decalogue is its specifically religious character. It is not an ethical code in and by itself, resting, as it were, on the bare imperative of God. The preamble brings the affection to Jehovah, in view of what He has done redemptively for the people, to bear through a responsive affection upon their conduct. If we may apply the term 'Christian' thus retrospectively to the Decalogue, we should say, what it contains is not general but Christian ethics. Ethics is represented as the redemptive product; something else, lying behind, as the source. That there is implied, apart from this, a hegemony of religion over ethics, appears from the far greater volume of elaboration devoted to the four opening words, dealing with the specifically religious side. Our Lord recognized this, when distinguishing in the law between the first and second great commandment. In the light of this redemptive purport the negative form of most of the commandments likewise receives additional significance. Of course, this has a meaning in itself, altogether apart from redemption, in that it issues a protest against sin. But the very fact of God's issuing such a protest admits of the inference, that He will not leave sin in possession of the field.

It should be observed, however, that not all the words are clothed in this negative form of 'thou shalt not'. The fourth word, that relating to the Sabbath, has positive import. And the majestic appendix to the second word reaches down into the very depths of the love of God for His own, as well as of His jealousy towards them that disobey the law out of hatred of God. The charge, therefore, is not warranted that the Decalogue is a purely negativistic document, evincing no positive interest for what is good, merely opposing that which is evil. Our Lord implied that the law requires love towards God and man, and love is the most positive of all forces. The practical nature of the Decalogue, both on its religious and on its ethical side, is revealed in the way it addresses itself to concrete external sins. But this again is not meant to deny the organic unity of sin in its root. On the contrary, this unity is distinctly recognized in tracing the transgression back to the hatred of God. It is likewise implied in the last word of the ten, where the overt sins of killing, stealing, committing adultery, bearing false witness, are reduced to their one source of coveting, evil lust having its seat in the heart.

THE TEN WORDS

As to the distribution of the text of the Decalogue over the ten words various views are held. The text informs us that there are ten, but does not number them singly, for the system of dividing the text of the Old Testament into verses is, of course, not original. The Greek Catholic and the Reformed Churches consider the preamble as standing outside of the circle of ten. The first word then applies to the prohibition of worshipping other gods, the second to the prohibition of images, and so on to the end in the manner familiar to us. This division is as old as the time of Philo and Josephus. The Roman Catholic and Lutheran Churches count as one what we reckon as the first and second words. Inasmuch as the number ten is required, this compels the dividing up of what we call the tenth commandment into the ninth ('thou shalt not covet thy neighbour's house') and the tenth ('thou shalt not covet thy neighbour's wife, etc.'). This is necessary because no other word lends itself to a similar division, except perhaps the fourth, and neither the Romanists, nor the Lutherans, want to count in the preamble. Still a third division, now common among the Jews, reckons the preamble as the first word. This would, of course, ordinarily yield eleven, but this result is avoided through taking the first and second together. The same numbering, with the preamble included was at one time resorted to by some critics, who had lost one word through assigning a later origin to the second word. Of these three plans the first deserves the preference.

The introduction cannot be strictly called a commandment. Still, this difficulty might be relieved by observing that the law does not speak of commandments but of words (Decalogue means 'ten words'). Probably however, 'word' is used in this connection for 'commandments', a meaning it not infrequently bears. The objection, therefore, remains. And it is strengthened by the fact that counting the preamble as one of the ten would cut its very vital relation to all the other words. Something can be said in favour of closely drawing together the first and the second words, as will be presently shown, but nothing speaks in favour of dividing the tenth word into two. It exposes, one might urge, to the objection of separating between house and wife as non-covetable objects, but this is more of an apparent than a real objection, because house here does not mean the mere building, but stands for the entire household-establishment, including, of course, and that in the first place, the wife. Augustine was somewhat over gallant, when not perceiving this, he gave preference to the text of Deuteronomy, where the wife precedes the house. But, assuming that 'house' means 'household', no reason exists why this general term should receive for itself an entire separate word, and then in a next word the enumeration of its several constituent parts be made to follow. The structure of the Decalogue is not of that kind, as may be seen by comparison with the text of the fourth word. And Augustine has improved the matter only in a sentimental respect, for, with all due regard for the honoured position of the wife in the family, it would hardly be in keeping with the feeling of the Old Testament in such matters to give the wife a separate commandment all to herself, especially since her position in one respect had been already defined in the, on our reckoning, seventh commandment.

THE FIRST WORD

Our discussion of the several separate words confines itself to the first four. The following six, regulating the relation between man and man, belong to the department of Ethics. These first four words deal specifically with the relation of man to God. The first three form a group by themselves, protesting as they do, against the three typical and fundamental sins of paganism, the sin of polylatry, that of idolatry, that of magic.

It will be observed, further, that the first word is not a theoretical denial of the existence of other gods besides Jehovah. Neither is it, of course, an affirmation, either directly or impliedly, of the existence of other divine beings. It leaves this whole question to one side, and confines itself to the injunction that Israel shall have only one object of worship: 'there shall be no other god (or gods) to thee before me'. But if this, theoretically or legislatively considered, falls short of the abstract enunciation of the principle of monotheism, and reaches, logically speaking, only up to monolatry, it were pedantic to seize upon it, lawyer-like, as evidence of the lawgiver's intent to leave polytheism untouched. And yet precisely this the critics have been doing, when building on this innocent form of expression the view that Moses had not yet reached the stage of monotheism. When afterwards the dating of the Decalogue came down to much later times this exegesis involved its adherents in a somewhat serious difficulty. It seemed difficult to assume that the prophetic spirits who produced the Decalogue at so advanced a juncture should not yet have reached the standpoint of monotheism. The critics save themselves out of this impasse by saying that, although monotheism had been in process of development since the times of Amos and Hosea, it had not been explicitly formulated until the age of (pseudo-) Deuteronomy and Jeremiah. As for Moses, it becomes doubtful, on this hypothesis, whether he had reached the standpoint of as much as monolatry in his day, for the testimony of the Decalogue to that effect has fallen away.

All this is readily corrected by the simple reminder that the Decalogue, while law, is not law in the modern technical sense of that term. It takes no pains, by means of involved clauses and piled up qualifications, to stop up every loophole for misunderstanding or evasion. Moses was a lawgiver, not a scribe. The plane on which the matter is put by not raising the problem of abstract monotheism is in reality a higher one than would have underlain the commandment otherwise. To say: there are no other gods in existence, therefore you are shut up to serving me alone, motivates the allegiance of Israel to Jehovah less worthily, than to say, as the Decalogue actually does, 'I am Jehovah, thy God, who has brought thee up out of the land of Egypt, out of the house of bondage. Thou shalt have no other gods before me'. Besides the appeal to the sense of gratitude for deliverance received, there shines through also an allusion to the offended honour of Jehovah, in case other objects of worship should be placed by His side. The words 'before me' or 'beside me' express the indignity such transgression would offer to Him, subjectively.

THE SECOND WORD

There is some uncertainty in regard to the syntax of the second word. In the Authorized and Revised Versions the word 'likeness' is made dependent on 'thou shalt not make', and thus co-ordinated with the preceding object 'graven image'. The likeness, then, is something that can be made; it must be a manufactured object. Attention has, however, been called to the fact that the Hebrew word thus translated may also properly be rendered by 'shape', i.e., natural, non-manufactured shape, any one of the forms or likenesses nature offers. If this be adopted, and it seems to be favoured somewhat by the distinction of the 'shapes' in three groups – those in heaven above, those in the earth beneath, and those in the water under the earth – then plainly those shapes cannot be the object of the verb 'thou shalt not make', since they are not the product of human making.

Consequently the syntactical construction of the sentence must on this view be changed. It will have to read as follows: 'Thou shalt not make unto thee a graven image, (and), as to the likeness of anything (prefixed accusative phrase of reference) that is in heaven above, etc . . . thou shalt not bow down thyself unto *those*, nor serve them, etc.' Two things are on this view forbidden: the worship of a graven image (graven means 'made out of metal'), and the worship of any of the forms of nature.

It must be admitted that this new construction does not read very smoothly. On the other hand the usual interpretation labours under the difficulty of explaining satisfactorily why a 'graven' image should have appeared more objectionable than any other kind of made likeness. Still, it seems to be a fact attested also elsewhere in the Old Testament that graven images awakened a special aversion among the opponents of idolatry. Wellhausen thinks the difficulty can be removed by adopting as original the text of Deuteronomy which reads: 'Thou shalt not make unto thee a graven image of any of the shapes, etc.' But even in Deuteronomy the Septuagint and Samaritan versions have the 'and' before 'likeness': 'image and all likeness'.

More interesting and important, however, is the enquiry into the ground on which idolatry is forbidden here. The traditional exegesis of the second commandment is wont to find the reason in the spiritual (non-corporeal) nature of God, which causes every bodily representation to be a misrepresentation, and one moreover to the disparagement of God, because in the scale of being the incorporeal ranks above the corporeal, the so-called 'flesh'. While acknowledging the truth of this idea in itself, we cannot regard it as a completely satisfactory exegesis of the second word. On such a view of the motive the appendix ought to read, 'for I, Jehovah thy God, have no body'. Instead of this it is the *jealousy* that is warningly referred to. And 'jealousy' cannot here have the general significance of 'fiery zeal' which it has sometimes elsewhere, for that would not have made the introduction of the idea more appropriate in this than in any other word of the Decalogue. There must be a special reason why the making or worship of images awakens the jealousy of Jehovah. The word means conjugal zeal specifically, jealousy in the married relation. It implies that, when images come into play, for the monogamic relation between Jehovah and Israel, a polygamous, or even meretricious bond with other religious lords has been substituted.

The question before us, therefore, is why and in what sense image-making detracts from the undivided devotion of Israel to God, and places other divine objects of devotion beside Him. Now it is plain that this cannot be satisfactorily explained on the basis of the image being a symbolic copy of the Deity, so that after all the latter would be but all the more worshipped through the image. For us who think in modern terms admiration or even worship bestowed upon one's photograph could scarcely excite jealousy. It would be much more apt to give rise to selfish satisfaction. We must set aside this whole modern way of thinking about the matter, and endeavour to reproduce for ourselves the feelings with which the ancient idolatrous mind regarded and employed the image it possessed of its god. This is a far more complex thing than the formula of reality and symbol is able to express. While not easily described in its true inwardness, we may perhaps define it by subsumption under the category of magic. Magic is that paganistic reversal of the process of religion, in which man, instead of letting himself be used by God for the divine purpose, drags down his god to the level of a tool, which he uses for his own selfish purpose. Magic is full of superstition, and, after a fashion, full of the quasi-supernatural, but it is void of true religion. Because it lacks the element of objective divine self-communication from above, it must needs create for itself material means of compulsion that will bring the deity to do its bidding. From the nature of the case these instruments of magical compulsion will indefinitely multiply. Taking these instruments for his practical use, man will further begin to feel that the powers habitually working through them are somehow subtracted from the deity and stored up in the forms of magic. Thus the magically manipulated image will inevitably tend to become a second god by the side of the original one, and will even tend to outgrow the latter in potency of usefulness. The image is not the symbol; it acts as the rival and substitute of the god. Thus the sensual representation of Jehovah by becoming mixed up with magic leads straightway to polytheism.

In so far, the Romanists and Lutherans correctly sensed that there existed an intimate connection between the first and the second commandment. Jehovah's retention of the exclusive right to Israel's worship became endangered as soon as images were introduced. It is not impossible that the 'graven image' refers particularly to Jehovah-images, and that the 'likenesses' or 'shapes' refer to alien deities. The former no less than the latter excites the divine jealousy, and both are referred to in the commandment, no matter whether this suggestion in regard to 'graven image' be correct or not. The first commandment enjoins the having of one God; the second strikes at the chief source of danger for the observance of this. Even in the double-faced meaning of the word 'idolatry' this connection of the two things still reflects itself; it means partly the worship of other gods, partly the worship of images. These facts are sure.

THE THIRD WORD

The transition from the second to the third word is a natural one, for we are here still in the sphere of magic. This time it is word-magic that is forbidden. It is not sufficient to think of swearing and blasphemy in the present-day common sense of these terms. The word is one of the chief powers of pagan superstition, and the most potent form of word-magic is name-magic. It was believed that through the pronouncing of the name of some supernatural entity this can be compelled to do the bidding of the magic-user. The commandment applies the divine disapproval of such practices specifically to the name 'Jehovah'. 'To take up' means to pronounce. 'In vain' literally reads 'for vanity'. Vanity is a quite complex term in which the ideas of the unreal, the deceitful, the disappointing, the sinful, intermingle. It designates a large sphere of paganism, which must have occupied a place also in Israel's past, and must have continually threatened to encroach upon the true religion. The use of the name Jehovah for such a purpose was particularly dangerous, because it seemed to lend the protection of legitimacy.

Although the antique and the modern may in this matter appear to lie at a great distance from each other, nevertheless what we call swearing and blasphemy is not essentially different from this ancient name-magic, and consequently falls under the condemnation of the third commandment. We must remember that originally the habit of swearing served a far more realistic purpose than at present. If it has become conventional, and therefore, as some would pretend, innocent, this is largely because the modern man has retained such a small amount of religion as to make him feel that swearing cannot at bottom be irreligious. In ages not so very long ago the employment of supernatural names for the purpose of execration and objurgation had a quite realistic intent. The names served to call out the supernal powers for injuring the enemy or for miraculously attesting the truth of a statement. It is from such practices that all our survivals of swearing have descended. And, even where the swearer professes to attach no real significance to his formulas, yet there still clings to the most thoughtless use of them always more or less of the feeling that it does not matter much if the name of a god, perhaps no longer believed in, can be harnessed to the service of man in the most trivial of affairs. This may be the pale shadow of name-magic, but it is in principle not different from the realistic thing. The core of the sin does not exclusively lie in its believed efficacy, but in the disrespect for God that is implied. It is, as all magic is, the opposite to true religion. Hence the emphatic condemnation: 'Jehovah will not hold him guiltless that pronounces His name for vanity'.

THE FOURTH WORD
The fourth word has reference to the hallowing of the seventh day

of the week. This duty is based in Exodus (but cp. Deuteronomy) not on something done to Israel in particular, but on something done in the creation of the world. This is important, because with it stands or falls the general validity of the commandment for all mankind. Traces of a previous Sabbath-observance are not found in the Pentateuch [but cp. *Ex.* 16.23]. It is certain that the week of seven days was known before the time of Moses [cp. *Gen.* 29.27]. This mode of reckoning time may have had for its forgotten background the original institution of the Sabbath.

Outside of the circle of Special Revelation two views have been taken as to its origin. By some it is associated with the role played by the planets in astral religion. Saturn, being the chief planet, would have had the last and principal day assigned to him. According to others the seven-days-week is derived from the four phases of the moon, the twenty-eight days divided by four yielding seven. On either view the development would have been a transfer of the worship due to the Creator from Him to the creature. The Assyrians observed the seventh, the fourteenth, the twenty-first, and the twenty-eighth day of the month as a day of rest. This differed, however, from the Old Testament Sabbath observance in two respects: it was dependent on the phases of the moon, and the abstention from labour was due to the supposed ominous character of the day, which rendered working on it inauspicious.

It has been claimed that in two passages of the Old Testament the Sabbath is represented as of Mosaic origin, viz., in Ezek. 20.12; Neh. 9.14. But these passages mean no more than that the institution in its specific Old Testament form dates from the time of Moses. It must be remembered that the Sabbath, though a world-aged observance, has passed through the various phases of the development of redemption, remaining the same in essence but modified as to its form, as the new state of affairs at each point might require. The Sabbath is not only the most venerable, it is likewise the most living of all the sacramental realities of our religion. It has faithfully accompanied the people of God on their march through the ages. With regret it must be admitted that the beauty and comfort of this thought seem to have impressed themselves more deeply upon the Jewish than upon the Christian consciousness.

The principle underlying the Sabbath is formulated in the Decalogue itself. It consists in this, that man must copy God in his course of life. The divine creative work completed itself in six days, whereupon the seventh followed as a day of rest for God. In connection with God, 'rest' cannot, of course, mean mere cessation from labour, far less recovery from fatigue. Such a meaning is by no means required by the Old Testament usage of the word. 'Rest' resembles the word 'peace' in this respect, that it has in Scripture, in fact to the Shemitic mind generally, a positive rather than a negative import. It stands for consummation of a work accomplished and the joy and satisfaction attendant upon this. Such was its prototype in God. Mankind must copy this, and that not only in the sequences of daily existence as regards individuals; but in its collective capacity through a large historic movement. For mankind, too, a great task waits to be accomplished, and at its close beckons a rest of joy and satisfaction that shall copy the rest of God.

Before all other important things, therefore, the Sabbath is an expression of the eschatological principle on which the life of humanity has been constructed. There is to be to the world-process a finale, as there was an overture, and these two belong inseparably together. To give up the one means to give up the other, and to give up either means to abandon the fundamental scheme of Biblical history. Even among Jewish teachers this profound meaning of the Sabbath was not entirely unknown. One of them, being asked what the world to come would be like, answered that it would resemble the Sabbath. In the law, it is true, this thought is not developed further than is done in the primordial statement about God's resting on the seventh day and hallowing it. For the rest, the institution, after having been re-enforced in the Decalogue, is left to speak for itself, as is the case with most institutions of the law. The Epistle to the Hebrews has given us a philosophy of the Sabbath on the largest of scales, partly in dependence on Psa. 95 [Heb. 3, 4].

The Sabbath brings this principle of the eschatological structure of history to bear upon the mind of man after a symbolical and a typical fashion. It teaches its lesson through the rhythmical succession of six days of labour and one ensuing day of rest in each successive week. Man is reminded in this way that life is not an aimless existence, that a goal lies beyond. This was true before, and apart from, redemption. The eschatological is an older strand in revelation than the soteric. The so-called 'Covenant of Works' was nothing but an embodiment of the Sabbatical principle. Had its probation been successful, then the sacramental Sabbath would have passed over into the reality it typified, and the entire subsequent course of the history of the race would have been radically different. What now is to be expected at the end of this world would have formed the beginning of the world-course instead.

From what has been said about the typical, sacramental meaning of the Sabbath it follows that it would be a mistake to base its observance primarily on the ground of utility. The Sabbath is not the outcome of an abnormal state of affairs in which it is impossible, apart from the appointment of a fixed day, to devote sufficient care to the religious interests of life. On such a view it might be maintained that for one sufficiently at leisure to give all his time to the cultivation of religion the keeping of the Sabbath would be no longer obligatory. Some of the Continental Reformers, out of reaction to the Romish system of holy days, reasoned after this fashion. But they reasoned wrongly. The Sabbath is not in the first place a means of advancing religion. It has its main significance apart from that, in pointing forward to the eternal issues of life and history. Even the most advanced religious spirit cannot absolve itself from taking part in that. It is a serious question whether the modern church has not too much lost sight of this by making the day well-nigh exclusively an instrument of religious propaganda, at the expense of its eternity-typifying value. Of course it goes without saying that a day devoted to the remembrance of man's eternal destiny cannot be properly observed without the positive cultivation of those religious concerns which are so intimately joined to the final issue of his lot. But, even where this is conceded, the fact remains that it is possible to crowd too much into the day that is merely subservient to religious propaganda, and to void it too much of the static, God-ward and heaven-ward directed occupation of piety.

The universal Sabbath law received a modified significance under the Covenant of Grace. The work which issues into the rest can now no longer be man's own work. It becomes the work of Christ. This the Old Testament and the New Testament have in common. But they differ as to the perspective in which they each see the emergence of work and rest. Inasmuch as the Old Covenant was still looking forward to the performance of the Messianic work, naturally the days of labour to it come first, the day of rest falls at the end of the week. We, under the New Covenant, look back upon the accomplished work of Christ. We, therefore, first celebrate the rest in principle procured by Christ, although the Sabbath also still remains a sign looking forward to the final eschatological rest. The Old Testament people of God had to typify in their life the future developments of redemption. Consequently the precedence of labour and the consequence of rest had to find expression in their calendar. The New Testament Church has no such typical function to perform, for the types have been fulfilled. But it has a great historic event to commemorate, the performance of the work by Christ and the entrance of Him and of His people through Him upon the state of never-ending rest. We do not sufficiently realize the profound sense the early Church had of the epoch-making significance of the appearance, and especially of the resurrection of the Messiah. The latter was to them nothing less than the bringing in of a new, the second, creation. And they felt that this ought to find expression in the placing of the Sabbath with reference to the other days of the week. Believers knew themselves in a measure partakers of the Sabbath-fulfilment. If the one creation required one sequence, then the other required another. It has been strikingly observed, that our Lord died on the eve of that Jewish Sabbath, at the end of one of these typical weeks of labour by which His work and its consummation were prefigured. And Christ entered upon His rest, the rest of His new, eternal life on the first day of the week, so that the Jewish Sabbath comes to lie between, was, as it were, disposed of, buried in His grave. (Delitzsch.) If there is in the New Testament no formal enactment regarding this change, the cause lies in the superfluousness of it. Doubtless Jewish Christians began with observing both days, and only gradually the instinctive perception of the sacredness of the day of the Lord's resurrection began to make itself felt.

The question can be raised, whether in the fourth commandment there is an element that applies to the Old Testament Church only. The answer depends on the precise construction and exegesis of the words. Is the distinction between six days of labour and one day of rest merely a matter of proportion, or is it likewise a matter of sequence? The latter view seems more probable. In so far, we shall have to say that in this element of prescribed sequence there is a specifically Old Testament feature in the commandment which no longer applies to us. But the general principle on which the sequence, both under the old and the new dispensations, rests has not been changed. Precisely because it remains in force, the sequence required a change when the New Testament had arrived. Besides this, there are other prohibitions in the law, which by the very fact of their having not been incorporated in the Decalogue, are shown not to be universally applicable [Ex. 16.23; 34.21; 35.3; Num. 15.32; cp. also Amos 8.5; Jer. 17.21]. Nor must it be forgotten that the Sabbath was under the Old Testament an integral part of a cycle of feasts which is no longer in force now. The type embodied in it was deepened by the Sabbatical Year and the Year of Jubilee. On the Sabbath man and beast rest, in the Sabbatical Year the very soil rests; in the Year of

Jubilee the idea of rest is exhibited in its full positive import through the restoration of all that was disturbed and lost through sin. From all this we have been released by the work of Christ, but not from the Sabbath as instituted at Creation. In this light we must interpret certain New Testament statements such as Rom. 14.5, 6; Gal. 4.10, 11; Col. 2.16, 17.

[5] The Ritual [ceremonial] Law

The Ritual Laws: This is what by another name is called the ceremonial law. It forms an integral part of the Mosaic legislation. The elements composing it were not, however, necessarily introduced *de novo* at the time of Moses. Much of older custom was probably incorporated. Some have thought that the ordinances here prescribed did not originally belong to the structure of the theocracy, but were imposed upon the people as a punishment after their sin with the golden calf. This view has been held in two forms, a more innocuous and a more serious one. Several of the Church fathers, perhaps out of reaction from Judaism, embraced it. Later the Reformed theologian Cocceius adopted it. In both these instances this was not accompanied by a low or depreciating view of the content of these laws *per se*.

More serious was the form of the theory proposed by Spencer, stated previously in connection with the redemption from Egypt. Spencer joined, of course, to this view of the pagan provenience of the ritual practices a very sceptical attitude in regard to their typical significance. According to our previous interpretation of the structure of the theocracy it is precisely in these ritual institutions that the greater part of the gospel of Moses is enshrined. The rejection of them as not willed by God, therefore, de-evangelizes the Mosaic revelation to a large extent.

In more recent times the error in question has played a considerable role in the critical appraisal of the several parts of the Old Testament. The Wellhausen school derives many of the ritual customs from the Canaanites, and this again has for its background the extreme, wellnigh exclusive stress placed upon the ethical teaching, which is held to be alone of enduring value. The proof for this last interpretation is found in the general construction of the history of Old Testament religion by this school. By the older advocates of the view Scriptural authority was sought for its adoption. Such was discovered in the time of their introduction, namely, immediately after the idolatry with the golden calf had been committed. It is true that a chronological conjunction exists here. But there was no causal connection as the theory would have us believe. In fact the contents of this part of the law were communicated by God to Moses while he was upon the mount, and it was only after his return that he learned about what in the meanwhile had taken place. In the intent of the Lawgiver, then, the incorporation of all this in the religion of Israel could not have been an afterthought.

Sometimes Ezek. 20.25 is quoted in proof of the penal character of the observance of these things. The prophet here distinguishes between ordinances the Israelites had rejected and 'statutes that were not good, and judgments wherein they should not live'. Jehovah gave them the latter in punishment for their not keeping the former. These punitive statutes and judgments are then identified with the ritual law. This is an impossible exegesis, especially if we remember that Ezekiel was the priest-prophet, for whom it must have been impossible to treat the very things among which his occupation lay, as things purely imposed for punishment. It is another question what precisely is meant by 'the statutes that were not good and the judgments whereby they should not live'. Perhaps these words refer to the idolatrous customs which in their later history, for instance in the time of Manasseh, the people adopted. Causing their children to pass through the fire is mentioned as one of them, vs. 26. It is said, however, that Jehovah 'gave' them these evil ordinances. This is not easy to explain. Perhaps it may be understood of the providential ordering of the history by God, which led to their apostasy to such heathen cults.

SYMBOL AND TYPE

In determining the function of the ceremonial law we must take into consideration its two large aspects, the symbolical and typical, and the relation between these two. The same things were, looked at from one point of view, symbols, and, from another point of view, types. A symbol is in its religious significance something that profoundly portrays a certain fact or principle or relationship of a spiritual nature in a visible form. The things it pictures are of present existence and present application. They are in force at the time in which the symbol operates.

With the same thing, regarded as a type, it is different. A typical thing is prospective; it relates to what will become real or applicable in the future. In the New Testament the word 'type' occurs only once [Rom. 5.14] where Adam is said to have been a type of Christ. This is the technical, theological meaning of the word, which, therefore, must have been in use before the time of Paul. The Jewish theologians doubtless had their system of typology. The word came to this technical meaning after a very natural fashion. Its primary, physical sense is that of a mark or impression made upon some soft substance by a thrust or blow (*tupto*, 'to strike'). This meaning occurs in John 20.25. Out of this developed the sense 'form', 'image', possibly from the fact that the impression struck on coins produced an image [*Acts* 7.43]. But the meaning 'image' easily passes over into that of 'model', 'example' [*Acts* 23.25; 2 *Thess.* 3.9]. To this third usage the technical use, observed in Rom. 5.14, attaches itself.

To 'type', the impression, corresponds 'antitype', the counter-impression. This also is used technically in the New Testament. Both Peter and the Epistle to the Hebrews employ it. It stands for the copy taken of the technical type. There is, however, a difference between these two writers. Peter finds the technical type in the history of the Old Testament. The water of baptism to him is the antitype of that of the deluge [1 *Pet.* 3.21]. The writer of Hebrews finds the type, the model, in the heavenly world. To him, therefore, the same Old Testament things that Peter would call types are already antitypes [*Heb.* 9.24]. The former is a more theological, the latter a more purely historical view of the relationship.

The main problem to understand is, how the same system of portrayals can have served at one and the same time in a symbolical and a typical capacity. Obviously this would have been impossible if the things portrayed had been in each case different or diverse, unrelated to each other. If something is an accurate picture of a certain reality, then it would seem disqualified by this very fact for pointing to another future reality of a quite different nature. The solution of the problem lies in this, that the things symbolized and the things typified are not different sets of things. They are in reality the same things, only different in this respect that they come first on a lower stage of development in redemption, and then again, in a later period, on a higher stage. Thus what is symbolical with regard to the already existing edition of the fact or truth becomes typical, prophetic, of the later, final edition of that same fact or truth. From this it will be perceived that a type can never be a type independently of its being first a symbol. The gateway to the house of typology is at the farther end of the house of symbolism.

This is the fundamental rule to be observed in ascertaining what elements in the Old Testament are typical, and wherein the things corresponding to them as antitypes consist. Only after having discovered what a thing symbolizes, can we legitimately proceed to put the question what it typifies, for the latter can never be aught else than the former lifted to a higher plane. The bond that holds type and antitype together must be a bond of vital continuity in the progress of redemption. Where this is ignored, and in the place of this bond are put accidental resemblances, void of inherent spiritual significance, all sorts of absurdities will result, such as must bring the whole subject of typology into disrepute. Examples of this are: the scarlet cord of Rahab prefigures the blood of Christ; the four lepers at Samaria, the four Evangelists.

These extravagances have produced in better-trained minds a distaste for typology. In order to weed out the worst, it was proposed to deal only with such types as were recognized to be types in the New Testament. These were called *typi innati*, 'inborn types'. The others whose typical significance had to be discovered by research were called *typi illati*. Then the Rationalists went one step further, claiming that all instances of typology in the New Testament are but so many examples of Rabbinical allegorizing exegesis. This would discredit our Lord and His Apostles as fanciful exegetes. But even the distinction between *typi innati* and *typi illati* cannot be upheld. The mere fact that no writer in the New Testament refers to a certain trait as typical, affords no proof of its lacking typical significance. Types in this respect stand on a line with prophecies. The New Testament in numerous cases calls our attention to the fulfilment of certain prophecies, sometimes of such a nature that perhaps we might not have discerned them to be prophecies. And yet we are not restrained by this from searching the field of prophecy and looking in the New Testament for other cases of fulfilment. The instances of typology vouched for by the New Testament writers have nothing peculiar to themselves. To recognize only them would lead to serious incompleteness and incoherency in the result. A system of types is something rational, the shaping of which we may expect from a God of wisdom, but the insertion here and there of a few isolated allusions would be out of harmony with the evidence of design in revelation.

We have, besides, the direct encouragement of the New Testament to heed the typical import of the Old Testament Scriptures. On the way to Emmaus, our Lord, beginning from Moses and from all the prophets, interpreted to the disciples in all the Scriptures the things concerning Himself. Since the law of Moses is included, some of these things must have been of a typical nature. He rebuked his companions, because they were slow of heart to understand and believe these prefigurations concerning His work and career. The author of

Hebrews intimates that about the tabernacle there was much more of typical significance than he was able to work out [9.5]. After the same manner he speaks of Melchizedek as a typical figure whom his readers had failed to appreciate [5.11ff.]. Of course, it is inevitable that into this kind of interpretation of Old Testament figures an element of uncertainty must enter. But after all this is an element that enters into all exegesis.

Besides ritual types there are in the Old Testament historical types. With some of these we have already become acquainted from the foregoing narrative. There had been also ritual types previously. But all this had been more or less sporadic. The new thing is that now, in the time of Moses, a system of types is established, so that the whole organism of the world of redemption, as it were, finds a typical embodiment on earth. The types are shadows of a body which is Christ. If the body called Christ was an organism, then also the shadows of it, that came before, must have borne the same character. In Gal. 4.3, Col. 2.20 Paul speaks of the ritual institution as 'first rudiments of the world'. He ascribes this rudiment-character to them because they were concerned with external, material things. In a certain sense (though not in point of formulation) Paul placed the ceremonies of the Old Testament on a line with similar customs of pagan religions. In paganism the religious rites possessed this character through their general dependence on the inclination towards symbolism. In the Mosaic institutions this natural symbolism also lay at the basis, but here there was a special divine control in the shaping of the materials. Because thus the truth found expression in physical forms, we say that it came on a lower plane. Under the New Testament this outward mode of expression has been retained in the two instances of Baptism and the Lord's Supper only, but the entire Old Testament still moves in this physical sphere. Hence, in Heb. 9.1, the tabernacle is called 'a worldly sanctuary', that is, a sanctuary belonging to this physical world. It was appropriate that after this fashion a sort of artificial substratum should be created for the truth of redemption to rest upon. The truth shuns suspension in the air. In the New Testament it has the accomplished facts to attach itself to. While these were yet in the making a provisional support was constructed for them in the ceremonial institutions.

From the foregoing it follows that the symbolic and the typical understanding of the ceremonies could not be expected to keep equal pace. Its symbolical function the law performed in virtue of its own inherent intelligible character. It was different with the types. Even though the defective provisional efficacy of the ceremonies might be to some extent perceived, it was far more difficult to tell what was intended to take their place in the future. Here the types needed the aid of prophecy for their interpretation [cp. *Isa.* 53]. We must not infer from our comparatively easy reading of the types that Israelites of old felt the same ease in interpreting them. It is unhistorical to carry back into the Old Testament mind our developed doctrinal consciousness of these matters. The failure to understand, however, does not detract from the objective significance these types had in the intent of God. But it is also possible to commit the opposite error, that of perpetuating the Old Testament typical form of religion through importing it into the New Testament. This the Romish Church does on a large scale. And in doing so, instead of lifting the substance of the types to a higher plane, it simply reproduces and repeats. This is destructive of the whole typical relation.

THE TABERNACLE

The tabernacle affords a clear instance of the coexistence of the symbolical and the typical in one of the principal institutions of the Old Testament religion. It embodies the eminently religious idea of the dwelling of God with His people. This it expresses symbolically so far as the Old Testament state of religion is concerned, and typically as regards the final embodiment of salvation in the Christian state. The tabernacle is, as it were, a concentrated theocracy. That its main purpose is to realize the indwelling of Jehovah is affirmed in so many words [*Ex.* 25.8; 29.44, 45]. It derives its most general name from this, namely, *mishkan*, 'dwelling-place'. The English versions render this too specifically, in dependence on the Septuagint and the Vulgate, by 'tabernacle'. But 'tabernacle' signifies 'tent'; every tent is a *mishkan*, but not every *mishkan* a tent. For 'tent' there is another Hebrew word, *'ohel*.

The dwelling of God in a house must not be, and was never, conceived, as Spencer would understand it, on the basis of the primitive idea that the Deity needs comfort and shelter. Even as regards the shrines of paganism this can hardly have been the original conception. A shrine is always and everywhere a place established or appointed for intercourse between a god and his worshippers. Had the Israelites associated with their *mishkan* so low an idea of the Deity, then they could hardly have failed to introduce into the *mishkan* some image of God, for a god thus physically conceived as needing shelter cannot have been conceived without a body. In the passages quoted it is most distinctly stated, that not a need which God has for Himself, but a need created by His relation to Israel is served by the establishment of the tabernacle. The tabernacle does not symbolize what Jehovah is in His general Being and operations. Hence also it does not circumscribe or limit Him in any way. The sense in which it is to be understood becomes clear by having regard to the metaphorical sense which the verb 'to dwell' frequently has. It means intimate association [*Gen.* 30.20; *Psa.* 5.4; *Prov.* 8.12]. The dwelling with His people is to satisfy God's desire to have a mutual identification of lot between Himself and them. Thus understood, the concept helps us to feel somewhat of the inner warmth and God-centred affection, and on the part of God, the man-seeking interest of Old Testament religion.

Because such identification of lot is the underlying idea, we can understand that the form chosen for the divine *mishkan* should be an *'ohel*, a tent. For, since the Israelites lived in tents, the idea of God's identifying His lot with theirs could not be more strikingly expressed than by His sharing this mode of habitation. Further, the materials out of which the tent was constructed had to come from a free-will offering of the people, so as to symbolize that they desired their God to dwell among them. More precisely the religious intercourse is defined in still another name of the tent: *'ohel mo'ed*, 'tent of meeting'. The meeting does not refer to the meeting of the people together, but to the meeting of Jehovah with the people. Here again, curiously, the Septuagint and the Vulgate, anticipating the next name, have rendered 'tent of the testimony', but in this case the English versions have not followed them. The word that is rendered 'meeting' does not designate an accidental encounter, but something previously arranged. It implies that Jehovah makes the provision and appoints the time for coming together with His people. The idea is of importance, because it is one of the indications of that conscious intercourse between God and man which characterizes the Biblical religion [*Ex.* 29.42, 43; *Amos* 3.3].

That the coming together is for the communication of thought, the third name, just mentioned, 'tent of the testimony', *'ohel ha'eduth*, shows. Testimony is a name for the law. The law was present, and through it a perpetual testimony of Jehovah, in the Decalogue, put within the ark of the testimony. It was likewise present in the book containing the law as a whole, which was put by the side of (not inside) the ark [*Deut.* 31.26]. But, while the 'testimony' is a synonym for the law it is also a synonym for the *berith*, and in harmony with this its purport will have to be determined. In part a testimony against Israel

[*Deut.* 31.26, 27], it must be on the whole a testimony in their favour; it emphasizes in this connection the gracious, redemptive nature of God's revelation to Israel, Psalm 78.5; 119 (*passim*).

THE MAJESTY AND HOLINESS OF GOD

While all this emphasizes the condescending, friendly nature of Jehovah's approach to and abode with the people, and brings, as it were, an echo of the Abrahamic mercies, yet there is another side to it, which was only partially brought out in the patriarchal period. The tabernacle still bears another name. It is 'a holy place', 'a sanctuary', *Mikdash*. It is somewhat difficult to understand the bearing and full reach of this term, because in New Testament usage the conception of 'holiness' has been more or less narrowed, and monopolized by the ethical sense. The older application, out of which the ethical one has sprung, denotes the majesty, the aloofness of God, not, however, as something arbitrarily assumed or maintained, but as something inherent in and inseparable from the divine nature. One might almost say, God's holiness is His specific divinity, that which separates Him from every creature, as distinct in place and honour.

The state of mind in the creature answering to this is the feeling of profound reverence and fear. The effect may best be seen from such a context as Isa. 6. It is more in evidence in Old Testament revelation and religion than in the New Testament, although in the latter also it is sufficiently present to show that the tendency of modern religion toward an exclusive stress upon the love of God is unwarranted [cp. 1 *John* 4.18]. The awe or fear inspired by the holiness of Jehovah is not first due to the sense of sin. It is something deeper, lying behind that, although the consciousness of sin is profoundly stirred and intensified by the feeling of this deeper fact. A comparison between the seraphim, who experience only the sense of the majesty of Jehovah, but have no sin, and the prophet, who has both, is very instructive [*Isa.* 6]. The sanctuary-character of the tabernacle is expressive of both elements in the idea. The people, though in favour with God, must yet remain at a distance, in fact are confined to the court, excluded from the tabernacle proper. Only the priests may enter, but this is due to the necessity of their ministering within, not to their being outside of the reach of the divine holiness in its exclusive effect. Even the expiation that continually takes place, and whereby the ethical disqualification is in a measure removed, cannot overrule this anterior principle that a proper distance must be maintained between God and man.

The coexistence of these two elements, that of trustful approach to God and that of reverence for the divine majesty, is characteristic of the Biblical religion throughout. Even the religious attitude exemplified by Jesus retains it, for if He teaches us to address God as Father, He immediately adds to this the qualification 'in heaven', lest the love and trust towards God should fall to the level of irreligious familiarity with God. Especially the presence of the *cherubhim* upon the ark in the most holy place gives a majestic expression to the majesty-side of the divine holiness. These *cherubhim* are throne-attendants of God, not 'angels' in the specific sense of the word, for the angels go on errands and carry messages, whereas the *cherubhim* cannot leave the immediate neighbourhood of the throne, where they have to give expression to the royal majesty of Jehovah, both by their presence and their unceasing praise [*Isa.* 6.3; *Rev.* 4.8, 9]. The second, more ethically coloured aspect of the holiness idea is exhibited likewise in the tabernacle. It is, as already stated, in part responsible for the exclusiveness observed. Positively it finds expression in the demands of purity made of the priests and in the ceaseless expiation of which the tabernacle is the scene.

THE PLACE OF WORSHIP

Still another application of the idea of the presence of Jehovah in the tabernacle appears in this, that it is the place where the people offer their worship to God. It is the palace of the King in which the people render Him homage. This feature belongs more particularly to the 'holy place', where it is symbolized in the three pieces of furniture there placed, the altar of incense, the table of the bread of the Face (i.e., the Deity in revelation) and the lampholder. The incense stands for prayer. The symbolism lies partly in that the smoke is, as it were, the refined quintessence of the offering, partly in the ascending motion of the same. That the altar of incense has its place nearest to the curtain before the 'holy of holies' signifies the religious specificness of prayer as coming nearest to the heart of God. The offering was of a perpetual character. The notion of the grateful smell of the burning incense in the nostrils of Jehovah is somewhat removed from our own taste of religious imagery, but should not on that account be overlooked, since it is not in the slightest degree felt to be inappropriate by the Hebrew sense of religion. The table of the bread of the Face [*Ex.* 25.30; *Lev.* 24.5–8] represents a meat- and drink-offering. As our study of the sacrificial law will show, this is the class of offering symbolizing the consecration of the activities of life to God. What the lampholder precisely represents is not so easy to determine. Its offering must be something on a line with the other two, that of prayer, and that of the good works of Israel, but the problem is to discover in what it differs from the last-named of these two. In connection with Zech. 4.2ff., Rev. 1.20, it may be found in this, that here the reflex effect of the good works of the congregation upon those without, and thus resulting indirectly in the ascription of praise to God, may be intended [*Matt.* 5.14]. Light has perhaps more symbolical association in Scripture than any other natural element. It figures significantly in all of the three spheres of religious manifestation. It appears as the light of knowledge, as the light of holiness, as the light of joy.

These various things were symbolized in the tabernacle with close dependence upon Jehovah's dwelling there. The symbolic character, however, must not be understood as purely symbolic, excluding the element of real efficacy. There was in all of them a sacramental use; they were real means of grace. For this reason the question becomes interesting, how the divine presence in the tabernacle is to be understood. Was this a symbolical thing, or at least a purely spiritual thing, or was it embodied in some realistic supernatural manifestation? This is the problem of the so-called *Shekinah*. From very ancient times a realistic view concerning this has prevailed both among Jewish and among Christian theologians. In 1683 Vitringa abandoned this venerable belief and substituted for it the belief in a purely spiritual, invisible presence. He did this on the basis of a modified exegesis of Lev. 16.2, which passage had served up to that time as the main support of the realistic interpretation. His opinion was that the 'cloud' spoken of in this verse was the cloud of incense, to be produced by the high priest, not a theophanic cloud of supernatural character. People at that time were sensitive on the point of supernaturalism, and this, on the surface innocent, exegetical innovation roused such a storm of protest that Vitringa retracted his proposal and returned to the old view. About the middle of the eighteenth century the controversy was renewed and this time the anti-realistic opinion prevailed. Since the first quarter of the nineteenth century the realistic view has found new defenders, but some of the objections previously raised against it weighed heavily enough in the somewhat rarified air of the 'supernaturalism' of those days to lead to a compromise. It was now thought that the divine glory was actually present by way of supernatural manifestation in the most holy place, but that it had not resided there continuously, being confined to the annual occasion of the high priest's entrance behind the curtain.

It is plain that opinions in this matter have been influenced more by theological predisposition than by exegetical evidence. Vitringa seems to have been almost the only one who approached the question with an unprejudiced exegetical mind. His exegesis of Lev. 16.2, is, however, untenable. It rests on the identification of the cloud in vs. 2 and in vs. 13. This equation is unfounded, for the mere occurrence of the identical phrase, 'lest he die', in both verses does not, in view of the totally different connection, suffice to prove it. The meaning of vs. 2 is: Aaron must not come at all times within the veil; if he should come at any other than the one appointed time, he exposes himself to the danger of death, for there is within a manifestation of the presence of Jehovah embodied in a cloud. The caution 'lest he die' is occasioned by the presence of the cloud. In vs. 13 Aaron is warned that, when entering, he must not enter without veiling himself with a cloud of incense, because disregard of that will expose him to danger of death. The caution 'lest he die' here is directed to the production of an artificial cloud of incense. Moreover it will be observed, that in vs. 2 'the cloud', and in vs. 13 'a cloud' is spoken of. 'The cloud' must mean the well-known cloud spoken of previously in the history. This can only be the cloud which had accompanied the people on their journeys, namely, the supernatural, theophanic cloud. The cloud of incense had never before been mentioned in the narrative; therefore in vs. 13 'a cloud' was in place. Wherever in the Old Testament the terms 'cloud' and 'appearing' occur together the reference is always to the theophanic cloud. The construction of vs. 2 must be strained to the utmost to make it speak of a cloud of incense and the necessity of producing it. On the occasion of the inauguration of the tabernacle and of the temple it is distinctly stated that the divine glory entered into the sanctuary [*Ex.* 40.34, 35; 1 *Ki.* 8.10–12]. True, on both occasions the glory must subsequently have withdrawn, for the priests, who could not serve on account of its presence at first, afterwards served again. But that the glory entirely withdrew, and no part of it remained, is not stated either. After all, the latter assumption is a most natural one. Ezekiel relates that at the time of the captivity he saw the glory of Jehovah departing from the temple [10.18; 11.23]. Haggai implies that in the post-exilic temple something was lacking in comparison with the temple of Solomon [2.7]. The Psalmists speak of the sanctuary in terms implying that it and the glory belong together [63.2]. And to corroborate all this we have the testimony of Paul, who mentions among the great privileges distinguishing Israel the *doxa*, 'glory' [*Rom.* 9.4; cp. also *Acts* 7.2; *Rev.* 15.8; 21.11, 23].

The tabernacle, then, represented not merely symbolically the indwelling of God among Israel, but actually contained it. But we must enquire more particularly, whether it was Jehovah's house exclusively, or the joint house of Him and the people. The correct answer to this is that the tabernacle is in its entirety Jehovah's house. There are not in it two apartments, one for God and one for the people, for the holy place, no less than the holy of holies, is the place which Jehovah owns alone. At the same time it must be maintained that the people are received into God's house as His guests. That this under the Old Testament was not carried out literally, but only symbolically, cannot alter the fact. For reasons of emphasizing the sinfulness of the people and the provisional nature of their sanctification, this could as yet be only symbolically expressed, but the thought was there as an ideal none the less. As an ideal privilege this belonged to every Israelite [*Psa.* 15; 24; 27]. If the tabernacle symbolized the heavenly habitation of God, and the ideal destiny of God's people has always been to be received of Him to the most consummate fellowship there, then there must have been at least an ideal reflex and foreshadowing of this in the tabernacle. In accordance with this principle the names given to God's celestial palace and to the earthly sanctuary are identical. *Ma'on, hekhal, zebhul* are used indiscriminately of both. The point raised is not without theological importance. It touches the question of the nature of religion, and the part played in it by God and man respectively. In the ideal covenant-fellowship, here portrayed, the divine factor is the all-controlling one. Man appears as admitted into, adjusted to, subordinated to, the life of God. Biblical piety is God-centred.

CHRIST IS THE ANTI-TYPICAL TABERNACLE

The typical significance of the tabernacle should be sought in close dependence upon its symbolic significance. We must ask: where do these religious principles and realities, which the tabernacle served to teach and communicate, reappear in the subsequent history of redemption, lifted to their consummate stage? First we discover them in the glorified Christ. Of this speaks the Evangelist [*John* 1.14]. The Word become flesh is the One in whom God came to tabernacle among men, in order to reveal to them His grace and glory. In John 2.19–22 Jesus Himself predicts that the Old Testament temple, which His enemies by their attitude towards Him are virtually destroying, He will build up again in three days, i.e., through the resurrection. This affirms the continuity between the Old Testament sanctuary and His glorified Person. In Him will be for ever perpetuated all that taber-nacle and temple stood for. The structure of stone may disappear; the essence proves itself eternal. In Col. 2.9, Paul teaches that in Him the fulness of the Godhead dwells bodily. With these passages should be compared the saying of Jesus to Nathanael [*John* 1.51] where He finds in Himself the fulfilment of what Jacob had called the house of God, the gate of heaven. In all these cases the indwelling of God in Christ serves the same ends which the Mosaic tabernacle provisionally served. He as the antitypical tabernacle is revelatory and sacramental in the highest degree.

THE TABERNACLE ALSO A TYPE OF THE CHURCH

But what is true of the Christ is likewise true of the Church. Of that also the tabernacle was a type. This could not be otherwise, because the Church is the body of the risen Christ. For this reason the Church is called 'the house of God' [*Eph.* 2.21, 22; 1 *Tim.* 3.15; *Heb.* 3.6; 10.21; 1 *Pet.* 2.5]. An individual turn is given to the thought where the Christian is called a temple of God [1 *Cor.* 6.19]. It ought to be noticed that 'house of God' is not in the New Testament a mere figure of the fellowship between God and the Church, but always refers specifically to the Old Testament dwelling of Jehovah. The highest realization of the tabernacle idea is ascribed to the eschatological stage of the history of redemption. This is depicted by the Apocalypse [21.3]. The peculiarity of the representation here is that, in dependence on Isa. 4.5, 6, the area of the tabernacle and temple are widened so as to become equally co-extensive with the entire New Jerusalem. The necessity of a tabernacle or a temple symbolic and typical, presupposes the im-perfection of the present state of the theocracy. When the theocracy will completely correspond to the divine ideal of it, then there will be no more need of symbol or type. Hence the statement 'I saw no temple therein', vs. 22. This does not, however, make it 'the city without a church'. Using Scriptural terminology, we should rather say that the place will be all church.

THE SACRIFICIAL SYSTEM OF THE LAW

The second main strand entering into the ceremonial law is that relating to sacrifice. The sacrificial ritual forms the centre of the rites of the tabernacle. The altar is in fact a house of God, a tabernacle in miniature. Hence it is described as the place where God records His 'Name', and meets with His people [*Ex.* 20.24]. The laws about the tabernacle in the closing chapters of the Book of Exodus are immediately followed by the sacrificial laws in the opening chapters of Leviticus.

Sacrifices as such did not, of course, begin with the Mosaic law. We read of Cain and Abel bringing their offerings, and of Noah offering sacrifices after the flood. Still it will be observed that these sacrifices belong to the state of sin. From this it may be inferred that the idea of sacrifice has an intimate connection with the fact of sin. In order to determine this connection accurately, we shall have to distinguish between the two main ends served by sacrifice, for the connection with sin is not entirely the same in each. These two main ends are expiation and consecration. It is plain that expiation cannot exist without there being sin to expiate. The expiatory element in sacrifice, therefore, takes its origin from sin. It is somewhat different with the element of consecration. Consecration is not first made necessary by sin. It is as old as religion itself, nay, constitutes the very essence of religion. But from this original existence of consecration in the exercise of sinless religion we may not infer that the specifically sacrificial form of consecration is as old as the practice of the idea itself.

The correct way of putting it is that the externalized form of consecration is a result of sin. In the sinless intercourse between God and man everything is direct and spiritual; no symbol intervenes between the worshipping creature and the Creator. This difference between the two aspects of sacrifice has its bearing upon the question of the purely human origination of sacrifice or its divine institution. For the expiatory use of sacrifice a positive divine institution was obviously required. Even if man could have conceived the idea of expiation of himself, there still would have been required explicit divine sanction to put it into practice. On the other hand, the idea of consecration was innate in man, and it is perhaps conceivable, that, after the fall, man of his own accord proceeded to give to this a new externalized embodiment, because he felt sin to have made such a separation between God and himself as to preclude the direct offering of himself to God.

It must be admitted, however, that the Pentateuch contains no record of the institution of sacrifice either as to its expiatory or as to its consecratory aspect. Some profess to find it in Gen. 3.21. The covering provided by God from the simple skins of animals would have carried the implication that animal life is necessary for covering sin. Agaicst this speaks the fact that the word used for this act of God is not the technical term used in the law for the covering of sin by sacrifice. It is a word signifying 'to clothe', a term never employed in the law for the expiation of sin.

While the law does not appoint a separate class of sacrifice for expiation alone, it does devote the vegetable, bloodless sacrifice to the purpose of consecration alone. In the animal, bloody sacrifice, the two ideas find joint expression, and the intimate union between the two is also brought out in the rule that no vegetable sacrifice shall be brought except on the basis of a preceding animal sacrifice. The unbloody sacrifice does not negate the idea of expiation; it presupposes it. Of course, the exclusive use of animal sacrifice for expiation is due to the presence of blood in it. Without blood there is no sacrificial expiation under the law.

OFFERINGS – GIFTS – SACRIFICES

The general category under which sacrifices are subsumed is that of *qorban*, 'offering' (literally, 'that which is brought near') or that of *mattenoth qodesh*, 'gifts of holiness'. This classification seems primarily to have been taken from the consecration element in them. That consecration is a gift seems natural, but that expiation should bear the same name is not so easy to understand, although there must be some meaning in this also, as we may discover later. This gift character is of the greatest importance for our understanding the nature of sacrifice. The point here to observe is that 'offerings' and 'holy gifts' are generic terms. They cover sacrifice, but they cover much more than sacrifice proper. All that is devoted in any way whatsoever to the service of Jehovah can be called by these names, but not everything of this nature can be called sacrifice. Every sacrifice is a holy gift, but not every holy gift is a sacrifice. It is unfortunate for our understanding of the matter that the law has no separate, single term for this specific subdivision of the holy gifts, so that in order to satisfy our desire for specification we must fall back on the Latin word 'sacrificium', which originally was also far more comprehensive than the use we now put to it. But, if we cannot name the 'sacrifice' in one Biblical word, we can at least by way of description single it out from the cognate, but by no means identical, things.

What distinguishes the sacrifice from all other things, however sacred these may be, is that part or the whole of its substance comes upon the altar. Without the altar there would be no sacrifice. This coming upon the altar is a most significant thing: it means the direct consumption of the sacrifice by Jehovah, for Jehovah dwells in the altar. In anthropomorphic language the law expresses the principle of assimilation of the sacrifice by Jehovah, when it speaks of it as 'food for Jehovah' or as yielding 'a firing for the savour of satisfaction for Jehovah'. Much later the prophets still had to protest against a naturalistic interpretation of this conception, as though Jehovah were by nature in need of food and the gratification of His sense of smell. The meaning of the law is that in virtue of His relation to Israel, as the God of Israel, He cannot exist without this, since for this very purpose He has chosen Israel and instituted the ritual service, that there might be a never-ceasing supply of praise and consecration for Him. The whole tenor of the law is to that effect. Its spirit, especially in the system of sacrifice, is that of a God-centred religion. Since, in the Old Testament, the man-ward activities of religion were relatively restricted, the impression made by this is all the stronger. It belongs, however, to the entire Biblical religion under all circumstances. In it all activity is service, not according to the modern depleted, humanitarian sense of the word, but in the sense of its being in the last analysis directed toward God, a sacrifice in the profound Old Testament understanding of this term.

It is, however, a one-sided exaggeration of this thought, when some have endeavoured to define sacrifice as worship. There is worship in sacrifice, but worship by no means constitutes the whole of sacrifice. Worship covers only the one half of the act, that which extends from man to God. The other half, extending from God to man, is not prayer, but a sacramental transaction, something God does, and in regard to which man is purely receptive, passive. Instead of prayer, it is rather the divine answer to prayer. In this respect again the modern connotation of the word has become deceptive. It savours too much of the pagan etymology, for in *sacrificium* the notion of *facere*[1] is too prominent, and that as a human, not a divine *facere*. Still the designation of sacrifice as worship may be turned to good use. It may help to explain how, even in the case of expiatory sacrifice, a giving on the part of man is involved. Man must put his aspiration and desire and trust into the proceeding; he gives in so far back to God what God has first given to him as a means of grace.

The regulation of the material for sacrifice will further make plain the sense in which it is regarded as a gift to Jehovah. The first requisite is, of course, that all things offered must be technically 'clean'. But not all that is clean is allowed for sacrifice. Within the animal kingdom the following species are allowed: oxen, sheep, goats, pigeons. From the vegetable kingdom: corn, wine and oil can be brought. The

[1] Doing.

principle expressed in this selection is two-fold. The sacrifice must be taken from what constitutes the sustenance of the life of the offerer, and from what forms the product of his life. To an agricultural people like the Israelites in Canaan (and to this the law looks forward) the things named naturally came under consideration from the two-fold point of view indicated. Reducing these two, however, to their unitary root, we have to say that they characterize sacrifice as the gift of life to God. Short of the impossibility under the Old Testament of human sacrifice, the principle in question could not have been better expressed than in the way it was. Both negatively and positively an important truth was thus enunciated. Negatively it was brought out that sacrifice is not transfer of value to Jehovah, not a present, in the pagan sense of the word. Jehovah protests against such a perverted notion with the reminder that all the contents of the world are antecedently His property. There is no possibility of enriching Him. And positively it emphasizes that God is not satisfied in the religious converse between Himself and man with anything short of the consecration of life itself.

THE RELATION BETWEEN THE OFFERER AND HIS SACRIFICE

The next point to discuss is the relation assumed by the law to exist between the offerer and his sacrifice. There are varying theories about this, not so much because the law itself is equivocal on this point, but because the argumentation from the ritual law in favour of or against certain theories of the atonement has influenced opinion on this question. This is made possible through the absence from the law of any outspoken philosophy of sacrifice. Here as in other points the law is left to speak for itself. Abuse is made of this, when interpreters, as it were, interrupt the law or even silence it, presuming to speak for it. No preconceived theory of atonement should be allowed to colour our understanding of the law, but the reverse should happen. There is only one qualification of this: the New Testament in certain points speaks so plainly in regard to the fulfilment of certain traits of the ritual in the atonement, as to render it impossible for us to disregard this. For the rest, however, we must gather our philosophy of sacrifice from careful observation of the manner in which the ritual proceeds. This we shall do presently. By way of preface it may be explained here, that there are three general opinions in regard to the inner meaning of the ritual and the relation it establishes between offering and offerer.

The first may be designated the purely symbolical theory. According to it the sacrificial process exhibits in a picture certain things that must be done to the offerer, and that can and will be done to him with the proper effect. The picture, as a mere picture, must needs remain within the sphere of subjectivity; it exhibits in no way what must take place outside of man for him, but only what takes place within him; we, therefore, call this the purely symbolical theory. Speaking in dogmatic language we might say, that on this view of the matter sacrifice is a pictorial representation of such things as sanctification and return to the favour of God. The utmost that this theory could possibly concede would be, that the ritual perhaps depicts some objective obligation, that might have been imposed upon man, of which by way of a lesson he is reminded in the sacrifice, but which is not further carried out or exacted from man, not even symbolically, in the further process. This interpretation of the sacrificial procedure lies on the line of the moral and governmental theories of the atonement.

The second theory may be designated as the symbolico-vicarious theory of sacrifice. It has in common with the other the assumption of subjectively-turned symbolism at the opening. According to it the ritual begins with portraying the subjective state of man, chiefly as to his obligation. But right there it parts way with the purely symbolical view. If the latter assumes that the further steps continue to portray what will be done within man to modify this, the symbolico-vicarious theory presupposes the recognition by ritual itself that nothing can be done in man himself with the proper effect, and that, therefore, a substitute must take his place. All the successive acts of the ritual apply to this substitute, not to the offerer. Consequently the entire transaction assumes an objective character. It becomes something done, to be sure, for the benefit of the offerer, but done outside of him. It will thus be seen, that the objectivity and the vicariousness of the process go together. On the same principle adoption of the purely symbolical theory carries with itself exclusion of the vicarious element and of the objectivity.

To be distinguished from these two theories is a third attitude towards the law of sacrifice. This, however, can by no means be co-ordinated with the two preceding views, for it denies that in the law, or the Old Testament in general, any coherent, consistent theory of sacrifice is to be found. This is the opinion, on the whole, of the Wellhausen school of critics. The sacrificial laws are said to be the precipitate of a long development. They contain, loosely conglomerated, customs dating from widely distant times, and based on discordant principles. It belongs, therefore, to the very essence of this hypothesis to deny that the law itself has any intelligent view of the meaning of sacrifice. All that these writers presume to offer is a history, not a theory of sacrifice. During the most ancient, nomadic period, sacrifices were nothing else but means for establishing or strengthening the blood-communion supposed to exist between the deity and its worshippers. This was effected by making both partake of a common blood, the blood of the sacrificial animal. The act did not mean expiation; it meant a sacrament. In a later stage of religious development a considerable change took place in the conception of sacrifice. This change was connected with the settlement of the Hebrew tribes in Canaan. Previously their religion had been a nomadic religion, now it became an agricultural one. The sacrifices were presents bestowed upon Jehovah, the richness and frequency of which assumed great importance. The cult became complicated and luxuriant. Underlying it was the naïve popular belief that God could be influenced by the presentation of such gifts, irrespective of the spirit in which they were brought.

This view of sacrifice was essentially of Canaanitish origin. The prophets protested against this popular delusion, and from the ethical conception of the nature of Jehovah attained by them, drew the inference that sacrifices were not only an unnecessary but even a dangerous form of religious service, something disapproved of by Jehovah. At first this remained a purely theoretical preaching, which never gained any acceptance with the people. The prophets soon saw that in order to make any headway against the popular cult they would have to stoop to some form of compromise. This consisted in pruning, purifying, and elevating as much as possible the practised religion. The results of this compromise are embodied in the various law-codes now found in the several Pentateuchal documents. Especially in the later codes the grosser conceptions of the earlier period were made to the largest possible extent vehicles of ethical, spiritual truth.

THE STAGES OF THE SACRIFICIAL RITUAL

Now, coming to the various acts or stages making up the ritual process, we first consider the selection of the particular animal from within the limits of allowance above specified. The animal must be a perfect specimen of its kind. Both as to age and as to condition it must be free of anything that would detract from its value. This is conceivable from the naïve popular conception of sacrifice as a gift to Jehovah, for to one's God one gives of the best only. But it is not easily explainable from the standpoint of the purely symbolical theory. According to this the sacrifice must be viewed as a picture, a replica of the offerer.

Now the offerer is at the same time supposed to come with an offering, because he feels himself abnormal and imperfect. How then can the perfectly normal and flawless animal figure as his double? At this point, certainly, the symbolico-vicarious view has the advantage; it substitutes for the imperfect offerer the perfect animal-substitute, in order that through its perfection something may be accomplished that would be otherwise impossible. To be sure, the animal exhibits ethical perfection after a very negative fashion only; in that it is not subject to moral distinctions it is incapable also of symbolizing moral defects. It is innocent simply because it cannot be good or bad. But this is inseparable from a process in which an animal takes the place of a man. And in part it is symbolically obviated by the positive stress laid upon the physical normality and perfection of the animal. Isaiah in chapter 53 speaks of the sacrificial lamb, as though it had semi-ethical qualities, but even these are negative, innocence and meekness, and besides, the description is modelled after the character of the Servant of Jehovah. Still this suggests how the negative could serve as a symbol of the sinlessness of the antitype. And Peter declares that believers are redeemed with the precious blood of Christ, as of a lamb without blemish and without spot. And this blameless and spotless character the Apostle does not represent as merely in general enhancing the value of the offering, but as enhancing its efficacy for redemption [1 Pet. 1.19].

The next step in the ritual, after the animal had been brought to the sanctuary, was the so-called laying on of hands by the offerer. The Hebrew phrase is stronger than the English rendering suggests; it literally means 'the leaning on' of the hand or the hands [Lev. 16.21]. This ceremony took place in every ordinary animal sacrifice, and in animal sacrifice only. This points to a close connection between what was peculiar to animal sacrifice and the act in question. Peculiar to animal sacrifice is the use of the blood for expiation. With this, therefore, the laying on of hands must have something to do. The significance of the act is indicated by the analogy of the other occasions on which it was performed [Gen. 48.13, 14; Lev. 24.14; Num. 8.10; 27.18; Deut. 34.9]. From these instances it appears that laying on of hands always symbolized a transfer from one person to another. What the thing transferred was depended on the occasion, but the one to whom something was transferred appears everywhere as a second person, distinct from the one whose hands are laid on. This decidedly favours the vicarious interpretation of sacrifice. It means that the animal cannot have been considered the mere double of the offerer; it must have been a second person different from the offerer.

In answering what was transferred to the animal-substitute we cannot, of course, be guided by the above analogies. There is independent evidence to show that the transferred thing was nothing else but the sin, i.e., the liability to death-punishment on the part of the offerer. In the ritual of the Day of Atonement, which we may consider the culminating occasion of the whole ritual system, Aaron is told to lay his hands on the head of the second goat, and confess over him all the iniquities of the people. This second goat was not a sacrifice to be slain after the ordinary manner; it was sent away into the wilderness for the purpose of symbolically removing the sin. Yet it formed with the other goat in reality one sacrificial object; the distribution of suffering death and of dismissal into a remote place simply serving the purpose of clearer expression, in visible form, of the removal of sin after expiation had been made, something which the ordinary sacrificial animal could not well express, since it died in the process of expiation. We are certainly warranted, when here the hands convey sin, and where the same ceremony occurs in ordinary sacrifice, in drawing the conclusion that on every such occasion sins are transferred.

The interpretation followed is of such great importance, because it virtually determines the construction to be placed upon the next following step in the ritual, the slaying of the animal by the hands of the offerer. The act has thus given the altar its name *mizbeach*, 'place of slaughter'. The importance is attested also by the careful injunction that the slaying must take place at the altar and particularly at the north side. The symbolical meaning of this may not be clear, but, unless weight was attributed to the act, the place would have been treated as indifferent. Both these features tell strongly against a theory defended by even such safe interpreters as Keil and Delitzsch, to the effect that the slaying of the animal forms no significant part of the ritual, but is simply the inevitable means for obtaining the blood and the fat, the use of which *is* truly significant, ritually considered.

In connection with the laying on of hands transmitting sin the slaying of the sin-bearing animal could scarcely have any other purpose than to signify that death is the penalty of sin, vicariously inflicted in sacrifice. And that this point of view is not foreign to the law appears from such cases as that related in Deut. 21.9 (where there is expiation and yet no shedding of blood, but death by the neck being broken), and the offer of himself by Moses to die in the place of Israel [*Ex.* 32.30–34].

The error of Keil and Delitzsch is due to the fact that the law does not name the slaying, but everywhere the blood, as the means of expiation. This is a correct observation, but the inference drawn from it is wrong. The blood is the most eloquent symbol of death, so that the antithesis, not death but blood, is fundamentally wrong. To be sure, blood can likewise be the symbol of life. But it does not so appear in the ritual. Nor is it fit to appear in such a capacity, because it figures as blood flowed out, and this stands everywhere for the life departing, i.e., for death. Blood in its normal state, blood in the integral animal does not expiate. It expiates as blood that has passed through the crisis of death, and is therefore fit to be the exponent of death. The rule, there is no expiation without blood, cannot be reversed, so as to make it say, there is no blood without expiation. If it still be urged that blood conceived as the exponent of expiating death ought to have had its effect when flowing out of the animal slain, at the moment of its direct conjunction with death, the answer lies in a correct appreciation of what the Old Testament term designating 'to expiate' stands for.

We are inclined to draw distinctions here which are necessary for dogmatic precision. Thus we distinguish between the atonement itself and the application of the atonement. The symbolism of the ritual takes these two in one. When it says that 'blood covers' (that is the technical term of the law for expiation), it means to describe in one word the atonement as we call it, plus the application of the atonement (which we call justification). Now in this inclusive sense the process of covering is not completed until the blood, as the symbol of death, has been applied to the altar, i.e., brought into contact with God, who dwells in the altar. This is the simple reason why the law refrains from saying that the slaying atones, and why it is so careful to emphasize that the application of the blood to the altar has this effect. But this cannot be held to prove that the slaying has nothing to do with the effect. Besides, there is also an external reason why the law dwells more upon the manipulation of the blood than upon the slaying of the animal. The latter was simple and the same in all cases, whereas the former was complex, varying in the various classes and for the various occasions of sacrifice. It needed discriminating attention.

So far from negating the expiatory power of death in a vicarious sense, the constant references to the blood rather illuminatingly confirm this. To the conception of the ritual 'blood' and 'life' are identical. And 'life' and 'soul' are likewise identical. We need, therefore, only to inquire into the Old Testament signification of 'soul' to reach the inwardness of the matter on this point. Besides several others, the classic passage on the subject is Lev. 17.11. Here we read: 'For the life of the flesh' (i.e. living flesh) 'is in the blood; and I have given it to you upon the altar to make covering for your souls; for it is the blood that makes covering by reason of the life'.

What, then, is the Old Testament conception of 'soul'? In that the reason is placed for the blood's efficacy to cover for souls. The two associations of the term 'soul' are in the first place that of individuation, secondly, that of sensibility. Both are, of course, physiologically, and hence symbolically, intimately connected with the blood in the body. 'Soul' is that which results when the general spirit of life joins breath to a body. This is not meant for an affirmation of trichotomy; it is a practical distinction between spirit and soul, not as two entities, substantially considered, but as two aspects of the same thing. And in the same practical way soul and sensation, feeling, are associated.

The question, therefore, is simply reduced to this: what makes the principle of individuation and of sensibility the proper instrument for expiation? It will be seen at a glance that the answer to this is found in the vicarious theory, and in it alone. That which is a substitute for another person must be an individual, and that which undergoes punishment for another must be capable of feeling, of suffering. Taking it together, then, we may say, that the blood has its rich symbolism in sacrifice, first, because it stands for death, secondly because it stands for the death of an individual, substitutionary person, and thirdly because it stands for a death involving suffering. All this is given in the slaying, but slaying or dying are abstract conceptions, that cannot be made subject to sight symbolically, whereas 'blood' and 'soul' and 'life' are concrete things.

VICARIOUSNESS DEFINED

The passage Lev 17.11 also contains the most explicit statement of the principle of vicariousness to be found in the law anywhere. It virtually amounts to saying: soul works covering for soul. The inherent vicariousness of the statement is recognized by all exegetes, even by such as have no theological use for its teaching. Still a certain latitude of interpretation, within the limits of vicariousness, seems possible.

There are, in the abstract, three possibilities. One can say the passage teaches that for the integral life of the offerer, due to God, another integral life, that of the animal is substituted. This it will be observed, while retaining the principle of vicariousness, rules out entirely the idea of vicarious death, vicarious suffering. Antitypically speaking it would amount to saying that for the positive gift of our life in consecration to God, which we had failed to bring, Christ has, by way of substitution, given God His life of service, to reimburse God for ours, but that the suffering of the Saviour played no part in the matter, inasmuch as God was simply concerned with receiving consecration, and had no interest in the payment through suffering for offences committed. In other words, the justice of God is entirely ruled out. Christ was our substitute in His active obedience only.

Again one may say: God does indeed reckon with sins but not in the sense of punishment being required for them; the only way in which He reckons with them is by desiring a positive gift that will compensate for the injury offered Him. This would amount to saying that Christ's active obedience had served for making God forego the punishment of our sins, in view of the rich obedience rendered by Christ. It is again the active obedience that plays the exclusive part, but on this view it plays it at least with a side-reference to the sin that was committed, and had to be made good somehow.

Or, finally, one may say: the sacrificial animal in its death takes the place of the death due the offerer. It is forfeit for forfeit. Christ not merely in His positive service, but through His suffering and death made up for the abnormality of our sin. He satisfied the justice of God. We maintain that the first and second interpretations, while not perhaps absolutely ruled out by Lev. 17.11 alone, do not place the most natural construction upon the words, and, taken together with the general trend of Biblical teaching on the atonement are not plausible.

THE MEANING OF 'COVERING'

Our next enquiry addresses itself to the precise symbolical conception the law frames for what we call expiation, that of 'covering'. The Hebrew word is kapper, piel infinitive of kaphar. Covering can be of two kinds, obliterative and protective. It is thought by some that the latter is the idea originally underlying the use of the word for expiation. The symbolism would convey that the offerer through the interposition of the blood between God and himself obtained safety from the reaction of the divine anger against sin. The obliterative interpretation is that the stain of sin and its impurity are put out of the sight of God through the blood smeared over them. It is not a matter of grave doctrinal importance, but one of historical interest largely, which of the two figures lies at the basis of the Biblical usage. It is not even certain that in Biblical times the etymological associations were still distinctly remembered. The word may have become a purely technical ritual term.

Most seem to speak in favour of the original understanding of the process as one of obliteration. In secular use the term seems to have this for a background. Jacob 'covers' the face of Esau through sending a present before himself. In this way the anger on Esau's face is 'covered', put out of sight [*Gen.* 32.20]. There is further a religious usage outside of the sphere of sacrifice, and in this also the idea of obliteration shines clearly through [cp. *Psa.* 32.1; 65.3; 78.38; *Isa.* 22.14; *Jer.* 18.23]. In these cases the object is almost uniformly the sin, not the sinner, and to the former the idea of protection afforded by God could not properly apply. Then there are the various synonymous phrases in which the Old Testament describes the removal of sin on the part of God. These are most of them of an obliterative sort [*Neh.* 4.5; *Isa.* 6.7; 27.9; 38.17; 44.22; *Jer.* 18.23; *Mic.* 7.19].

We may infer from all this that in the province of sacrifice likewise the idea of removal of sin through obliteration was the originally prevailing one. A striking difference should be noted, however, between the secular and the religious use of the conception. Outside of religion it is the offender who does the covering, and the person offended is covered. Jacob covers the face of Esau. In the sphere of religion, ritual or otherwise, God, the offended Person, procures the covering, and it is applied to the sinner. Man cannot cover the face of God. The idea, as though man could do anything whatsoever in order to effect a change in the disposition or attitude of God towards sin or the sinner, is utterly repugnant to the spirit of Biblical religion. Between man and man that may be possible, but not between God and man. If the normal relation is to be restored, it is the prerogative of God to resolve this and to put His resolve into operation.

In paganism all this is different. Here the figure employed is that of 'smoothing' the gods, that is of removing the wrinkles out of their frowning face. Thus the Greek says *hilaskesthai tous theous*, the Latin says *placare deos*. This figure underlies the technical pagan term of 'expiating'. If the translation of the Scriptures into Greek, or Latin, or the modern languages, could have avoided such terms, there would have been less danger of perverting the Biblical idea through giving it a pagan equivalent grown on a totally different root. But the translators, perhaps, had no choice. Their use of 'covering' would probably have made the language unintelligible to the Greek or Roman reader. This state of affairs imposes the duty upon us of not relying on the Greek or Latin or English sound of a term used in such connections, but carefully to consult the Hebrew, and make our construction of the process on the basis of that alone. To neglect doing this exposes in the present case to a very dangerous misconception.

When the Bible says that God 'expiates' man, not man God, the inference is easily drawn that the whole abnormality consists in the ill-disposition of man, and that all that is required consists in God's smoothing this out. The whole process of atonement would become in this way subjectivized. The resulting concept is a hybrid: it has the Biblical construction, and the pagan mould of thought. To escape from the misunderstanding all that is required is to go back from the term 'expiating' to the term 'covering'. Man needs 'covering', God needs no 'covering'. God is the subject, man is the object of the act. The reason why man needs covering is something that lies in him, but it is not something that lies in man considered in itself. It creates the need of covering, because of something that is in God. The sin in man, as calling forth a reaction from the offended holiness of God, is what renders the covering necessary. It is a real help here to keep in mind the full formula in which the law itself describes the process: 'the priest shall cover upon him on account of his sin' [Lev. 4.35].

While the protective view of the transaction fits equally well into the true doctrine of the atonement as the other, Ritschl has worked it out in a manner which leads far away from the Biblical premises of sacrifice. He assumes that the protection which man needs and the law provides does not arise from man's sinfulness, but from his finiteness as a creature, which endangers his life when entering into the presence of the majesty of God. But, when man appears with the prescribed gifts, and the priests perform for him the appointed rites, he receives adequate protection from this danger, and is enabled to exercise fellowship with God. And from this fellowship with God he receives, besides other things, also the favour of the forgiveness of sin. It will be noticed, that this reverses the usual order of things. We are accustomed to say, and understand the Bible as saying, that forgiveness is the source from which fellowship flows. Ritschl would turn this around, making fellowship the source from which forgiveness proceeds. The whole tenor of the law is against this. As we have seen, the covering is kept by the law in the closest connection with the fact of sin. To deny this is to void the sacrificial system of all ethical content.

The next step in the ritual after the covering is the burning of certain parts of the animal upon the altar. What was the symbolical meaning of this act? Some would find in it a further carrying out of the idea expressed in the slaying of the animal. The consumption of it by fire would then symbolize that more intensified experience of death which awaits the sinner in the hereafter. Against this there are fatal objections. After expiation had once taken place, and the offerer's soul had been effectually covered, the end of the penal transaction had been reached. Had the meaning of the burning been what is assumed on this view, then the act of expiation ought to have followed, not preceded the burning. The covering ought to have been made by means of the blood and ashes combined. In the vegetable offering the burning was exactly the same as in the animal offering, and yet no expiation entered into the former.

The verb descriptive of the burning is everywhere *hiqtir*. This verb does not describe burning of the consuming kind, but of the sublimating kind, a process whereby something is changed into a finer substance. The verb for destructive burning is *saraf*, and this is actually used for the burning of parts of the animal outside the camp, but never of the burning upon the altar. Moreover, the law speaks of the altar-burning as yielding a sweet odour of delight to Jehovah. While Scripture teaches that the punishment of sin is required by the justice of God, it never speaks of this as giving delight to God. On the contrary, that which is represented as yielding delight to Jehovah is the surrender of man's life in consecration of obedience. In this sense, therefore, we must understand the burning upon the altar.

The question, however, may be raised, whether this consecration is the vicarious one offered God by the substitute of the offerer, or the consecration of the offerer himself. If the latter were true, we should have to say that at this point the symbolico-vicarious significance of the ritual came to an end, and the purely symbolical one took its place. But this would inevitably have introduced a certain ambiguity and confusion into the ritual. And there is no reason whatever for finding a conflict between vicariousness and consecration. Although expiation cannot be made by man himself, and consecration by the grace of God can be subjectively inwrought into the life of man, yet we also know of an active consecratory obedience offered to God on behalf of sinners by Christ. Our Lord employs ritual language, when affirming that He sanctifies Himself for them (i.e., for the suffering of His death) [*John* 17.19]. And Paul does the same, when, speaking of Christ's active obedience, he says: 'Christ also loved us, and gave Himself up for us, an offering and a sacrifice to God for an odour of a sweet smell' [*Eph.* 5.2].

The final stage in the ritual of sacrifice consisted in the sacrificial meal. This was peculiar to the peace-offerings. In speaking of the

Passover we have already noticed the main characteristics of this class of sacrifice. The Hebrew name for it is *shelamim*. The adjective corresponding to this is *shalem* meaning 'integral', 'uninjured', 'living in peace and friendship with somebody'. It is natural to think, in connection with this, first of all of the state of forgiveness following the expiation. But, while this is not excluded, since in the sacrifice preceding the meal there is real expiation, yet we must take care not to stress this side of the matter one-sidedly.

'Peace' is in Scripture a far more positive conception than it is with us. The peace-offering accordingly symbolizes the state of positive favour and blessedness enjoyed in the religion of Jehovah, which at all times includes more than the sacrificial relief obtained from sin. In the Orient a meal can signify both the cessation of hostility and the communion of friendship. The rendering 'peace-offerings' in the English Bible, on the basis of Septuagint and Vulgate, is most felicitous; that of other versions, German and Dutch, is less faithful. These render 'thank-offerings', but the thank-offerings are only one species of the genus peace-offerings. The state of peace in its two-sided significance is symbolized as a gift of Jehovah, for it is He, not the offerer, who prepares the meal. Hence the meal is to be held at the tabernacle, the house of God. We may compare the meal partaken of by 'the nobles of Israel' on the mount [Ex. 24.11] where also Jehovah is obviously the host. Paul in 1 Cor. 10, by implication calls the meal the table of Jehovah, for he compares the Lord's supper, where Christ is the host, and the pagan sacrificial meals, where the 'demons' give the feast at their table, with the practice of the ancient Israelites, who have 'communion with the altar'.

THE VARIETY OF OFFERINGS

The classification of animal sacrifices represents an ascending scale, beginning, as it were, with the worst point, religiously considered, in the state of the offerer, and ending with the acme of his religious blessedness. The distinction between the classes is not a distinction of exclusive expression of single points, but one of emphasis on particular points, which in the succeeding classes are not dismissed from view, but recapitulated, so that the final class contains the whole in proper arrangement of the several elements. In the sin-offering the idea of expiation stands in the foreground, but, after this has first been stressed, the consecration-idea receives attention likewise, through the burning upon the altar. The intent upon working expiation before all else is seen in the elaborate manipulation of the blood, not present to that extent in the following classes. The animal in the sin-offering was invariably one, but the species and sex differed according to the persons involved and their rank in the congregation, not, however, as though the guilt of the sin were proportionate to the station of the sinner, but because the more highly-placed member of the theocracy involves more individuals in his sinning [*Lev.* 4.3].

The distinction between the sin-offering and the trespass-offering is difficult to define. Two features stand out in the latter: on the one hand, it is the only sacrifice of which an appraisal is made; on the other hand, it is the only one to which a sum of money must be added. The value-feature, therefore, is in evidence. This suggests the theory, that it forms the complement of the sin-offering in giving to God the positive thing withheld from Him through sin. Every sin offers to God what ought not to be offered, an offence, and at the same time it withholds from God what ought to have been given to Him, obedience. If the sin-offering rectifies the former, the trespass-offering would then make restitution for the latter. In its ritual procedure it closely resembles the sin-offering, as we might expect on this view. The trespass-offering derives a unique interest from the fact that it is the only class of sacrifice with which the sacrificial death of Christ is directly connected in the Old Testament. In Isa. 53.10, the self-surrender of the Servant of Jehovah is designated an '*asham*, a trespass-offering, and this is quite in harmony with the idea, prevailing in the context, that the Servant not merely atones for the sins of the people, but gives to God what by their disobedience they have withheld.

Finally it will be noticed, that not every sin-offering had a trespass-offering joined to it, as the above theory might seem to imply. The trespass-offering was only required where an actual property-value had not been paid. The material substance in a limited sphere was thus made to symbolize the spiritual in the general sphere of sin.

In connection with the burnt-offering we notice the strong emphasis placed upon consecration, which found expression in the burning of the entire sacrifice upon the altar. With this agrees, that it is the one sacrifice perpetually kept burning. In fact from the latter feature one of its names, the *tamid*, is derived.

Of the peace-offering all that is essential has been said in discussing the Passover and the sacrificial meal. Three distinct classes of peace-offerings are named: the praise- or thank-offering, the votive-offering, and the freewill-offering. The principle of division is not a strictly logical one, inasmuch as the first class is denominated from the purpose served, the second and the third are named from the subjective attitude of the offerer, which was either obligatory, as in the case of the votive-offering, or spontaneous, as in the case of the freewill-offering. An interesting fact to notice is that the Mosaic law makes no provision for prayer-offerings. Perhaps this was due to a fear of fostering the superstition that the offering could through its natural inherent power compel the bestowal of the blessing desired. As to the votive-offering the sacrifice seems not to have accompanied the making of the vow, but to have been the object promised in the vow, so that it becomes a special kind of thank-offering.

The vegetable offering was considered, like the animal sacrifice, as symbolically food for Jehovah. Hence it is not offered in an unprepared condition, but in the shape of roasted ears, or as fine wheaten flour, or as loaves or cakes prepared in the oven or in the pan. Every meal-offering must be attended with oil. A wine-offering forms its complement. Taking these ingredients together, some have thought to discover in the vegetable offering an exact copy of the animal sacrifice, the meal standing for the meat, the oil for the fat, the wine for the blood. On a line with this the Romish theologians found in the meal-offering a special type of the Lord's Supper. Both opinions are untenable. In the case of the substitution of a vegetable sin-offering, on account of extreme poverty, the law enjoins that no oil shall be put upon the flour. Had the fat been represented by the oil, then the latter could not have been lacking in the substitute-sin-offering. There is, of course, a typical connection of these sacrifices with the Lord's supper, but this it has in common with all other parts of the system. It is true, the elements are vegetable in both, but they are so for a different reason in each case. In the Lord's supper they are so, because of the substitution of the unbloody for the bloody sacrament under the new dispensation. In the Old Testament vegetable offering the vegetable material was selected, in order to give expression to the idea of consecration in works. In the animal sacrifice too, as we have seen, there is consecration, but there, in harmony with the animal gift, it is a consecration of the entire life as a unit. Here, in the vegetable offering, it is a consecration of fruit, that is, of the diversified product of life. That part of the vegetable offering which is burnt upon the altar bears the name of *azkarah*, 'that which calls to remembrance'. Though sometimes in the law the term may be used in an unfavourable sense [*Num.* 5. 26], in the vegetable offering it has favourable meaning. In the Greek it is rendered by *mnemosynon*. This relates to alms and prayers especially. Thus the angel says to Cornelius that his prayers and alms have gone up for a 'memorial' before God [*Acts* 10.4].

UNCLEANNESS AND PURIFICATION

The third main strand distinguishable in the ceremonial law is that relating to uncleanness and purification. Together with the indwelling of Jehovah in the theocracy, and the process of sacrifice, it forms a fundamental conception, which as such has entered into the permanent fabric of Biblical religion. At the outset we must guard against identifying the unclean and the forbidden. There are processes and acts absolutely unavoidable, which nevertheless render unclean. The law rather seems to have multiplied the occasions for contracting uncleanness, that thus it might increase the material on which to operate the distinction and teach its lesson. Further, we must avoid identifying cleanness with cleanliness, uncleanness with dirtiness. Sanitary significance the distinction does not have. It offers no excuse for identifying Christianity with hygiene. Positively, we may say that the conception has reference to the cult, that is, to the ritual approach to Jehovah in the sanctuary. We must not view it from the standpoint of inherent content or quality. 'Clean' means qualified for the worship of Jehovah in the tabernacle, 'unclean' the opposite. The effect which these predicates produce is the thing stressed. If we say that the contrast is symbolical of ethical purity and impurity, it still will hold true that this symbolized contrast is not simply equivalent to goodness and badness as such, but to goodness and badness from the particular point of view that the one admits into, the other excludes from fellowship with God. This is one of the ideas in which the intimate connection between religion and ethics finds expression. From the Biblical standpoint ethical normalcy or abnormality should, before aught else, be appraised with the question in mind: What effect does the state, designated in ethical terms, have on one's intercourse with God?

There is a distinction between the antithesis 'clean' versus 'unclean' and that of 'holy' versus 'unholy'. And yet there is a close connection between the two pairs of opposites. Cleanness is the prerequisite of holiness. Nothing unclean can be holy, while it remains in that state. But, suppose it to be made clean, this would by no means *ipso facto* render it holy. Nor are things clean by nature necessarily holy. There exists a large territory between the unclean and the holy, full of things clean but not on that account holy. But from this territory things are taken and constituted holy by a positive act of God. The Hebrew vocabulary bears out the relation thus defined. It offers distinct terms for the two contrasts involved. The terms for 'holy' and 'unholy' are *qadosh* and *chol*, those for 'clean' and 'unclean' are *tahor* and *tame*.

Being thus related to the service of Jehovah, the distinction between

173

cleanness and its opposite obtains for the life of every Israelite comprehensive significance, for in reality the Israelite exists for nothing else but the continual service of God. It creates a bisection of the entire congregation to apply to it this ritual test. The people at each moment divide themselves into two halves, one composed of the clean, the other of the unclean. This finds striking expression in one of the formulas for designating the people comprehensively. The phrase '*atsur we'azubh* means 'every Israelite'. It is rendered in the A.V. somewhat mysteriously by 'shut up or left', in the R.V. by 'shut up or left at large'. Its simple meaning is 'shut out from access to the sanctuary and left free to go' [*Deut.* 32.36; *Jer.* 36.5].

The objects and processes causing uncleanness are regulated by the law chiefly in Lev. 11 and Deut. 14. They belong to the following classes: certain sexual processes, death, leprosy, the eating of certain species of animals, or the touching of otherwise clean animals when these have not been slaughtered but have died of themselves. The distinction, as applied to these several classes of things, is evidently much older than the Mosaic law. The law does not profess to introduce the matter *de novo;* it simply regulated usages and observances of long standing. Many of these observances must have changed their character in the course of the ages, and the meaning attached to them, if such there were, must have changed likewise. Perhaps there is no sphere of conduct tending more strongly towards the petrification of once significant acts than this world of the clean and unclean.

From the original or subsequently acquired meanings we must, therefore, distinguish the lawgiver's motives in incorporating these practices into the legislation. First we devote some attention to the possible previous meanings attributed to them, either forgotten, or still remembered at the times of Moses. The subject occupies a very large place in recent study of primitive religion. Not a few writers bring it into connection with what they consider the origin of religion itself. Our remarks confine themselves to the field of Shemitic religion, and that with special reference to the Old Testament laws of uncleanness and purification.

TOTEMISM

A first theory on the basis of which, besides other things, the distinction between clean and unclean has been explained is that of totemism. Totemism is a form of superstition in which savage tribes and families derive their origin from some animal or plant or some inanimate object, to all the specimens of which they pay religious reverence, after which they name themselves, and which they abstain from killing and eating. Various phenomena in Old Testament popular religion have been explained from it, and then appealed to as traces of its ancient existence among the Hebrews. It is not believed that within the period covered by the Old Testament tradition such things were practised, but survivals, no longer understood, are supposed to occur. As regard animals, the eating of which is forbidden in the law, the view is that these animals were originally sacred to the various totem-groups among the Hebrews. When several tribal groups united, and adopted the cult of Jehovah, the interdiction of eating them was continued, but the motive for the interdict was changed: they were forbidden as food because of their idolatrous character. On this theory the notions of uncleanness and holiness appear materially identical. What is holy in one cult is unclean in another, and it is unclean in the latter precisely because of its holiness in the former. The adherents of this view are wont to apply to these two ideas the common term 'taboo'. The two ideas have in common not merely the element of prohibition, but also that of contagiousness, and of necessary removal through lustration, holiness as much as unholiness.

Objections that may be urged against this theory in its Old Testament application are numerous. The lists of unclean animals in Lev. 11 and Deut. 14 are so long that all these animals could not any time have been totems within Israel's ken. The names of persons among Israel derived from animals form a small proportion of the names borne. Even in Arabia the majority of the tribes do not bear animal names: of the big tribes only a few; of closely related tribes the one will have an animal name, the other not. No plants were unclean to the Hebrews, yet totems were made of plants as well as of animals. The tribal names among Israel in which a reminiscence of totemism has been found are Leah, Rachel, and Simeon. The first two of these precisely name clean animals.

ANCESTOR-WORSHIP

A second, likewise partial, explanation of the phenomena of uncleanness is that from ancestor-worship. This is believed to lie at the basis of the uncleanness of the dead. Also the prohibition of certain mourning rites is attributed to worship of the dead, whereas others are supposed to have sprung from some other attitude towards the dead to be spoken of subsequently. On the principle that what is sacred in one cult becomes taboo in another, ancient worship of the dead, particularly of ancestors, is believed to account for the taboo of the dead in the cult of Jehovah.

Of the mourning customs that come under consideration here is the wearing of a 'sack', signifying' primitively religious submission, therefore extended to the dead as gods. The veiling of the head and the covering of the beard spring from the same motive that leads a person obtaining sight of the deity to veil himself. The putting off of sandals was a common act in stepping on holy ground. Hence, if it occurs in connection with the dead or their graves, it must have been a religious act. The shaving of head or beard is of the nature of an hair-offering. Fasting plays a role in the worship of Jehovah, in mourning it likewise must have been a part of religion. Nakedness and self-mutilation appear elsewhere as religious rites; in mourning they cannot have any different meaning.

Here again the objections that arise are numerous. We mention the following only. There are many of these things, e.g. fasting, that are not forbidden in Israel. On the principle of their being descended from such a pronounced form of idolatry as worship of the dead they most certainly ought to have been. This applies to all practices for which analogy in the service of Jehovah is found. Further the uncleanness arises from the dead body, but the worship of ancestors or the dead in general was not rendered to the body. It addressed itself to the 'soul' or 'spirit' of the dead. We can verify this from other circles where worship of the dead existed. To the Greeks the dead body, in one period of their history at least, was unclean, and yet, in spite of this belief, there was worship of the dead. That the cutting off of the hair was preparatory to an offering to the dead is not proven, since nothing is said anywhere of such hair being left at the grave or in any other way given to the dead. The putting off of sandals is not, strictly speaking, an act of worship. Nor can the blood made by incisions have been considered an offering to the dead. There is no evidence that this blood was brought in contact with the dead. A number of the customs mentioned are not interpretable as acts of worship. Nakedness, the rending of garments, the rolling on the ground are such. That the dust and ashes put upon the head were obtained from the grave or funeral pyre is not proven. But, even if they were, that would not render the custom an act of worship. There must be some other explanation of these things on the basis of superstitious idolatry in general.

Still further, the way in which the matter of mourning for relatives has been ordered for the priests forbids us to derive these mourning customs from ancestor-worship. The high-priest could not come near a dead body at all. But the ordinary priests were permitted to perform the mourning rites for their near relatives, not for remoter ones.

Had a protest against ancestor-worship been involved, then the prohibition ought to have been most stringent with regard to near relatives, for these precisely would be likely to receive worship of this sort.

THE ANIMISTIC THEORY

Still a third theory offered in explanation of the facts of uncleanness is the animistic theory. This theory appears in two forms. Both have in common the assumption that to the primitive mind certain things appear as bearers of a sinister supernatural influence that is to be shunned. According to the one form of the theory these bearers are of a personal, demonic kind. According to the other the danger resides in impersonal soul-matter, diffusing itself and attaching itself in certain preferred ways, and in reality as dangerous as the influence of a personal demon. The nature of the first form of the theory brings with it that the forms of uncleanness are, especially the mourning-practices, but so many self-disguising attempts to escape the notice of these demonic powers. To say that it renders unclean to do this or touch that, only means that danger lurks in the vicinity where uncleanness is held to be contracted. It is an indirect discipline, administered as to children for teaching them to avoid danger by dissemblance in their appearance. The other form of the theory finds in these practices likewise a sort of self-defence, not by means of camouflage, but rather by prophylaxis.

The personal form of the theory attaches itself chiefly to the uncleanness of death and to the mourning customs. The dead body should be held unclean, because the soul hovers around it for some time in not altogether too pleasant a spirit. It is jealous of the relatives, who have entered upon possession of its estate, a feeling extending even to the personal relict of a man, his widow, who therefore, was cautioned not to remarry for a considerable period.

While this theory in the first form may give a fairly plausible explanation of some of the facts, it by no means explains all. There are some mourning customs that cannot have sprung from the desire of self-protection through disguise. Fasting scarcely can have aimed at that, a mistaken exegesis of Matt. 6.16 notwithstanding. The most various explanations of fasting as a religious practice have been presented, none of them so far satisfactory in every respect. Some say it springs from regarding the food in a place where some one has died as unclean. Others say, the fasting person considers himself unclean, and does not want to defile the food. According to still others, it is originally the preparation for a sacrificial meal, on the principle that no other food should come in contact with the holy food. Others again see in it an effort to induce ecstatic conditions. Still others consider it a species of ascetic practice. All this shows how precarious it is to maintain that it must have meant a form of self-disguise.

Nor can the sounds made by the mourners very well be accounted for on such a principle. A person's voice, when crying or wailing or shouting, may not be as easily recognizable as ordinary speech, but silence would have rendered it far more unrecognizable still. The rending of garments does not hinder identification very much. Nor does walking on bare feet. Nor do incisions made on the body. Nor does the beating of face, breasts or hips. Nor does the putting of dust and ashes on the head. Perhaps the treatment of hair on head or beard most easily lends itself to this explanation from disguise. But in that case the mourning women ought to have treated the hair differently from the mourning men, as was actually the custom elsewhere.

Apart from these individual points of criticism, the theory labours under one general difficulty. How could the spirit of the dead supposedly be ignorant of the simple fact that the people in the immediate surroundings were relatives? If it wanted to injure relatives, the mourning observances would have been the simplest and surest way of informing it where to strike. Personal identification was unnecessary. People could hardly fail to credit the dead with so much knowledge as to be aware of this, the less so, since the dead were known to have been mourners themselves during life on frequent occasions. And why should the dead be jealous of the survivors for entering upon possession of what they had left behind? As a rule among primitive people no such extreme individualism in the matter of property-relations exists. The average man, primitive or civilized, is not jealous of his heirs, but glad to have heirs. Besides, the theory implies that mourning customs are more recent in their origin than the existence of private property. This would be hard to prove. The same mourning practices are found among most nomadic as among settled agricultural tribes.

The impersonal form of the animistic theory holds that the ascription of uncleanness to things and places is a means to bar soul-matter out. When separated from one body this substance seeks to slip into or attach itself to another. Every avenue of entrance is carefully closed up. The openings of the body are covered up, or made inaccessible. Fasting precludes the hostile fluid from slipping in with the food. The first food eaten after the fasting was not derived from the house of the dead. It was supposed that the soul-matter disliked attaching itself to anything torn or burst. The bystander rent his garment at the very first moment after death had taken place. The simplest, shortest, straightest garment was put on; all folds and creases were avoided; shoes were discarded, so as to leave nothing for the soul to nestle in. The hair was cut off the head with the same fear in mind. The nails were pared. Incisions were made in the body, that the blood might freely flow out. Attention is called to the distinction the law makes between covered and uncovered vessels. The uncovered vessel becomes unclean, the covered one escapes the contagion [*Num.* 19.15].

It must be admitted that this form of the theory on the whole succeeds better in explaining things than the preceding one. Many of these primitive practices really look like means of seclusion and fortification against an invading spirit-power. This principle admits of application at several points where that of concealment breaks down. Even so, however, many things remain unaccounted for. The rending of garments, one would think, rendered ingress all the easier. To say, that the soul-matter does not like a broken or torn thing, may be true, but this itself requires an explanation which is not given. Entire nakedness also would have been felt as giving the spirit free play upon the body. The taking off of the sandals would be dangerous for the same reason. The rolling on the ground, as well as the putting of dust and ashes on the head, would have been an unsafe act. The self-mutilations, by opening up the body, made only new avenues of ingress.

The theory is distinctly weaker than the other form, when it comes to explain the greater exposure of relatives to attack. If it is a question of personal jealousy, there is at least some apparent reason for this. If, on the other hand, it is a question of soul-matter seeking some lodgement, then it is difficult to see, why precisely relatives should have felt themselves in danger above others. The range of uncleanness is wider than the mourning circle. Why do the relatives in particular mourn? If the soul-matter, being unintelligent, has no personal feelings about it, if it only seeks some hole or crevice to slip into, then, when a taboo is erected against this through the assumption of uncleanness, and this is further strengthened through the observance of mourning, it becomes difficult to explain why only the relatives engage in the latter. It might be said that the relatives are nearer to the body, therefore subject to greater exposure, whereas the others can simply keep away. But if so, then the rule ought to have been that, not blood-propinquity, but local propinquity, was the decisive consideration. All who came near the dead ought to have mourned.

Besides these three theories, which endeavour to account for groups of phenomena comprehensively, there are attempts to account for single facts. Altogether apart from totemism, certain unclean animals may have derived their taboo from their figuring as sacred animals in some idolatrous cult. This may apply to single cases, although to the entire collection of unclean animals it is not applicable. Many of the unclean animals belong to the smallest species, and certainly never were cult-objects. With bigger animals, such as swine, it is different. Isa. 65.4ff. speaks of a cult, which included the eating of pork. In the circle there referred to, undoubtedly pork was regarded, not as unclean, but as holy. Some similar practice of more ancient date may have occasioned the regulation of the law, that swine shall be unclean animals to the servants of Jehovah. The interdict on unclean animals is in Lev. 20.22ff. significantly brought into connection with the difference between the Israelites and the Canaanites. This indicates that the latter did not treat the animals tabooed in Israel as unclean. On the contrary these very animals must have played a rather prominent role in their religion. It further suggests that on that very account they were debarred from the ritual of the true religion.

The uncleanness of leprosy occupies a place by itself. This cannot be explained from sanitary motives. True, although modern medical science teaches leprosy to be only slightly contagious, the ancient people might have thought differently about it. But a serious objection is, that other equally serious, and obviously contagious diseases did not render a person unclean, notably the pestilence. It has been suggested that leprosy was ascribed to a special stroke from Jehovah or some evil spirit, and that even the name of the disease bears witness to this; *tsara'ath* and *nega'*, the two names for leprosy, both come from roots meaning 'to strike'. But according to others these terms have no religious significance, being taken from the spots and swellings characteristic of the disease. If the idea of a demonic or divine stroke came into play, we should expect that the same instinct would have expressed itself in regard to insanity and epilepsy. Yet these do not render unclean. Possibly leprosy may have been associated with uncleanness, because of its being, as it were, a living death. In that case the uncleanness of the leprosy would have to be classified with that of death. The words used about the leprosy of Miriam [*Num.* 12.12] suggest something like this.

But why does death with all that accompanies it render unclean? On the principle that both birth and death cause uncleanness, it has been plausibly suggested that through the uncleanness of these two termini of life the entire natural life as such is declared unclean. The objection has been raised, that on this view of the matter, the law should not have declared giving birth, but being born, as bringing with it uncleanness. It does only the former. The mother is unclean, we are told, not the child. The objection has not much weight. We may observe that the child is actually unclean. This, however, having received a most pointed expression through circumcision, there was no need of stating it separately, and by attaching the uncleanness to the mother the additional truth was taught of the uncleanness not merely of life in its entire course, but in its very source.

While the points of view indicated may contain elements of truth, they do not profess to give a satisfactory solution of the whole problem. Some older explanations, frequently discarded by modern writers with amusement and contempt, are not so summarily to be dismissed as is done by them. Certain animals, like snakes and birds of prey, awaken a natural aversion in the human mind at primitive stages, and this may have had something to do with the shaping of the law.

Far more important than these insoluble problems and their tentative solutions is the consideration of the manner in which the law makes these strange things subserve its purpose of revealing the true religion of the Old Testament. The first thing the law does is to give the whole distinction a religious aspect, no matter whether this inhered in it from the beginning or not. When the law undertakes to regulate a thing, it obtains from that very fact religious significance. The principle is explicitly affirmed. The matter is brought into relation with the holiness of God [Lev. 11.44, 45; *Deut.* 14.21]. Hence also the process of cleansing is called a 'sanctifying'. The unclean are debarred from the sanctuary and from the feasts. From the tithes nothing can be taken for the dead, nor eaten in mourning [*Lev.* 22.4; *Num.* 9.6; 19.12, 20; *Deut.* 26.14]. The removal of uncleanness is in part accomplished by ritual 'covering' [*Lev.* 12.7, 8; 14 (*passim*); 16.29, 30; 15.14, 15; *Num.* 8.5ff.]. The role played by the number seven in the periods of purification is evidence of the religious character of the latter. The stringency of the regulations with reference to the priests proves that a religious motive was the determining one [*Lev.* 21.1ff.; 22.2, 3].

The uncleanness, thus related to the service of Jehovah, is associated with ethical sin. This is done in two ways. On the one hand the ritual uncleanness is treated as sin. On the other hand the ethical abnormality is made to borrow its vocabulary from the ritual law. We do not always clearly appreciate the latter. When sin of a distinctly ethical kind is called 'impurity', we are apt to think this a self-explanatory metaphor. In reality it is a direct borrowing of ritual language. God teaches people to feel about sin as they are accustomed to feel about an ignominious and uncomfortable exclusion from the ritual service. Thus circumcision is made a lever of ethicizing and spiritualizing in Deut. 10.16. This incipient spiritualizing of the ritual vocabulary is further carried out by the Prophets and Psalmists. Isaiah speaks of 'unclean' lips in an ethical sense [6.5]. The earth is 'defiled' by transgression of the fundamental laws of God [*Isa.* 24.5]; blood (i.e. murder) 'defiles' the hands [*Isa.* 1.15; 59.3]; the temple is 'defiled' by idolatry [*Jer.* 32.34; *Ezek.* 5.11; 28.18]; the people *pollute* themselves by their sins [*Ezek.* 20.7, 8, 43; 22.3; 39.24]. Ethical purity is symbolized by 'clean hands' and 'a pure heart' [*Psa.* 24.4]. The ethical cleansing is described in terms of ritual purification [*Psa.* 51.7; *Ezek.* 36.25; *Zech.* 13.1].

The Old Testament

PART TWO
THE PROPHETIC EPOCH
OF REVELATION

ONE:
THE PLACE OF PROPHETISM
IN OLD TESTAMENT
REVELATION

Next to Mosaism, Prophetism marks an epochal onward movement in Old Testament revelation. In order to understand why this should be so, we must call to mind how the process of revelation is articulated. Revelation follows events. But not all happenings in the history of Israel, even though apparently momentous, give rise to a large influx of new revelation. What is necessary for this is, that the new happenings shall leave something new, that is of lasting significance, behind. When the acts of the exodus lead to the setting up of the theocratic organization, a large volume of revelation follows in their wake. We must, therefore, ask, what was the great event in Sacred History, that could call forth such a new body of revelation of the most far-reaching importance.

This event can be nothing else but the new organization of the theocratic kingdom under a human ruler. In the days of Samuel this movement began; it found provisional embodiment in the rule of Saul, but was not consolidated on a firm basis until the accession of David. Henceforth the idea of this kingdom remains central in the hopes of Israel. This human kingdom, however, is only a representation of the kingdom of Jehovah Himself. At first, when the people asked for a king, Jehovah disapproved of the un-theocratic spirit in which the request was made, and declared it tantamount to rejection of Himself. Nevertheless the desire was granted, obviously in order that through the wrong conduct of the office by Saul, its true conception might be the more clearly taught.

This was also the reason why for such a long time during the period of Joshua and the Judges the institution of the kingdom was kept in abeyance. Only after in this twofold manner – first by withholding a king, and next by allowing a wrong sort of king – the ideal of the king after the heart of Jehovah had been carefully inculcated, did the actual permanent thing arrive. The kingdom is in its intent an instrument of redemption as well as the embodiment of the blessedness of

Israel. To it the Messianic expectations attach themselves. It is a serious mistake to conceive of the kingdom as something accidentally arrived at, and merely tolerated for a time at the expense of democracy. The thing was too large and deep to have aught of the unessential and dispensable about it. It touches, through the kingship of Christ, the very acme and perfection of the Biblical religion.

A KINGDOM-PRODUCING MOVEMENT

To this kingdom-producing movement the rise and development of prophetism attach themselves. The prophets were guardians of the unfolding theocracy, and the guardianship was exercised at its centre, the kingdom. The purpose was to keep it a true representation of the kingdom of Jehovah. It sometimes almost appears as if the prophets were sent to the kings instead of to the people. From this interlinking of the prophetic office with the national interests of Israel, summed up in the kingdom, we can best explain the peculiar circumstances under which prophecy arose at the time of Samuel, in a deep patriotic movement, with a large admixture of national aspirations, shaping itself collectively at the first as well as individually. The bands or so-called 'schools' of the prophets were centres of religious and patriotic life in one; but, in harmony with the purpose of Israel's existence, the religious dominated the patriotic, not the reverse. The case of Deborah in the period of the Judges furnishes an earlier example.

It is a mistake, however, to infer from this national function, that the prophetic office was a sort of diplomatic, political office. This has been done by Winkler, who appeals wrongly in support of it to the enumeration of offices in Isa. 3.2. As developed by him, the view in question would throw a rather unpleasant light upon the prophetic activity during the later critical days of the kingdom. He believes that the great Oriental powers availed themselves of the prophets as agents to further their own interests among the smaller kingdoms. Hence the phenomenon that so often the counsel given by the prophets in political complications coincided with the plans pursued by these powers. Elisha is assumed to have received his instructions from Damascus, Isaiah from Nineveh, Jeremiah from Babylon.

But there is no evidence that such relations of a diplomatic or semi-diplomatic kind were ever cultivated by the prophets. What we find is rather an aversion to all political entanglements and alliances. But this is not based on superior political insight on the part of the prophets. It simply results from their staunch maintenance of the theocratic principle, that Jehovah is King, and Israel bound to rely exclusively on Him [*Isa.* 7; 30.1–5; *Hos.* 7.11; 12.1]. Already in the times of David and Solomon such prophets as Nathan and Gad worked largely through the kingship. By Elijah and Elisha afterwards the same method was pursued. That whatever there seemed to be of political interposition was not at bottom political, but religious, appears from the fact that its procedure is open. There is no secret understanding, no conspiracy about it. Politics as such is unable to dispense with the element of secret procedure. It must be admitted, however, that there is some difference in this respect between Elijah and Elisha. The latter did enter into a conspiracy against the dynasty of the house of Omri. But even what Elisha aimed at was not improvement of the political situation. The end in view was to eradicate the cult of Baal by fire and sword through the supplanting of the Omrites by the house of Jehu. One need only compare the conduct of the prophets of Israel with that of the seer Balaam in the Mosaic period, to acquit the former of all charges of diplomatic intrigue. Balaam let himself be hired by a king, something no prophet of Israel could ever have contemplated.

THE WORD AS THE INSTRUMENT OF PROPHETISM

Prophetism, in restricting itself to the word as its instrument, while seemingly limited as to efficacy in this respect, in reality did more than anything else towards the spiritualizing of the relation between Jehovah and Israel. The prophets did not create facts, they upheld principles; and whatever future facts they spoke of were placed by them in the pure ideal light of prediction. Through prophecy Biblical religion has first come to be, to the extent it is, the religion of truth, of faith, of Scripture. In this respect the prophets were the precursors of Protestantism, at least from a formal point of view. More than ever before, the religious consciousness of Israel felt itself bound up with the cardinal fact of revelation. Jehovah's approach to Israel is eminently the approach of speech; God gives Himself in the word of His mouth.

The word, while being primarily intended for an official purpose, secondarily also becomes a means of grace for the prophet himself. The intimacy of the intercourse which the prophet needed and enjoyed in virtue of his task, could not fail at the same time to minister to his own religious growth. Still, the stressing of this feature can be over-done. It is suspicious, when joined to a neglect or implicit disavowal of the revelation-significance of the prophet. Religious heroism is not what Scripture puts foremost among the phenomena of prophecy. And where a high degree of religiousness is shown, we are distinctly given to understand that it was the result of the privileges of the office, rather than the prerequisite of investment with the office. The prophets were not primarily chosen because of their signal piety. They became pious above the average as a result of the exercise of their God-ward function.

A FACTOR OF CONTINUITY

Prophecy is a factor of continuity in the history of revelation, both through its retrospective and through its prospective attitude. Its preaching of repentance, and of the sin of apostasy from the norms of the past, links it to the preceding work of Jehovah for Israel in the patriarchal and Mosaic periods. Through its predictive elements it anticipates the continuity with the future. Although the name 'prophet' may not mean 'foreteller', none the less foretelling is an essential part in the prophet's task. The prophets themselves emphasize this so much that one cannot consider it to be incidental [*Amos* 3.7]. The initiation into the secret of the coming things forms part of that religious intimacy into which the prophet has been received with Jehovah. But objectively also the prophet could not be a true revealer if the substratum of facts, which all revelation requires, were absent from his consciousness. And this substratum is given partly in the future facts.

Modern interpreters but too frequently make the prophet stand as a disinterested 'teacher' historically, forgetful of all things except his own present lesson. This is a distortion of his figure. Teachers in this sense the prophets never were and 'schools' they never kept. The error in question frequently springs from a failure to observe how closely the doctrinal principles of the prophet's preaching shape his forecast of the future. Mere arbitrary exhibitions of pretended foresight the predictions never were. They cannot be removed from the preaching without disarranging and deforming the latter. And here again the personal equation must be taken into account. The prophets felt to a large extent that they were living in times out of joint, and among a people out of sympathy with what was most precious to themselves. Their instinctive desire would be to seek compensation in the future for what the present denied them. A warmth of emotionally-coloured interest not seldom suffuses their predictions. And there is also perceptible a desire for contemplating in advance the vindication of the truth, assailed and scorned in the present. Religious decadence and degeneracy have always stimulated occupation with the future. Eschatological interest is sometimes a species of comfort to the pious soul. For all these reasons it is a cheap modernizing tendency to belittle the predictive element in prophecy.

TWO MAIN PERIODS OF PROPHETISM

The principle of continuity within the plan of revelation in its double form of linking on to the past and reaching out into the future, can be distributed over the two main periods in which the history of prophetism divides itself. The former of these periods extends from the great prophetic revival in the time of Samuel to the date of the first writing-prophets about the middle of the eighth century B.C. The second extends from there onwards until the close of Old Testament prophecy. The difference between these two periods is that in the earlier one the possibility of repentance and conversion, in response to the prophetic preaching, is still reckoned with. The prophets speak out of the consciousness of being reorganizers, reconstructionists. That something better will come and must come they know, but they are not aware as yet of the extent to which, when come, it will swallow up the past.

In the second period, although the call to repentance never ceases, yet it acquires a more or less perfunctory tone. The prophet now knows that, not repair, but regeneration of the present lies in the womb of the future. But the main thing to be observed is that this rebirth is not equivalent to a new setting up of the past, not even in an idealized form. Occasion is taken from the prediction of overthrow to introduce into the picture all the absolute values of eschatology. As the divine method in general is not to bring out of the chaos and dissolution of sin the return simply of the former state of affairs but the attainment of a higher order of things, so the same rule on a smaller scale is illustrated here in the history of Israel. God made use of the impending destruction of the Mosaic theocracy to create room for something far transcending the original structure.

The arrival of this new phase of prophecy coincides with a series of new, momentous developments on the scene of history. The first phase opened with the record-breaking events of the age from Samuel to David. The second opens with the appearance upon the horizon of the great, humanly-speaking irresistible, Eastern power which God had chosen to be the instrument of His judgment. How important was the change thus brought about in the outlook of prophecy may be seen from this, that it has left its impress even upon the outward form of communicating the message. From the middle of the eighth century onwards the prophets begin to be writing prophets. Amos, Hosea, and, somewhat later, Isaiah and Micah for the first time committed the prophetic word to writing. The word of the earlier prophets, though a truly divine word, had been largely a transient word, intended for

189

their own day and generation. But from this second crisis onward the word ever increasingly obtained reference to the new creation of the future, and consequently dealt with things in which future generations would have a share and supreme interest. And even their own contemporaries, who refused the prophets a hearing, were through the witness of the written word to be convicted of the truth spoken of them. In these ideas the prophets begin to grasp more clearly than had been done before the principle of the continuity, that is, of a history of redemption and revelation.

The true principle of history writing, that which makes history more than a chronicling of events, because it discovers a plan and posits a goal, was thus grasped, not first by the Greek historians, but by the prophets of Israel. Hence we find also that the activity among these circles includes sacred historiography, the production of books like the Books of Samuel and Kings in which the course of events is placed in the light of an unfolding divine plan. Good meaning can thus be found in the ancient canonical custom of calling these historical writings 'the earlier prophets'.

TWO:
THE CONCEPTION OF
A PROPHET: NAMES AND
ETYMOLOGIES

THE HEBREW TERM 'NABHI''

The Hebrew word for prophet is *nabhi'*. It is doubtful whether the etymology can render us much assistance towards determining the fundamental conception of the office. Various proposals have been made by exegetes. We mention the following:

(*a*) Connection is sought with a root-group in which the first two radicals are *nun* and *beth*. The meaning fixed upon is 'to spring', 'to gush forth', or passively 'to be sputtered, bubbled or gushed against'. The *nabhi'* then might be 'the one gushed upon by the Spirit' (so Keil). Kuenen seeks to give an active turn to the idea. He thinks the *nabhi'* may have been so called because he was rushing and gushing in his gestures and speech. The passive view is excluded by the intransitive meaning of these verbs, which are not capable of a direct object. Nor does the active sense particularly suit the purpose to which Kuenen would put it. He seeks in it support for considering the earliest prophets a sort of raving men, dervish-like in their behaviour. 'To gush' is scarcely strong enough for that. At the utmost the copious flow of speech could perhaps be referred to, but on this there is no clear reflection anywhere. 'To drop', as a synonym for prophesying, seems rather to describe the constant iteration of the message [*Ezek.* 20.46; 21.2], but even this is not certain.

(*b*) Recourse is had to the Arabic. In it *naba'a* means 'to announce'. But the ideas of 'bubbling' and 'sprouting' are also represented in this root-circle, so that adherents of view (*a*) may find additional support here. A difficulty arising in connection with 'to announce' is that *nabhi'* is restricted to the announcer for the Deity, whilst the verb, in order to give us help, would have to signify 'to announce' in general. The suspicion arises that perhaps the verb is derived from *nabhi'* in its technical religious sense, which latter then might very well have had another etymology. Nor is it impossible that the word entered into the Arabic from the Hebrew.

(c) Derivation from the Assyrian has been advocated. *Nabu* here signified 'to call', 'to proclaim', 'to announce'. The element of authority seems to be regularly associated with the word. The ideas of 'gushing', 'springing' are likewise represented in the root: *manbau* is 'a fountain', *nibhu*, 'a sprout'. The concurrence of the Hebrew, Arabic and Assyrian in expressing this idea in the same root to which *nabhi'* belongs is certainly remarkable, but we are not able to point out the transition from this root-concept to the specific meaning of *nabhi'* 'prophet'.

(d) A special derivation from the Assyrian is that attaching itself to the name of the god Nebo. Some think that Nebo bears his name as speaker and herald for the gods, but this is not proven. He does appear as the god of wisdom, inventor of the art of writing, carrier of the tablets of destiny. Sayce says: he was interpreter of the will of Bel-Merodach; he reads the oracles and interprets dreams. He might, however, carry all these predicates, and yet there might be no etymological connection with his name.

(e) Hupfeld proposes to identify the roots *naba'a* and *na'am*, from which latter comes the well-known phrase *ne'um Jahveh*, 'oracle of Jehovah'. The identification of the two roots is precarious, because it involves both interchange of *mem* and *beth*, and exchange of place between these two radicals. On Hupfeld's view *nabhi'* would mean 'oracler'.

(f) Certain Jewish scholars, and more recently Land, bring *nabhi'* into connection with the verb *bo'*, 'to enter in'. It is taken by them as the Niphal participle of this verb, 'one entered in', that is, by the Deity. But on this view the most important part of the conception would have remained unexpressed or been lost sight of through long usage. '*Nabhi'* of the Deity' or '*nabhi'* of the Spirit' nowhere occurs.

In view of this uncertainty of the several derivations it is exceedingly fortunate that from a few Old Testament passages we can gather with certainty the meaning attached to the word by Scripture in the sphere of revelation. These passages are: Ex. 4.16; 7.1; Jer. 1.5, 6. From these we learn that *nabhi'* was understood as an appointed regular speaker for a divine superior, whose speech carries the authority of the latter. In the first-named passage, it is true, the term *nabhi'* is not used explicitly. None the less a definite view of what a prophet ought to be with reference to God underlies it. Aaron will serve Moses as a mouth, and Moses will be to Aaron as a god. It is not a question of the relation between some sender and his ambassador in general, but a question of an ambassador of God. Aaron shall be the substitute-mouth for the Moses-god. It is only because Moses, so to speak, occupies the place of God, that Aaron can be spokesman in this absolute sense. And within the terms of the figure the infallibility of the result is safeguarded, for Jehovah says: 'I will be with thy mouth and with his mouth.' The second passage is still more convincing. Moses is made a god to Pharaoh and Aaron is to act as Moses' *nabhi'*. Aaron can be *nabhi'* only because a god stands back of him. The same, without figurativeness, follows from the relation between Jehovah and Jeremiah defined in the third passage. God says, He has ordained Jeremiah a prophet. Jeremiah answers: I am a child; I cannot speak. Then Jehovah declares that He has put His words in Jeremiah's mouth by touching it with His hand. Thereupon the words become divinely-powerful: Jeremiah stands over the nations, to root out and to pull down, to build and to plant.

It will be noticed that in all three passages it is a question of speaking. This alone introduces into the second the figure of the *nabhi'*. The disqualification pleaded is in each case an inability to speak. The prophet's business lies in the sphere of speaking. And this speaking is not ordinary speaking, as in ordinary life one man might speak representatively for another. It is a unique representation conveying divine authority and, in a measure, divine omnipotence, and these are based on divine communication. Jehovah touches the mouth and puts the words there, and they acquire the effect of divine words.

The point is thus clearly established, that even to the pre-Mosaic Hebrew consciousness a *nabhi'* is an authorized spokesman for the Deity, and that in his word a divinely-communicated power resides. Jehovah does not endeavour to teach Moses what a prophet is. He takes for granted that Moses knows this, and on that supposition constructs the analogy, wherein Moses figures as a god and Aaron as a prophet. Whatever the etymology of the name in its origin, to the Old Testament mind the prophet stood from beginning to end as the authoritative speaker for Jehovah. What the implications of this general conclusion are, we shall investigate presently, when dealing with the mode of prophetic revelation. But the general conclusion in itself is of the highest importance. It marks the religion of the Old Testament as a religion of conscious intercourse between Jehovah and Israel, a religion of revelation, of authority, a religion in which God dominates, and in which man is put into the listening, submissive attitude.

Within the process of carrying the divine message *nabhi'* names the active factor. The *nabhi'* is one who does something; he speaks. True, in order to be able to do this, he must have been first passive; he must have received or experienced something. But that the name does not express; it only presupposes it. In fact the receiving of a divine message does not necessarily imply that it must be communicated. It can be for the recipient himself, or intended to be kept unspoken. Only when with the message there goes, explicitly or implicitly, the charge to transmit it, is there a case of prophecy. The prophet is a speaker to others. In other names the reverse, passive side of the process, the receiving of the message may stand in the foreground. In 'prophet' it does not. And *nabhi'* has become the prevailing name. Not the mysteries of the background, but the issue in the open, where it reaches the mind of man, is the main consideration. The term is practical through and through, and so is the religion of the Old Testament which it so largely colours.

Some of the etymologies above reviewed differ from this conclusion. They would lay the stress on the passive side of the prophetic experience. Apart from etymology, two motives underlie this un-biblical preference. By representing the prophet as chiefly passive the way is prepared for conceiving him after a rude, primitive fashion, as not in control of himself, being powerfully affected by a strange extraneous compulsion. On the other hand, the passivizing of the form suits the modern desire for assimilating the prophetic experience as much as possible to the common experience of religion, for that can be done only through bringing out the subjective, experiential side.

The two linguistic arguments adduced for the passive understanding are, in the first place, that *nabhi'*, after the pattern of *qatil*, must be meant passively, and in the second place, that the only verbal forms occurring in connection with the word are the Niphal and Hithpael species. It must be conceded that the *qatil*-form often has passive meaning. For example, *mashiach* is, not the one who anoints, but the anointed one. Still this is by no means uniformly so. There are quite a number of active nouns of this formation, such as *paqid*, 'overseer'. In the Arabic, Ethiopic, and Assyrian languages *qatil* is the regular form for the Qal active participle. As to the verbal forms, we must remember that, while the Niphal is both passive and reflexive, the Hithpael is never passive, but always reflexive. The fact is that both are reflexive, being derivatives from the noun *nabhi'*, and signify simply 'to conduct oneself as a *nabhi'*.

THE GREEK TERM 'PROPHETES'

With this enquiry into the meaning of *nabhi'* we may combine a brief discussion of its Greek equivalent, *prophētēs*, from which our word prophet has come. We associate with this mostly the idea of 'foreteller'. This is not in accord with the original Greek etymology. The preposition 'pro' in the composition does not express the time-sense of 'beforehand'. It has local significance; the *prophētēs* is a forth-teller. The Greek term, however, has religious associations no less than the Hebrew one. *Prophētēs* is the one who speaks for the oracle. Thus it might seem, that with the 'pro' correctly understood, the Hebrew *nabhi*' and the Greek *prophētēs* were practically synonyms. This, however, would be misleading. The Greek *prophētēs* does not stand in the same direct relation to the deity as the Hebrew *nabhi*' does. In reality he is the interpreter of the oracular, dark utterances of the Pythia, or some other inspired person, whom, from the depth underneath, the godhead of the shrine inspires. The Pythia would thus stand at the same remove from deity as the *nabhi*', but the *prophētēs* is separated from the deity by this intervening person. *Prophētēs* is therefore rather an interpreter than a mouth-piece of what the god speaks through the one he directly inspires. He adds of his own, not merely the illumination of the oracle, but also the form in which he clothes the meaning apperceived.

Those who scorn the idea of what they contemptuously call 'verbatim inspiration' move rather along the Hellenic than along the Biblical line. It is precisely the Greek *prophētēs*, and not the Old Testament *nabhi*' who has this freedom of movement they think so desirable. And not merely are the *nabhi*' and the *prophētēs* different, but this difference is in the last analysis due to the difference between the Biblical Jehovah and the pagan god. Phoebus Apollo speaks, or rather speaks not. He utters dark, incomprehensible sounds. Then the Pythia, herself upon her tripod under the influence of the narcotic fumes arising from the cleft, needs likewise a *prophētēs* for rendering the oracular noise intelligible to ordinary mortals. But the Biblical God is light in Himself and His word gives light to all who seek it, although He uses the *nabhi*' as His transmitter. Somewhat of the savour of subjectivity always clung to the Hellenic term. A philosopher is *prophētēs* of immortal nature. Poets are *prophētai* of the Muses. These are, of course, metaphors, but none the less they arise out of the apperception of the vague character of divine inspiration, belonging to the whole complex of pagan experience from which they spring.

It is no wonder, then, that the word *prophētēs*, taken into the service of Biblical religion, had to undergo a baptism of regeneration, before it could be properly used. And, since so much of the task of the Old

Testament *nabhi'* consisted, as a matter of fact, in prediction, the Biblical-Greek usage naturally put this into its regenerated *prophētēs*. Although this was etymologically wrong, it was not so theologically. The New Testament already puts a quite perceptible chronological stress on the preposition *pro*. There can be no doubt but, when the Evangelist Matthew writes numerous times, 'this happened in order that it might be fulfilled that was written by the prophet', etc., he associates with the word 'prophet' the idea of foretelling, which the Hebrew word *nabhi'* has not, although the *nabhi'*-function has.

Some of the Greek fathers, who might have been more sensitive to Greek idiom, forgot the locally-projectory sense of *pro*, and substituted for it the chronological sense. Thus Chrysostom observes: 'For *prophēteia* is nothing else but the proclamation beforehand of things to come.' Augustine, as a matter of etymological definition, quite correctly says: 'The prophet of God is nothing else but the enunciator of the words of God to men.' When he, however, adds: 'men, who either are not able to, or do not deserve to hear God', this goes beyond the import of both *nabhi'* and the Biblical *prophētēs*. Although thus the New Testament and the fathers may have sacrificed somewhat of etymological correctness, we should remember that their interest lay not in philology. The modern tendency to minimize the predictive element, and lay well-nigh exclusive stress on the teaching function, is far more one-sided and misleading than the popular impression that the prophets were foretellers of coming events. Still the original meaning of *prophētēs* as an exact translation of *nabhi'* is by no means entirely lost sight of in the New Testament [cp. *Heb.* 1.1].

THE TERMS 'RO'EH' AND 'CHOZEH'

So much for *nabhi'* and its equivalent, *prophētēs*. We now come to two other names, *ro'eh*, and its synonym *chozeh*. These two names are translated into Biblical English by 'seer' without distinction. For determining their import the point at issue is: do they refer to super-natural insight (metaphorically), or are they descriptive of a specific visionary mode of receiving what is conveyed by God? In themselves the two verbs could easily bear a metaphorical interpretation. But it is not so easy to apply this notion to the noun. We do not usually say that a person has, or has had, a sight, when we simply mean that he evinces deeper insight into certain matters than the average man. Yet the object-nouns of the verbs are quite freely used. The verbs must at first have related to a visionary process or product in the technical sense. Later on their sense was generalized; they came to mean 'revelation' by whatever process obtained, through hearing no less than vision. But this did not make them metaphors. We shall see, later on, how this generalizing came about in the regular development of the mode of prophetic revelation. The word 'seer' refers to an extraordinary influence brought to bear on the seeing-faculty of the prophet, by which he was made to see things, instead of hearing them, with the same result that through this seeing a message of divine provenience was introduced into his consciousness. The two terms differ from *nabhi'* in that the latter describes the active function of speaking for transmission of the message, whereas 'seer' describes the passive experience of being made acquainted with the message ocularly. To this, of course, would correspond the hearing which receives the speech of God.

Koenig, in his work entitled *The Old Testament Conception of Revelation*, has endeavoured to establish a distinction between *chozeh* and *ro'eh*. He thinks that *ro'eh* is used of true prophets only, whereas *chozeh* would, if not exclusively, yet predominantly be applied to false prophets. Isa. 28.7 shows that *ro'eh* is not avoided with reference to false prophets. According to Isa. 30.10, the two terms are quite synonymous [cp. further 2 *Chron.* 16.7, 10]. And the nouns for 'vision' are taken from both roots without any perceptible difference.

There are other designations of the prophets, more of a descriptive nature, and not rising to the rank of formal names. Such are *tzopheh*, *metzappeh* (outlooker, watchman); *mal'akh Jahveh* (messenger of Jehovah); *ro'eh* (shepherd); *'ish haruach* (man of the Spirit); *'ish ha'elohim* (man of God). These either explain themselves or will find their explanation in connection with those features of prophecy of which they are descriptive.

THREE:
THE HISTORY OF PROPHETISM:
CRITICAL THEORIES

The term 'prophet' is not always used in the stiff, strict technical sense we are accustomed to combine with it. As 'vision' came in course of time to stand for revelation in general, so 'prophet' could be equivalent to 'instrument of revelation' without particular regard to technical sense, distinguishing a prophet from other organs of revelation. Moses is called a prophet, and yet is set over against the prophets as to his communication with God [*Num.* 12.6ff.]. In Gen. 20.7, Abraham is called a prophet. The meaning here seems to be one who has special acquaintance with God, and can intercede for others. To this Psa. 105.15, refers, where the synonym is 'anointed ones'. Amos speaks of prophets raised up in the distant past [2.11]. Hosea calls Moses a prophet [12.13]. Peter, in Acts 3.21, 24, uses in succession the wider sense and the specialized application: 'holy prophets which have been since the world began', and 'all the prophets from Samuel and them that followed after'. This recognizes that there was an incision in the history of revelation in the time of Samuel, that prophecy in a new form began from that date. The reason for this has been explained above.

THE HISTORY OF PROPHETISM
We can take our point of departure for the history of prophetism in the time of Moses. Not only were there prophets at that time among Israel, but they represented, with the exception of Moses, whose case was unique, the prevailing form of revelation. Their position was a privileged one. Nor was this entirely due to pre-eminence of office. It is evident that a religious pre-eminence was involved. Moses, in Num. 11.29, expressed the desire that all the Lord's people might be prophets. This clearly shows that from the first there was a religious as much as a functional value found in the appearance and exercise of the office. This appraisal runs through the entire history of prophecy from beginning to end. The divine promise in Joel 2.28–32 extends it

into the eschatological age. Not only is Israel honoured by having prophets, the greater honour is that the people are intended to become prophets. Jer. 31.34 is of the same tenor. Afterwards the functional position of the prophets is raised. From inferior to Moses, they become in prospect like unto Moses, with an approach even to the prophetic dignity of the Christ [*Deut.* 18.15; *Acts* 3.22].

During the first stage of the new epoch in the history of prophetism, which dates from Samuel, the difference from what had existed before lay in two points. On the one hand, the office obtained a more public theocratic background for its activity in the newly-established kingdom. On the other hand, the number of prophets shows a large increase, especially if we count in the groups of collective prophets associated with such men as Samuel. Prophetism, as attached to the kingdom, did not on that account lose any of its independence. The events in the reigns of Saul and David in turn, upheld and restrained by the prophetic leaders of the time, are sufficient proof of this. A mere religious appendix of the kingdom prophecy never was. In course of time, as the occupants of the throne degenerated, it became the very opposite, an institution to counterbalance and reprove, or even to reject. But on the whole, during this first stage of development, the attitude of the prophets towards the kingdom was a friendly, fostering, protective one. Especially was this the case in the line of the Davidic succession.

As apostasy reared its head, both in the kings and among the nation, the relationship was altered. Prophets and kings stood over against each other. The keynote of prophecy having become the message of overthrow, the kings, who naturally believed in the conservation of what existed, could not fail to regard the prophets with suspicion and antagonism. The prophets were from their standpoint lacking in patriotism, in fact traitors. This change of base on both sides is followed by the invasion of apostasy into the ranks of the prophets themselves. The contrast between true and false prophets begins to play a role. False prophecy encroached to such an extent upon the true, as to bring the whole office into discredit. Zechariah predicts that in the better order of affairs to come, parents will disavow a son laying claim to prophetic calling, nay, that the quasi-prophets themselves shall be ashamed of the calling. Prophesying and an unclean spirit are put on a line [13.2–6]. This is quite a different reason for the supersession of prophecy from that forecast in Jer. 31.34, and the opposite of the favourable forecast of Joel, which hearkens back to the Mosaic era.

It has been attempted to derive the corruption of prophecy in some way from the collective form which the latter developed. This is unjust so far as the earlier stage of the history of this movement is concerned. It coincides, as we have seen, with the religious and patriotic revival that occurred in the age of Samuel, and can scarcely be discredited without discrediting in principle the whole movement of which it formed a part. The same observation can be made in regard to its intensified activity in the age of Elijah and Elisha. The historical writers plainly stamp it with their approval [1 Sam. 3.1]. It is not easy, however, to define the exact relation between individual prophetism and group-prophetism. We meet with the group-prophets first in 1 Sam. 10.5. The word here used is *chethel*, 'band', 'company'. The same meaning belongs to another word, *Lehaqah*, found in 19.20. A 'school' in any academic sense these words cannot describe. After this these designations are not met with again. But something analogous appears in the history of Elijah. The name here is 'sons of the prophets' [1 *Ki.* 20.35; 2 *Ki.* 2.3; 4.38; 6.1]. The only subsequent reference to this name is in *Amos* 7.14.

'Sons of the prophets' might be descriptive of the relation of submission and attachment in which these bands lived with great individual leaders. Or it might be simply an instance of the Hebrew idiom, which, by putting 'son' before some noun, indicates that a person is possessed of the character the noun expresses. In that case 'sons of the prophets' might not differ from the simple 'prophets'. Of course, the phrase is not a genealogical designation. But the second view also meets with the objection that some sort of distinction is clearly suggested. Amos even makes the statement that he was at the time of his calling neither a prophet nor a prophet's son disjunctively. What is the distinction? Some have attempted to seek it along the line of prophets as recipients of revelation and as cultivators of religious enthusiasm. Koenig has characterized the leading prophets as 'primary', the group-prophets as 'secondary'. He thinks the secondary prophets were mere preachers. Supernatural disclosures were not confined to the leading prophets.

The term 'preachers' is apt to obscure the very point in which perhaps a difference between individual prophets and band-prophets can be discovered. The group-prophets do not seem to have been employed in the transmission of truth as the others were. The individual prophets, therefore, were the 'preachers'. That the collective bodies were recipients of supernaturally-communicated truth is plain, nevertheless. They 'prophesied', and this can scarcely mean anything else than that they had been touched by the Spirit in a supernatural manner.

The strange bodily manifestations that took place among them likewise bear witness to that fact. These extraordinary phenomena must be attributed to the Spirit as much as were the analogous peculiar phenomena in the early New Testament Church. The Spirit has not his exclusive function in moralizing and spiritualizing. He can work also in the sphere of the semi-intelligible. Music played a part both in the production and the expression of the enthusiasm characteristic of these circles, and music lies on the border-land of that reign of feeling where mysterious forces play upon the soul, of which even he who experiences them cannot give a clear account to himself. We must not classify such things depreciatingly. They were different from bodily convulsions of purely pathological origin. They have their contact with the centre of the religious, spiritual life. As regards music, it is interesting to note that, according to 1 Chron. 25.1, the temple-singers by their singing 'prophesied'.

Taking these things into account, we shall be kept from drawing too sharp a line of division between the individual and the group-prophets. Individuals from the groups were selected to execute errands for the others. Sometimes a group-prophet was made an individual one. There seems, however, to be no evidence that the functions and experiences of the collective prophets were life-occupations. The call of such men as Isaiah and Jeremiah was obviously a call to life-long service. The assumption that Amos, after prophesying at Bethel, returned to his secular occupation at Tekoah finds no real support in 7.14. A point of difference between the two kinds of prophets may perhaps be found in this, that those belonging to the band-prophets had no power to do miracles [2 *Ki.* 6.5].

It has been asserted that Amos disavows every connection between himself and 'the sons of the prophets' [7.14]. This cannot be a correct exegesis, for the same disavowal would also include the prophets in general. Amos speaks of the sending of prophets to Israel as one of the bounties bestowed upon the people by Jehovah [2.11]. It has been overlooked that in the Hebrew form of the statement there is no predicative verb. It is just as grammatical to render: 'I was no prophet', etc.' as to render: 'I am no prophet,' etc. He was no prophet before his call, but precisely in virtue of the call he is one now. The only implied criticism that Amos seems to make of the prophets or prophets' sons of his day lies in the indignant repudiation of the priest's charge that he prophesies in order to eat bread, i.e., to support himself, and therefore should not stay at Bethel, but return to his own Judean country. We may even infer from this that Amaziah means to intimate,

'Do not take away the bread from such prophets as are native here'.

This is the first trace we discover of a deterioration within the prophetic circles. Micah later on criticizes the prophets of his own day on the same ground [3.11; Jer. 6.13]. When serious corruption of this nature appears, we are obviously on the eve of the approach of 'false prophecy' in general. The court and temple prophets at Bethel cannot have deserved the name of true prophets. And yet there is no particular reason for finding the source of such corruption among the group-prophets. We find Isaiah gathering around himself a band of disciples. Evidently there did not attach any stigma in his day to the group-formation as such [8.16]. And in the time of Jeremiah we observe that the false prophets had individual leaders, leading them astray, so that it was no matter of individuals or groups either for good or for evil. The collective movement had as good a reason of existence as the activity of individual prophets. The crisis through which Israel passed in the time of Samuel, and again of Elijah-Elisha, was but a form of expression of a religious crisis. The issue between Philistines and Israel, and that between Canaanites and Israel, was at bottom a religious issue. We must look upon the assemblies of prophets as centres of religious life. As the priestly representation of Israel was entrusted to a tribe and family, so it was quite appropriate that companies of men, under the influence of the Spirit, should represent and typify the new Israel, through their endowment with extraordinary gifts and powers. To the individual prophets such a symbolico-typical significance likewise belonged, but in their case it was to some extent obscured by their messenger and speaker function. And herein may lie a reason why the reception of truth was common to both orders, whilst the transmission of it fell outside of the province of the prophetic groups.

The modern critical reconstruction of the history of Israel's religion has laid hold upon prophetism at two vital points. The first concerns the origin of *nabhi*'-ism among Israel. The second relates to the role the prophets are believed to have played from the eighth century, B.C. onwards as creators of ethical monotheism. These two points deserve separate investigation.

THE ORIGIN OF 'NABHI'-ISM' IN ISRAEL

First, then, we have the hypothesis, widely spread in critical circles, of the Canaanitish derivation of prophetism. It is believed that the movement was not an indigenous one in Israel, but by a sort of contagion passed over from the Canaanites. The arguments adduced in favour of this hypothesis are chiefly the following four:

(a) There is in Hebrew no etymology for *nabhi'*; the thing therefore, as well as the name, must have been an exotic thing:

(b) the peculiar phenomena of the movement remind of the wild, orgiastic character of Canaanitish nature-worship;

(c) the time of its emergence coincides with the time of closest contact and conflict with the Canaanites;

(d) the subsequent history of prophetism, its gradual purification, is most readily explained on the theory of its foreign provenience.

Our answer to these arguments is as follows: the absence of the Hebrew etymology *nabhi'* has in common with other offices of a religious nature. It simply proves that the function is exceedingly ancient. The word *kohen*, priest, likewise has no ostensible root in Hebrew, but nobody infers from this that the priesthood was a foreign importation; there is no etymology in the Canaanitish idiom any more than in the Hebrew. The enthusiastic elements of the prophetic phenomena of the period of Samuel are much exaggerated. The gusher-etymology is too uncertain and too variously-interpretable to furnish any solid support. Much reliance is placed on the following contexts for bearing out the view in question [1 *Sam.* 10.10; 19.23; 1 *Ki.* 18; 2 *Ki.* 9.11; *Jer.* 29.26; *Hos.* 9.7; *Zech.* 13.6]. The first two show Saul encountering bands of prophets, prophesying with them, and engaging in certain movements peculiar to their behaviour. In 1 Ki. 18 we have the account of the story of the orgy of the Baal-prophets at Carmel. 2 Ki. 9 gives the story of the officers in camp with Jehu, who spoke of the young man sent to them by Elisha as 'this mad fellow'. Hos. 9.7 has: 'the prophet is a fool, the man of the Spirit is mad.' Jer. 29.26 reads: 'every man that is mad, and makes himself a prophet.' Zech. 13.6 speaks of the wounds (received in prophesying) which the young man will ascribe to some other cause, when disavowed and threatened with death by his parents.

It must be granted that there are some strange phenomena here. They are, however, by no means homogeneous in character. There is nothing, for example, in the remainder of the material resembling the actions of the Baal-prophets at Carmel; notice the phrase 'after their manner'. Such a thing as the cutting of themselves with knives nowhere else occurs, except, perhaps, in the decadent post-exilic period. Our danger and difficulty spring from this, that this whole group of phenomena lies so far removed from the customs and habits of our religion, that, out of astonishment at the mere facts as such, we lose sight of the great difference between the features displayed among Israel and similar features observed in pagan religion.

At the outset we should frankly acknowledge this mysterious 'irrational element' to have been an integral part of prophetism for those times. It was not a thing disapproved of, but created and sanctioned by God and the great leaders of Israel's faith. It stood in close connection with the collective form that prophetism assumed, and the fundamental significance for Old Testament revelation of which we have endeavoured above to point out.

As to the phenomena in detail some special observations may be added here. The descriptions in 1 Sam. 10 and 19 give no warrant for speaking of 'roving bands', or 'wandering dervishes'. Saul met a procession of prophets. That they roved over the whole land or through certain parts of it, is not proven by this. On the contrary, 19.20–24 indicates that at Naioth, near Ramah, they had a fixed habitation. Of 'dancing' and 'leaping' there is no mention. A distinction must further be made between what the prophets did and what happened to Saul. The passage reads: 'the Spirit of God was upon him also [that is, in like manner as upon the prophets], and he stripped off his clothes also [in like manner], and prophesied before Samuel in like manner, and lay down naked all that day, and all that night.' Observe that with the last statement the 'also' is not repeated. The lying naked for twenty-four hours, therefore, need not have been of common occurrence among the band-prophets. It seems to have been rather a special judgment visited upon Saul, something moreover which furnished David an opportunity to escape. The ancient Versions omit the 'also' in vs. 20 likewise; if this be adopted as an emendation, the stripping off of clothes may as well have been something peculiar to Saul. At any rate the 'nakedness' was not quite the same as what we understand by that term. It need mean no more than the laying aside of the upper garment. From all this to wild, orgiastic ecstasy there is still considerable distance. Raving behaviour is reported of Saul in 1 Sam. 18.10: 'And it came to pass in the morning that the evil spirit from God came upon Saul, and he prophesied in the midst of the house . . . and Saul cast the javelin', etc. The verb rendered 'prophesied' is in reality a denominative from *nabhi*'; it means 'he behaved like a *nabhi*'. The point of comparison is that he behaved like one possessed of a spirit, whose words and actions are beyond his own control. But this cannot prove that the prophet in all respects was like a 'raving madman'. It only proves that a madman could be characterized by certain symptoms of prophesying.

There is still further the term *meshugga*' used by the officer in Jehu's camp of the messenger sent by Elisha. It means 'a mad fellow', and is

still used every day as a slang term in the Yiddish language. It is now
an expression of disrespect, but was not necessarily so in everybody's
mouth at the time of Elisha. It is only the smart young officer in the
camp who applies it with contemptuous connotation. This is not
different from the way in which a company of drinking men might
speak of a preacher who appeared with a message to some person of
their number. It might be best rendered by 'fanatic'.

The word recurs in Hos. 9.7, in parallelism with *'ewil*: 'The prophet
is *meshugga'*, the man of the Spirit is *'ewil*, for the multitude of thine
iniquity and the great hatred.' These words either describe the desperate
state of mind overwhelming the prophet when he sees the judgment
come (in which case the true prophet is meant), or they describe the
madness and foolishness of the prophet who encourages the people in
their iniquitous course of action (in which case the false prophets are
meant).

A third passage containing *meshugga'* is Jer. 29.26. It occurs here in
the letter sent by Shemaiah to the priest Zephaniah. It gives the latter
authority to put into prison 'every *meshugga'* and *mithnabbe'*. Vs. 27
shows that the writer reckons among this category also the prophet
Jeremiah. Translating strictly, the two terms are not quite synonymous;
the pair means, 'every one that is mad and pretends to be a prophet'.
Besides, this is a judgment passed by a false prophet, and does not
reflect the average opinion among the people. Shemaiah was the bitter
enemy of Jeremiah.

Disrespect for the prophetic office has also been found in the question
of 1 Sam. 10.11, 12: 'Is Saul also among the prophets?' and the further
question to which it gave rise: 'And who is their father?' [cp. 19.24].
The context in which the narrative occurs makes it difficult to believe
that, at least on the narrator's part, real disrespect is intended. If there
originally was such to his knowledge, he would scarcely have incorporated into his account the quaint saying embodying it from mere
archaeological curiosity. Samuel is depicted as standing on a footing
of familiarity with these prophets: he causes the just-anointed Saul to
be brought into their company. The meaning of the proverb is obscure,
but it can hardly mean: 'How does such a decent man get into such
disreputable company?' Equally obscure is the import of the other
question. That would, on the assumption of intended disrespect, have
to mean: These fellows are people of no extraction; no one knows
their father. Neither of these two interpretations has anything particularly in its favour, except the circumstance that a better one has not so
far been found. Proverbs are often the hardest things to interpret.

The alleged disavowal of connection with the prophetic order by Amos has been touched upon above. This disposes of the first and second arguments in favour of the derivation of nabhi'-ism from Canaan.

The third argument requires but little comment. In reality it tells much more strongly against the hypothesis under review than in favour of it. At the alleged time of the rise and spread of the movement there was strong antagonism between Israelites and Canaanites. Is it likely that a man like Samuel, who stood at the head of the theocratic-patriotic movement, should have encouraged borrowing from the enemy? In order to make this credible, it would first be necessary to assume that the entire figure of Samuel, as drawn by the historian, is a caricature.

The fourth argument is easily the most feeble of all. That foreign origin presents more favourable opportunity for improving a movement of this kind, than its indigenous character, would be hard to prove. With equal, nay, greater, force one might contend that the native growth will have more of the gradualness and native attachment, which are the basis for a desire after improvement.

DID THE LATER PROPHETS CREATE ETHICAL MONOTHEISM?

In the next place we will consider the theory of the same critical school as to the role played by the prophetic movement at a later point in history. The prophets, from the age of Amos and Hosea onwards, are credited with the discovery and establishment of the great truth of ethical monotheism, in which the distinctive and permanent value of Old Testament religion is held to reside. We here must endeavour to sketch the genesis of this belief in the prophetic circles as the critics conceive of it. The phrase 'ethical monotheism' should not be misunderstood. It is not constructed on the principle of addition, as though the prophets had stood, in the first place for monotheism, and in the second place for the ethical character of Jehovah. The real meaning is: an ethical conception of Jehovah giving rise to monotheism. It will not be overlooked that in this opinion concerning the later complexion of prophetism, the critics assume towards the movement a favourable attitude, whilst, as just shown, the critical appraisal of its origin is highly unfavourable. This is the reason why it is so necessary, from the critical premises, to speak of gradual purification and improvement. Once the fact of ethical improvement, in an idealizing direction, has been established, there can be, perhaps, no serious difficulty about deducing monotheism from it. But the problem lies in the ethicizing of the conception of God from the starting-point of an ethically-indifferent or sub-ethical conception of Jehovah's nature and character. The construction we are offered by way of solving this problem is as follows:

The ethical element must have come in between the days of Elijah and Elisha on the one hand, and the age of Amos and Hosea on the other. Before the time of Elijah and Elisha Jehovah was only the national God of Israel. He was neither a particularly ethical being, nor the only true God. Some of His features were even ethically repellent. The prophets like Elijah and Elisha stood up for Jehovah, simply because they were greater patriots and more confirmed nationalists than the rest. Elijah's main trait is his insistence upon the exclusive right of Jehovah to the national service of Israel. Neither he nor his lesser successor protested against the calves set up at Dan and Bethel. Of course, they did represent Jehovah as the avenger of gross injustice. But this is by no means to be confounded with the prophetic view of a a century later, which made the entire relation of Israel to Jehovah rest on an ethical basis, and believed that it served a moral purpose. It did not differ in principle from the way in which a heathen deity might have been invoked in a similar situation elsewhere.

What then happened to create a difference in this respect? The course of external events became the great ethicizer in the prophetic mind. Israel suffered serious reverses in war. Such a thing, especially when of a protracted nature, was difficult to explain on the old basis of national favouritism alternating with autocratic caprice. As soon as the existence of the nation was threatened, the unsatisfactory nature of such a crude, incalculable relationship became apparent. The smaller nations, when conquered by the large powers, not only themselves passed from the scene of history, but with them vanished their gods. The problem of the threatened existence of Israel assumed the character of a religious problem. The national god has no other reason of existence than to protect his people. Failing in this, his usefulness is at an end. The situation became even more acute when, after the danger from Syria had been averted, the Assyrian power appeared on the horizon. From Damascus one might possibly hope to escape.

The national god was not equal to such a crisis. The alternative became: Israel is saved, and then Jehovah remains, or Israel is conquered, and then Jehovah likewise is eliminated. While only the latter seemed within the range of historical possibility, the prophets of that age shrank from even contemplating such a terrible issue. They were so attached to their God, that they dared not think of His perishing.

To escape from this desperate thought it was evidently necessary to detach in some way the national existence of Israel from the religious existence of Jehovah. This, of course, could be done in one way only: by incorporating some other superior element in His character, such as would surmount the ideas of national championship and favouritism towards Israel, in which no one could possibly believe any longer. It was not sufficient to say: Let Israel be sacrificed, but let Jehovah continue. What was needed in addition was a new and super-national content to fill up the gap created in the concept of Jehovah through the prospective fall of Israel.

Now it was this service which the ethical conception of God rendered to the prophets. For, if Jehovah were supremely ethical, then the ethical aims He pursued could be thought of as requiring the destruction of Israel. In that case the destruction of the nation would no longer involve the destruction of Jehovah. On the contrary, from the new standpoint, it would mean the vindication of Jehovah as to His innermost character. The prophets thus sacrificed Israel in order to save their God. At an almost exorbitant rate, as it were, they insured their religious conviction in regard to the indestructibility of God. At bottom, and sharply looked at, it was not so much positive interest in the idealism of ethics that made them reason as they did. In reality their ethicizing of the character of Jehovah was but the indispensable prerequisite for keeping a hold upon Him. They adored Him religiously, with a deep traditional attachment, so strong, that in the case of an enforced choice they would rather lose their people than their God. The ethical character of God was a means to an end.

But how did they come to seize upon the ethical element as precisely fitted to render them this service? The answer is that the prophets were somewhat ethically gifted above the mass. They had a greater sensitivity to right and wrong. But even this was not so much to their credit as might be at first supposed. It was rather a case of goodness arising from reaction against extreme evil. For, as a fact, the moral conditions among Israel offered abundant warrant for such a reaction. Riotous living and licentiousness prevailed, especially among the upper classes. The administration of justice was thoroughly corrupt. The rich oppressed and exploited the poor. All the elements were therefore given for framing a new conception of God. The newness consisted in this, that the prophets clearly enunciated the absolute supremacy of the ethical aspect in the nature of Jehovah. The entire religion of Israel was placed by this on a new basis. All the distinctive tenets of the prophetic theology are supposed to have sprung from it. It lies at the root of the monotheism differentiating the prophets of the eighth century from the monolatry of the preceding age, beyond which even an Elijah and Elisha had not advanced. With His character of ethical absolutism Jehovah now stood unique among the gods.

Most critics agree that this monotheistic inference is clearly drawn from Jeremiah's time onward. Some difference of opinion exists as to the period between Amos and Jeremiah. According to some the writers of this period are practically monotheistic, so far as Israel is concerned, but without as yet reflecting upon the sphere outside of Israel (so Baudissin). According to others this period is one of nascent monotheism, the prophets not expressing themselves consistently, but only occasionally passing the line between monolatry and monotheism (so Kuenen). Still others think that the whole problem had no existence for the pre-exilic prophets, that not Jeremiah, but Deutero-Isaiah, during the exile, was the first actual monotheist (so Stade). But all agree that the genesis of monotheism was after the manner described.

It ought to be further noticed that, according to the critics, the ethicism that thus came to be ascribed to Jehovah, was extreme ethicism, hyper-ethicism, as it were. It was concentrated, not in the benevolent, gracious aspects of the ethical consciousness, but in the strictly retributive aspect of the same. The Jehovah of the prophets is not so much a good Being in the sense of 'well-inclined', as a good Being in the sense of his insisting upon obedience. He has little of the genial warmth of love about Him. The emphasis weighs heavier upon the inevitable consequences of disobedience, than upon the joy of obedience. The whole view of God's moral nature has a certain unamiable one-sidedness about it. The ethics exclude the love and grace of God. This is the reason for the divisive criticism practised by certain writers of this school upon the text of the prophetic books. On the principle that a promissory, gracious attitude of Jehovah towards the people would have been utterly irreconcilable with the ethical premises of the prophets, these writers proceed to eliminate from the prophetic discourse everything that, in their opinion, would belie the manner in which the ethical convictions had been acquired. Large sections of a promissory, eschatological nature are exscinded.

In still one further respect the ethical absolutism of the new-school prophets powerfully affected the reconstruction of religion. Ethicism tends of itself to spiritualizing, and spiritualizing, carried to an extreme, resulted in the rejection of all religious usages among Israel that were not spiritual, at least not on the surface. All ritual observances, the sacrificial cult, the feasts, all images made of the Deity, were represented by the prophets, not merely as ineffective, but as reprehensible and exciting the wrath of Jehovah. Notice carefully: it is not the spiritual knowledge of Jehovah that has produced the correct ethical ideal as to his demands; the reverse process took place: because Jehovah was ethical, therefore He must be spiritual.

There is at this point also some dispute as to the more or less absolute nature of the prophetic opposition to the cult. Some hold that it was rejected *in toto* as intolerable to Jehovah. Wellhausen admits that the prophets reject the sacrificial cult of the people, because it was so grossly corrupt. Smend declares: 'The prophets reject the sacrificial cult of a people with whom Jehovah is on the point of suspending all fellowship.' But others think more radically on this point.

Finally, although this is supposed to have been a more gradual development, the ethically monotheistic conception of God gave birth in course of time to whatever there appears of individualism and universalism in the prophetic religion.

So far the hypothesis represents the movement of prophetism as tending towards a better and ideal goal. The remainder of the story is of a different nature. For prophetism proved unequal to the combat with the unethical popular religion it had ventured upon. The perception gradually dawned upon the prophets, that as pure idealists they could not accomplish anything. A more pragmatic tendency appeared as a result of this. The prophets now addressed themselves chiefly to the cult as the root-seat of all the evils denunciated. An attempt was made to turn the cult, which could not be entirely abolished, to the best possible use by making it a vehicle of ethical and spiritual ideas. For this purpose it had, of course, to be pruned of its most naturalistic excrescences. Unfortunately this pragmatism, aiming at compromise, bore in it the seeds of decay. It meant, regarded from the original prophetic standpoint, an abandonment of the absolute distinction between right and wrong. The several law-codes of the Pentateuch, with their strange mixture of the moral and the ritual, are the product of this compromise. In this way prophetism obtained its first external hold upon the popular mind, but the strength inherent in its former uncompromising attitude was broken. In accepting a fixed law for regulating the religion of Israel it sacrificed its idealistic freedom. It succeeded to some extent in uprooting the cult from its soil of naturalism, but the cult, however much modified, remained something external. The antithesis between the ritual and the prophetic loses its sharpness, until in the post-exilic prophets it vanishes almost entirely. Thus were laid the first foundations of Judaism.

The foregoing must suffice as an outline of the later history of prophetism from the eighth century onward, as the critics construe it. The criticism of its several positions is so interwoven with our positive presentation of the prophetic teaching, that we cannot help deferring it until then.[1]

[1] See pp. 234ff.

FOUR:
THE MODE OF RECEPTION
OF THE PROPHETIC
REVELATION

The prophets affirm and imply everywhere a real communication from Jehovah to themselves. They believe themselves recipients of revelation in the solid, unmodernized, unsubjectivized, original sense of the word. We proceed to enquire into the specific forms of statement in which the prophets describe this experience, and the mode in which they conceive it to have come to them from God.

That the prophets had a conviction concerning the objectivity of the process is acknowledged with practical unanimity even by those whose theological or philosophical standpoint leads them to deny the supernatural source from which the prophets derived it. This being so, it becomes incumbent on all those unable to accept the simple, straightforward explanation submitted by the prophets, who had the experiences themselves, to attempt a different solution of the problem. It is true, the old form of reasoning which simply reduced the whole matter to the alternative: either the prophets were untrustworthy characters, and then their writings are a tissue of lies, or they were honest, reliable men, and in that case we must accept their testimony at its face value with all the supernaturalism involved – this reveals a sort of historical naïveté, somewhat remote from our modern way of thinking. Not all honest, sincere testimony, backed up by a good reputation of the witness can in this way be absolutely identified with the reality of what happened, although in our ordinary relations of life it still remains. and will doubtless remain, the simple and only means of verification. But even in judicial proceedings the matter becomes easily complicated far beyond the reach of such simple tests.

Modern psychology is said to have made many things comprehensible, on which our forefathers looked as profound mysteries. But modern psychology has also revealed depths in the inner life of man, of the existence of which rationalism, with its easy-going way of accounting for things, could not have any suspicion. Modern science in this

212

matter applies in both directions: the rationalistic explanation of prophecy is as thoroughly discredited by it as any superficial and naïve demonstration of the reality and truth of the phenomena, that was current among the orthodox at one time.

There are three elements entering into the problem to be solved.

(a) The first is the psychological fact of the conviction on the part of the prophets.

(b) The second is the continuity of the prophetic movement with its claim to supernaturalism during so many centuries.

(c) The third is the remarkable body of predictions, that has accompanied the movement in its course, the whole teleological trend of it towards a distant consummation, in point of which no movement in the history of religions can be compared with it.

If we keep these three points in mind, it ought not to be difficult to show that prophetism still remains a mystery, unsolved as much as ever, and that it casts no stigma of being unscientific or outdated upon anyone, if he prefers to accept the testimony of the prophets themselves, that the revelations came to them from above.

THE VIEWS OF KUENEN EXAMINED

Kuenen recognizes the fact that the prophets sincerely believed in the direct divine source of the message they proclaim. But he thinks they must have been mistaken in this, because many of their predictions have not been fulfilled, nay, are incapable of fulfilment at the present day, or at any future day. Yet he recognizes with true scientific temper that the uniformity and continuity of conviction on the prophets' part require a psychological explanation of greater dignity than the easy verdict: they were mistaken. But the explanation he offers is a very poor one. It consists in this, that the great sureness expressed is the reflex of the earnestness and unshakableness of their ethico-religious belief. The prophets were aware, literally speaking, that no such communications from God took place, but they desired, by the representation of objectivity employed, to impress the people, that their teaching was true. The explanation is open to serious criticism both as to its reconcilableness with the antique cast of mind, and to its moral excusability. It is too modern a conception to try to convince people of the truth of the thing preached not only by earnestness of preaching, but to do so by way of a pretended direct derivation of the thing from God. The earnestness would stand in inverse ratio to the consciousness of the preacher, that he had to resort to pretence. The prophets would, no doubt, have discovered sooner than modern preachers seem to be able to do, that every such mental reservation broke the force of their enthusiasm, and moreover cut through the bond of sympathetic self-identification of their hearts with the hearts of their audience. It is easy to see that what such an explanation ascribes to the prophets is something that a high-minded man like the critic in this case would hesitate to admit as his own mental attitude.

Further there is here a failure of understanding the prophets from a purely literary point of view. Their avowals sound so positive, and realistic also, that the conscious intent of utilizing them for the purpose of persuasion seems out of the question. Such positiveness and realism are not the product of rhetorical craftsmanship.

Nor must we forget into how difficult a position the consciousness of using such methods would have brought the prophets in their controversy with the false prophets. Against them the burden of prophetic criticism was that they prophesied 'out of their own hearts'. Can that have meant that the false prophets lacked the earnestness of conviction which their criticizing opponents ascribed to themselves? Is the point not rather this, that they questioned the supernatural provenience of the message proclaimed by the other prophets? And that, while all the time they must have been aware of their own having prophesied out of their hearts, with this difference only, that they believed their heart to be a better one!

Finally on any theistic scheme that believes in a real contact of God with the prophets, however much 'psychologized' it may have been, the stigma of half-true representation would inevitably involve God Himself. How could He have indulged in or connived at such a procedure as would have lain beneath the plane of business ethics supposed to be in force between the principal and his agent?

As to the argument from non-fulfilment or impossibility of fulfilment of certain prophecies, that is a chapter by itself. Reasoning from this is very deceptive and precarious, because the fundamental premises of supernaturalism and naturalism enter into the very determination of what 'fulfilment' of a prophecy means, and as to whether it is absolutely unfulfillable at any point of time. The adoption of pre-millenarianism would greatly limit the field of the impossible in this respect, chronologically speaking. Upon the problem of 'fulfilment' we cannot here enter. The question under debate ought to be staked on the self-testimony of the prophets alone.

'KERNEL-REVELATION'

Another serious attempt in the same direction is made by the theory of 'kernel-revelation'. God is believed to have imparted to the prophets the essential kernel of the truth only, and to have left the working-out of this kernel to the subjective prophetic reflection. This would conserve at least a portion of the claim of the prophets that their message came supernaturally from God. The 'kernel' is usually identified with the ethico-religious principles of the preaching. In this case likewise the prophets must have been aware of the distinction in provenience between the two elements of their message. But here again the criticism applies that such a distinction between kernel and envelope lies far from the mode of antique religious thought. The prophets everywhere insist on their word carrying the authority of God, but nowhere indicate that this claim must be understood with the qualification named. The prophets must have been conscious of the contribution made out of their own minds to the resulting product, and yet they speak of this product in its entirety as invested with absolute divine authority. Finally, this hypothesis requires the intervening of a considerable period between the communication of the truth-kernel to the prophet and the state of ripeness of it, through reflection, for transmission to the people. As a matter of fact we find frequently that, no sooner is the message received, than it is made known to the hearers. Such instantaneousness the theory renders impossible.

THE 'DIVINATION' THEORY

In the third place we consider the 'divination' theory. This places the prophetic knowledge on a line with extra-biblical instances of a mysterious knowledge, so that the former would lose its unique character. It is a theory particularly devised for explaining the predictive element in the prophetic writings. It ranks higher, from a religious point of view, than the two preceding views, in that it places the phenomena at least in a mysterious light, and disdains to make use of rationalistic devices to account for them. The contact between Jehovah and the prophet is, indeed, a highly mysterious thing. Some of the mystery escapes us because we are led to speak of it in anthropomorphic language. Smend and others would stake the whole issue of prophetic prediction on this one analogy.

It is true, there are some well-authenticated instances in history of foresight or insight into matters far out of the range of ordinary human knowledge. In Deut. 13.1, 2, Scripture itself speaks of 'prophets' and 'dreamers of dreams', giving a sign and wonder that comes to pass, who yet seduce the people through the prestige thus obtained to idolatry. Yet a certain degree of divine influence in their activity cannot

H   215 be denied, for we are told that through this experience God proves the people. It is added, however, that such a quasi-prophet must be put to death. But to explain the phenomena of Old Testament prophecy as a whole on the basis of such a faculty of insight or foresight is not to be thought of. There are certain features differentiating all that has been discovered of this nature from the facts of prophetism. The naturalness, clearness and immediacy of the latter are here looked for in vain. Magical preparations and manipulations regularly accompany these alleged analogous processes. Much that seemed at first unaccountable has been explained on the basis of 'suggestion' or 'autosuggestion'. This field, however, while to some extent explored, remains still full of mystery. It is foolish to build upon it a comprehensive explanation of the phenomena of Biblical prophetism. Perhaps it may throw light on the development of false prophecy among Israel. False prophecy is probably not entirely made up of fraud. Self-delusion may have had something to do with it. On the other hand, there is among the true prophets a clear and not seldom expressed consciousness that the God of Israel alone can make true predictions of the future and lay bare the secret things to which the created mind has no access. Were prophecy to be explained as 'divination', then we should have to say that in this respect it has thoroughly misunderstood itself.

REVELATION THROUGH SPEECH AND HEARING

We now proceed to register the statements of the prophets themselves as to the manner in which the truth came from God to them. We must distinguish here between what falls in the sphere of speaking followed by hearing, on the one hand, and what falls in the sphere of showing followed by seeing, on the other. References to the speech of Jehovah are frequent in the records of the prophets. Sometimes Jehovah's speaking is a comprehensive formula for the whole process of bringing the message into the mind of him for whom it is intended, including every step leading up to this. He is said to speak to the people, although in reality He at first spoke only to the prophet, commissioning the latter to repeat His words in the ears of the people. For the present we are concerned only with what passed from God to the prophet. [Cp. for the distinction *Hag.* 1.1; *Mal.* 1.1; with *Hos.* 12.10.]

The most frequent formulas used of the divine prophetward address are *amar Jahveh, dibber Jahveh, ne'um Jahveh*. The first and second of these are in the perfect tense and mean 'Jahveh has said', 'Jahveh has spoken'. The third is a passive participle signifying 'that which has been oracled'. The perfect tense is important, because originally, and probably always, related to revelations imparted before the prophet spoke. That this speaking of God was meant by the prophets, not in any mere figurative, but in the literal sense appears in various ways. They distinguished between Jehovah as the speaking God and the idols as dumb gods. This antithesis entirely loses its point, if the divine speech was not to, but only through the prophets. The contrast drawn is a piece of popular apologetic. For as regards speech through the prophets, the heathen laid claim to receiving this as much as Israel, and there was no way of proving the difference with regard to indirect provenience. The difference lay precisely in this point, that in paganism there was no objective speech coming from the gods to the prophets, because the whole structure of pagan religion and revelation lacks reality [*Isa.* 41.22–26; 43.9; *Jer.* 10.5; *Hab.* 2.18].

Further the divine speech is represented by the prophets as the expression of the thinking and planning of Jehovah. Just as in man thought and speech belong organically together, so in God [*Isa.* 19.17; 23.9; *Jer.* 51.29; *Amos* 3.7]. Still more realistically, we find a mouth ascribed to Jehovah, which, while not implying a corporeal nature, yet admits of no other interpretation than that He exercises the faculty of speech in the literal sense [*Isa.* 58.14]. The prophets describe this speaking of Jehovah as coming with various degrees of emphasis. Such a variety could be predicated of a real act only [*Isa.* 5.9; 8.11; 14.24; *Jer.* 25.30; *Amos* 3.7, 8].

Once more, the prophets not merely say in an indefinite way that God has spoken, but add the indirect object: Jehovah spake unto me [*Isa.* 8.1; 18.4]. The speaking of Jehovah is assigned to a definite point both in space and time [*Isa.* 5.9; 16.13, 14; 22.14; *Jer.* 1.13; *Ezek.* 3.12]. According to 1 Sam. 3.8, 9, the voice was so external that Samuel mistook it once and again for Eli's voice. Isaiah distinguishes explicitly between his hearing from Jehovah and his declaration to others of the thing heard [21.10].

It has been objected to this mode of argument, that neither Deuteronomy nor Jeremiah places the criterion for distinguishing between a false prophet and true prophet in the reception of divine communications, but, on the one hand, in the agreement of the oracles with the principles of the true religion, on the other hand in the fulfilment afterwards. This, however, relates not to the prophets themselves, but only to those to whom they were sent. Of course, the people could not tell what had or what had not taken place in the private chamber of the prophet's intercourse with God.

There is ample ground, then, to assume that in a number of cases the speech of Jehovah was not only objective but external. The externality implies the objectivity, but this cannot be turned around, so as to make the objectivity in every case involve externality. Koenig takes the ground that all speech of God to the prophets must have been external, because thus only could an infallible assurance be produced of the divine source of the revelation. But this *a priori* ground is not sufficient to prove his thesis. Externality of revelation would not exclude every possibility of self-deception. Hallucinations of hearing are not uncommon things in excited states of mind. If the testimony of the prophets claimed an external speech as underlying every communicated message, we should have to accept this, no matter whether it was to our taste or not. But this the prophets do not claim. The resulting problem arises, how objective speech can be conceived without externality.

At the outset the confusion of thought should be guarded against, as though the inward speech of Jehovah to the prophet were identical with the product of reflection or emotion in the prophet's mind, so that it welled up from his own consciousness. This would not so much internalize as subjectivize the whole process, and as a rule it is stressed by those whose faith is not quite equal to belief in a solid revelation from God. They feel that, if somehow it could flow up as a part of the natural mental processes, the thing would appear more normal and credible. But this is not meant by 'internal speech'. The phrase is here taken to designate an inner occurrence in which, apart from the bodily ear, the prophet perceives a divine voice addressing him, and that with such objectivity as to enable him clearly to distinguish its content from the content of his own thinking.

The possibility of such a thing rests partly on the theological, partly on physiologico-psychological grounds. Theologically speaking, it is not impossible for God to convey to the soul directly sounds of words expressing a certain thought. God has control of the soul in its whole internal organization. And we must endeavour to realize that the conveying of sound to the soul *ab extra* through the ordinary process of air-vibration and nerve-conduction and brain-impression and soul-reaction is in itself a most wonderful, to us unintelligible, thing, so long as we believe in the difference between matter and soul. Hearing is a psychical, not a physical act. It has ordinarily certain physical prerequisites, but is not identical with these. What then should hinder God from producing the psychical experience of hearing in other ways than the ordinary one? The case is precisely the same in the sphere of sight-production and seeing as a psychical act. The prerequisites of seeing are physical, the seeing is psychical. It is a difficult question to answer, how the prophet could have distinguished between internal voices and speech externally conveyed. But it certainly would be presumptuous, with our limited knowledge of the borderland between matter and mind, to declare it impossible.

The grounds on which it has been assumed that not infrequently such an inner speech came from God to the prophet's soul are as follows. The root from which comes the well-known phrase *ne'um Jahveh* is cognate with roots that signify 'to rumble', 'to grumble'. It might, therefore, well be expressive of a dull, low sound, and in so far appropriate of low, whispered tones heard from within. True, we must not appeal to 1 Kings 19.12, because here 'the sound of a gentle stillness' is symbolical, the actual revelation coming afterwards. Job 4.12–16 might rather be compared: 'Now a thing was secretly brought to me, and mine ear received a whisper thereof . . . fear came upon me and trembling . . . a form was before mine eyes: silence, and I heard a voice.' The analogy of revelation through vision suggests a double mode of revelation by sound. The vision was not always seen with the bodily eye; most likely the speech was not always received through the bodily ear. The force of this analogy is further strengthened by the circumstances that in both cases, of seeing and hearing, a preparatory operation on ear and eye was required. Jehovah 'opens the eye', but He likewise 'wakes the ear' [*Isa.* 50.4].

The Spirit of God is sometimes specified as the organ for communicating the word of God. This favours the view, that in such cases at least the revelation was an inward one. The Spirit works usually *ab intra*. Koenig has denied that the Spirit anywhere appears as a source of revelation. He would restrict the Spirit's work in connection with revelation to the preparatory sphere, and excludes from it the impartation of truth itself. But there are some passages which speak of the Spirit as Revealer [2 *Sam.* 23.2; 1 *Kings* 22.24; *Isa.* 61.1; *Joel* 2.28 (English Bible); *Zech.* 7.12; *Neh.* 9.30; 1 *Pet.* 1.11]. Of course, there was such a thing as an antecedent operation of the Spirit for the endowment of the prophet with necessary gifts, such as courage, force of utterance and similar qualifications [*Mic.* 3.8].

In what proportion verbal revelation took place by external or internal speech cannot be determined. It has been suggested that, as verbal revelation gradually supplanted visions, so the increasing use of the internal word may have marked an advance in the development of prophetism. It might be said that in the inner word God comes nearer to man than in any other mode of self-disclosure. But positive evidence to that effect we do not possess. Which were the motives for the preference on each several occasion of the one to the other is hard to determine. Where the communication occurred in privacy, both forms may have appeared equally appropriate. The choice may have depended on the momentary psychical or religious condition of the prophet. There are moods in the spiritual life, even of the ordinary child of God, where the desire for an external approach of God is felt strongly. This desire is at bottom the desire for something substantial, suited to meet the weakness of faith. Every external approach of God to His people is more or less of the nature of a sacrament. On the other hand, the religious state of the prophet may have been at times so spiritualized, that the desire for touch with God took the inward direction, and the voice perceived within produced a feeling of unique satisfaction.

Where the contact occurred in public, in the presence of other witnesses, and of the people for whom the communication was intended, the natural mode of address would be the inward one. Here the prophet had to repeat the words. Suppose they had been given to him by an external voice, then this voice would have reached the ear of the others no less than his own, and the transmission of the message to these others would have become an unnecessary duplication. The function of the prophet would have been in that case superfluous.

Further the internal speech may have secured, through its immediate precedence of the delivery of the message, the exact correspondence of word received and word transmitted. The prophet could simply utter straightway what the internal voice supplied. There was scarcely an interval of remembrance; the whole thing became, as it were, one living process; the prophet became in a veritable sense the mouth of God, while lending his ear to God within. Perhaps in the writing of prophecy also the inward voice played a part. The main point to affirm is that the prophet indiscriminately calls whatever he utters in the discharge of his function 'the word of Jehovah', and means this in a strict, literal sense. The product is to him the essential thing, not the variable process. But the prophet never makes the freedom observed in the process an excuse for impugning the absoluteness of the product.

REVELATION THROUGH SHOWING AND SEEING

Side by side with the revelation through speech and hearing goes the other form, that through showing and seeing. Visions are recorded of the canonical prophets in the following instances: Isa. 6; Jer. 1.11–12; 24.1; Ezek. 1–3; 8–11; 37.1–10, 40–48; Dan. 2.19; 7; 8; 10; 11; 12;

Amos 7.1–9; 8.1–3; 9.1; Zech. 1.8; 6.1–8. No visions occur in Hosea, Joel, Obadiah, Jonah, Micah, Nahum, Habakkuk, Zephaniah, Haggai, Malachi. Taking the extended visions of Ezekiel and Daniel as units we obtain a comparatively small number. This, however, leaves out of account the cases where 'visions' are spoken of in the prophets, and uncertainty exists as to whether the word means visions proper, or is a general term for revelation. But, even counting these in, there are not enough to bear out Hengstenberg's view that the visionary form was the constant form of prophetic revelation, and that whatever speech there is must be considered as intra-visionary speech. In some cases the visionary mode of receiving a message would seem to have belonged to the introductory act of the prophet's career.

There is evidence that in ancient times visions were of common occurrence. Balaam's revelations were received in a visionary state. In the time of Moses, according to Num. 12.6, the ordinary converse of Jehovah with prophets was in a vision, and the parallelism with dreams, in which the term here occurs, shows that visions in the technical sense are referred to. For the period immediately preceding Samuel, 'word of Jehovah' and 'frequent (or open) vision' were synonyms. These facts have been construed as indicating a steady progress in revelation from the more external and sensual media to the more internal and spiritual vehicles, because sound and hearing come closer in their nature to the spiritual world than perceptible objects and sight. This is open to the objection, however, that with both Ezekiel and Zechariah the visionary mode preponderates, and that in Jeremiah visions are somewhat more frequent than in Isaiah. The personal equation probably had something to do with this phenomenon. Some of the prophets may have been of a more imaginative type of mind than others. Jeremiah relates of himself that he lived constantly amidst the scenes of the coming destruction, and that they were so vivid to him as to become exceedingly painful. He could no longer participate in any social pleasure, was 'full of the fury of Jehovah', weary with holding in [6.11].

It has already been observed that in course of time 'vision' lost its technical meaning, and became simply synonymous with 'revelation', in whatever form received. The title standing at the head of the Book of Isaiah: 'The vision of Isaiah, the son of Amoz' certainly does not mean to cover the whole book as the product of visionary experiences. The content of much of the book excludes this. It simply means 'the revelation of Isaiah'; the verb in the clause 'which he saw' has the same generalized sense: it means 'which he received'.

We can distinguish in visions proper between the nature of some objects perceived and that of others. Realities of the supersensual world may have been momentarily brought within the range of sight of the prophet. This may have been the case in 2 Kings 6.17, where Jehovah at the prayer of Elisha opens the eyes of his servant, so as to make him see the supernatural host encompassing the city of Dothan. A purely symbolical picture, had he been told that it was such, would hardly have satisfied the boy. But surely in other cases there was no need of bringing forth the supersensual realities and laying them open to the beholder. We gain the impression from the account just referred to that the prophet himself either did not need to have his eyes opened, because he had this faculty of 'second sight' constantly, or that for this particular occasion his eyes had been opened some time before. The opening of the eyes would suit equally well the beholding of supernatural realities as the apprehension of supernaturally produced pictures. There can be no doubt that in many cases the wonder was an internal one. It was then placed before the inner vision of the prophet, an inner field of vision, as it were, consisting of pictures.

But even here a distinction is possible: the things thrown upon this screen might have been psychical reproductions, portraits of the realities submitted, or they may have been symbolic figures shadowing forth the realities but not copying them. This yields various possibilities. Similar distinctions may be drawn as to the organ of perception employed in a vision. This may have been the external bodily eye. If there was external reality *ab extra*, though of a supernatural kind, it would seem that the organ of external vision would have been the proper instrument for perceiving it. It might have been supernaturally qualified for the act, but it would be none the less the bodily eye. If, on the other hand, the things to be shown were spread out on the inner field of vision, then the inner eye, the soul-eye, would be the organ of vision indicated. The outer eye for the outer things, the inner eye for the inner things, would seem to be a natural rule to follow. Still there is something of logical constructiveness about this, so that we may well hesitate to lay it down as a hard and fast rule. The whole region is a field of mystery, and other processes than we can imagine may have characterized it.

REVELATION THROUGH RAPTURE

Notice, however, that there is conceivable, as to the field of vision, still a third possibility besides the two mentioned above. A rapture of the prophet's entire personality into the region of heaven is not out of the question. In that case he would have seen not merely a piece of objective supernaturalism, descended for his own benefit, but he would have himself ascended, either in the body, or, what is more likely, in the spirit to the very realm of heaven. There has been much dispute along this line in regard to the vision of Isa. 6. Was this a vision in the temple on Mount Zion, or an opening up to the prophet of the heavenly sanctuary into which he had been transported? It is good to keep these various possibilities before one's mind in order to avoid confusion of thought, but not commendable to yield to the urge·of curiosity, where Scripture withholds details. Paul, who had had the visionary experience in a most realistic form, up to the point of rapture into heaven, modestly disclaims knowledge as to whether the rapture was in or outside of the body [2 Cor. 12.1–4].

BODILY EFFECTS

The visionary mode of receiving a message differed in one important respect from the process of audition, namely, as to the manner and extent in which it affected the body. Perhaps there was in hearing also a clearing or closing up of sense from the outside world, with entire concentration upon the one voice heard. But on its negative side this has not found expression. It is not uncommon to say in ordinary connections, that a person closes his ears or has his ears closed. Still no reference is made to this, where the hearing of divine speech is described. Only the 'waking' of the ear is mentioned, not its being put to sleep, or being closed to the outside world. With the seeing-process it is different. Here we have somewhat detailed and objective description of what happens to the body during the visionary state. First of all, of course, comes the shutting of the bodily eye. No sooner does the prophetic vision set in than the external sight is suspended, and this is not due simply to psychical concentration upon the shown image; there is a physical closure of the eyelids. Balaam describes himself as 'the man whose eye was closed', and also as 'the man which saw the vision of the Almighty, having his eye open' [Num. 24.3, 4]. The seer's inner eye was opened, whilst the bodily eye was closed. But the bodily peculiarity was not confined to the eye, for Balaam mentions as a further characteristic of this visionary experience his 'falling down'. We read of this also in the accounts of Ezekiel and Daniel. This was not a voluntary act of worship, but obviously an effect of the over-powering divine influence coming upon him. As such, of course, it was not necessarily a symptom of the visionary state. Further, however, goes what is related about Ezekiel's sensation of being carried off to a far away place, whilst yet the elders in Tel-Abib remained sitting before him [8.1ff.]. This looks like a regular rapture of the soul while the body remained where it was, and, if so, involves a separation between soul and body.

Frequently the prophetic vision in its subjective side is associated with the revelation-dream [*Num.* 12.6; *Dan.* 2.19; *Joel* 2.28]. Although the association shows that the two were in some measure cognate, the distinction shows them to have been different in other respects. In the dream there is no abnormal, disturbed relation between body and soul. In the vision there probably was, at least at times. What it consisted in is not easy to determine. The vision seems to have exhausted the body much more than would happen through a dream. In order to interpret to him a new vision the angel had to awaken Zechariah, as a man that is awakened out of his sleep. The appearance of the body after the vision was like that of a sleep. Still this does not describe here the bodily condition during the vision. It is an after-effect of something not itself described [*Zech.* 4.1]. After receiving a revelation Daniel was sick for some days [7.28; 8.27]. Jer. 31.26 is also peculiar: the prophet after depicting the delights of the future, says, 'I awaked, and beheld; and my sleep was sweet unto me'. Is the use of 'sleep' instead of 'dream' here significant?

THE INTRA-MENTAL STATE

So far, however, all this relates to the commerce between body and spirit. Much more delicate and difficult the problem becomes when the intra-mental state during the vision is enquired into. Even if we go so far as to conceive of the body as having lain in a trance, with apparently suspended animation (which does not happen in a dream), even then this would not teach us anything as to how the soul felt and reacted under the things shown within the vision. In attempts to answer this question, altogether too much has been built on the Greek term *ekstasis*. The influence of this term is due, not so much to its summing up in itself a group of Biblical phenomena, as rather to its having served at first as the translation of the Hebrew word *tardemah*, 'torpor of deep sleep' in the Greek Bible, and to its having, once in, carried with itself many associations acquired in its previous or subsequent extra-biblical usage. *Tardemah* occurs twice, first of the sleep God made to fall upon Adam before the removal of his rib, and the second time of the sleep into which Abram was put previously to his vision of the theophany that passed between the pieces of the animals [*Gen.* 15.12]. In Adam's case the sleep had nothing to do with

224

any visionary state. It simply acted as an anaesthetic. In Abram's case, on the other hand, we actually have a sleep introducing and accompanying the vision.

But *tardemah* here does not throw any light on the patriarch's mental state during the vision, although we learn from the situation itself that he did not, while in this visionary sleep, lose consciousness of things around, as would be the case in an ordinary sleep, for the very purpose of the transaction was that he should observe and notice. But the apparent source of information began to flow, when the word *ekstasis* replaced *tardemah*, for *ekstasis* is an extremely pregnant and suggestive term in the Greek consciousness. It expresses in classical Greek the state of insanity, mania, although this does not seem to have been particularly applied to the oracular process in religion. The word has also both in ordinary Greek and in the Greek Old Testament the weaker sense of 'dread'; 'astonishment'; a figurative and toned-down meaning, which presupposes the stronger one, as when we say that we are 'beside ourselves' under sudden, strange occurrences. Originally the *ekstatis* was real abnormality, insanity. Perhaps something of this crept into the popular conception of the prophetic state, since it easily appeared as a condition of lack of self-control. But that insanity has lack of self-control, and the prophetic state shows the same feature, does not, of course, identify prophecy with insanity.

Stronger, however, than popular usage, was the effect produced by the philosophical handling of the word. Philo gave it a prominent place in his system, and that in a peculiar well-defined sense. According to Philo *ekstasis* is the literal absence of the *nous* from the body. His view of the transcendental nature of God and its incompatibility for close association with the creature necessitated this view. When the divine Spirit arrives in the prophet, he observes, the *nous* takes its departure, because it would not be fitting for the immortal to dwell with the mortal. Now this Philonic conception of ecstasy received wide acceptance in the early Church, although in a somewhat moderated form. Its widest spread it obtained through the Montanists, who in the second century cultivated a type of prophecy rendering the prophet out of his senses. In order to justify the phenomena current among themselves, the Montanists claimed that the Biblical prophets had been subject to the same law. They expressed their view in the belief that the prophet was *amens*, in the visionary state. Tertullian sided with them, and spoke, like them, of the *amentia* of the prophets.

In more recent times Hengstenberg has been a strenuous defender of the realistic 'ecstasy', and in the first edition of his '*Christology of the Old Testament'* even approaches the Montanist position, although in the second edition his statements are more moderate, and he here concedes that, as between the Montanists and the Church fathers, the truth lay in the middle. In order not to do injustice to this type of view, we must carefully note the philosophical provenience of the term *amentia*. It was not meant as a synonym of *dementia*. Far less is it the equivalent of 'mania'. It simply means that the prophet for the time being is 'without his mind'. This at least was the philosophically oriented theory of Philo, although much cruder and wilder notions may have gathered around it, when handled by less cultivated minds.

It is plain on the surface of the Biblical data that ecstasy in the Philonic or Montanist sense had no place in prophetism. The Biblical prophets coming out of the visionary state have a distinct remembrance of the things seen and heard. Biblical prophecy is not a process in which God dislodges the mind of man. Its true conception is that it lifts the human mind to the highest plane of intercourse with God. And it is of the very essence of Biblical religion that its exercise lies in the sphere of consciousness. The prophets, while in the visionary state, retained the faculty of reflection and introspection. Isaiah compares with the holiness of Jehovah, sung by the seraphim, the sinful state of himself and his people. Ezekiel in later visions was aware of the similarity of what he actually saw to things shown him before [3.23; 8.4; 10.15, 22; 43.4]. Interesting from this point of view is Isa. 21.6–10. Here the prophet, as it were, becomes a double personality, one for receiving the vision, another for reflecting upon it and speaking about it to God. In the New Testament we have the explicit declaration of Paul, that the spirits of the prophets are subject to the prophets [1 *Cor.* 14.32]. A glossolalist needs an interpreter, the prophet interprets himself.

We have found in the above enquiry that the mode of seeing, while the older of the two main forms of prophetic revelation, yet continued to accompany the mode of hearing, in later times. The prophets did not cease to be *ro'im*, henceforth to remain *nebhi'im* exclusively. The coequality of the one with the other is proven by the constant double usage till the latest times. This result seems to be upset by the passage, 1 Sam. 9.9: 'Beforetime in Israel, when a man went to enquire of God, thus he said, Come and let us go to the *ro'eh*: for he that is now called a *nabhi'* was beforetime called a *ro'eh*.' The verse is an interjected remark of the writer to explain why in vs. 11 Saul and his servants say to the young maidens, 'Is the *ro'eh* here?'

Here *ro'eh* and *nabhi'* appear as two successive designations of the same office in the course of history.

The critics have not been slow to make use of it in support of their theory of the importation of *nabhi'*-ism from Canaan in the time of Samuel. This the passage could never prove, for the writer, certainly later than Samuel's time, speaks from his own historical standpoint: what was customary in his (the writer's) time had not yet been so in Saul's time. Between the period of Saul and his own a change of usage had taken place. But what he does not say is that the change had come in the time of Saul or thereabouts. It might have been later, and have had nothing to do with any importation from Canaan.

But, while for this reason of no use to the critics, the verse causes difficulty. Negatively it seems to imply that *nabhi'* was not yet in use at the time of Saul. And it would also create some difficulty to determine about what date the change of usage came in and what occasioned it. When and why was the designation *ro'eh* dropped and *nabhi'* uniformly used? These two difficulties are met by substituting for the Massoretic text that of the Septuagint. The latter reads: 'for the people called the *nabhi'* the *ro'eh*'. In the text followed by the Septuagint translators, in the place of *hayyom*, 'today', there stood *ha'am*, 'the people'. Through this emendation the statement becomes clear in its import. Of the two, so to speak official, names in use for the prophet the people had preferred for a long time to employ the *ro'eh*-title. This was still their habit in Saul's day; it was no longer so in the time of the writer. Because his readers might not be familiar with the ancient popular way of speaking, he explains its early prevalence. It was entirely a matter of popular habit of address. In no way does this contradict the statements in earlier history that there were *nebhi'im* long before, say in the time of Moses.

Perhaps we can even surmise in what this popular habit of avoiding *nabhi'* was rooted. The common people would come to a man like Samuel in the ordinary, in a certain sense trivial, difficulties of their daily life, as was the case with Saul seeking his father's animals. To that kind of enquiry the name *ro'eh* may well have seemed more fitting than the stately, serious *nabhi'*. And the man of God would also naturally obtain the information sought through vision-process rather than through speech-address from God. Such things Jehovah supplied to His servants by letting them see, for instance, the place where something lost could be found. A state of mind like this, so far from proving the non-existence of *nabhi'* rather presupposes it.

There is no occasion, moreover, for looking down upon this part of the prophet's function as something beneath his dignity, and putting it on a line with pagan soothsaying. It was God's desire to furnish the people with light even on such homely subjects. They were a people among whom revelation dwelt, and it was one of their privileges to reap this practical benefit from it. The *ro'eh* of Israel could be at the same time the *nabhi'* in the important affairs of national and religious life. It is instructive to read Isa. 8.19ff. in this connection. There is false soothsaying among Israel, but the prophet maintains not only that it is evil; he likewise maintains that it is unnecessary, because normal provision has been made for its supply: 'Should not a people seek unto their God?'

EXTREME CRITICAL VIEWS ANSWERED

Two extremes may be observed in the critical attitude towards the visionary phenomena of prophecy. The latest tendency is to approximate what took place among Israel as much as possible to the abnormalities of pagan prophecy, and to reduce the phenomena in both quarters alike to the pathology of religion. Interpreters of the prophets have turned themselves into medical students in order to discover what specific type of neurology can throw light on the symptoms. Hysteria, epilepsy, catalepsy and several other more recondite states are studied from the records of medicine, in order to make the abnormal from the physiological or psychological point of view the normal from the pathological standpoint. When a prophetic strangeness has been classified as a disease, it is supposed to be sufficiently accounted for. Hoelscher's book, *Die Propheten*, is so excessively technical in this respect as to be unreadable to the theologian who is not at the same time an expert in a highly specialized branch of medicine.

Before this psychiatric development took place, the diametrically opposite tendency existed, namely, to consider the visions of the prophets, not real experiences, but a species of literary composition employed in order to add vividness and force to their message. Some have applied this to all visions. Others would restrict it to the later period of prophetism, holding that in earlier times the visions were real. The argument in support of this theory is as follows. Some visions, it is believed, are so circumstantial and elaborate, that they cannot possibly have been perceived. They betray in numerous points the workmanship of the free composer. Some are made up of such fantastic and grotesque features that no degree of imaginative power could enable us to combine them into a real picture. They elude the painter's skill, for the simple reason that they are not real pictures, just aggregates of single scenes loosely combined. The connection between the vision and the message is often far-fetched and artificial. The complicated and artificial visions occur largely in the later prophets, Ezekiel and Zechariah, the simple and more natural ones belong to the older period.

Over against such considerations we should take into account other equally pertinent facts. We are not fitted to determine from the range of our own imagination how far the visualizing power may have extended in the prophets. The prophets were Shemites. The ecstatic state allowed of intense concentration upon a single scene. Our inability to reproduce the vision into a picture proves or disproves nothing as to what the prophets were capable of in that respect. The argument from looseness in combining, closely looked at, proves the opposite of what it is intended to prove. In the case of free literary composition a prophet like Jeremiah would certainly have been capable of producing more natural and striking symbols. This suggests that such visions are the work of God, whom in this matter we do not presume to measure by the rules of pictorial or literary composition. It may be true that the unnatural visions are found largely in the later prophets, but these same prophets on other occasions see visions of striking vividness and charm. On the theory of literary composition it becomes difficult to explain why the prophets have, on the whole, made such rare use of this form of representation. The prophets draw a clear distinction between symbolic actions and objects figuring in the reality, and symbolic visions seen by themselves. Why this distinction, if the visions were inventions? Why did not Jeremiah exhibit the almond rod, or Amos the basket of summer fruit? Most writers now admit that the older prophets did see visions. But the later prophets speak of theirs in precisely the same language. This would have been somewhat misleading, had they not actually seen them.

FIVE:
THE MODE OF
COMMUNICATION OF
THE PROPHECY

SPEECH

We have already seen that the name *nabhi'* places the emphasis upon the communication of his message by the prophet. Where the form in which the message had been conveyed was that of speech, the most natural form for delivering it would be that of reproductive speech. That divine speech can thus naturally pass over into human speech is a wonderful thing in itself. But man has been made in the image of God, and the faculty of speech forms a part of this. In all speech outside of God there is something divine-like. Besides, the prophets stood under the special control of the Holy Spirit, who plays upon the human organ where and as He will. Especially if through inner speech the oracle came at the very moment preceding delivery, there would remain no time to translate it into other language. And the retention of the same form was of official importance.

The prophets, of course, must have done considerable work in writing their prophecies. This would remain true, even if the modern theory of the redactional character of the books named after them were to be adopted. The written prophecies were in the first instance delivered in speech, to some extent at least. And the cause why writing was resorted to was a peculiar one which had nothing to do with the original form of transmission. Ezekiel has sometimes been singled out as a type of the rhetorical writing prophet, especially in his eschatological deliverances, but he was none the less a great speaker too. His audiences were so impressed and excited by the address made to them as to be daily talking against him by the walls and in the doors of the houses, and representing his speech as a very lovely song of one that has a pleasant voice and can play well on an instrument [33.30–32]. It would not be useless to study even Ezekiel for homiletical instruction.

Just as the spoken divine word calls for verbal delivery, so the vision calls for a special kind of verbal delivery, in which its pictorial

230

origin shall be reckoned with. For words were necessary here also. The prophets could not set up a stage or throw on a screen that inner film they had looked upon in the vision. The optical experience is, however, reproduced in words as closely optical as possible, and frequently the prophet leaves it at that without further explanation. He simply says, I saw. The visionary form obviously was chosen for the people's sake, no less than for the prophet's sake. Hence both in parables and allegories the medium of the objective work is likewise employed. Isaiah probably had not seen in vision the vineyard of Chapter 5. Still further the prophets are sometimes directed to turn their persons and their actions into the form of symbolism. Here is the incarnate vision.

It must be admitted, however, that some of these actions are of a most extraordinary nature, so as to raise doubt as to the possibility of their having been actually carried out. The two conspicuous examples of this are what is related in Jer. 13.1–7 and in Ezek. 3.26. To these may be added, though of less difficult interpretation, Isa. 20.3, and Hos. 1.3. It would take too long to rehearse in detail the difficulties and possibilities of these instances. The commentaries should be consulted on this subject by the curious.

MIRACLES

Under the head of the communication of the divine purpose, also the miracles performed by the prophets should be considered. The Old Testament is not precise in its definition of what constitutes a miracle or in distinguishing among the several types of miracles. The several names in Hebrew reveal this indefiniteness on the theological side. These words are: *pel'e*, something peculiar, extraordinary; *mopheth*, something creating surprise or attracting attention; *nora'*, something that inspires awe; and the comprehensive name *'oth*, sign, which is generic for the preceding more special terms. The importance obviously lies in the effect to be produced, not in the precise manner of its production.

Besides the sign of omnipotence there is the sign of conjunction, consisting in the prediction that two (possibly both natural) events will come together in time, and which in the last analysis is reducible to the omniscience of God, showing His supernatural presence in the course of things as clearly as the sign of omnipotence. All predictions are wonders, that is, when taken together with the fulfilment. This does not, however, necessarily imply that the fulfilment must be brought about through supernatural interposition. The supernatural

231

here lies in the foreknowledge; it is a species of omniscience-miracle. In such cases the name 'sign' is transferable to the fulfilling event itself [*Isa.* 41.22ff.; 42.9].

But we shall have to conceive of the connection between prophecy and fulfilment as closer still. The representation emerges here and there, that there is a causal nexus between the predictive word spoken and the event following at its own appointed time. The divine word here appears invested with a self-realizing, omnipotent power: it is a word that works miracles. Of course, this is not the word entered into matter or bound to paper, but the living word that issued from the divine mouth, and is never detached from Him.

Finally, it should be observed, that the record of the prophetic miracles is found not so much in the prophetic writings themselves, as in the historical books dealing to a large extent with the prophets. The inference has been drawn from this that we cannot place reliance on the miracle accounts, because they are not borne out by the prophets' own testimony. This is an unwarranted inference. The difference is due to the different character of the two sources. History is an account of acts, prophecy an account of words. Hence, where a piece of history-writing has been inserted in a prophetical book, the miracles are as much in evidence as in the history elsewhere [cp. *Isa.* 36–39]. The case of the New Testament is analogous. Here we find the miracles in the historical document of Acts, rather than in the Epistles. The wonders that do appear in the prophetic writings are those most intimately connected with the word, viz., the wonders of prediction. In the earlier part of Daniel, which is historical in character, the wonders occupy more space than in the later part, which bears a different impress. The idea that the disappearance of the wonder element would be one of the symptoms of the gradual purification and spiritualization of prophecy has no support in the phenomena. As prediction prevails especially in the later prophets, and prediction is regarded as a wonder-thing, one might be inclined to reverse the judgment in question, and affirm that the element of miracle appears not on the decrease but on the increase in the history of prophetism.

Besides the apologetic and a soteric purpose served by the miracles themselves, the prominence of this element in its teaching has also a typical significance belonging to the sphere of eschatology. It bears witness to the prophets' interest in the great supernaturalizing world-change expected from the future. The specifically eschatological predictions of the prophets are steeped in the atmosphere of the supernatural. Modern criticism likes to call this the apocalyptic element in the prophetic writings. While it must be granted that the later apocalyptic (non-canonical) writers have run to excess in this matter, they probably would not have done so, had there not been a solid basis for it in the canonical books. The more up-to-date criticism, which is succeeding the school of Wellhausen, has already made a much-needed correction at this point. Through showing that there was an indigenous eschatology in Israel before the time of the great writing prophets, it has greatly changed the aspect of the ancient religion that used to be placed back of the prophetic movement by the critics. Still this sense for the supernatural, as is now being realized and recognized more clearly, lies at a far remove from the pagan sphere of magic and divination. Against the latter the prophets uniformly protest. The prophetic miracle is wrought after prayer, and in dependence on the power of Jehovah working freely [1 *Kings* 13.5; 17.20ff.; 18.36ff.; 2 *Kings* 4.33; 20.11]. Of compulsion of the Deity there is no trace anywhere. And in the future epoch it will not be otherwise.

SIX:
THE CONTENT OF THE
PROPHETIC REVELATION

We confine ourselves in this place to the teaching of the great prophets of the eighth century. Coming as these do at the great turning-point of the Old Testament history of redemption, their study is of fundamental importance, and in point of newness anticipates much of the teaching of the later period.

The subject easily divides itself into the following parts:

[A] The Nature and Attributes of Jehovah.

[B] The Bond between Jehovah and Israel.

[C] The Rupture of the Bond: The Sin of Israel.

[D] The Judgment and the Restoration: Prophetic Eschatology.

[A] THE NATURE AND ATTRIBUTES OF JEHOVAH

It goes without saying that the prophetic orientation is God-centred. This is but another way of saying that it is religious, for without that, no religion deserving that name can exist. The prophets feel this so instinctively that they have no need nor occasion for reflecting upon or expressing it. It is only when reaching its highest point, and becoming a veritable passion for Jehovah, that it sets its crown upon itself by reflecting upon its own nature and delighting in its own expression. For in religion everywhere, not the instinctive, unreflected, but the clearly-recognized, the thoroughly illuminated, constitutes the finest product of the process. That is the cause why a religious experience uncoloured by thought and doctrine necessarily means an inferior thing, and may even reach the vanishing-point, where doubt arises whether it still deserves the name of religion or not. This does not mean that there is not much in religion lying below the surface of consciousness, or belonging to the spheres of volition and feeling. But it can prove its title only by the urge of ascending into the light of day and the region of praise, for in no other way can it reach the place where the divine glory finds recognition and the movement of religion attains its summit. God is not a philanthropist who likes to do good in secret without its becoming known; His delight is in seeing Himself and His perfections mirrored in the consciousness of the religious subject. No compromise is possible here. The only other comprehensive principle is that man finds his supreme pleasure in seeing himself and his excellencies recognized and admired by God. He who chooses the latter standpoint will never understand the prophets.

The one among the prophets who has most clearly apprehended this and expressed it is Isaiah. If we compare his consciousness in this respect with Hosea's, we shall find that the latter dwells more upon what Jehovah is and does for Israel, the former is centred in what Israel is for Jehovah [*Isa.* 5; *Hos.* 13.8]. While Jeremiah in his inaugural visions sees things, Isaiah in his temple vision sees Jehovah Himself. And he sees Jehovah in His temple, that is to say, in the place where everything is subordinated to God, and God sets the stamp of His presence upon everything, the place of worship. In keeping with this, Isaiah is pre-eminently the prophet of the highest type of religion. His religious sensibilities are most finely and strongly affected by the message he brings to others.

Further, this religious reaction is in Isaiah of a peculiarly fundamental character. Three primal ingredients enter into it. First there is a vivid perception of the infinite majesty of Jehovah. In the second place this has for its correlate a deep realization of the immeasurable distance between the majesty of Jehovah and the creaturehood, as well as the sinfulness, of man. Thirdly, there enters the element of unqualified surrender to the service of the divine glory. It is a significant fact that the noblest conception of religion is represented in the circle of the prophets by him who was unquestionably the greatest of the prophets in every respect.

MONOTHEISM

Coming now to the first head of the prophetic teaching on the nature and attributes of Jehovah, we begin with the principle of monotheism. As has been shown above, there is agreement on this point between us and the critical school, inasmuch as the latter not only grants the prophets to have been monotheists, but even regards them as the discoverers and first champions of the belief. Controversy as to the point of fact could arise with the left wing of the school only, namely, with those who make explicit monotheism an exilic or post-exilic product. With the others the further question might be debated, as to whether the pre-exilic monotheism from Amos downward was only a nascent, inconsistent, or an explicit, confirmed monotheism. It remains, therefore, still of importance both for a positive and for a controversial purpose to state the facts as furnished by the early prophets.

We find in them explicit statements in which at least the divinity of the pagan gods is denied, although this, of course, does not deny to these gods absolutely every sort of existence. Amos calls the false gods after which the ancient Judeans had walked 'their lies' [2.4; cp. *Isa.* 1.29, 30]. Isaiah has a sarcastic term for naming the idols, *'elilim*; this, though not of the same etymology as *el*, yet reminds of it, but by making out of the word a diminutive, represents the pagan gods as 'godlets', or (etymologically taken) as 'good-for-nothing-ones'. The false god fails to measure up to the conception of full deity [2.8, 18, 20; 10.10ff.; 19.1, 3; 31.7]. In Hosea, who comes chronologically between Amos and Isaiah, we have no such explicit statement, apart from his references to the images. In chapter 1.10, however, he calls Jehovah 'the living God' in which there may be a reflection on the 'dumb' idols.

Monotheism is likewise presupposed by the way in which the early prophets express themselves about images and image-worship. The images are represented as the work of man's hand and their worship is ridiculed. This polemic against idols is found in both Hosea and Isaiah [*Hos.* 2.10; 4.12; 14.3; *Isa.* 2.18, 20; 17.7, 8; 31.7]. It might be objected that such ridicule strikes only at the images, with which the gods were not identified. The objection might also be raised, that the same polemic is directed against the images of Jehovah, in whose case it cannot have implied denial of His existence or Deity. With reference to the first caption it should be answered that such a distinction between the god and his image is a thoroughly modern idea. The idolatrous mind forms a far more realistic concept of the image than that of a symbolic reproduction of the deity. In some way, not always comprehensible to us, the image and the god are seen in one; through the image, control is exercised over the deity. This alone, after all, makes the ridicule of Hosea, Isaiah and some of the Psalmists, fair and to the point. Where the theological distinction between image and what is imaged forth is introduced, it immediately becomes unfair and beside the point. But the ridicule of the prophets through the image is intended for the pagan gods. If it is a disgrace for the god to be manufactured out of matter, then this must be because the god is actually bound up with matter; a more remote or refined association with matter, on the principle of symbolism, would not warrant it.

We may here refer back to what was said in connection with the second word of the Decalogue.[1] To the pagans the magically-divine presence in the image exists. A deity which lets itself be manufactured or encased in this manner, to be manipulated by man, exposes itself to ridicule. This ridicule, then, proves proximately only that the pagan god is falsely invested with deity by his worshippers. In the somewhat later stage of the polemic this has apparently become different. Here the language employed is such as to suggest that there is nothing to the image besides mere matter. From this latter standpoint the ridicule becomes, of course, more poignant and incisive: it leaves nothing un-annihilated. But perhaps in the earlier period the subject had not been thought through thus far by the popular mind.

The second caption made upon the argument was, that it would seem as if the prophets through their ridicule of the images had struck at the existence of Jehovah Himself, since what they say is not seldom, nay, primarily, addressed to the cult of Jehovah-images. This caption likewise is unwarranted. The prophets actually meant to strike at 'Jehovah', that is, at the false Jehovah represented by the images, such as stood at Dan and Bethel. Hosea places the Jehovah of Dan and Bethel entirely on a par with the foreign gods or the imported deities in Israel or the indigenous gods of Canaan. He calls him outright 'Baal'.

There are a number of statements in the early prophets, as there are in other parts of the Old Testament, which vividly speak of other gods and ascribe actions or movements to them seemingly implying existence. It is possible, that this may be due to belief in subdivine, demonic existence. It is also possible, however, that such statements must be explained on the basis of rhetorical personification. It is not always easy to say which of the two is involved. Sometimes the context will tell [cp. *Isa.* 19.1; 46.1; *Mic.* 7.18]. In Psa. 96.4, we read: 'Jehovah is to be feared above all the gods', yet vs. 5 soon adds: 'All the gods of the peoples are things of nought, but Jehovah made the heavens', and in vs. 7 all the peoples are invited to give glory and strength unto Jehovah [cp. *Psa.* 135.5, 6, 15ff.].

The unlimited power ascribed to Jehovah in every place and sphere has for its correlate the monotheism of the prophets. To be sure, these affirmations do not exactly cover what we understand by 'the universe', as in its vast extent it has become known to us in the course of history. But this objection is not relevant. The sole question is, whether any

[1] See pp. 135–137.

rival power was attributed in any known sphere of reality to any other divine or sub-divine being. Of this there is no trace.

If the critical theory of a gradually developing monotheism in the era of the prophets were true, we should expect that the monotheistic belief would appear in the earlier writers in a less developed, in the later writers in a more developed form. We might be prepared for finding Amos and Hosea less consistently monotheistic in their forms of statement than Isaiah and Micah. Or, as between the eighth and the seventh centuries, we might anticipate a progress in Jeremiah beyond Isaiah. But no difference of this kind is found. Further, the monotheism of the prophets is nowhere associated by them with the unique ethical nature of Jehovah. The modern theory holds that stressing the ethical at the expense of the gracious character of Jehovah brought forth the monotheistic conviction. Mic. 7.18 reasons in precisely the opposite way.

THE NATURE AND ATTRIBUTES OF JEHOVAH

Next to the question of monotheism the prophetic teaching on the nature and attributes of Jehovah claims attention. Jehovah is called 'spirit', but this has a somewhat different connotation from what it has in our doctrinal terminology. It does not express immateriality, but the energy of life in God. Its opposite is 'flesh', signifying the innate inertia of the creature, considered apart from God [Isa. 31.3]. 'Flesh' is not yet, as later in the New Testament, associated with sin.

Among the attributes distinguished there is no attempt at classification. In Isa. 57.15, two aspects of the divine manifestation towards man are distinguished, the transcendental one, in virtue of which God dwells on high, and the condescending one, in virtue of which He bends down and dwells with the humble ones of His servants. This approaches in a broad way the well-known distinction between incommunicable and communicable attributes. To the class of transcendental attributes belong omnipotence, omnipresence, eternity, omniscience, holiness.

OMNIPOTENCE

The unlimited power of Jehovah is strongly emphasized by Amos, largely for the ethical purpose of magnifying the terror of the approaching judgment. A word for the conception of omnipotence the Old Testament does not possess. But Amos in a figurative, descriptive way succeeds in vividly conveying the impression of what it consists in. Jehovah forms the mountains, creates the wind, makes the Pleiades and Orion. He calls for the waters of the sea, and pours them out upon the face of the earth. The change from day into night and from night into day obeys His will. As a conqueror controls the land through occupying its high places, so He treads upon the high places of the earth. He sends fire, famine, pestilence, and all plagues and evil, all this again as instrumental in the execution of His judgment [2.5; 3.6; 4.6, 9, 10, 13; 5.8; 7.4].

Similar statements are met with in Isaiah in similar connections. Especially the suddenness, the immediateness of the effect produced, are stressed by this prophet. Jehovah works by a word, and this is but a way of saying that He works supernaturally. He sustains to the creature the relation of a potter to the clay, a great figure expressive of omnipotence as well as of sovereignty. In the future He will change the whole face of the earth, making Lebanon a fruitful field and the fruitful field a forest [2.19, 21; 9.8; 17.13; 29.5, 17]. The strongest statements are in the second part of the prophecy [40, 42, 45]. For Micah we may compare 1.2–4.

'JEHOVAH OF HOSTS'

One of the standing names of Jehovah is associated with this attribute of omnipotence, the name 'Jehovah of Hosts'. It occurs in several forms, some fuller, some more compact in form. It is difficult to tell whether the variety is due to a process of enlargement or of abbreviation. The longest form is 'The Lord Jehovah the God of the Hosts'. This (with the article before 'hosts') is found in Amos 3.13 only. Most common is 'Jehovah Zebaoth'. This is a specifically prophetic name of God, which does not appear in the Pentateuch, Joshua, or Judges. We meet with it first in Samuel and Kings, next in eight Psalms, in all four of the early prophets, in all the other prophets, except Joel, Obadiah, Jonah, Ezekiel. Finally, it occurs in three passages in Chronicles. Jehovah Zebaoth is probably an abbreviation, since a proper name cannot stand in the construct state. A further abbreviation is that into the simple 'Zebaoth', but this is not found in the Old Testament. The Septuagint has in a number of cases transliterated 'Zebaoth', and this has passed over into two New Testament passages [*Rom.* 9.29; *Jas.* 5.4]. Where the Septuagint translates it, it has either 'The Lord of the powers', or, 'the Lord, the All-Ruler'.

The word *tsabha'* has outside of the name four meanings, and to each of these one of the four interpretations of the name attaches itself. These four meanings are: an army of human warriors, the host of super-human spirits, the host of the stars, the sum-total of all created beings. The last-named view, proposed by Wellhausen, is thought to

239

be borne out by Gen. 2.1, where the writer speaks of 'the heavens and the earth and all the hosts of *them*'. While the plural of the pronoun shows that hosts of the earth is not an unconceivable phrase, yet it is evident that the preceding reference to 'heavens' has by way of zeugma induced the writer to draw 'the earth' into the same construction. It is not proven thereby that this was a common way of combining 'hosts' with the earth. There is, however, truth in Wellhausen's observation that in Amos the name has most comprehensive cosmical associations. Only, this is due to another cause, as we shall see presently. Some have found two other instances of this cosmical use, one in Psa. 103.20–22, the other in Psa. 148.1–4. In these passages, however, a clear distinction is drawn between the works of Jehovah in heaven and on earth, and his hosts, which shows that the latter must be sought in a specific sphere of the intelligent creation, namely, among the heavenly servants of God.

Wellhausen, besides putting upon it this peculiar interpretation, has also advocated the view that the name was coined by Amos. But this is unlikely, because already in Amos the name has several forms, and because the prophet nowhere seeks to explain it. Both features indicate that the name was in use before him. As a matter of fact it does occur in passages which on Wellhausen's own view, would be older than the date of Amos. In order to carry through his conjecture he has to declare these passages interpolated or altered from their original form. For this no literary necessity exists.

The interpretation which understands the hosts of the astral bodies has some things in its favour. 'The host of heaven' occurs most frequently in passages where astral idolatry is spoken of [*Deut.* 4.19; 17.3; *Jer.* 8.2; 19.13; 32.29; *Zeph.* 1.5]. In pagan religion this is usually based on the belief that the stars are living beings or somehow identified with superhuman spirits. It has been suggested that this reference of the phrase 'host of heaven' is originally identical with the reference of it to angels. It would then date back to a time when a similar belief still prevailed among the ancestors of the Hebrews. Its use in the name of God would involve a protest against this species of idolatry, it being intimated that Jehovah is superior to these beings, Lord over every creature. There was also a belief, not seldom associated with the preceding, that the star-angels had been set over the pagan nations to rule them under the permission of God, and the belief in this form seems to have existed and survived late among the Jews. There are some contexts in Deuteronomy, where this belief is referred to. In chap. 29.26, we read: 'they went and served other gods . . . whom He had not divided unto them.' In 32.8, the Septuagint has a text diverging from the Hebrew, which reads: 'When the Most High gave the nations their inheritance, when He separated the children of men, He set the bounds of the peoples according to the number of the angels of God.' The Hebrew reads, 'according to the number of the children of Israel'. But the difference in reading between the original and the Greek Version rather suggests that here the Septuagint translators or readers stood under the influence of this peculiar idea, and changed the text accordingly. And there are several serious objections to the idea that the name was in ancient Israel understood in this sense. In the early prophets it does not occur in contexts where the stars are mentioned. Amos in 5.8, where he speaks of Pleiades and Orion, does not employ it [cp. also *Isa.* 40.26]. The stars are uniformly called the 'host' of heaven in the singular. And they are never called 'the host of Jehovah'.

Much more can be said in favour of a view, enjoying considerable vogue at the present day, that the 'hosts' are the armies of Israel of which Jehovah is the captain. The wide acceptance accorded to this is due to its favouring the critical idea, that Jehovah was originally a wargod. Still this need not hinder us from accepting it. There is a warlike side to the conception of God in the prophets; Isaiah especially reveals a certain delight in describing the martial features of Jehovah. It would by no means imply, as the critics seem to think it does, that Jehovah had once been a war-god exclusively. An argument in favour of this interpretation has been taken from the fact that of the military 'hosts' only, the word is used in the plural, whereas of stars and angels it always occurs in the singular. The name has the plural; what else then can these 'hosts' be than the 'hosts' of Israel? [cp. *Ex.* 7.4; 12.41; *Psa.* 44.9; 60.10; 108.11].

Two things, however, somewhat detract from the force of this argument. The first is that in the Exodus passages, not the soldiers of Israel, but the multitude of the people in general are spoken of as 'the hosts of Jehovah'. The use of the noun 'hosts' is not, then, due to military associations; it arises simply from the numerousness of the people. And in the Psalm passages the hosts are not called Jehovah's hosts, but 'our hosts'. A counter-consideration is this, that precisely those passages where God is named 'Jehovah of Hosts', when they have occasion to refer to the armies of Israel, do not employ the term 'hosts', but some different word (1 *Sam.* 4. 16, 17].

Another argument adduced in favour of the military sense is, that in several instances 'Jehovah of Hosts' occurs in significant combination with the ark, which was a palladium of war (1 *Sam.* 1.3, 11; 4.4;

2 *Sam.* 6.2]. The first two passages do not speak of the ark in particular, but only of the tabernacle, and for its association even with the ark another reason would have to be found, since there is nothing military in the story of Hannah. As to 1 Sam. 4.4, and 2 Sam. 6.2, where the surroundings are more or less warlike, it yet seems unlikely that the use of the name Jehovah of Hosts is induced by the ark as the exponent of this. In the sequel of these references the ark is spoken of repeatedly, and yet it does not draw in its wake the name under discussion. There must then be another reason why it should do this in precisely the two passages cited. And the reason is not difficult to discover, for in these two there are mentioned, together with the ark, the cherubim upon it. And that points to another explanation presently to be looked into.

A further argument, and one to which some force cannot be denied, is taken from 1 Sam. 17.45, and Psa. 24.10. In the former David says to Goliath: 'I come unto thee in the name of Jehovah of Hosts, the God of the armies of Israel, which thou hast defied.' Here 'The God of the armies of Israel' seems actually to be explanatory of 'Jehovah of Hosts'. The Psalter passage is not equally convincing. 'Jehovah of Hosts' in vs. 10 is not necessarily the equivalent of 'Jehovah mighty in battle' of vs. 8. The structure of the passage seems to be rather climacteric, so that 'Jehovah of Hosts' is made out to mean far more than 'Jehovah mighty in battle'. If we assume that for David the martial sense was really associated with it, we shall have to regard this as probably the older interpretation put upon the name, one, however, which in course of time, in Prophets and Psalms gave way to another, felt to be more adequate in describing the central character of Jehovah.

Nor need the reason for such a substitution have lain exclusively in the enlarged conceptions of this later period of revelation. There is something else to be taken into account. The prophets probably felt that the times had changed. Whilst in the time of David the whole trend of the religion of Israel was towards the forcible shaking off of a foreign yoke, in the period of the prophets, when altogether too much reliance was placed on military resources, and the divine purpose was to break this unreligious, untheocratic frame of mind, the stress could no longer be laid upon what should be done with human help, but rather upon what Jehovah would miraculously accomplish. And therefore the 'hosts' become of a different complexion; they are now exponents of the heavenly, supernatural interposition of God in the affairs of His people. This is quite in line with the condemnation of political alliances, which is a constant ingredient of the prophetic preaching of our period.

So far as the prophets are concerned, then, we are led back to the older view, which interprets the 'hosts' of the multitude of angels. This best satisfies all the facts in the case. We have already found that the occurrence of the name in 1 Sam. 4.4 and 2 Sam. 6.2, is due to the mention of the cherubim. A number of other instances show the same conjunction. It is Jehovah worshipped by the seraphim whom Isaiah calls Jehovah of Hosts. In Isa. 37.16, Hezekiah's prayer, Jehovah is called Jehovah of Hosts as sitting upon the cherubim. The only place where the name occurs in Hosea stands in a context which mentions the angel of Jehovah [12.4, 5]. In Psa. 89 the name occurs only once, vs. 8, and in the preceding context the angels stand in the foreground.

Further, this interpretation most easily explains the several features associated with the name. The war-like flavour arises from the fact that the God of the angels is the omnipotent King of the heavenly multitudes, who can conquer His enemies, when earthly resources fail, nay, can even turn His hosts against Israel, if need be [Isa. 31.4]. Jehovah of Hosts is His royal name. It designates Him as the almighty King both in nature and history [Psa. 103.19–22; Isa. 6.5; 24.23; Jer. 46.18; 48.15; 51.57]. In the Orient the might of a king is measured by the splendour of his retinue.

JEHOVAH'S RELATION TO TIME AND SPACE

Next to Jehovah's omnipotence His relation to time and space come under consideration. In regard to God's presence in space two representations occur. He abides in Zion, whence He roars [Amos 1.2], and where He has His royal throne [Isa. 2.3; 8.18]. Hosea calls Canaan Jehovah's land [9.3]. These statements do not involve any earthly limitation of God's presence. They are not remnants of a crude theology. These writers elsewhere represent God as dwelling in heaven [Hos. 5.15, of a return to heaven; Isa. 18.4; 33.5; Mic. 1.2, 3]. In Zion there is a presence of gracious revelation. Of course, the same is true with reference to heaven, for heaven, no more than any locality on earth, can circumscribe or bind God. The heaven is His throne, and the earth His footstool. According to Amos 9.2, the reach of Jehovah's power is absolutely unlimited by space. True, this is expressed in anthropomorphic popular language. There is no hint of the idea that God is above all space, and strange to it in His own inner life. He, of course, recognizes space as an objective reality in the existence of the creature, but His own divine mode of existence it does not affect.

The same relation applies as between Jehovah and time. In popular language, such as the prophets use, eternity can only be expressed in terms of time, although in reality it lies altogether above time. Some have found in Isa. 57.15, the theological conception of eternity as a sphere enveloping God, in the same manner as time is that in which, by reason of the structure of his consciousness, man necessarily dwells. But the words rendered in the Authorized and Revised Versions by 'that inhabits eternity' are also capable of the rendering, 'that sits enthroned for ever', which would yield only the ordinary idea of duration without beginning and without end. Among the early prophets it is only Isaiah who reflects upon this mysterious and majestic divine attribute. In the description of the Messiah [9.6], the title *abhi'ad*, now frequently rendered by 'father for eternity', might perhaps mean 'father of eternity', although this would be an even higher flight into the realm of the transcendental than the idea of God's inhabiting eternity.

Indirectly the eternity finds expression in various ways. Inasmuch as Jehovah is the Creator of all things, He must have existed before every creature and be prior to every development in history. He is the first and the last, because He has laid the foundation of the earth and spread out the heavens [*Isa.* 44.6; 48.12, 13]. He calls the succeeding generations of men from the beginning [*Isa.* 41.4]. Together with these statements sometimes occurs the divine self-designation, 'I am He', which is interpreted to mean, I am the same, not subject to change through the flux of time, especially as implying a warrant for the unchanging faithfulness of Jehovah. This would be the same thought which we found expressed in Ex. 3.14, in the phrase 'I am that I am', and that is thenceforth associated with the name Jehovah as such.

OMNISCIENCE

Jehovah's omniscience finds expression in connection with His omni-presence, and His ability to predict things. Because He is everywhere, He knows whatever occurs. He declares unto man what is his (man's) inward thought [*Amos* 4.13]. Hosea says, 'The iniquity of Ephraim is bound up, his sin laid up in store'. Every sin committed by the people is present before God; it cannot be lost any more than can money kept carefully in a bag [*Hos.* 13.12]. God's eternity comes into play here also. Being before all that happens, He has been able to foretell many things that came to pass, and now challenges the pagan gods to measure themselves with Him in further predictions [*Isa.* 41.22–24; 43.9–13; 44.6–8]. This implies that His foreknowledge is intimately connected with His purpose. It is no magical divination of uncertain contingencies, but the natural concomitant of His plan. 'Jehovah does nothing, but He reveals His secret unto His servants the prophets' [*Amos* 3.7]. It is in vain to seek to hide one's counsel from Jehovah, as the politicians try to do, who work in the dark and say: Who sees us, and who knows us? This is in vain, because Jehovah is, in reference to all plotting of man, as the potter is to the clay: He fashions the very mind that conceives the thought of hiding from Him. Man's hiding from Jehovah is an object of Jehovah's own purpose [*Isa.* 29.15, 16].

HOLINESS

Another transcendental attribute is the 'holiness' of Jehovah. The Hebrew for the adjective is *qadosh*, the corresponding noun '*qodesh*'. Of the verb the Niphal, Piel, Hiphil and Hithpael species are in use. But all these verbal forms are derivatives from the noun or adjective; they therefore can afford no help towards ascertaining the fundamental meaning beyond what the noun and adjective give, and these give nothing by way of etymology, because the whole root with all its derivatives has been monopolized by religion, leaving us to guess what, outside the sphere of religion, its physical root-signification may have been. And such is the case not only in Hebrew, but likewise in the cognate languages. Some compare the radicals with those of the root *chadash*, 'to shine', from which is formed the adjective for 'new', the new thing being the shining thing. This would be in accord with the positive aspect of the Biblical idea of 'holiness', that of purity, and to it the ethical application of the idea would naturally attach itself. Others make the derivation from a root-group having for its first radicals the combination *qad*, in which inheres the idea of 'cutting', of 'separation'. On this view the branch of the concept which denotes aloofness, majesty, lies nearer the root-concept. The latter of these derivations deserves the preference.

The reasons for this preference are, first: it is easier to subsume all that pertains to the idea of holiness under the concept of separation, than, pursuing the reverse order, to start with the notion of purity. The transition from majesty to purity seems easier than that from purity to majesty. In the next place, the opposite of *qadosh* is *chol*; the latter means 'loose', 'open', 'accessible': it is natural, then, to assume that *qadosh* is originally 'separated', 'cut off'; 'non-trespassible' [1 *Sam.* 21.5; *Ezek.* 42.20; *Amos* 2.7]. And thirdly, a certain synonymity can be observed between the idea of holiness and that connected with the root *cherem*. The Hiphil of this latter root means 'to devote', and this starts from the idea of separating (cp. 'harem' and 'Hermon').

Starting then with the concept of 'cutting off', we must endeavour to trace the development of the word, and in what manner it came to be applied to the Deity. The original sense is a negative one. And it is a practical one, describing a rule of behaviour to be observed with relation to the Deity and His surroundings. Beginning to speak of an 'attribute' of God can only lead to misunderstanding. 'Holiness' is not in the first instance what a god is, but it teaches what ought not to be done to a god, that is, come too familiarly near. 'Unapproachability' would best express it. But the further feeling is that this rule of exclusion is not something arbitrary; it is due to the fact that the divine is divine, and that it insists upon having this distinction between itself and the creature recognized. Here, then, a positive element enters in through the consciousness on God's part of His distinctness and His resolve to maintain the distinction and give it external expression. A shrine is not indiscriminately open, the entourage of the deity and of the shrine constitute a barrier for approach, which, when violated, excites the resentment of the deity.

Thus far the notion is not one of Special Revelation; it is not confined to Israel or the Old Testament. The Phoenicians, for instance, speak of 'the holy gods'. But under the influence of Special Revelation the idea is immeasurably deepened. It is safe to say that no Shemitic pagan ever looked upon his god in the same manner that Isaiah did when having the vision in the temple. Since ascription and feeling of holiness are at the bottom a recognition of deity, it must follow that the true, inward, consummate sense of it can be reached only there, where the conviction of the uniqueness, not of a god as such, but of Jehovah as the only true God, exists. As Deity obtains a new meaning, when we pass over from paganism to Israel, so does holiness. Notice that the idea of majesty and exaltation above the creature is not abandoned; it is only deepened and purified, and remains a standing safeguard against every vulgar familiarity with God, such as would undermine the very basis of religion.

Taking the divine holiness in this form, we can easily perceive that it is not really an attribute to be co-ordinated with the other attributes distinguished in the divine nature. It is something co-extensive with and applicable to everything that can be predicated of God: He is holy in everything that characterizes Him and reveals Him, holy in His goodness and grace, no less than in His righteousness and wrath. An attribute, strictly speaking, holiness becomes first through its restriction to the ethical sphere.

There are certain passages in the Old Testament that clearly illustrate this general conception of the majesty-holiness of Jehovah. The Song of Hannah [1 *Sam.* 2.2], addresses God in these words: 'There is none holy as Jehovah, for there is none beside Thee, neither is there any rock like our God'; again, Hos. 11.9: 'I am God and not man, the Holy One in the midst of thee (Israel).' We can explain from this general meaning the association also between holiness and God's dwelling on high [*Isa.* 57.15]. The heavens are the highest and most intimate shrine, where Jehovah dwells alone; hence the striking contrast, when over against this is set His condescension to the humble. The same association exists with Jehovah's eternity. This likewise is something so specifically divine that it sets Him apart from all that is created and exists in time. In the passage just quoted, God's being enthroned for ever and His holiness stand side by side. Habakkuk exclaims: 'Art not Thou from everlasting, O Jehovah my God, mine Holy One; we shall not die' [1.12]. It is the same with the divine omnipotence, for this too belongs to Jehovah alone. In the song of Ex. 15 God is celebrated as 'glorious in holiness, fearful in praises, doing wonders'. According to Num. 20.12, Moses and Aaron are rebuked for not having 'sanctified' Jehovah (that is to say, for not having recognized and proclaimed Him as 'holy'), when they failed to ascribe to Him the omnipotence that could make water flow from the rock at a simple word of command. Especially in the prophet Ezekiel this association with omnipotence is frequent. One might almost say that here holiness is equivalent to almighty power. God complains that His holy name has been profaned among the nations through the captivity of Israel, because it made the heathen doubt His omnipotence to protect and defend and deliver His people. Hence in order to sanctify His name again (that is to say, to exhibit Himself as omnipotent), He will gather them and bring them back into their land. 'My great name' is now interchangeable in this prophet with 'my holy name'. The subjective response from man to this majesty-holiness consists in awe and reverence [1 *Sam.* 6.20; *Isa.* 6.2, 3], where even the seraphim, though not sinful, recognize it with trembling [*Isa.* 8.13].

More familiar to us is the specifically ethical aspect of 'holiness'. This is due to its having almost monopolized the word in the New Testament. Still it has not entirely supplanted the general majesty-holiness, as the second petition in the Lord's prayer may remind us. But, what is of more importance, the ethical meaning does not stand in the Old Testament simply co-ordinated with the majesty-meaning, as if these represented two disconnected ideas. On the contrary, the ethical sense bears very plainly upon its face the impress of its development out of the majesty-idea. The development starts with the

I   247 experience that by a sinful being the majesty of God is far more keenly felt than by a sinless one. The seraphim in Isa. 6 feel the majesty and react to it with awe; the prophet feels this same thing, but feels it as a sinner; hence his exclamation, 'Woe is me! for I am undone; because I am a man of unclean lips and I dwell in the midst of a people of unclean lips.' This is a sense, not of general fear, but of moral dissolution. The reaction upon the revelation of Jehovah's ethical holiness is a consciousness of sin. But this consciousness of sin carries in itself a profound realization of the majesty of God. It contemplates the holiness not as 'purity' simply. It were better to define it 'majestic purity' or 'ethical sublimity'. It is associated with exaltation no less than the other branch. Especially in Isaiah this intermarriage between majesty and purity is clearly observable. The prophet likes to speak of it in terms of dimension rather than of intensity. 'Jehovah of Hosts is exalted in judgment, and God the Holy One is sanctified in righteousness' [5.16; cp. *Psa.* 15.1; 24.3].

From this interweaving with the idea of majesty we may further explain that holiness becomes the principle of the punishment of sin. From mere purity, which is a negative conception, this could never follow, for purity might satisfy itself with a mere revulsion from sin or a shutting up of itself against sin. As soon, however, as the element of majesty is made to mingle with that of purity, the latter becomes an active principle, that must vindicate itself and uphold its own honour. Holiness thus operating is represented as the light of divine glory turned into a flame devouring the sinful [*Isa.* 5.24; 10.17; 33.14, 15]. The same colouring received from the majesty of God is perceptible in the other, benevolent, ethical attributes. According to Psa. 103.1ff., the 'holy name' of God underlies such gracious manifestations as are enumerated in vss. 2–5.

Side by side with holiness in God Himself, holiness is predicated of certain things that are more or less closely related to Him. The temple is holy, heaven is called holy, the sabbath is holy, the mountain of Jehovah is holy. We have already seen how this is a natural consequence of the primary meaning of the word. If Jehovah is unapproachably majestic, then it becomes important to draw a circle of holiness around Him, which shall bar out the 'profane'. On our view the holiness predicated of God is the primary, original conception, the holiness of the other things is derivatory. The divine holiness radiates, as it were, in every direction, and creates a light inaccessible.

Some writers, however, have taken the opposite view of the sequence of these two ideas. They assume that at first certain objects entering into the cult of the deity were considered holy, and that afterwards this way of speaking passed over from the objects to the god into whose cult they entered. It has even been suggested that the transfer may have been brought about through the images, which were both sacred things devoted to the worship of the deity, and identified with the gods themselves. But this would have been an utterly unintelligible procedure. What could the holiness of an object, considered as ante-dating the custom of calling the gods holy, have meant? To say that they were 'consecrated' is no answer, for it presupposes that the deity is sacred. The only answer that could be given would be that the things were set apart as the property of the god, in other words, 'holiness', when predicated of a thing, would be equivalent to 'the property of the god'. But on this view it becomes quite incompre-hensible how the transition of the attribute to the deity ever took place. If the thing is holy, because it is exclusive property, what could it mean that Jehovah was exclusive property? The proximate answer to this would probably be: He is the property of those who are holy, that is Israel. But on that view the idea would become a purely reciprocal one, in which the god would have no priority to man.

This certainly is not the impression we receive from the Old Testa-ment usage, which stresses so strongly the exclusive application of the idea to God. Moreover, the difficulty arises, that on this view of the matter the existence of private property must have preceded in time the rise of the idea of holiness. Diestel, who advocates the priority of thing-holiness or at least its simultaneity with god-holiness, seeks to prove his theory with two arguments. The one is derived from the name 'the Holy One of Israel', frequent in Isaiah, occurring also in Jeremiah and the Psalter. He takes it to mean, 'the One who conse-crates Himself to Israel'. Grammatically this is possible, for on the same principle the sabbath is called 'the holy one of Jehovah', that is to say, dedicated to Him. So is Aaron. Still, the usual construction on such an understanding would have been with the preposition *lamed*, 'holy to Israel'. But an objection to Diestel's view is that Isaiah uses the name not exclusively with favourable reference to Israel; sometimes the opposite is the case [5.19, 24].

On account of this it is better to interpret the name as joining two thoughts in one: Jehovah is the Holy One, and Jehovah is the God of Israel. His appurtenance to Israel is indeed affirmed, but it finds expres-sion in the phrase 'of Israel', and 'Holy' stands in the ordinary (ethical-majestic) sense to describe His nature. The other fact relied upon by Diestel has already been touched upon above. He thinks that because holiness can be associated with benevolent divine intent towards Israel, this must rest on its being a name for Jehovah's consecration to Israel. We saw that this combination has no other purport than to ascribe to the attributes in question a unique richness and quality.

The derived holiness of things and persons in the service of the deity or in the neighbourhood of its dwelling-place occurs, as has been shown, both in the circles of paganism and in revealed religion. But there is a difference in principle as to the manner in which the idea has been worked out. The background of the concept in paganism is of a physical, naturalistic kind. The derived holiness was conceived as a vague influence passing over to persons and things. One might compare it to an electrical current, with which everything in the vicinity of a shrine is charged. It makes things dangerous to the touch. It is different among Israel. Though the same dangerous character may belong to certain things (for instance, the ark), yet this is due only to a free sanctifying act of God. Thus God 'hallowed' the sabbath, not because it inherently possessed a peculiar character, to which magic and superstition could attach themselves, but because it was His will that the day should bear a peculiar significance reminding of and binding it to the service of God.

The specific connotation of 'holiness', as predicated of man, both in the Old Testament and the New Testament, should be carefully noted. When a man is declared to be ethically holy, even where the conception has been thoroughly spiritualized, the meaning is never simply that of moral goodness, considered in itself, but always ethical goodness seen in relation to God. The idea marks the consecration of ethics to religion.

RIGHTEOUSNESS

Midway between the transcendental and the communicative attributes stands the righteousness of Jehovah. The Hebrew words are *tsedek* and *tsedakhah*; the adjective is *tsaddiq*. First of all it ought to be observed that when righteousness is predicated of Jehovah, the analogy is not the duty of fair dealing between man and man, but always the procedure according to strict justice on the part of a judge. There are only apparent exceptions to this, as when, for the sake of metaphor, God is represented as Himself appearing in court seeking a verdict on His own action [Psa. 51.4]. As a rule the righteous God is the righteous judge. Now a judge among men is not called righteous simply because he follows an instinct of fairness towards the parties before him, but because he rigidly adheres to the law above him. Thus the question arises how this idea can be transferred to God, who has no law above Him. Still, the prophets and the Old Testament in general adhere to this form of representation. Nor is this with them a convenient anthropomorphism simply. The idea lies behind it, that underlying the decisions of Jehovah lies His nature. That is the law, not, to be sure, above Him, but yet truly within Him. And the same presupposition applies when not merely in a case of decision under the law, but also in the making of the law Jehovah is called righteous. The law was not made according to arbitrary fiat, it is a righteous law, because conforming to the divine nature, higher than which there is and can be no norm [*Deut.* 4.8].

This forensic or judicial righteousness of Jehovah further branches out in several directions. We can distinguish

[1] a righteousness of cognizance,
[2] a righteousness of retribution,
[3] a righteousness of vindication, and
[4] a righteousness of salvation, shading off into
[5] a righteousness of benevolence.

[1] *First, then, the righteousness of cognizance*
By this we mean that Jehovah is held to take notice and keep account of all moral conduct. This applies both to individuals and to nations collectively. All conduct falls under the divine jurisdiction. Here it should be remembered that God, while functioning as judge, none the less remains God, and His being God cannot be separated from His procedure as judge. In ordinary life it is not the business of a judge to watch the conduct of men subject to his jurisdiction. From Jehovah's oversight nothing escapes. Nor is He in any relation a disinterested spectator: the cognizance is with a view to corresponding action.

Amos has given most emphatic expression to this. To him the divine omniscience has practically become the pervasiveness of ethical appraisal and ethical control on the part of Jehovah. Righteousness and God are identical; to seek the one is to seek the other [5.4, 6, 14]. To such an extent does the prophet feel righteousness to be the inward governing principle of world-control, that it appears to him as the normal, the departure from which is monstrous and absurd [5.7; 6.12]. God stands beside every wall of conduct, a plumbline in His hand [7.8]. In this figure, however, the cognizance-aspect is seen at the point of turning into that of retribution, for the plumbline was used not merely for measuring, but likewise for tearing down [*Isa.* 28.17].

[2] *Secondly, therefore, Jehovah is righteous as the One who punishes sin*
The modern ethical admiration for the prophets but too often over-

looks this feature of their teaching. Ritschl has even denied that the punishment of sin appears anywhere in the Old Testament, except in some of the latest writings, as a result of the divine righteousness. He would interpret the attribute as a benevolent one. Going back to the physical root-meaning of 'straightness' he defines it as 'the order and normal consistency with which God acts to secure for the righteous and pious the attainment of salvation through protection from the wicked'. Only incidentally, because the positive beneficial end cannot be attained otherwise, the destruction of the wicked results. They stand in the way of God's plans and must be swept aside.

Our criticism upon this interpretation should not be that it is entirely wrong. There is a meaning of the term 'righteousness' imparting to it benevolent character and sometimes losing sight in doing so of the retribution administered to the wicked. We shall presently see what there is of this in the prophets. Ritschl's mistake does not lie in this either, that the later writings of the Old Testament evince a keener sense of this terrible side of the divine treatment of sin. The later generations had learned through the bitter experience of the judgment how true and inavertible the execution of this principle was. The more frequent occurrence of the word itself, for instance, in the penitential prayers of that period, may serve as proof of this [2 *Chron.* 12.6; *Ezra* 9.15; *Neh.* 9.33; *Lam.* 1.18; *Dan.* 9.14]. But the mistake of Ritschl lies in his taking part for the whole. Still, so far as the actual occurrence of the idea in the Old Testament is concerned, he was not mistaken.

We must, however, emphatically insist that there is a retribution for sin in the prophets and that this is for them associated with the word 'righteousness'. In fact Amos and Isaiah are all emphasis on this. The word is not lacking, but its relative infrequency is proof of its un-worded presence to the mind of the prophets. There are things so self-understood that scarcely articulate expression is required for voicing them. The term is found in Amos 5.24: 'let justice roll down as waters and righteousness as a mighty stream.' This should not be interpreted as a demand for uprightness from Israel. Israel, being so degraded and corrupt as the prophet represents it to be, it would have been strange to ask for uprightness of such sudden and copious production as the figure implies. The idea is rather, that, the time for reasoning and expostulation having gone by, nothing remains but divine judgment rushing down and sweeping away the sinners. The thought of the absolute necessity of this has made so deep an impression on Amos' mind, that he almost loses sight of everything else. There is a grandiose one-sidedness in this prophecy; Amos is the preacher of justice and retribution *par excellence*. His mind is carried away by the unparalleled energy, one might almost say impetuosity, of the divine resentment against sin. Jehovah, according to Amos, executed righteousness, not from any lower motive, such as safeguarding the structure of society, or converting the sinner, but from the supreme motive of giving free sway to the infinite force of his ethical indignation. In Isaiah we meet with essentially the same conception, although not perhaps in such impressive grandeur as with Amos. In two passages the divine righteousness is explicitly named as bringing the judgment on sin [*Isa.* 5.16; 10.22].

[3] *The third aspect of righteousness in the prophets is that of vindication*
Jehovah decides between two causes, puts the one in the right, the other in the wrong. He does this as part of His world-government, to which all issues are subject, but more particularly, because the fulfilment of His purpose is involved. The idea is soteric, though having in it a principle of universalism. It may be applied to individuals, but also collectively. The Psalmists sometimes claim that they are righteous, and appeal to Jehovah to acknowledge this and treat them accordingly. This has caused difficulty with interpreters on account of its seeming to run athwart the principle of unmeritoriousness in God's dealing with His people. The difficulty is relieved by giving such statements their proper setting. It is not over against God in the abstract, that the pleaders claim to be righteous, but over against their adversaries, who persecute them, not, however, for private reasons, but on account of their identification with the true religion.

The same holds true where the claimant is not an individual but the personification of Israel. In the Psalms it is not always easy to determine whether the praying subject is an individual or the congregation of Jehovah. The principle, however, is the same in both cases. However sinful against Jehovah, Israel stands in the world for the true religion, the cause of God is bound up with her destiny. Over against her oppressors and persecutors she is in the right, although these at the same time are the instruments of God in pressing His claim against Israel. But they go too far and do not understand the merely instrumental nature of the service they render. It is the part of the divine righteousness to declare this, in doing which, for a moment, the issue between Jehovah and Israel may be put to one side. But not seldom also the sight of Israel's humiliation and sorrow seems to move Jehovah to deep compassion, and becomes the occasion for a signal display of grace towards His suffering people. An instructive and touching passage in this connection is Mic. 7.9, where Israel speaks: 'I will bear the indignation of Jehovah, because I have sinned against Him: until He plead my cause, and execute judgment for me: He will bring me forth to the light, and I shall behold his righteousness' [cp. for the righteousness of vindication, *Isa.* 41.10, 11; 50.8; 51.5; 54.1, 14, 17; 59.16, 17].

[4] *Out of this reasonable righteousness of vindication, that of salvation easily develops*

So far, even in the vindication of Israel against her enemy, the setting is plainly forensic. God acts in the instances cited plainly in the capacity of a judge. There are, however, cases where righteousness is spoken of as a source of salvation without particular reflection on the righting of the people's wrongs from the side of their enemies. This saving righteousness can appear as an attitude or intent in God [*Isa.* 46.4, 13]. But it can also be objectified, so as to acquire existence and embodiment outside of Jehovah, the product of the righteousness as it is in Him. Nay, it can even appear in the plural: 'righteousnesses' [*Isa.* 45.24; *Mic.* 6.5 *Heb.*]. It is synonymous with such terms as salvation, light, glory, peace [*Isa.* 46.12; 51.5, 6, 8; 56.1; 59.9, 11; 61.3, 10; 62.1, 2]. Isaiah 49.4 is the only passage where the salvation-idea and the judicial-award-idea intermingle: 'Yet surely the righteousness due to me is with Jehovah, and my recompense with my God.'

These passages, all in the latter part of Isaiah, furnish Ritschl with the evidence for his benevolent construction of the idea of 'righteousness' in general. It cannot be denied that here his contention is right, and credit due to him for having brought light into the facts. But his recurring upon the root-idea of 'straightness', and framing his definition upon it, is not thereby proven correct. It reflects his desire to cut the whole idea loose as much as possible from its forensic moorings. It need not be absolutely rejected, however, on that account. To us a sufficient explanation seems to be found in this, that the judge is commonly expected to be the saviour of the wronged and oppressed. When it is forgotten that he does this as a judge, and only the beneficent intent and the desirable result are remembered, the judge, as it were, disappears from the scene, and only the saviour remains. To us the association of righteousness in God as Judge on the one hand, and saving procedure on the other, [*Psa.* 51.14] appears more or less incongruous, just as the same combination of holiness with saving procedure, previously observed, has something strange for us. Compare, however – and it is found in the New Testament [1 *John* 1.9] – 'He is faithful and just to forgive us our sins.'

For the pluralizing of the idea noticed in Isa. 45.24, and Mic. 6.5, analogies have been discovered outside of the prophets [*Judg.* 5.11; 1 *Sam.* 12.7; *Psa.* 11.7; 103.6]. According to some writers, however, this is a different usage, with its own peculiar etymology, and the rendering ought to be 'victories'. But the two ideas, perhaps, do not lie so far apart as is imagined. Even if the term be rendered 'victories', there may be reflected in this the belief, so common in war, that victory is a practical verdict from the deity, declaring the victor in the right. On this view the instances cited should be classified with the preceding rubric, the righteousness of vindication.

[5] One step farther still, *the term 'righteousness' is removed from its forensic origin where it comes to stand for 'generosity', 'alms-giving'* This is a late development. Instances occur in Dan. 4.27 (Aramaic); Psa. 112.3, 9; Prov. 10.2; 11.4. Examples of it also occur in the New Testament [*Matt.* 6.1; 2 *Cor.* 9.9, quoting freely from the Psalm]. Undoubtedly in Judaism there was connected with the usage as such a sentiment of self-righteousness. Hence our Lord's criticism of the spirit, while retaining the current word.

EMOTIONS AND AFFECTIONS

The next group of attributes consists of what may be called the 'emotional' or 'affectional' dispositions in Jehovah's nature. Most of the material for this is found in Hosea and the second part of Isaiah. Hosea's temperament was strongly emotional, and therefore adapted for giving expression to this side of the divine self-disclosure. We are here in a sphere full of anthropomorphism, but this furnishes no excuse for neglecting or glossing over the subject. An anthropomorphism is never without an inner core of important truth, which only has to be translated into more theological language, where possible, to enrich our knowledge of God.

The prophet Hosea was not unaware of the relativity and limitations of this mode of description, as may be seen from 11.9: 'I will not execute the fierceness of mine anger . . . for I am God, and not man, the Holy One in the midst of thee.' What other prophets affirm concerning God in terms of will and purpose, Hosea expresses in language suffused with emotion. He speaks of the divine resentment of sin as 'hating' [9.15]. God's intention to punish Israel is 'a strong desire' [10.10]. 'Anger' appears as a motive for judgment [11.9; 13.11]. The strongest expressions are found in 5.14; 13.7, 8. Still the tendency towards this is not wholly absent from Isaiah either [42.13, 14; 59.17; 63.3–6].

The terms are usually derived from violent physical processes, but we must not forget that the language formed such words before the prophet, and the latter only made use of them. As to anger, *chemah* means 'a boiling heat within'; '*aph* is 'the snorting quick breathing' of an angry person; as its opposite, '*erekh* '*appim*, literally 'long breathing', means 'longsuffering'; *za'am* is 'seething heat'; '*ebhrah*, 'the overflowing of passion'.

But not only the dangerous, likewise the friendly, benevolent manifestation of Jehovah's nature is expressed, in similar terms. The most general term for this is *chesed*, a word which has received the most varying renderings, but, taking all in all, is best rendered by 'loving-kindness'. It expresses the warm, affectionate feeling that should exist between persons bound together in a previous bond of love. It presupposes love, but is even more than that. Compare Job 39.14–16; the pinions and feathers of the ostrich have no *chesed*, because she leaves her eggs in the sand. '*ahabhah*, 'love', is distinguished from *chesed*, in that it expresses the spontaneous, free origin of the divine affection. Into *chen*, 'grace', the element of the unworthiness of the recipient enters. Still further we meet *rachamim*, literally 'bowels', for mercy and compassion. The importance of 'loving-kindness' is seen in this, that it underlies and enriches and makes more tender other disclosures of the divine affection [*Hos*. 2.19]; for the New Testament, cp. Eph. 2.4, 5.

[B] THE BOND BETWEEN JEHOVAH AND ISRAEL

According to the prophets a close and unique bond exists between Jehovah and Israel. This is so self-understood as not to need explicit affirmation. Indirectly its existence is expressed through references to its origin. Jehovah chose Israel, they are His people; He married her, they are like a vineyard which He cultivates for the sake of its fruit. A technical term for it is *berith*,[1] usually rendered by 'covenant', although this is not always the proximate association. Of forms of some inter-human *berith* mention is made in Amos, Hosea and Isaiah. The term does not appear in Micah. Of a *berith* between Jehovah and Israel we learn only in Hosea and Isaiah.

Of etymologies proposed for *berith* the chief ones are as follows. It has been derived from *bara*, 'to cut'. The reference to 'cutting' is

[1] See pp. 122–4.

then explained from the ceremony spoken of in Gen. 15.17 and Jer. 34.18, 19. The phrase *karath berith*, 'to cut a cutting', for making a *berith*, has been thought to favour this etymology. Usually, however, in such phrases, when verb and noun repeat the same idea, the identical root is employed for both, so that we should on this view expect *bara berith*. Others go back for their derivation to the same verb 'to cut', but give a different turn to the signification, cutting being interpreted as determining, defining, from which would result as the primary sense 'law', 'ordinance'. Still others go back to the Assyrian *beritu*, 'to bind', *birtu*, 'bond'. The etymology is not of overmuch importance, although it may sometimes do harm by unduly tying the conception down to one hard and fast meaning. The only common idea, always present, is that of a solemn religious sanction. Where this is present, a promise, law, agreement, may all be called *berith*. The main question is, how does it occur in Hosea and Isaiah?

As regards Isaiah, the emphasis and reason for introducing the idea lie largely in the association of the absolute sureness of the divine promise. The *berith* with Noah and the *berith* of Israel's coming redemption are put on a line with this as the point of comparison [54.9, 10]. Similarly, 55.3; 59.21; 61.8. In 24.5, on the other hand, the idea of law, ordinance prevails. There may be an allusion here to the Noachian *berith*. It will be noticed, however, that even so the emphasis rests on the perpetual obligation of the ordinances, constituting an 'everlasting' *berith*. Only in 56.4, 6, *berith* seems to signify in Isaiah the general legal relation between Jehovah and His servants, for here observance of the sabbath and other ordinances is specified as pertaining to the 'holding fast' of God's *berith*.

Difficult of interpretation are 42.6, and 49.8. In both the Servant of Jehovah is designated as *berith 'am*, a 'covenant of people'. The two most plausible views about this phrase are either that in the future through the Servant the *berith* will be realized anew or restored, or, laying emphasis on the word 'people', that through the Servant the *berith* will once more assume the form of a relationship into which Israel enters as a people, in contrast with its present scattered, disorganized state of existence. On both interpretations the *berith* here also appears as the comprehensive, fundamental name for Israel's religious organization. It will be seen from this that the idea of the *berith* in this sense, while by no means absent, is neither particularly conspicuous nor pervasive in the prophecy.

As to Hosea we have the explicit statement [8.1]: 'They have transgressed my *berith*, and trespassed against my law'; here *berith* is legal organization of the ancient religion as a whole. For the rest all depends for this prophet on the question, whether the marriage-idea is at all to be equated with the *berith*-idea. The prophet works out everything belonging to the union of Jehovah with Israel on the basis of the marriage between the two. It is incapable of proof that in his day every marriage was *per se* a species of *berith*. Still, this does not exclude the possibility of Hosea's having made the equation.

The marriage-idea as a form of religious expression is old in Shemitic religion. For this reason Wellhausen's theory that Hosea, under the influence of his sad marital experience, had by brooding over it come upon the possibility of utilizing the figure for depicting the course of Israel's religion in past, present and future, is untenable. The whole setting of the figure from the very beginning proves its familiar nature. We have learned from the Decalogue about the conjugal jealousy of Jehovah.[1] The figure is not even characteristic of revealed religion. Like that of fatherhood and kingship, it was current in paganism in Israel's neighbourhood. The name 'Baal' for the Canaanitish deity is based upon it, for this name means the husband-lord, through whose union with the land fruitfulness is obtained, or who from another point of view has the people for wife so that the individual members of the people become his sons and daughters [*Num.* 25.2–9; *Jer.* 2.27; *Mal.* 2.11]. On one of the Phoenician inscriptions the phrase *Bresyeth Baal*, the 'Spouse of Baal', has been found, but this is individual, the name of a woman.

Isa. 54.1; 62.5; *Jer.* 31.32, may further be compared, but in all this there is so far no explicit combination of the *berith*-idea and the marriage-idea. Moreover, these last-cited passages are younger than Hosea and would not be conclusive with regard to him. It is first in Ezek. 16.8, that entering into *berith* with Israel is called a marrying her. Jeremiah also almost certainly associated the two conceptions, although not doing so explicitly anywhere. Prov. 2.17 calls marriage a *berith*, and so does Mal. 2.14. With the exception of Proverbs, we know that these writings are later than Hosea, and might have borrowed from him the combination. But this in itself would put it beyond question that Hosea was understood by them to have long ago made it. The critics can doubt this only because they have cut out from Hosea the passage 8.1. If this passage is genuine, and there is no reason for doubting it except that furnished by the critical desire to remove from Hosea all traces of acquaintance with a legitimate statutory religion, then it becomes almost impossible to deny that the prophet identified the

[1] See p. 136.

berith-idea and his favourite idea of marriage between Jehovah and Israel. Only the expurgated Hosea could have lived in such naïve unconsciousness that the marriage meant a *berith*-union between the two.

Still in the pre-Jeremianic period we must acknowledge, always leaving Hosea to one side, that there is a scarcity of references to the *berith*-form of the religion, and the critics find support in this for their contention that the origin of the idea is as late as the latter part of the seventh century. We have already looked into this contention under the head of the Sinaitic *berith*-making. How, without impugning the latter as a historical fact, can the phenomenon of relative scarcity be explained? We have on that occasion already noted that in the subsequent prophets, excepting Jeremiah and Ezekiel, the conception again suffers eclipse. This shows that there must have been something in the prophetic teaching that temporarily forced it into the background.

The cause for this need not have been the same in each individual prophet. We shall presently see why the *berith*-thought was peculiarly adapted to the trend of Hosea's teaching, and that particularly in its specific form of a marriage-union. But with Isaiah it is different. His whole point of view is theocentric, emphasizing that Israel lives for the sake of Jehovah, and possibly the *berith*-idea with its strongly stressed mutualness did not appear to him peculiarly adapted for bringing this God-centred characteristic of religion to the front. In Amos and Micah again the rupture of the union between Jehovah and Israel appears so certain and inevitable, and so much in need of emphasizing, that perhaps a steady reference to the *berith*, with its inevitable reminder of the unbreakableness of the bond, may have been found to be less in line with their teaching.

But, apart from all such individual considerations, we must remember the general character of the prophetic revelation. The law institutes and commands, prophecy explains the reasons and motives on which institutions and obedience are based. Behind the *berith* lies something deeper and more fundamental, the nature and will of Jehovah. For the *berith* is after all an institution, which can be temporarily kept in the background, for sufficient reasons. Such a procedure does not convict the prophets of ignoring or opposing the *berith*-idea. It only shows that their teaching moves on deeper lines.

HOSEA'S TEACHING ON THE MARRIAGE-BOND

Hosea, on the supposition that marriage and *berith* with Jehovah are to him identical, is the chief source of our information in regard to the nature of the union. We learn from him:

[1] *The union originated on the part of Jehovah*

Not Israel offered herself to Him, He sought out Israel. Theologically speaking, we would say that the *berith* had its source in the divine election. Election is spoken of by Isaiah [14.1; 43.20; 49.7]. With Amos and Hosea, however, a more characteristic and intimate term is chosen to convey somewhat of the religious depths and value of this idea. This term is *yada'*, 'to know', not in the intellectual sense of 'to be informed about', but in the pregnant, affectional sense of 'to take loving knowledge of' [*Hos.* 13.5; *Amos* 3.2]. This act is not yet represented as an eternal act on the part of Jehovah; in keeping with their standpoint in the midst of history, the prophets think of it as something emerging in time. The New Testament makes out of this 'knowing' a 'fore-knowing'. But this is simply putting the act back into eternity. To cut it loose from its Old Testament antecedents and to intellectualize it in the interest of a Pelagianizing theology is an utterly unhistorical proceeding. The 'pro' in the Greek rendering does not serve to give God His standpoint in time, from which He then is able to look forward and base His decision on what the creature is foreseen to be about to do at a certain point in time; it serves the precisely opposite purpose of giving God His standpoint before, that is to say, in Old Testament language, above time.

[2] *The relation had a definite historical beginning*

Israel had not been always thus united to Jehovah. The *berith*-conception as here conceived does not belong to General but to Special Revelation. Israel entered into this special union with Jehovah at the time of the Exodus [*Hos.* 13.4; cp. 11.1, and *Amos* 2.10]. It is characteristic of the prophetic point of view, that the origin is sought, not so much in a concrete act of ratification, although that is presupposed, but in the events of the Exodus with all their rich implications. It was not a blind transaction, but one full of intelligence. The idea of marriage was eminently fitted to emphasize the historical birth of the union, better than that of fatherhood and sonship. Father and son never exist apart from each other. Husband and wife do so exist at first, and then are brought together at a definite point of time.

[3] *Though the union originated effectually on Jehovah's part, yet Israel was led freely to enter upon it*

The marriage-*berith* is to Hosea's mind a spiritualized union. We should, however, realize that this feature was not necessarily given with the idea of marriage as such. In Hosea's time marriage did not partake of the same spiritual character it has acquired in the course of time, chiefly through the regenerating influence of the subsequent Biblical religion. There was less of equality between the sexes, and less freedom of choice on the woman's part. It is all the more remarkable that Hosea, while utilizing the conception, has not allowed it to remain upon the level of the common custom of his day. If we adopt the realistic view of chapters 1–3, we shall have to assume that the prophet was by special grace enabled to live on a higher plane of love towards his wife than the average Israelite of that time [cp. *Jer.* 3.1]. If on the contrary we choose the allegorical interpretation, we must say that, at least in his understanding and vision of the matter, he was led by the Spirit to frame a conception of the divine-marriage-love towards Israel, far transcending, not only his own, but every ordinary experience known to him. The dispute between allegorists and realists is interesting, but doctrinally the points of arrival on each view coincide.

We can only rapidly sketch the features in which this spiritualized character of the union reveals itself. Jehovah is represented as having wooed Israel, sued for her affection [2.14]; as having drawn her with the cords of man [11.4]; here the figure of sonship comes in to supplement and enrich that of marriage. Jehovah strengthened Israel's arms and taught her to walk [7.15]; although the Giver of all nature-blessings, of corn, wine, oil, silver, gold, wool, and flax, Jehovah is distinguished from the Baals, in that He has something more and finer to give than these: loving-kindness, mercy and faithfulness [2.19]; in reality He gives, in and through all these things, Himself after a sacramental fashion [2.23]; He is personally present in all His favours, and in them surrenders Himself to His people for never-failing enjoyment. Even after Israel becomes unfaithful, He continues to appeal to her heart by proofs of his love; 6.4 is the language of divine disappointment at the failure of these efforts.

To these divine approaches corresponds the attitude expected from the people. The state of mind which the people ought to cultivate, by reason of their union with Jehovah, is described by Amos, Isaiah and Micah on the whole from an ethical, by Hosea from an affectional point of view. When Amos, Isaiah and Micah say: not sacrifices but righteousness, Hosea says: not sacrifices but the knowledge of Jehovah. All the demands made of the people are summed up in this one thing, that there should be the knowledge of God among them, and that not as a theoretical perception of what is Jehovah's nature, but as a practical acquaintance, the intimacy of love. It is that which corresponds on Israel's part to the knowledge of Jehovah from which the whole marriage sprang [13.4, 5]; this knowledge is intended to make Israel like unto Jehovah, it has a character-forming influence. This is so fundamental a law that it holds true even in idolatry [9.10].

[4] *Although the berith is thus traced back to its highest ideal source in the nature and choice of Jehovah, it nevertheless established a legally defined relationship*

The marriage exists under a marriage-law. Israel is charged not merely with having been deficient in love and affection, but with having violated distinct promises. She is legally guilty. Jehovah has a *ribh*, 'controversy at law' with Israel [4.1]. This presupposes a law giving the right to sue. In fact the prophet proceeds to enumerate the points in which the people are indictable. Amos likewise speaks of the *torah* and the *chuqqim* which the Judaeans have rejected [2.4] and this cannot be understood of prophetic instruction, as is possible in Isa. 5.24. In the second part of Isaiah there are indisputable references to the law as the norm under which Israel lives [42.21, 24; 51.7; 56.2, 4, 6]. Hosea puts the *berith* and the *torah* together [8.1]. Since this is a marriage-law, it must have been imposed at the time of the Exodus. Hosea, therefore, bears witness to the existence of an ancient *berith*-law among Israel, and in so far refutes the contention of the critics, that no law was recognized as in force by the prophets.

Of course, nothing can be determined from this passage alone as to the extent and nature of this law. From 8.12, however, we learn that it was of considerable compass, and had been given in written form: 'Though I write for him my law in ten thousand precepts, they are counted as a strange thing.' Certain statutes of the Mosaic *torah* are clearly presupposed in the early prophets [4.2]. Hosea considers it a calamity for Israel, that in the coming exile she will be debarred from fulfilling her ceremonial duties [9.3–5]. Isaiah also had a high regard for the temple-service, and was on a friendly footing with Uriah, the priest [8.2]. To mark Egypt as belonging to Jehovah he predicts that an altar shall be in the midst of the land and a *matstsebhah* at its border [19.19]. The Egyptians shall in that day worship with sacrifice and oblation [vs. 21]. Zion is the city of 'our solemnities and appointed feasts' [33.20]. For the second part of Isaiah cp. 56.2, 4, 7; 60.6, 7; 63.18; 66.20–24. About the passages alleged to condemn the sacrificial cult on principle, see the next chapter of the discussion.

[5] *The covenant is, according to Hosea, as it is to all New Testament writers, a national 'berith'*

It was made when the descendants of Abraham had come to form a nation [11.1]. Nevertheless Hosea has become instrumental in imparting an individualizing direction to the teaching about it. His emotional temperament was a potent factor to this effect. From its emotional side, more than in any other aspect, religion is a personal, individual matter.

Even where Hosea speaks of the people collectively, the impulse towards this is so strong as to make him personify and individualize Israel. Several of such passages the individual believer may appropriate even now almost without change [2.7, 16, 23; 6.1–3; 8.2; 14.2, 4, 8]. This will be the less surprising if we remember that, at the basis of such impersonations lay, at least on the realistic view, the intensely personal experiences with his wife, which were to him a mirror of the intercourse between Jehovah and the pious. Jeremiah, who in this poetic, emotional temperament so strongly resembles Hosea, has subsequently taken up this line of thought, and consequently consciously developed further what to Hosea bore the nature of an intuition.

The marriage-idea worked towards individualism in still another manner. If Jehovah is the husband and Israel the wife, then individual Israelites will appear as Jehovah's children [2.1; 11.3, 4]. Very strongly the trend towards individualism asserts itself in the closing words of the book [14.9].

Finally, it should not be forgotten, that the prophetic doctrine of the coming judgment bore in it a fertile seed of individualism. In the approaching catastrophe the majority will perish. Those that inherit the promise are only a small remnant, and the differentiation rests on a spiritual basis. Isaiah has carried this doctrine of the saved remnant to its ultimate root in the divine election [4.3]; those that escape of Israel are every one that is written (in the book of life).

[C] THE RUPTURE OF THE BOND: THE SIN OF ISRAEL

The early prophets predict clearly that the bond of the *berith* will be suspended. It will not, to be sure, be irreparably broken off. Were the critical contention correct, that all connection between Jehovah and Israel is based by the prophets on inexorable justice, excluding every exercise of grace, then plainly the thought of restoration must have been intolerable to them, since it involved nothing less than the abandonment of the supreme principle in the divine nature, a principle moreover that they had learned to uphold only after a long struggle with the opposing forces of grace and favouritism. On that view the prophets would have gone back on themselves, and what is worse, have made Jehovah go back on Himself. That they nevertheless proclaim with obvious delight the idea of grace proves that the critical construction must be, to say the least, one-sided.

The judgment comes on account of the sin of the people. Itself it belongs, as we shall see, to the eschatological perspective. But the sins leading up to it belong to the present stage. The prophets nowhere deal with sin in the abstract. It is always the concrete sin of Israel with which they are concerned. This, however, they most strictly relate to Jehovah. Strictly speaking, there is no sin except against God. The prophets deal with certain large aspects of the sinful conduct of the people. This, however, is a division on the external side, which does not contribute much to the psychology of sin. In fact the material for this is more largely to be gathered from such writings as the Psalter. Still, as compared with the law, there is more of reflection on the inner nature of sin in the prophets. From the groups of sin that the prophets single out for attack something can be learned concerning the motives of condemnation, and this opens the possibility of drawing inferences as to the real sinfulness of what they protest against. We further can distinguish in the individual prophets a peculiar view-point from which each regards the sin inveighed against. We shall therefore first have to look into the large groups of sin dealt with, and then, in the second place, examine the two prophets who reveal an individual way of judging sin.

COLLECTIVE NATIONAL SIN

The sin which the prophets condemn is largely collective national sin [Amos 2.6–8; 3.1; 7.15; 8.2]. And where not the whole nation in its solidarity is rebuked, certain classes are attacked. Still this is not collectivism pure and simple, as some writers assert, for the distinction between class and class, which accompanies this mass-treatment, proves that the judgment is a qualitative one, and qualitativeness bears in itself the beginning of individualism. We find distinctions drawn between the profligates, the rich oppressors, the voluptuaries, the corruptors of justice, the externalists in the worship of Jehovah. And, on the other hand, we learn of the righteous, the needy, the poor, the meek [Amos 2.6, 7; 5.11, 12; 8.4]. [While this is a collective treatment of sin, it is generically collective. The collectivism of the Old Testament is enforced, however, in this, that when the catastrophe comes, the pious are made to suffer with the wicked. But this is a problem that afterwards staggered Jeremiah and Ezekiel. All we can do is to recognize that there is solidarity in punishment, and that, following the principles of revelation, we must posit, behind solidarity of judgment, a solidarity of guilt, though we may not be able to reckon this out in detail. It is at bottom the question whether ethical laws or physical laws are supreme in the government of the universe.

The problem is apt to be realized more keenly to the extent that the organic structure of a community falls into pieces. At the time of Amos such a process was not as yet visible on the surface. At the time of Jeremiah and Ezekiel it had become different. The critical judgment on this point has been warped by the assumption that the prophets stood absolutely alone against the whole nation. But this is merely theory. The prophets recognize gradations in the moral and religious condition of the people. Amos knows of a sifting that will take place, although he refers to this not so much in order to console, as rather to frighten: it will be as bad as sifting, the saving of two legs or the piece of an ear out of the mouth of the lion [3.12; 9.9, 10]. For Isaiah compare 3.10. In Micah there is not the same clear distinction of classes, but this is due not so much to an excess of nationalism as to the perception that there are no good individuals left [7.2]. The beginning of the individualized treatment of sin is most clearly perceptible in Hosea, just as the individualization of the *berith* received from him a powerful impulse [14.9].

THE CORRUPTION OF RITUAL WORSHIP

One great source of sin unanimously attacked by the prophets is the cult, the ritual worship of Jehovah. As stated above, in connection with the sacrificial system of the Mosaic law, the Wellhausen school takes the ground that the prophets opposed sacrifices and similar rites on principle, and that consequently they cannot have looked upon these as ordained by Jehovah, which again amounts to saying that the Pentateuch did not exist in their time. It is admitted, of course, that some passages speak of specific features of the cult, and cannot be quoted in support of such a generalizing theory. Thus images and other paraphernalia of idolatry are denounced [*Mic.* 1.7; 5.13, 14]. The corruptness of the priests is rebuked [*Mic.* 3.11]. According to Amos 2.7, religious prostitution of a particularly aggravated kind occurred, probably in connection with the cult of Jehovah. Amos 2.8, may be compared with Ex. 22.26, 27. These denunciations, as referring to special forms of misconduct, must be kept separated from the passages in which the critics find an unqualified condemnation of the cult expressed. The main passages thus interpreted are: Amos 4.4; 5.5, 21–26; 8.14; Hos. 6.6; Isa. 1.11ff.; Mic. 6.6–8. In the later prophets the passage most frequently appealed to is Jer. 7.21–23.

In endeavouring to estimate the purport of these passages it is necessary at the outset to warn against the attempt to break their force made from the apologetic side, namely, that all these condemnations are turned against a wrong technique with which the sacrifices were handled. This is a highly implausible exegesis, for the prophets are not as a rule concerned with forms, or the correct observance of forms, as such. They deal with principles of spiritual significance only. Thus Amos 4.4–5 discloses a ritual flaw in the offering of leavened things. This is against the law [*Lev.* 2.11]. But what the prophet censures is not this; he makes use of it only to ridicule the excessive ritual impulse, unable to satisfy itself with the ordinary requirements. Similarly, the advertising of sacrifices brought is condemned, not because any law existed forbidding this, but because of the perversion of the principle of true sacrifice observable in it. Again in the second half of vs. 4, not the bringing of tithes every third day, instead of every third year, is made an object of serious criticism by the prophet. It was, of course, impossible to bring tithes every third day. The prophet on purpose exaggerates, in order to mock the perverted zeal of the offerers. Hos. 10.1 is another example of the same kind of polemic; disapproval of the multiplication of altars has the support of the law, but the prophet has in mind the sinful tendency behind it: multiplying o altars is a piece of religious adultery, which spreads itself over a number of degrading liaisons [cp. vs. 2: 'their heart is divided'].

This conservative apologetic is therefore not in accord with the facts. What the prophet ridicules is sometimes in harmony with the Mosaic law, sometimes not: hence the point must have lain in something else, as suggested above. Still the critical exegesis is not thereby justified. In carefully examining the passages under debate we shall find that the disapproval of the cult on the part of the prophets is not based on principle, but due to one of the three following considerations: Either, the cult is conducted in a materialistic, mercantile spirit, in order that by giving so much value for return-favour to be obtained, certain benefits may be purchased from the deity after a semi-magical fashion;

or, the cult is conducted, jointly with gross immoral practices, so as to divorce Jehovah's religious interest from his ethical requirements;

or, finally, the cult is employed in order to secure escape from the approaching judgment or to avert the latter entirely.

If we now look into the passages it will become clear that the presence of one or other of these three thoughts is sufficient to account for the phenomena.

AMOS 5.25

Amos 5.25 is of uncertain interpretation as to the meaning of the question proposed by God: 'Did ye bring unto me sacrifices and offerings in the wilderness forty years, O house of Israel?' Some take this as a protestation on Jehovah's part that the wilderness-journey proves sacrifices unnecessary for securing or obtaining the divine favour. This would imply that Amos regarded the wilderness-journey, in contradiction to the Pentateuch, a period of divine favour for Israel. The critics profess to find this view in Hosea and Jeremiah, and so take for granted that it must be likewise the view of Amos. But this by no means follows. Amos' words must be interpreted by themselves. If so taken, the situation immediately takes on another aspect. Its natural meaning becomes: Did you endeavour in the wilderness, after having been rejected by me, to propitiate me by sacrifices and offerings? If at that time ye were not foolish enough to attempt this, why do ye act on this principle now? Such an exegesis makes the question only negate the effiaccy of the cult as a means for regaining the favour of Jehovah, once forfeited by sin. The law itself precludes this delusion, when it allows no sacrificial covering for sin committed with a high hand, and that was precisely the sin which both the generation of the wilderness-journey and the contemporaries of Amos had committed. The words of vs. 26 also favour this exegesis, when, passing from question to affirmation, God proceeds: 'Yea, ye have borne Sakkuth, your king [R.V. "the tabernacle of your king"], and Kaiwan, your images, your star-god, which you made unto yourselves.' This rendering of the verb as a perfect tense, 'ye have borne', simply excludes that Amos should have regarded the period of such idolatry as a period of high favour with Jehovah. It is true, some exegetes render vs. 26 as relating to the future: 'so ye shall take up Sakkuth, your king', etc., that is, you will have to take all your idolatrous paraphernalia into exile (cp. R.V. in the margin).

While this interpretation is possible grammatically, the perfect being taken as a perfect consecutive, it is by no means necessary, and it would involve an unusually harsh transition to make the statement as a whole mean: the wilderness-journey proved that sacrifices are not essential to right standing with God, therefore ye shall go into captivity with all your idols. This is certainly a strange way of speaking, that might be perhaps tolerated in Hosea; but in Amos, with his closely consequential thought, it seems oddly out of place. What a harsh sentence for such a mere mistaken opinion! And the mild description of the state in the wilderness, as one proving no sacrifices to be necessary, sounds oddly tame for Amos with all his vehemence of expostulation in the context. If our exegesis, on the other hand, be adopted, the preceding context can also be interpreted to the same effect: God hates, despises their feasts, because these things cannot avail to stem the judgment, as the foolish people believe they are able to do. Not sacrifices but retribution will satisfy Jehovah: 'Let judgment roll down as waters, and righteousness as a mighty stream.'

ISAIAH 1.10–17

Isa. 1.10–17, sounds even stronger than the language of Amos just considered. But in this case likewise there is nothing to indicate that the statement is meant as a pronouncement on the value or worthlessness of sacrifices in the abstract. The words 'who has required this at your hand?' in vs. 12 might, at first sight, seem to imply a divine declamation, 'I have never required it', and that would rule out the revelation-origin of the sacrificial laws. But the added qualification, 'to trample my courts', clearly shows what is meant. Ordinary frequentation of the temple Isaiah would hardly have stigmatized as a trampling of the temple-courts. Isaiah himself visited the temple, as chapter 6 proves. And how absurd it is to impute to the prophet a sweeping condemnation of all the acts enumerated here! Prayer is one of the things that God refuses to receive! This alone suffices to prove, that not these acts in the abstract, but some peculiar accompaniment of them, rendered them unacceptable in Jehovah's sight. What this attending feature is the prophet clearly enough indicates. It is the joining together of all these things with flagrant iniquity. Vs. 13 should be rendered: 'I cannot away with iniquity joined to a solemn meeting.' When they pray God will not hear. This is not because prayer is wrong as such, but because the hands lifted up in prayer are 'full of blood'.

It should never be forgotten that in the prophets God speaks the language of burning indignation. If all sorts of qualifications and safeguarding of the words had been added, the entire force of the denunciation would have been broken. What the critics demand, as necessary for our exegesis to stand, is that the prophet should have made Jehovah speak on this wise: 'Although in the abstract I do not disapprove of ritual worship, and even demand it, yet in the way you offer it to me I cannot accept it.' What the critics have failed to appreciate psychologically is the rhetorical absoluteness of the condemnation. They have made a precisely-formulated theological deliverance out of it. What we have in such passages is the anthropomorphic speech of one whose indignation has been aroused to the point

268

of refusal to consider the question in the abstract or with nicety of distinctions. No man, no preacher, truly capable of resentment against sin, would have stopped to add qualifications under such circumstances.

HOSEA 6.6

In Hos. 6.6, the difference between the two members of the sentence is a difference in form but not in reality. The meaning is not that when mercy comes under consideration, God absolutely rejects all sacrifice ('mercy and not sacrifice'), whilst, when it is a matter of the knowledge of Himself, He has only a relative preference, which does not absolutely reject the sacrifice ('knowledge of God more than burnt offerings'). There is here simply an idiomatic variation of the same thought in both clauses. The second clause is a way of speaking such as anyone might employ: I want acts rather than mere promises. It therefore should not be regarded as weaker than the 'not' makes the first, but be interpreted in harmony with it: Jehovah desires knowledge of God and not burnt offering. The rejection is absolute in both cases. But the point at issue is on what this double rejection is based. The context furnishes the answer. What God here scorns is sacrifice as a means for appeasing His righteous displeasure, sacrifice moreover offered without true repentance. When their goodness is as a morning cloud and the dew that goes early away, offerings cannot avail to avert the judgment. Therefore God hewed them by the prophets, and slew them by the word of His mouth. It is to this train of thought that, by means of 'for' the sixth verse is joined. The *chesed* here points back to the false *chesed* of vs. 4, and the knowledge of God to the pretended knowledge of vs. 3. When the words are thus interpreted in the light of the context, they no longer prove the contention of the critical theory.

MICAH 6.6–9

In Mic. 6.6–9 likewise everything depends on a correct apprehension of the context. The question, 'Wherewith shall I come before Jehovah', etc. is not asked by the prophet himself, but by someone representing the people. It is not permissible at the outset to put into it the expectation of a negative answer, and to make this negative answer the opinion of the prophet; I will not come before Jehovah with any of these things. If it is a question asked by the people, we must understand it as meant in all seriousness; the speaker wants to know what would be the proper way of approaching Jehovah under the circumstances, and to what limit of exertion and expense he ought to go. The structure of the discourse is dramatic. The offer of the speaker in vs. 6 is induced by the expostulation of Jehovah voiced in vss. 1–5. Jehovah has a controversy with Israel, the point of which is that they have been ungrateful for ancient favours received. In response to this charge of ingratitude the prophet introduces the representative of the people, who asks how he can make amends for an acknowledged delinquency. He offers to reimburse Jehovah by ritual service of a most excessive kind, and to conciliate Him by means of a pagan form of expiation, the sacrifice of the first-born.

The prophet is the third speaker. He opposes to the twofold offer of vss. 6, 7, the declaration, 'He has showed thee, O man, what is good, and what does Jehovah require of thee, but to do justly, to love kindness, and to walk humbly with thy God?' Does such an answer imply disapproval of sacrifice on principle? The law itself nowhere represents sacrifice as a sufficient return for the favour of God. Besides this, the idea of lavishness in ritual to make up for past neglect and ingratitude is offensive on every right interpretation of sacrifice. The words, 'He has showed thee, O man, what is good', etc. do not refer to the time of the Exodus, so as to carry the implication that these things were the only things taught Israel at that time, to the exclusion of sacrifice. They refer to prophetic instruction of later date.

It has been suggested that in the three things named the characteristic burden of each of the three great prophets, Amos, Hosea, Isaiah, can be recognized. To do justly would then sum up the message of Amos, to love kindness that of Hosea, and to walk humbly with one's God, that of Isaiah.

AMOS 4.4

It is far from certain that in Amos 4.4, sacrifice is called 'transgression'. The form of statement, 'Come to Bethel and transgress, to Gilgal and multiply transgression' does, it is true, permit of this exegesis. But it does not require it. The words lose nothing of their point, when the transgression is found, not in the act of sacrificing *per se*, but in the character which this act had habitually come to bear at Bethel and Gilgal. To sacrifice there was, under the circumstances, to transgress, to do so lavishly involved the multiplying of transgression. To be sure, the transgression cannot in this case, as in Isa. 1.13, have consisted in some sinful manner of life added to the sacrifice. The context in Amos shows that the sin must have been something entering into the sacrificial act itself. We cannot render: 'Come to Bethel, sacrifice there, and then lead a dissolute life.' But the sin that increased at the same ratio with the sacrifice need not, for all that, have lain in the sacrifice as such. Apart from the wrong ritual spirit prevailing at the sanctuaries named, we must not forget that precisely at Bethel and Gilgal Jehovah was notoriously served under the form of an image, and that may well have vitiated every sacrifice brought there from the prophet's point of view. This also would not amount to a denial of the legitimacy of sacrifice in the abstract.

The last-named consideration will have to be remembered likewise in interpreting Amos 5.4, 5. A pointed contrast is here drawn between seeking Jehovah, and seeking Bethel or entering into Gilgal or passing over to Beersheba. In the sanctuaries named Jehovah is not to be found. Why? Not necessarily because sacrifices are brought there, for that happened at many another place in Amos' time, but because through their officially legitimatized idolatry and the frequency of visits paid to them, they had become the special exponents of what the prophets regarded as the wrong type of religion.

Even less reason is there to infer from Amos 8.14, and 9.1, that the prophet regards all sacrificial worship as *per se* sinful. On the contrary, the former passage confirms the suggestion just made, that the image-worship practised at Samaria, Dan and Beersheba, provoked his irony. 'To swear by the sin of Samaria' cannot mean to swear by the cult of Samaria. Swearing is usually done by the name of a god, and less frequently in the name of a custom or practice. Probably the 'sin' is here the image of the Samaritans, though it may have stood at Bethel, for that was the official sanctuary of the capital. In the formula, 'as thy God, O Dan, liveth', we may find a confirmation of this view as to 'the sin of Samaria.' Only in the third clause we read of swearing by something that is not directly a god. The exact formula here also is given: 'As the way of Beersheba liveth.' It is not easy to tell what 'the way' means here. The use of the verb 'liveth' makes us expect a reference to something personal. But there is no evidence, so far as we know, of a god or idol having been designated as 'a way'. There are writers who think that 'the way' can mean the type of religion prac-tised at a certain place; here: 'the cult-way of Beersheba'. This use of *derek* for religion (cp. the Greek *hodos* in a similar sense) cannot be proven to have been familiar at the time of Amos. Probably 'the way of Beersheba' means the pilgrimage to Beersheba. One could swear by that, even as the Moslem of the present day swears by the pilgrimage to Mecca. But, however interpreted, the phrase gives no countenance to the idea that the prophet meant any condemnation of sacrifice on principle.

JEREMIAH 7.21–23

We find, therefore, that in no passage of the four early prophets is the cult of sacrifice denounced as in itself and under all circumstances sinful. The most convincing passage, however, from their point of view, the critics find in Jeremiah, a prophet of the seventh century [*Jer.* 7.21–23]. Here Jehovah first declares, 'Add your burnt offerings to your sacrifices and eat ye flesh', and then explains, that in the day of His bringing up Israel out of Egypt He did not speak unto them, nor command them aught about sacrifices. On the contrary, these were the things He had required: 'Hearken unto my voice, and I will be your God, and ye shall be my people, and walk ye in all the way that I command you, that it may be well with you.' And yet a moment's reflection will show how difficult it is from the critical standpoint itself to attribute to Jeremiah the opinion that the Mosaic legislation imposed no ritual demands upon Israel.

These critics generally assume that Jeremiah had a hand in the Deuteronomic reform-movement, which laid the Deuteronomic code upon the people. Now Deuteronomy does contain considerable ritual material. The code is said to have been a compromise. We ask: how could the prophet compromise on a matter that was to his view a matter of principle, beyond the reach of all compromise, namely, that sacrifices were sinful as such? Wellhausen believes that Jeremiah had cut himself loose from this reform movement, and he finds in 7.8 a characterization of its reprehensible methods from the prophet's later standpoint. 'The false pen of the scribes has wrought falsely' would then be a very bitter word spoken by the prophet against his own past. But there would be more than culpable inconsistency here; it would be a case of unparalleled audacity to dare to speak after such a *volte face* about anything commanded or not commanded at the time of Moses.

Further, in 17.26 the prophet foretells that in case of obedience to the sabbath law, Jehovah's favour will be shown in this, that men shall come from all quarters of the land to bring Jehovah burnt offerings and sacrifices and meal offerings and frankincense and thank-offerings. Similarly in 33.11 it is foretold that in the future there will be again heard in Jerusalem the voice of joy and gladness . . . the voice of them that bring sacrifices of thanksgiving unto the house of Jehovah. It will be necessary to declare these passages spurious, if Jeremiah on principle rejected every form of sacrifice. For these reasons we shall either have to let the passage in chapter 7 stand as an unsolvable enigma, or put another interpretation upon it.

The reference to the situation in Ex. 19 points the way to its under-

272

standing. It was at the very first approach of Jehovah to Israel with the offer of the *berith*, even before the Decalogue had been promulgated; it was at this earliest coming together of Jehovah and Israel that God refrained from saying anything about sacrifices, and simply staked the entire agreement between Himself and the people on their loyalty and obedience to Him [cp. *Ex.* 19.5]. Thus understood, the prophet means to affirm that the *berith* does not ultimately rest on sacrifice, but the sacrifices on the *berith*.

The fact that no explicit evidence for the prophetic condemnation of sacrifice can be adduced from their writings, gains in significance by observing that there are indubitable statements in which certain particular features connected with the cult are condemned. In Hos. 10.8 the high places of Samaria are called 'the sin of Israel'. In Hos. 10.10 it is said that the Israelites are bound to their two transgressions, that is to say, to the two calves at Dan and Bethel. In Mic. 1.5 we read in parallelism: 'What is the transgression of Jacob, and what are the high places of Judah?' But all this concerns cult-instruments; the cult as such is never declared sin.

Finally, by way of caution against drawing rash inferences from the prophetic passages discussed, reference may be made to analogous statements in the Psalter, and that in Psalms which the modern school itself regards as of post-exilic date, in which, therefore, the Psalmists cannot, on the critical view, have possibly meant to deny the existence or Mosaic provenience or divine authority of the laws of sacrifice (cp. *Psa.* 40.6; 50.7–15; 51.16–19]. If such statements could coexist with belief in the divine approbation and the religious value of sacrifice, when performed in the proper spirit, there is no reason to deny the possibility of the same mental attitude in the case of the prophets.

SOCIAL SIN

Side by side with the ritual sin of Israel, its social sin falls under the prophetic condemnation. Owing to the present-day sociological trend of religion, this side of the prophetic message has attracted considerable attention. At the outset the caution is necessary, that we may not expect overmuch light from this quarter on specific modern social and economic problems. The situation in the two cases is too widely different for that. The grave economic problems of modern society arise largely from commercial and industrial causes. The people of Israel were not a commercial nor an industrial community. Such a problem as that of the relation of capital to labour did not exist for them. A striking illustration of this is found in the rule that, while no interest may be taken from Israelite by Israelite, this is not forbidden in dealing with foreigners. What is allowed on economic grounds is forbidden on theocratic grounds: a higher rule exists for the people of God than that of economic rightness [*Ex.* 22.25; *Lev.* 25.36; *Deut.* 23.20; *Ezek.* 18.8]. Thus the cases where analogies can be drawn and applications made from ancient to modern conditions are few.

An exceptional case is, perhaps, what may be called 'the problem of the city'. Amos, and especially Micah, recognize that the city, while an accumulator of the energies of culture, is also an accumulator of potencies of evil [*Amos* 3.9; *Mic.* 1.5]. In the capital all evil is concentrated. Hence in the future all cities will have to cease to exist [*Mic.* 2.10; 3.8–12; 4.9, 13; 5.10, 13]. Men shall then sit in rural simplicity and security, each under his own vine and fig-tree, and none shall make them afraid [4.4]. The Messianic King will not proceed from the city of Jerusalem, but from the country-town of Bethlehem, as David did originally.

But even in this relative approximation to one of our modern problems, there are points of difference. The prophet has not in mind as one of the chief causes of evil in city-life the congestion of population of which modern sociologists make so much. It is moral evil that is congested there, and no attempt is made to reduce it, even in part, to physical causes. The cities are condemned for the specific reason of their being instruments of warfare, fortified places, perhaps also on account of their being exponents of a spirit of rebellious self-dependence over against God [*Mic.* 5.11; cp. *Gen.* 4.17]. The prophetic polemic against war has only in a subordinate sense the modern humanitarian and economic motive. The motive is largely religious: Israel must trust in Jehovah, not in its own strength. Of course, peace is better than war. In the great eschatological pictures, such as Isa. 2 and Mic. 5 the peace-ideal has its place. Swords will be beaten into ploughshares and spears into hoes, but this has nothing to do with the wickedness of war as such, except in so far as it is cruelly conducted. It stands on a line with the idea that devouring animals will cease.

The prophetic condemnation of the social sin of Israel does not have its deepest root in humanitarian motives. The humanitarian element is not, of course, absent. Nor could it be absent, for it is as old as the theocracy. The law takes the poor and defenceless under its special protection. It is in keeping with this, that the chief institutions of the theocracy, for example, that of the kingdom, bear a conspicuously humane, beneficent character. And we find this preserved and further developed in the prophets. Their rebuke of social sin attaches itself to

a figurative description of the idolatrous bent of the people: whoredom coincides with adultery. The principal cause of this adultery lies in sensual selfishness. Israel has withdrawn her affection from Jehovah. As He called them (the more He called them), so (the more) they went from Him; they sacrificed unto the Baals, they burned incense to graven images [11.2]. They knew no longer that Jehovah had healed them [11.3]. Their heart was exalted, they had forgotten Him (13.6]. To the Baals Israel ascribed what Jehovah had given her: 'I will go after my lovers that give me my bread and my water, my wool and my flax, mine oil and my drink' [2.5].

Israel ought to love Jehovah supremely for His own sake, and should seek the external blessings only because in them His love expresses itself. As it is, the very opposite takes place, the people care only for the gifts and are indifferent to the Giver. 'They sacrifice upon the tops of the mountains, and burn incense upon the hills, under oaks and poplars and terebinths, because their shadow is good' [4.13]. The sweet cakes of raisins, of which 3.1 says that they love them, are the figure for this sensual cult. Because inspired by this motive, it flourishes in times of plenty: 'Israel is a luxuriant vine which putteth forth his fruit; according to the multitude of his fruit he has multiplied his altars; according to the prosperity of his land he has made goodly pillars' [10.1]. When plenty and prosperity cease, the allegiance is lightly shifted from one god to another; 'I will go and return to my first husband, for then it was better with me than now' [2.7].

As to the cult Hosea condemns the selfish spirit in which it is conducted, and this for the sole reason, that it vitiates the relation between Israel and Jehovah at the very root. This type of polemic is peculiar to Hosea. What Ephraim brings is only a fleeting affection. Their *chesed* is like the morning-cloud and like the dew that goes early away [6.4]. Jehovah will not accept such service; it belongs to paganism. Hence the prophet says that she has loved the wages of religious prostitution upon every corn floor. She has sold herself to the strange gods for the produce of the land [9.1].

But the same principle determines Hosea's opinion with regard to the social and political sin of Israel. The prophet traces a connection between the faithlessness of the people to Jehovah and the dissolution of all social ties. This is the sequence of thought in 4.1, 2. Because faithfulness, lovingkindness (towards God) and knowledge of God fail in the land, therefore in the intercourse between man and man also, there is nothing but swearing and breaking faith and killing and stealing and committing adultery; they exceed and blood touches blood. Where the religious union with Jehovah is not kept sacred, there no human marriage can be secure. Sensuality produces religious whoredom, and religious whoredom again issues into physical whoredom [4.11, 14].

The sin of striving after riches and luxury, which Amos condemns for more obvious reasons, Hosea regards as an alienation of love from Jehovah. So we must understand 12.7–9, where Jehovah charges Israel with this sin, and then, by way of explanation, declares: 'I am Jehovah thy God from the land of Egypt', that is to say, I have remained faithful; ye have become faithless. They have become like the Canaanites, that is, like the Phoenicians, the traffickers of the ancient world. They have missed their theocratic vocation by striving to engage in trade. And their trading was dishonest; balances of deceit were in their hand [12.7].

Finally, in what Hosea says about the political sin of Israel it is not difficult to trace the influence of the same principle. A characteristic sin is in his view 'the pride of Israel' [5.5; 7.10]. This is the haughtiness born of self-reliance, the opposite to that spirit of dependence which ought to characterize behaviour towards Jehovah. Before all else, it is an act of disloyalty, when Ephraim seeks help with Assyria, whereas God ought to be her Saviour [5.13]. And, having once forsaken Jehovah, her heart has become so void of all constant attachment, that, while intriguing with Assyria, she at the same time seeks the favour of Egypt [8.9; 12.1]. Like a silly dove Ephraim is fluttering around; they call unto Egypt, they go to Assyria [7.11]. Hosea does not speak of faith positively, as Isaiah does, but this rebuke of the pride of Israel shows that the essence of the grace is familiar to him.

Among the political sins of Israel, the prophet further gives a prominent place to the manner in which they dealt with the institution of the kingdom. Not that he rejected the kingdom on principle, as some expositors claim. This can be maintained only by exscinding 3.5. If these words are genuine, then Hosea must have regarded the Davidic dynasty as the only legitimate one for Israel. But it is just as incorrect to assume that he condemned certain individual rulers of the northern kingdom for individual reasons alone. The terms in which he speaks are too general for that. It is not so much what the kings did, but rather what Israel did with the kingship and the kings, that meets with the prophet's disapproval. And he disapproves of it, because it was based on a wrong attitude towards Jehovah [8.4; 13.10]. The kingship was founded on the pride of Israel. This applies not merely to the later kings, rapidly succeeding one another; it applies to all the successive dynasties that the northern kingdom had seen. Hosea speaks in equally condemnatory terms of the kingship of Saul, for it had its origin in the same spirit [9.9; 10.9]. Only the kingdom of David escapes, because it was distinctly initiated by Jehovah, an instrument of the salvation He desired to give to His people.

Because thus viewing sin from the one principle of unfaithfulness to Jehovah, Hosea reaches a profound conception of its character as a disposition, an enslaving power, as something deeper and more serious than single acts of transgression. It is a bent, rendering its victims unable to reform [5.4; 7.2]. The 'spirit of whoredom' is within them, they are bent to backsliding [11.7]. 'Ephraim is a cake not turned'; he remains unconcernedly on the wrong, already burnt, side, however disastrous the consequences may be.

ISAIAH'S DOCTRINE OF SIN

We now turn to Isaiah and his conception of sin. It likewise reveals a point of view clearly his own. On the whole it is the deepest that the revelation of the Old Testament has to teach about sin. What the idea of the *berith*-marriage is to Hosea, that the thought of Jehovah's glory is to Isaiah. Sin appears to him as, first of all, an infringement upon the honour of God. The idolatrous practices of the people are denounced for this reason. God has forsaken Israel, because they are filled from the east (perhaps the emendation 'with divination', *qesem* for *qedem*, is to be preferred), and soothsayers like the Philistines [2.6; 8.19]. Note carefully what is to Isaiah the offensive feature in sin of this kind. Such practices are a slight put upon Jehovah's divinity. It is His right to supply all teaching and information of this sort to His people. They are to walk in His light, to be open always to the influx of divine truth [2.5]. The ideal in the prophet's mind is, that Israel as a whole shall live in such unbroken communication with Jehovah, as he was aware of possessing for himself (note the plural 'let us walk'). What they possess, or imagine themselves to possess, is a caricature of revelation.

In the same way idolatry is a caricature of religion in general, highly dishonouring to God. 'Their land is full of idols; they worship the work of their own hands, that which their own fingers have made' [2.8]. That God's people are capable of exchanging the living God for something lifeless, manufactured by themselves, appears to the prophet the height of irreverence and irreligion. Subjectively the offensive feature of this kind of sin consists in its humiliating, degrading influence upon man [2.9]. The true greatness of man consists in the service of Jehovah; this being abandoned for idolatry, a universal abasement takes place. The idols are to the prophet's view the opposite of all Jehovah stands for. As Jehovah is the Holy One, so the idols contract, as it were, a sort of positive unholiness; they are to be defiled, to be dishonoured [30.22].

It is, however, not through paganistic forms of divination and the cult of idols alone that Israel has dishonoured Jehovah. In 2.7 luxury, wealth and military pride stand between divination and idolatry, and the combination is very significant. Luxurious and riotous living are condemned from the point of view that these produce carelessness and forgetfulness of God. Those Judaeans who rise up early in the morning to follow strong drink, and tarry late in the night till wine inflame them, whose feasts are harp and lute and tabret and pipe, they are the ones who do not regard the work of Jehovah, neither have considered the operation of His hands. The work of Jehovah here is His work in history, the momentous issues that He is working out in regard to the lot of His people. Every truly religious man ought to have his eyes and ears open to what the course of history portends. Isaiah has here distinctly formulated the thought that history is a revelation of Jehovah, in which there is no place for accident or confusion. Primarily it is, of course, the task of the prophet to watch what is developing. But the specific task of the prophet is destined to be universalized. Had Israel complied with this requirement, they might have adjusted themselves to the coming events and have escaped. As it is, they go into captivity for lack of knowledge [5.13].

Isaiah speaks once and again of the sin of intoxication [5.11, 12, 22; 22.2, 13; 28.1, 3, 7]. Especially the last of these passages is extremely realistic in its picture of the drunken revels of the priests and prophets. The prophet does not, of course, condemn the use of wine as such. On the contrary, some of his noblest figures are derived from it [1.22; 5; 16.8–10; 18.5; 25.6]. But intoxication is irreligious and degrading, because it darkens the perception of the divine spiritual realities in man, and so renders him brutish. The drunkards at Jerusalem 'err through wine and through strong drink go astray; they err in vision, they stumble in judgment' [28.7].

An equally prominent form of sin with this prophet is pride. Isaiah speaks of the lofty looks of man, the haughtiness of men [2.11, 17], and of things in general in the land that are haughty and proud and lifted up, vss. 12–15. The daughters of Zion are haughty and walk with stretched-forth necks and wanton eyes. The glory and pomp of the Israelites are to be humbled [5.14]. 'Ephraim and the inhabitants of

Samaria say in pride and in stoutness of heart: 'the bricks are fallen, but we will build with hewn stone; the sycamores are cut down, but we will replace them by cedars' [9.9, 10]. Of the pride of intellect 5.21 speaks. Pride based on wealth and aesthetic pretence likewise comes in for rebuke. Isaiah himself was responsive to all things of beauty and grandeur that the world presented to his sight. And yet he condemns the silver and the gold, the pleasant pictures, the fine apparel of the daughters of Zion, so elaborately described in 3.16–24. Beauty, irreligiously esteemed, infringes upon the glory of Jehovah. To take any natural object or product of art, intended to reflect the divine beauty, so as to make it serve the magnifying of the creature is a species of godlessness. Pride and vanity are closely connected with each other. Pride is vanity, in so far as there is no real worth and greatness behind it.

Pride, however, is not found among Israel alone. To Isaiah it made no difference whether the boasters were the petty grandees of Judaea, or the mighty monarchs of the East. Because the Assyrian claims that by the strength of his hand he has done things, and by his wisdom removed the bounds of the peoples, Jehovah will punish the fruit of the stout heart of the king of Assyria, and the glory of his high looks [10.12]. The highest embodiment that this sin of pride had found, to the far-reaching vision of Isaiah, was in that King of Babel, who said in his heart: 'I will exalt my throne above the stars of God, I will sit upon the mount of congregation (the mythical mountain, where the gods assembled), in the uttermost parts of the north; I will ascend above the heights of the clouds; I will be like the Most High.' [14.13, 14]. Pride is in its essence a form of self-deification. Satanic sin, a type of Satan, has been found in the King of Babel thus described [cp. 14.12; *Rev.* 9.1], and because the King is here addressed as morning star, the name Lucifer has been transferred from him to Satan.

Still other forms of sin castigated by Isaiah are avarice and oppression [3.12, 15; 5.7, 8, 23]. With this we are familiar from Amos and Hosea. The commercial prosperity of the earlier part of Isaiah's ministry fostered this evil. During the first centuries of their settlement in Canaan the Israelites were a purely agricultural people. Later on, however, a trading class sprang up among them. As the structure of society still continued to be based on agriculture, the increase of wealth meant the acquisition of vast landed properties. The rich made the poor their debtors, and then drove them from their ancient estates. Now the use of the soil had among Israel a religious significance. Jehovah is Lord of the entire land. He gives the people only the usufruct of the soil. The massing of lands in the hands of a few, therefore, was not only an ethical evil because accomplished through foul means, nor merely a social evil because productive of great disparity, but it was likewise a religious evil because it deprived the poor man of the very basis of his religious existence. Deprived of his land, he could no longer bring his tithes, nor his firstlings, nor his sacrifices; he could no longer participate in the celebration of the feasts. Hence Isaiah calls a woe upon those that join house to house, that they may dwell alone in the midst of the land [5.8]. That Isaiah's motive is at least partly religious, may be seen from 3.13–15. Jehovah here enters into judgment with the elders of his people, because they have eaten up the vineyard. Chap. 5 throws light on this; it is called the vineyard, because in reality the property of Jehovah. The poor are called Jehovah's people. We can here already observe the religious colouring which the word gradually acquires [10.2; 11.4; 14.30–32].

ISRAEL'S SIN AS VIEWED BY THE PROPHETS HISTORICALLY

In conclusion we must look at the prophetic statements concerning the sin of Israel from a historical point of view. What light do they throw on the state and course of Israel's religion in the pre-prophetic period? Do these sins and errors appear to the prophets as a lower stage of development, quite natural and unavoidable at the time before the purer prophetic religion arose? This is the critical view.

It is admitted on all sides that the historical writings of the Old Testament contradict it on almost every page. Their testimony is that there was:

(a) a relatively perfect and pure beginning of Israel's religion in revelation;

(b) an almost immediate falling away from this;

(c) an effort on the part of the prophets to reclaim the nation.

What the adherents of the critical hypothesis claim, is that the writers or redactors of these historical books, under the influence of unhistoric views, so manipulated the sources, that these books no longer reflect the actual course of events, but instead a totally different, imaginary course of events, construed from the subsequent orthodox legalistic standpoint.

Now what we are interested in is, whether the prophets give an account of the history of Israel before their own times which agrees with the critical representation, or one which agrees with this testimony of the historical books.

The point at issue should be sharply formulated. The question is not whether the popular religion did or did not actually constitute a lower form of belief and practice than what the prophets stood for. That it did admits of no denial. The mass of the people lived on a low plane religiously. We may go further than this. This was not confined to the particular period or juncture at which the prophets arose; such had been the condition of the mass for a long time previously. Their actual religion may well have borne many of the features which the critics ascribe to it. We may even say that, through the critical controversy with the Wellhausenians, our eyes have been first opened to this in its full extent. We apprehend better now that during the entire course of Old Testament history the supernatural element introduced by revelation had to wage war with the paganistic tendencies of the people. And, since no false practice can in the long run exist without reacting on beliefs and conceptions, a paganistic cult must have had for its correlate a paganistic creed. In so far we and the critics need not widely disagree as to the state of affairs depicted in the prophetic writings.

But the difference between them and us concerns the question whether, over against this popular religion, there did, or did not exist a better historical tradition, going back to ancient times, to which the prophets could appeal, and on the ground of which they could charge the mass with apostasy. Do the prophets oppose to the degraded practices and belief of their time another type of religion, simply because it is better and their own, or because it is the only legitimate religion in Israel? Do they appeal to their own convictions, as to intuitive verities, in the judgments pronounced and in the ideals set up, or do they call back to a standard fixed before?

But even this does not quite suffice to formulate the point at issue. In a certain sense even our opponents admit that the popular religion in the days of the prophets represented a decline from a previous better state. It is believed that the Hebrews in their nomadic period, before they entered upon the life in Canaan, had had a much simpler form of religion than afterwards. Through adopting many of the customs of the Canaanites they deteriorated. There had been a downward process. For the simple, austere religion of the desert had been substituted the sensual, luxurious religion of the inhabitants of the land. But what the prophets preached was, according to the critics, not identical with this primitive nomadic religion. It differed from it as the ethical differs from the sub-ethical, the spiritual from the naturalistic. So that, while in one sense, the popular religion was a degenerated religion, in another sense, as compared with the prophetic religion, it was also a lower stage of evolution. There had never been something like those views of the prophets before. Consequently the question must be put as follows: Do the prophets teach that the people had fallen away from a relatively better faith, or do they claim that they had fallen away from an absolute norm, imposed upon them in the past by Jehovah and in substance identical with their own prophetic teaching?

In endeavouring to answer this question, we observe, in the first place, that the prophets charge the people with apostasy from a legitimate religion revealed to them at the time of the Exodus. This is the testimony of Amos 2.10; 3.1; 5.25; 9.7. It is implied also, as we have seen, in what Hosea teaches about the origin of the marriage-union, and the marriage-law resulting from it, in the same period. Israel's sin goes back, not merely to the time of the secession of the ten tribes, nor merely to the time of Saul ('the days of Gibeah' 10.9), but to the time before their entering Canaan [9.10]. Isaiah has numerous references to a better past, when the religious conditions were nearer to the ideal. This refers proximately to the time of David [1.21, 26]. But it reaches further back to the time of the Exodus and the wilderness-journey [4.5; 10.24; 10.26; 11.16]. Israel's first father already sinned, and her interpreters transgressed against Jehovah [43.27]. God knew from the beginning that Israel was very treacherous, called a transgressor from the womb [48.1–8, especially vs. 8]. Immediately after the redemption from Egypt they rebelled and grieved God's Holy Spirit, so that He turned into their enemy and fought against them [63.10]. Micah likewise appeals to the saving acts of Jehovah at the time of the Exodus, and appeals to them in order to call Israel back to obedience. Jehovah sent Moses, Aaron and Miriam before them and made known to them what is good [6.3–8].

The prophets view the people's religious condition, not merely as degraded and deplorable, but as a guilty condition. It is not necessary to point this out in detail; the threat of judgment against it is inconceivable on any other supposition. The moral indignation which so strongly colours their discourses can only have flowed from the knowledge that wilful transgression was involved.

The prophets identify this old ideal from which Israel has departed with their own teaching. Nowhere do they make a distinction between what Jehovah once demanded and what He now demands. None of the prophets ever betrays that his teaching appears to him in the light of an innovation. Though they were aware that their teaching marked an advance upon what lay before, yet they never indicate that there was an advance in the principles upheld. By these constant principles they judge the conduct of Israel. But not only this, explicitly and positively also they make the identification between their own message and the older one. Hosea says that in former times Jehovah has hewn Israel by the prophets, and slain them by the words of his mouth, because He desired lovingkindness and not sacrifice, the knowledge of God and not burnt-offerings [6.5, 6]. By a prophet Jehovah brought Israel up out of Egypt and by a prophet was he preserved, [12.13]. Israel made answer to Jehovah's approach unto her in the days of her youth [2.15].

It is the same in Amos. When Jehovah knew Israel among all the families of the earth, it was in order that among them righteousness should be cultivated [3.2]. Israel was originally a wall made by a plumbline; when Jehovah afterwards finds it otherwise, this is due to departure from the erstwhile rectitude [7.7]. Amos even declares that the same unresponsiveness and impenitence that met the prophetic teaching of his day, characterized the Israel of past generations [2.9–12]. The earlier prophets had preached along the same lines as he himself followed in his preaching. It is because Israel has rejected them, that he is now sent to announce the judgment. The earlier Israel had said to its prophets, 'Prophesy not'. Amos strongly feels his continuity with them as to the substance of the message. These prophets of old must have proclaimed unpleasant truths, otherwise there could not have been the same unpleasant reaction. And this could only mean that they, in the same manner as Amos, insisted upon the righteous nature of Jehovah, and foretold a judgment.

This carries back the knowledge of the ethical demands of Jehovah to a much earlier time than that of Amos. Isaiah in a similar way represents everything Jehovah has done to his vineyard as done for the purpose of reaping good fruit, namely, the fruit of righteousness [5.7].

The attitude assumed by the prophets towards the people precludes the idea of their having been conscious of innovation in the traditional faith of Israel. They boldly appeal to the popular conscience, while at the same time attacking the popular religion. Amos, in describing what had taken place in connection with the Exodus, including the raising up of unpopular prophets, asks: 'Is it not even thus, O ye children of Israel?' [2.11]. This means something more than that the people are asked to acknowledge the historicity of the facts; the appeal is to their consciousness of favours despised. This interrogative way of reasoning with the people is characteristic of Amos; 5.25; 6.2; 9.7. The last of these passages takes for granted that the people believe in Jehovah's control over the history of other nations than Israel.

But not only did the prophets expect the popular conscience to give at least a theoretical consent to their position; to some extent this assent must have been actually given; in other words, the people must have felt themselves in the wrong historically. There is no trace whatsoever of any defensive attitude assumed by the people, which nevertheless would have been unavoidable, had the prophets preached a new doctrine. There are not a few passages which give us glimpses of the struggle between prophets and people, but in none of these are the prophets charged with being innovators or iconoclasts in regard to the traditional faith of Israel [Amos 7.11–17; Hos. 9.8, 9; Isa. 28.1–13; 30.10, 11; Mic. 2.6–11]. How could Amos ever have adopted the interrogative form of speaking commented upon, had he been confronting a sceptical and gainsaying audience?

It might be said that the prophets whose writings we possess were not historians, that their aim was not to draw a faithful picture of the times with their conflicting forces and tendencies, but rather to present their own side in the controversy, and that in receiving their testimony without cross-questioning we do the people injustice. But this answer can not invalidate the above argument. For, unless the prophets have on purpose eliminated or obliterated every trace of this historical aspect of the controversy, we must expect to find traces of it in their record.

[D] THE JUDGMENT AND THE RESTORATION: PROPHETIC ESCHATOLOGY

THE VIEWS OF THE WELLHAUSEN SCHOOL OF CRITICISM
According to the Wellhausen school of criticism, eschatology resembles the ethical monotheism of the Old Testament in this respect, that it is a specifically prophetic creation. This implies that, as there was no ethical monotheism before the prophetic period, so there was no eschatology. And as an explanatory hypothesis has been devised to explain the origin of the former out of historical and psychological factors, so one has been constructed to explain on a basis of similar causes the rise of an eschatology among Israel. The difference, say the critics, is that in the construction of their ethical monotheism the prophets were more thoroughly ethical and spiritual than in their upbuilding of the eschatological scheme. While the ethical teaching, as to its substance, has perpetual validity and everlasting significance,

the framework of eschatology has in it much that is perishable. In the minds of the prophets it was, to be sure, largely a matter of fantastic expectations. In the sequel, however, it proved highly potential. In fact it has become the source of the supernaturalistic, theological, metaphysical world-view to which the Biblical religion has become wedded. Whatever there is in Christianity beyond ethical idealism and sentimental spirituality, all that transcends the present life and the evolutionary development of things, all that reckons from a definite beginning of creation and looks forward to a definite winding up of things, and, finally all that cleaves to the Messianic interpretation of Jesus, and has made of historic Christianity a realistic, concrete, factual religion, placing itself at the centre of the development of the world, all this in its last analysis springs from this one source. Hence eschatology, as the prophets preached it, has become in critical quarters not merely a problem for explanation, but likewise an object of criticism.

Since the ethical monotheism and the eschatology are two more or less incompatible things, the natural inclination, from the critical point of view, was to magnify the former and to minimize the latter, at least so far as the earlier prophets, the great heroes of the ethicizing of religion, are concerned. Much material of an eschatological complexion is eliminated by divisive methods from the writings of Isaiah and Micah especially, to a lesser extent also from the prophecies of Amos and Hosea. In the opinion of the critical school these books are not, as books, derived from the men whose names they bear, but are later crystallizations around nuclei of original, authentic material. In the long process of redaction they have undergone much of the accretion that is supposed to have come through the eschatological impulse. The original prophecies may have had a moderate admixture of this kind of material, but the rank growth of it that luxuriates in the present collections is of later origin. This principle finds especial application to the promissory pieces that lie scattered through the denunciatory, pessimistic material. If we distinguish in the full-grown eschatology between the two strands of threat and of hope, then the strand of threat is assumed to have been far more indigenous in prophecy than that of hope. In later times the element of threat was, however, also strongly elaborated as was the element of hope. In the original preaching of men like Amos and Hosea it was, if not less intense, at least more sober and kept subject to the ethical motive.

A distinction is made by the critics between the two strands of 'woe-eschatology' and 'weal-eschatology' as to their precedence of origin in the prophetic mind. The eschatology of woe always came

287

first, and remained first in order, even after the other had taken its place by the side of it. The eschatology of woe was the natural product of the prophets' ethical indignation at the corrupt moral and religious conditions they found prevailing. It all deserved to be swept aside in one great overwhelming catastrophe. From this, to the conviction that it would be, was not a great distance. The historical conjunction of forces favoured the expectation. Such a catastrophe was, of course, apt to be measured both in terms of intensity and in terms of compass by the urge of resentment in the prophet's heart.

Still, it is believed that the terms in which the early prophets described the coming woe were always derived from the national-political sphere. Their eschatology was a military one. Some earthly power would be the instrument of executing the judgment of Jehovah, and what it did would consist in national convulsions and overthrows. Later on, owing to the influx of all sorts of ideas of mythological origin from the Orient, this military picture was mixed with cosmical elements, and much more complicated schemes resulted. When, and in the measure that, this came about, the change from eschatology to what is called apocalyptic was made. Ezekiel marks the incision in this respect. Afterwards this mythological, cosmical element was retroactively introduced into the earlier prophets, so that the difference is now no longer clearly perceptible.

But the prophets were not entirely heralds of woe. They could not help remaining patriots, and had more of the traditional attachment to the old religion of Israel in them, than they themselves knew. Hence their own predictions of woe caused in them a reaction, and they began to soften these through holding in prospect a future of restoration to the favour of Jehovah and blessedness. Into this likewise crept later on the same mythological elements that had become mixed with the eschatology of woe. There was, however, a time at the beginning when the woe occupied the field alone. The earliest prophets were prophets of calamity pure and simple, and even found the distinction between themselves and the false prophets in this feature, that the false prophets prophesied of pleasant things to come.

Such is the Wellhausenian construction of the origin of prophetic eschatology. Of late it has lost its monopoly in critical circles through the influence of Babylonian archaeology upon the interpretation of the Old Testament. The views of men like Gunkel and Gressman have begun to supplant it. These men claim that there existed from ancient times an eschatology in the Orient, and that Hebrew belief, as it was influenced from this quarter in many other things, can not have escaped being so in the matter of eschatology. The Hebrews knew about these things long before the great prophets arose. And the prophets themselves knew about them and incorporated them into their message. These elements were from the outset mythological and cosmical.

The difference between the Wellhausen view and this modified view is that the streaming in of the ideas from the Orient is now put at a much earlier date, so early indeed, that it is believed that, before the prophets handled them, the ideas had become quite assimilated by the Hebrews. At first the prophets put them to an ethical and religious use. At a later stage the rank material outgrew their power of adaptation and the ideas were cherished and studied for their own inherent interest.

It will be felt that this shifting of critical opinion immediately made an important difference in the appraisal of the eschatological teaching of the early prophets. In two respects the method of treatment was changed. First, the mere fact of a prophecy being promissory and consolatory was no longer considered as prejudicial to its authenticity. Amos could promise and console, and so could Isaiah, for the material lay ready to hand, and it had acquired a sort of traditionalness and independence, which facilitated its introduction everywhere. There was no special motive required. It belonged to the general spirit of prophesying. Much of the material recently cast out as unworthy of the onesided ethicized prophets was thus reclaimed. And the same applies to the so-called mythological, realistic strand in the prophetic writings. There was now no longer any occasion to ascribe its introduction to a later vogue of apocalyptic.

THE ESCHATOLOGICAL TEACHING OF THE PROPHETS

After this brief orientation we may now study with equal brevity the eschatological teaching of two prophets, Hosea and Isaiah. It is sufficient to deal with Amos and Micah by way of side-reference only, because the material found in these is largely found in the other two likewise. The two topics with which we have to deal may be called the doctrine of the judgment and that of the restoration. In order to justify the characterization of these as eschatology, we should sharply mark what is the specific difference of eschatology from the Biblical standpoint. In the abstract it might seem more appropriate to fit in the crises described by the prophets with the general up-and-downward movement of history, each one being co-ordinated with preceding and following events. But this would miss the very point of the eschatological peculiarity. This consists in that the crises described are not ordinary upheavals, but such as lead to an abiding order of things, in which the prophetic vision comes to rest. Finality and consummation form the specific difference of prophetic, as of all other Biblical eschatology. The judgment predicted is the judgment, and the restoration is the restoration, of the end.

One other peculiarity to be noted is really a consequence of the one just stated. Whenever the prophets speak in terms of judgment, immediately the vision of the state of glory obtrudes itself upon their view, and they concatenate the two in a way altogether regardless of chronological interludes. Isaiah couples with the defeat of the Assyrians under Sennacherib the unequalled pictures of the glory of the end, and the impression might be created that the latter was just waiting for the former, to make its immediate appearance. The vision 'hastens' under their eye. The philosophy of this foreshortening of the beyond-prospect is one of the most difficult things in the interpretation of prophecy in Old Testament and New Testament alike. We cannot here further dwell upon it.

HOSEA

The manner of the description of the judgment varies according to the individual manner and style of the prophet. In Hosea the idea is more fully elaborated than with the others, precisely because there is more of the individual in it. Hosea, indeed, agrees with the others in declaring it 'punishment' inspired by wrath [9.15; 11.8, 9]. But on the other hand the same judgment also serves the opposite purpose. It serves as a chastisement imposed by love to discipline Israel, Jehovah's son. With reference to the former, notice that national death is specified as the wages of national sin [5.2; 7.9; 13.14]. The last passage should be rendered interrogatively: 'Shall I ransom them from the power of the grave, redeem them from death?' The answer required is negative, and Jehovah Himself proceeds to give it by summoning the plagues of death to overwhelm them: 'O death, where are thy plagues; O grave, where is thy destruction? Repentance shall be hid from mine eyes.' (Observe the magnificent manner in which Paul has turned this question into its triumphant opposite in 1 Cor. 15.55.)

Chap. 13.13 is the passage in which these two aspects of the judgment, the destructive and the disciplinary one, are most clearly distinguished. Here the new Israel is the son to be born, the old sinful Israel the mother, who dies in giving birth to the child. In dependence on the marriage-idea, all calamities of the judgment result from this, that Jehovah personally withdraws from Israel [5.6, 15; 9.12]. The judgment leads to conversion in more than one way. It enlightens as to the causes which have provoked Jehovah's wrath; it does this by striking the instruments of sinning involved in each, and thus prepares the way for conviction of sin [8.6; 10.2–8, 14, 15; 11.6]. Forcibly it separates Israel from the objects of her adulterous love [2.9, 12; 3.3–5]. Symbolically this is expressed by the feature that there is no intercourse between Hosea and his wife. But the prophet also keeps his wife isolated from himself after having received her back [3.3]: 'so will I also be toward thee.' Jehovah in like manner will keep Himself separated from the people during the exile, to enable them to obtain a truer conception of His character, for otherwise they would only have turned from the other gods to their own caricature of Jehovah. After these preparations Israel is won back by an unparalleled new revelation of Jehovah's love [2.14, 15].

The conscious results of these experiences are described in chap. 14. Here is the picture of Israel's conversion. It involves the profound recognition, not merely of sin, but sinfulness. In vs. 2 the word 'all' is to be stressed. The two principal forms of sin, pride and sensual idolatry, are specified [vs. 3]. The conviction is voiced that no external worship can buy back Jehovah's favour [vs. 2]. God's free forgiving love is the sole source of salvation. The profound humility suffusing the experience strikingly appears in this, that Israel does not call herself Jehovah's wife, nor even His son, but an orphan [vs. 3]; compare also 3.5 and 11.6, passages in which the same peculiar state of mind, penitence mingled with newly-awakened trust and fear, is finely depicted.

ISAIAH

In Isaiah the pictures of the judgment are, no less than with Hosea, in keeping with the general tone and temper of the prophet. His mode of thinking and seeing things is theocentric. The vision of the judgment in chap. 2 of itself turns into a theophany. The theophany comes in storm and earthquake. Here the political-military feature is absent. For the theophanic display of the majesty of Jehovah the prophet even loses sight of the destruction that overtakes the sinners, which in reality he had planned to describe. The judgment as to its intent is with Isaiah (and Micah) mainly a judgment of purification. But the purification is obtained through extirpation of the evil elements. It is the process by which the remnant is, as it were, distilled [4.3, 4; 6.11–13; 10.20–23; 17.6, 7; 24.13, 14; 28.5, 6, 23–29].

The comprehensive phrase for all this is 'the day of Jehovah' [2.12]. This phrase occurs also in Amos. It furnishes one of the proofs for the existence of an ancient pre-prophetic eschatology. It has become very important for New Testament revelation as 'the day of the Lord'. Some give it a general theocentric explanation for Isaiah [2.11]. It is quite possible that Isaiah gave the idea this turn, but the original sense can hardly have been such. A martial explanation has been suggested: the day monopolized by Jehovah as his day of victory; compare 'the day of Midian' [9.4]. A more plausible derivation, in dependence on Amos 5.20, is that it rests upon the contrast between darkness and light. These would be its two diverse manifestations, the one immediately preceding the other. An objection is that on this view it would have been denominated from its better side exclusively, whereas in Old Testament and New Testament alike the emphasis seems differently distributed. In Amos the doing away with all that is evil stands in the foreground, but with Isaiah it is rather the sweeping away of all that is a caricature of divinity. In the later pieces, chaps. 28–38. a more positive connection between the judgment and the conversion is traceable. The experiences of the Sennacherib-crisis will not only destroy the wicked and unbelieving; they will also teach the others how great is the sin of Israel and how great the grace of Jehovah.

In the second part of the book the captivity is represented as an atonement (in the Old Testament sense) for the sin of Israel, and this idea of expiation reaches its highest expression in the figure of the 'Servant of Jehovah' of chapter 53. The captivity is also represented as leading the true Israel to repentance [59.12–15]. The idea of 'the remnant' thus obtains for Isaiah a more positive aspect than it had for Amos. For Amos it means: 'nothing more than a remnant', for Isaiah 'only, but still a remnant'. In Micah, chap. 7.7–20 corresponds to the second part of the prophecies of Isaiah. Here a confession is put into the mouth of Israel, implying that the experience of the exile has produced a deep consciousness of sin.

Amos and Hosea do not reflect upon the consequences of either a favourable or unfavourable kind, which the judgment will entail for the foreign nations. Their negative and positive eschatology lack the universalistic element. Isaiah and Micah dwell upon both the adverse and the beneficent way in which the world at large will be affected by the crisis approaching for Israel.

Another difference is that the judgment-eschatology of Amos and Hosea is simple, that of Isaiah and Micah complex. The simple eschatology divides itself into two acts, the judgment and the restoration, both considered as units. With Isaiah and Micah this simple scheme becomes complicated. First of all a distinction is made between the judgment upon the Northern and that upon the Southern kingdom. These two are seen to fall apart in time. The complexity, however, arises from still another distinction. Both Isaiah and Micah expect a preliminary judgment of Assyria, which they do not identify with the final collapse of the world-power, and which, therefore, does not interfere with the continued hostile attitude of the latter toward Israel in the future.

From our standpoint we would say that this proximate deliverance stood in a typical relation to the final one. Isaiah and Micah begin to view the judgment after the manner of a process completing itself in successive acts. Assyria will not be the only, nor the last instrument wielded by God in judgment of Israel. After Assyria comes Babylon, mentioned by both prophets [*Isa.* 13 and 14; *Mic.* 4.10]. And, besides this specific mention made of Babylon, there still looms in the farther distance an ominous conglomeration of many nations preparing to come up for the attack, and to be destroyed in an even more mysterious, spectacular manner than the proximate foe [*Isa.* 17.12; 24–27, frequently called the Apocalypse of Isaiah; *Mic.* 4.11–13].

Finally, the most important difference arises from the appearance and activity of the Messiah in the judgment-drama of Isaiah and Micah, and his absence as a judgment-figure in the other two prophets [*Isa.* 9 and 11, *Mic.* 5.2ff.]. In Hosea he enters only as a static element of the future state [3.5].

THE 'LATTER DAYS' IN HOSEA

In outlining the make-up of the future state of the people we again consider Hosea and Isaiah separately. In Hosea the following points must be noted: a new union between Jehovah and Israel will be established. (Observe that this is not represented as the remarriage of the formerly divorced husband and wife. It is a new marriage altogether.) A new betrothal, like unto a first betrothal, precedes. In this the prophecy falls out of the setting of the story. But this is allowed to take place on purpose in order to indicate that the past will be entirely blotted out, so as not to cast forward its dark shadow on the future blessedness of the eschatological union. For this reason the prophet drops the recital of his own marriage-experience in chapter 3. He steps out of the picture, because to him the indelible stain of the former disruption clung, which should not cleave to the final relation between Jehovah and Israel. The new union will be absolutely undissolvable. This is nought but the expression of the eschatological in terms of the marriage-figure.

The personal, spiritual aspect of the new union is depicted in 2.18-20. The nature-aspect with its supernaturalistic colouring is found in vss. 21-23. In chap. 14 the two intermingle. The Israelites will become individually sons of Jehovah [1.10]. This promise is applied by Peter and Paul [1 Pet. 2.10; Rom. 9.25, 26] to the calling of the Gentiles, not, however, because Hosea was thinking of that, but because the underlying principle was the same, and because the Gentiles had been organically incorporated into the covenant of Israel.

A great increase of posterity will follow the restoration of Israel. [1.10]. The name 'Jezreel', which, according to 1.4, had an ominous, meaning, will obtain a favourable sense. Jehovah will sow the handful of remaining Israelites in the land to make of them a great multitude. Israel and Judah will be reunited. Thus the sinful disruption between them will be healed. The reunited people will appoint over themselves one head of the house of David. This also is the opposite to what their sin had consisted in; hence they are represented as doing it themselves. As they had chosen many heads, so now they will seek one head [1.11; 3.5]. Israel's rule will be victoriously extended over the neighbouring peoples [1.11].

As a comprehensive name for the approaching future Hosea uses the phrase 'acherith hayyamim, 'the latter days' [3.5]. It seems to denote in this place, not so much the future blessed state, but rather the final crisis leading up to it.

THE FUTURE 'GLORY' IN ISAIAH

Isaiah delights in depicting the era after the judgment as a supreme revelation of Jehovah's glory. His vision of it centres in the sanctuary and the city, whereas to Amos and Hosea, and even Micah, it rested upon the land. There is a priestly dignity about the prophet's language ultimately to be explained from the predominance of the note of the divine glory in his message. The future will be a state in which the people will be able to engage in the service of God without interruption. Over the whole of Mount Zion and over her assemblies will hang the protecting cloud and fire of the wilderness-journey, a covering for all the glory [4.5]. At the same time the prophet introduces the idyllic blessedness of an ideal life of agriculture into his picture. But this is done again with a clear reference to the greater opportunity such manner of life affords for maintaining the proper attitude of humbleness and simplicity towards God, in contrast to the luxury and artificial refinement which the prophet had learned to interpret as lying at the root of forgetfulness of Jehovah. Israel will in these perfect days put her pride in the fruit of the soil which Jehovah provides [4.2; cp. 30.23–26; 32.16–20]. The meaning of the phrase 'branch of Jehovah', which later in Jeremiah and Zechariah has a Messianic meaning, may be thus interpreted in Isa. 4.2 also, but according to others it means the produce of the soil with the associations just indicated.

In its most majestic form this thought appears where the prophet describes the future state as the restored paradise of the days of creation [11.6–9 in a Messianic context; 65.17–25]. Here the supernaturalizing of the entire state of existence is implied. The thought of the return of primeval golden conditions seems to have formed an ancient ingredient in much, even pagan, eschatology, with this difference, that in the latter there is a succession of cycles, from the highest to the lowest, whilst in Scripture things come permanently to rest in the consummation of the end. The transition from a restored Canaan to a restored paradise is not difficult because, from the outset, Canaan, the land flowing with milk and honey, seems to have been regarded as paradise-land [*Amos* 9.13; *Hos.* 2.21–22; 14.5–7]. A still higher flight the prophecy of Isaiah takes, where it speaks of 'new heavens and a new earth' created by Jehovah [65.17; 66.22].

The conception of a personal Messiah appears in Isa. 9.1–7, possibly also in chaps. 32, 33. It occurs in Mic. 5, and according to one interpretation in Hos. 3.5, where David might be a personal name of the Messiah. It is not found with Amos. The point of view from which the Messianic concept is introduced is in Isaiah the sacramental one: He is a pledge and constant vehicle of the gracious presence of Jehovah with His people. The name 'Immanuel' strikingly expresses this fundamental concept. Afterwards, in Isa. 53, under the name 'Servant of Jehovah' he becomes the sacrificial expiator of the sin of Israel on the principle of vicarious sin-bearing. But the original idea is larger in scope. In chap. 9 the Messiah appears as the ideal King. The prophet here seems to move his vision along from the dark scene of the deportation of a part of Northern Israel by Tiglath-Pileser to the scene of light, characteristic of the Messianic glory. Thick darkness has settled upon the territory of the north-eastern tribes, but the light, while first seen by them in its rising, shines in the end on the whole people. The Messiah is the central figure of this vision of light. His appearance explains all that precedes. (Notice the repeated 'for' in vss. 4, 5, 6, introducing each time an explanation of the immediately preceding, with the Messiah as the last factor, beyond whom no explanation is necessary.)

Further, emphasis is thrown on the Messiah's being the gift of God.

'A son is given.' He is identified with Jehovah in such a profound sense as to reveal His Deity. No one not possessed of the attributes enumerated could fulfil the sacramental function ascribed to Him. The names given are four: 'Wonder of a Counsellor', 'God-of-a-Hero', 'Father for Eternity', 'Prince of Peace'. The first two describe what the Messiah is in Himself, the last two what He is in reference to the people. Of the former pair again the first describes His wisdom to counsel and the second His power to execute. From the recurrence of some of these attributes in 10.21 and 40.28 as attributes of Jehovah Himself, it may be seen on how high a plane the Messianic teaching of the prophet here moves. In chap. 11, on the other hand, the emphasis is thrown on the equipment of the Messiah for his functions by the gift of the Spirit. The Spirit of Jehovah 'rests' upon Him. What He enjoys is not a temporary visitation of the Spirit, but His abiding influence [cp. 61.1–3].

One might say that the former of these two Messianic representations is reproduced in the Fourth Gospel, the latter in the Synoptics. The Spirit here also is a Spirit of counsel first, and a Spirit of might in the second place. To these are added the two phrases descriptive of His judging activity, which takes place in knowledge of the actual state of things, and in the fear of Jehovah, that is to say, under the controlling influence of the religious principle. His saving work for the poor and meek is stressed. Together with this, mention is made of the destruction of the wicked. The latter takes place after a supernatural fashion: 'With the rod of his mouth' and 'the breath of his lips' [cp. Ps. 2.9; 2 Thess. 2.8].

The New Testament

ONE:
THE STRUCTURE OF NEW
TESTAMENT REVELATION

There are three ways in which the structure of New Testament Revelation can be determined from within Scripture itself. To add 'from within Scripture itself'' is essential, for we dare not impose upon the divine process and its product a scheme from any outside source. If redemption and revelation form an organism, then, like every other organism, it should be permitted to reveal to us its own articulation, either by way of our observing it, or by our receiving from it the formula of its make-up, where at certain high-points it reaches a consciousness of its inner growth.

[1] *From indications in the Old Testament*
The first of the three ways spoken of runs through the Old Testament. The Old Testament dispensation is a forward-stretching and forward-looking dispensation. Owing to the factual character of Biblical religion its face is necessarily set towards new things. Prophecy is the best indicator of this, for prediction is not an accidental element in prophecy, but of its very essence. But more particularly eschatological and Messianic prophecy are pointed towards the future, and not merely towards the future as a relatively higher state, but as an absolutely perfect and enduring state to be contrasted with the present and its succession of developments. Here, then, the distinction between something old and something new, both comprehensively taken, is in principle apprehended. The Old Testament, through its prophetic attitude, postulates the New Testament. And there are passages in which the term 'new' emerges in a semi-conscious manner, as it were, to give expression to the contrast between what is and what shall be [*Isa.* 65.17; *Ezek.* 11.19]. This technical use of 'new' has passed over even into the vocabulary of the dispensation of fulfilment [*Matt.* 13.52; *Mk.* 16.17; 2 *Cor.* 5.17; *Rev.* 2.17].

There is, however, one prophetic utterance in which this form of thought crystallizes into the phrase 'New *Berith*': Greek, 'New

Diatheke'. This is Jer. 31.31–34. Although here the correlative 'Old *Berith*' does not explicitly appear by the side of 'New *Berith*', still the idea itself is clearly given in the words: 'Not according to the *berith* that I made with their fathers – to bring them out of the land of Egypt.' As a matter of fact, in this prophecy, besides the name 'New *Berith*', the two most distinctive features of the new order of affairs are described. The one is: Jehovah will create obedience to the law through writing it in the heart. The other is: there will be complete forgiveness of sin. And, what most closely concerns our present purpose, the 'newness' is applied not merely in a general way to religious status, but is most specifically extended to the sphere of revelation and of knowlege of God: 'They shall all know me, from the least of them to the greatest of them.'

[2] *From the teachings of Jesus*

After Jeremiah the phrase does not recur in the Old Testament Scriptures. We first meet with it again in the words spoken by Jesus at the Last Supper. His blood He calls 'my blood of the *diatheke*' (Matthew and Mark), the cup 'the new *diatheke* in my blood' (Luke and Paul). It is evident that our Lord here represents His blood (death) as the basis and inauguration of a new religious relationship of the disciples to God. While the former relationship is not referred to as 'the old', the implied allusions to Ex. 24 and Jer. 31, even apart from the use of the adjective 'new' in Luke (and Paul, 1 Cor. 11.25) reveal the presence in His mind of a contrast between something past abrogated and something new substituted. This is altogether independent of the choice between rendering *diatheke* 'testament' or 'covenant'. On either rendering the contrast between two distinct dispensations of religious privilege is involved.

Further, it is not obscurely intimated, that the new order of affairs, so far from being in its turn again subject to change or abrogation, is of final significance. It reaches over into the eschatological state, which of itself makes it eternal. This may be gathered from Jesus' solemn declaration about not expecting to drink of the fruit of the vine again, until He shall drink it new (Matthew adds 'with you') in the Kingdom of God (Luke, 'until the Kingdom of God shall have come'). What we call the 'New Covenant' here appears at the outset as an eternal covenant. Into the question of what induced our Lord, who had never before made use of the concept in His teaching, but exclusively spoken of 'the Kingdom', to employ it at this one late point, we cannot here enter.

It ought to be further noticed, that the contrast here drawn is not in the first place a contrast of revelation. The words speak of a new era in religious access to God. Of a new period of divine self-disclosure they do not speak, although that, of course, is presupposed under the general law that progress in religion follows progress in revelation.

[3] *From the teachings of Paul and the other Apostles*

From Jesus we pass on to Paul. Paul is in the New Testament the great exponent of the fundamental bisection in the history of redemption and of revelation. Thus he speaks not only of the two regimes of law and faith, but even expresses himself in the consecutive form of statement: 'after that faith is come' [*Gal.* 3.25]. It is no wonder, then, that with him we find the formal distinction between the 'New *Diatheke*' and the 'Old *Diatheke*' [2 *Cor.* 3.6, 14]. Here also, to be sure, we have in the first place a contrast between two religious ministrations, that of the letter and that of the Spirit, that of condemnation and that of righteousness. Nevertheless, the idea of difference in revelation, as underlying the difference in ministration between Moses and Paul, clearly enters. There is a 'reading' of Moses, that is, of the law, and a 'speech', a 'vision' of the Lord of glory [vss. 12, 14, 15, 16]. From the phrase 'reading of the Old *Diatheke*' in vs. 14, some have even inferred that the Apostle had in mind the idea of a second, a new canon to take its place by the side of the old. Vs. 15, however, shows that 'reading of the Old *Diatheke*' simply means reading of the Law, the Law being frequently in the Old Testament called by the name of *berith, diatheke*; hence in vs. 15 the 'reading of Moses' is substituted for the 'reading of the Old *Diatheke*'.

The Epistle to the Hebrews gives us the clearest information in regard to the structure of redemptive procedure, and that particularly, as based on and determined by the structure of revelation. It is not necessary to quote single passages, the whole Epistle is full of it.[1] We read here of the 'New *Diatheke*' [9.15[. The phrase 'Old *Diatheke*' does not occur, although other phrases, practically equivalent, do. How intimately to the writer the unfolding from the Old into the New is bound up with the unfolding of revelation, may be seen from the opening words of the Epistle. 'God having spoken – spake – in a Son – whom He has appointed heir of all things, who – when He had in Himself purged our sins, sat down', etc. The participle aorist 'having spoken' and the finite verb 'spake' link the old and the new together, representing the former as preparatory to the latter.

[1] Cp. G. Vos 'Hebrews, the Epistle of the Diatheke', *Princeton Theological Review*, XIII, 587–632; and XIV, 1–61; and *The Teaching of the Epistle to the Hebrews* (1956).

THE NEW DISPENSATION IS FINAL

It will be noticed that in Hebrews 1.1–2, as in the statements of the Old Testament, and of Jesus and Paul, the new dispensation appears as final. And this applies likewise to the revelation introducing it. It is not one new disclosure to be followed by others, but the consummate disclosure beyond which nothing is expected. After speech in 'a Son' (qualitatively so called) no higher speech were possible. Paul also speaks of the sending forth of God's Son from God as taking place in the *pleroma of the time* [*Gal.* 4.4]. Consequently there is nowhere any trace of the cumulative point of view: Prophets, Jesus, Apostles; the New Testament revelation is one organic, and in itself completed, whole. It includes the Apostles, who are witnesses and interpreters of the Christ, but does not have them *ab extra* added to itself as separate instruments of information. It is a total misunderstanding both of the consciousness of Jesus and of that of the New Testament writers, to conceive of the thought of 'going back' from the Apostles, particularly Paul, to Jesus. Such a thought is born out of the inorganic, arithmetical frame of mind, which knows only to work with addition of numbers, or at best with multiplication of witnesses. To take Christ at all He must be taken as the centre of a movement of revelation organized around Him, and winding up the whole process of revelation. When cut loose from what went before and came after, Jesus not only becomes uninterpretable, but owing to the meteoric character of His appearance, remains scarcely sufficient for bearing by Himself alone the tremendous weight of a supernaturalistic world-view.

As a matter of fact, Jesus does not represent Himself anywhere as being by his human earthly activity the exhaustive expounder of truth. Much rather He is the great fact to be expounded. And He has nowhere isolated Himself from His interpreters, but on the contrary identified them with Himself, both as to absoluteness of authority and adequacy of knowledge imparted [*Luke* 24.44; *John* 16.12–15]. And through the promise and gift of the Spirit He has made the identity real. The Spirit takes of the things of Christ and shows them unto the recipients. Besides this, the course of our Lord's redemptive career was such as to make the important facts accumulate towards the end, where the departure of Jesus from the disciples rendered explanation by Himself of the significance of these impossible. For this reason the teaching of Jesus, so far from rendering the teaching of the Apostles negligible, absolutely postulates it. As the latter would have been empty, lacking the fact, so the former would have been blind, at least in part, because of lacking the light.

The relation between Jesus and the Apostolate is in general that between the fact to be interpreted and the subsequent interpretation of this fact. This is none other than the principle under which all revelation proceeds. The New Testament Canon is constructed on it. The Gospels and the Acts of the Apostles stand first, although from a literary point of view this is not the chronological sequence. Theirs is the first place, because there is embodied in them the great actuality of New Testament redemption. Still, it ought not to be overlooked, that within the Gospels and the Acts themselves we meet with a certain preformation of this same law. Jesus' task is not confined to furnishing the fact or the facts; He interweaves and accompanies the creation of the facts with a preliminary illumination of them, for by the side of His work stands His teaching. Only the teaching is more sporadic and less comprehensive than that supplied by the Epistles. It resembles the embryo, which though after an indistinct fashion, yet truly contains the structure, which the full-grown organism will clearly exhibit.

The foregoing gives us the warrant for speaking of New Testament revelation and of its historic exposition, New Testament theology. It also explains to us the seeming disproportion in chronological extent of the Old Testament and the New Testament. This disproportion arises from viewing the new revelation too much by itself, and not sufficiently as introductory and basic to the large period following. Looking at it in too mechanical a manner, one might place the thousands of years of the Old Testament over against the scarce one hundred years of the life of Jesus and the Apostles. In reality, the New Testament revelation, being the final one, stretches over all the extent of the order of things Christ came to inaugurate, whence also the *Diatheke* which it serves is called an 'eternal *Diatheke*' [*Heb.* 13.20]. It is the eschatological *Diatheke*, and in regard to that, time-comparisons are out of place.

The disproportion is felt somewhat over-keenly by us, because we lack the eschatological point of view, which regards Christ as the 'Consummator'. Hence we are inclined to speak of the New Testament in its canonical, literary sense, extending, say, from the nativity of Jesus to the death of the last writer in the New Testament Canon. Still, we know full well that we ourselves live just as much in the New Testament as did Peter and Paul and John. For clearness' sake we may distinguish between the revelation-overture which opened the salvation-era, and the salvation-era itself, giving to both the name New Testament. In our Biblico-theological investigation the former alone is dealt with.

The first and great division within our field, then, is that between revelation through Christ directly and revelation mediated by Christ through the Apostolate. Calling this the overture of the New Testament dispensation, we can still distinguish certain preludes played before the setting in of the overture itself. All that precedes the public ministry may be considered in this light. The voices accompanying the Nativity, the preaching of John the Baptist, the baptism of Jesus by John, the probation (temptation) of Jesus, require preliminary attention before entering upon a survey of the revelation-content of His work. On the other hand, such matters as the question of development, and of the method of our Lord's teaching, are so vitally interwoven with the substance of the message brought as to appear of far more than preliminary importance. And to a still stronger degree, of course, this applies to the teaching on the Old Testament and on the Nature of God. This yields the grouping of the table of Contents prefixed to the present volume.

IS A FURTHER REVELATION TO BE EXPECTED?

The question may be raised, whether, within the limits of the principles here laid down, there can be expected still further revelation entitled to a place in the scheme of New Testament revelation. Unless we adopt the mystical standpoint, which cuts loose the subjective from the objective, the only proper answer to this question is, that new revelation can be added only, in case new objective events of a supernatural character take place, needing for their understanding a new body of interpretation supplied by God. This will actually be the case in the eschatological issue of things. What then occurs will constitute a new epoch in redemption worthy to be placed by the side of the great epochs in the Mosaic age and the age of the first Advent. Hence the Apocalypse mingles with the pictures of the final events transpiring the word of prophecy and of interpretation.

We may say, then, that a third epoch of revelation is still outstanding. Strictly speaking, however, this will form less a group by itself than a consummation of the second group. It will belong to New Testament revelation as a final division. Mystical revelation claimed by many in the interim as a personal privilege is out of keeping with the genius of Biblical religion. Mysticism in this detached form is not specifically Christian. It occurs in all types of religion, better or worse. At best it is a manifestation of the religion of nature, subject to all the defects and faults of the latter. As to its content and inherent value it is unverifiable, except on the principle of submitting it to the test of harmony with Scripture. And submitting it to this it ceases to be a separate source of revelation concerning God.

TWO:
REVELATION CONNECTED
WITH THE NATIVITY

The law above spoken of is, we repeat, that the event precedes, the interpreting revelations follow. What happened was nothing else than what theology calls 'the incarnation'. If nevertheless we prefer to speak of 'the nativity', this is in recognition of the point of view from which the accompanying disclosures present it. Not first in later theology, but already in the subsequent course of revelation itself, the incarnation-point-of-view is adopted. It describes, as it were, a vertical movement from heaven to earth, from the divine to the human, in which the pre-existent Messiah appears entering into human nature, the super-historical descends into the stream of history. In the teaching of our Lord (even in the Synoptics) there are references and allusions to this; in the Johannine teaching (of Jesus) these are much more numerous and plain; with Paul the doctrine emerges in rounded-off explicit form; in the Prologue to the Fourth Gospel and his Epistles the Apostle John gives it classical formulation.

But these all mark later stages in the progress of New Testament revelation. Here, at the point where the event actually occurs, the movement is seen to partake of a horizontal character. Without in any way excluding or denying the other aspect of the occurrence, which veiled itself behind the curtain of mystery, it preferred to continue speaking in terms of prophecy and fulfilment, thus moving along the level pathway of history. What Jehovah had promised to the fathers of Messianic eventuation, that came here to pass; the ideality of prediction now assumed the concrete form of the actual. This is not identical with saying that what happened in the course of history was on that account purely natural. The historical can be supernatural, the supernatural can enter history, and so become a piece of the historical in its highest form. There is no mutual exclusiveness. It is pure prejudice, when historians lay down the principle that they are allowed to reckon with the natural only.

ASPECTS OF THE NATIVITY

The pieces pertaining to this group are: the annunciation of the angel to Joseph [*Matt.* 1.20, 21, 23]; the annunciation of Gabriel to Zacharias, *Lk.* 1.11–22; the annunciation of Gabriel to Mary [*Lk.* 1.26–38]; the prophecy of Elizabeth [*Lk.* 1.42–45]; the Psalm of Mary (the 'Magnificat') [*Lk.* 1.46–55]; the prophecy of Zacharias [*Lk.* 1.68–79]; the announcement of the Angels to the shepherds, followed by the angelic song [*Lk.* 2.10–14]; the prophecy of Simeon (the 'Nunc Dimittis') [*Lk.* 2.29–35]; the prophecy of Anna [vs. 38]. The characteristic features of these pieces are as follows:

(*a*) There is in them a close adjustment to the Old Testament as to the mode of expression used. This feature brings out the continuity between the two revelations. The young dispensation begins with the speech of the fathers. This was inherently fit, but it likewise served the purpose of rendering the revelations more easily understandable by those to whom they were proximately addressed, people whose piety had been nurtured on the Old Testament. Thus the Magnificat is full of reminiscences from the Psalms, and from its Old Testament prototype, the prayer-song of Hannah, [1 *Sam.* 2.1–10].

(*b*) There is likewise a perceptible intent to fit the new things into the organism of the Old Testament History of Redemption. The nativity is connected with the house of God's servant David, as was spoken by the holy prophets, [*Lk.* 1.69, 70]; it is the fulfilment of the oath sworn to Abraham, [vs. 73]; the prophecy of which it is the culmination extends from the beginning of the world, [vs. 70]. In David, Abraham, the Creation, the dominating epochs of the Old Testament are seized upon; the chronological nexus is, as it were, the exponent of the oneness of the divine work through the ages and of the divine purpose from the outset to lead up to the Messiah.

(*c*) The new procedure to be ushered in is throughout described as bearing a redemptive character. This is accomplished, first of all, by giving it, both in the objective announcement by God and in the subjective apprehension of those addressed, the background of a state of sin and unworthiness, and the corresponding signature of grace and salvation. God's unique dealing with His people at this point is recognized as an act of sovereign mercy. This has found its typical expression in the words of Mary [*Lk.* 1.46, 51–53]. There is no trace of the view that anything well-deserving has evoked this visitation of God, least of all anything resembling faithful observance of the law. The gulf between the better Israel of ancient times and the apostate Israel of the present is realized. Zacharias is told that the child to be born to him shall turn many of the children of Israel to the Lord their God, and shall go before Him in the spirit and power of Elias to turn the hearts of the fathers to the children. The source of all blessedness is sought in the *berith*, which is but another way of saying that it flows from the free promise of God. God fulfils what He promised to the fathers (the patriarchs) [*Lk.* 1.54, 55, 72, 73].

(*d*) Equally significant is the absence of the political element from these pieces. In itself this element would not have been objectionable, for under the Old Testament theocracy national and religious interests intertwined. The nearest to a reminiscence from this comes in Lk. 1.71, 74 (salvation from enemies through the Messiah), but even here this feature is purely subsidiary to the end named in vs. 75.

(*e*) The legalism of Judaism is nowhere in evidence. It must be granted that even in Judaism this figures scarcely as an end in itself. It served as a means for bringing about the Messianic blessedness. The Jewish self-righteousness rested on the deeper basis of egoistic eudæmonism. But the legalism had become so inveterate, that to a considerable extent the vision of the other world remained coloured by it. Still, its main significance pertains to the pre-eschatological period. The Jewish sequence is: Israel is first to fulfil the law, then, by manner of recompense, the Messiah, with all that pertains to Him, will appear. The new sequence is: first the Messiah will appear, as a gift of divine grace, and through Him Israel will be enabled to yield the proper obedience. The effect of this is twofold: by shifting the law from the beginning of the process to the end the Jewish self-righteousness is eliminated; by vindicating for the law its permanent place at the end, the ethical import of the salvation is emphasized. Of John the Baptist, Gabriel predicts that he shall turn many of the children of Israel to Jehovah their God [*Lk.* 1.16]. To Joseph it is predicted that Jesus' chief work will consist in saving His people from their sins [*Matt.* 1.21].

(*f*) The closeness of the bond with the Old Testament is shown through the prolongation into these early revelations of the two lines of ancient eschatological prophecy. The one of these moves towards the coming of Jehovah Himself in a supreme theophany. The other moves towards the coming of the Messiah. It is by no means certain that even in Old Testament prophecy these were mutually exclusive: one writer or prophet might, under certain circumstances, favour the one, and under other circumstances the other representation. And it is even possible, that as the concept of the Messiah expanded into the supernatural and super-creaturely, the combinableness and somewhat of the identity of the two were perceived. On the whole, however, they are like two

307

separate streams. The full development of New Testament revelation has first fully disclosed their convergence through its teaching that in the divine Messiah Jehovah has come to His people.

In the pieces under review there is the beginning of this, but the coalescence has not yet fully been reached. It is to be observed that the two representations are so distributed, that in the circle of Mary and Joseph the Messianic kingship out of the line of David stands in the centre, whilst in the circle of Zacharias and Elizabeth the idea of Jehovah's coming prevails, although not exclusively (for the former compare Matt. 1.20; 2.1, 5, 8; Lk. 1.32; for the latter Lk. 1.16, 17, 76). For the entrance of the Davidic strain into the Jehovah-coming complex compare Lk. 1.32, 69; 2.4, 11. It is in accordance with the assignment of this line to the Baptist's family that the later word of God coming through John was so largely borrowed from Isa. 40. About 'the Lord' and 'the mother of my Lord' [*Lk.* 1.16, 17, 43] see later under the discussion of the name *Kyrios*.

Some intimation of the identity between Jehovah and the Messiah seems to be contained in the words of the angel [*Matt.* 1.21]. Here the name Jesus, to be given to the child, is understood in its etymological sense: 'Jehovah is Salvation.' In itself, of course, this need not by any means imply that the Messiah, as personally identical with Jehovah, will be the Saviour. For this identical name had been borne under the Old Testament by purely human servants of God, not to mark them as Jehovah, but simply to render their work symbolic of the fact that Jehovah in His own Person provides salvation for Israel. And in the abstract it might have been not otherwise in the case of Jesus. This exegesis, however, overlooks the important fact, that Jesus bears the name, as is explicitly stated, because He (Jesus) saves His (Jesus') people from their sins. We have, therefore, in close succession the statements, that Jehovah is salvation, and that Jesus saves, that Israel (Jehovah's people) are Jesus' people. On the other hand, the name Emmanuel in vs. 23 could be His merely on account of His being exponential of God's being with His people; moreover the words in this verse are not words of the angel, but words of Matthew who is quoting Isaiah.

(g) There are certain intimations of the universalism (destiny to include other nations) of the Gospel in these disclosures. Simeon speaks of the salvation prepared by God as a light to lighten the Gentiles, side by side with its being a glory for the people of Israel [*Lk.* 2.32], and announces to Mary, that the child is set for the fall and rising again of many in Israel, and for a sign that shall be spoken against [vs. 34]; yea, intimates that a painful experience described as a sword piercing

Mary's heart will contribute somehow to these effects [vs. 35]. An illumination of the Gentiles seems to be foretold, which will have for its foil the darkness of the unbelief of Israel. Not as if this were in any sense the first disclosure of universalism in Scripture, far less of the propaganda of missions. But the Judaistic proselytizing implied that whosoever was adopted from among the Gentiles could attain to a share in the privileges of Israel only through becoming a Jew. Here the idea is that through the unbelief of the Jew the Gentiles will be brought in [compare *Rom.* 11.11ff.].

(*h*) As a last element lending distinctive character to these revelations, we must mention the supernatural birth of the Messiah to be brought about without human paternity. We do not here discuss the objections raised against this event on historical grounds. That belongs to the department of Gospel History, as does likewise the critique upon the trends of thought and belief that, denying the fact as fact, are supposed to have produced the idea of the fact as a distinct phase in early Christology. All we propose here to deal with is what idea or ideas in the mind of God shaped the occurrence of the event, assuming it to have been an event in the way in which it is described as having come to pass.

Three elements offering an explanation have been thought of. The first concerns the sinlessness of the child through the estoppage of the transmission of sin. Reference to this may be found in Lk. 1.35, 'that which is begotten of thee shall be called holy', or 'that holy thing which is begotten', etc., provided 'holy' be taken in the ethical sense. It may, however, be taken in the sense of 'consecrated', in which case there would be no direct reference to the sinlessness of the child, although the 'consecration' would seem to presuppose the sinlessness. In so far we may assume that the action of the Holy Spirit spoken of had for one of its purposes the prevention of the transmission of the pollution of sin. But this does not yield an exhaustive explanation of the factors present, because the end could have been secured through some specific operation of the Spirit, not going to the extent of the elimination of the human paternity, unless the ground be taken (as it has been by some) that the paternal factor in the act of generation bears a special relation to the transmission of sin, not borne by the maternal factor. Discounting this, the fact that Joseph has nothing to do with the birth is too strongly stressed not to require some additional reason besides the motive just indicated.

We are thus led in the second place to think of the fitness which this mode of birth possessed for introducing into human nature One who was already antecedently in more than one sense 'the Son of God'. It was eminently appropriate that the human paternity of Joseph should give way to the paternity of God. In Matthew there is no reference to the divine Sonship of the child. In 1.21, 23, it is simply 'a son', that is a son of Mary. But in Luke, while 'a son' likewise occurs in 1.31, the other side of the child's derivation is specified in vss. 32, 35; 'the Son of the Highest', 'the Son of God'. And this is plainly brought into connection with the operation of the Spirit, represented more particularly as the transmitter of the power of the Highest over-shadowing her, so that no doubt is left as to the specific paternity of God being involved to the exclusion of that of man.

The third point of view from which the event is regarded is that of carrying back the supernaturalism of the whole Person and work of Christ into the very origin of His human nature, as directly derived from God. If even in Old Testament history this principle finds expression as regards the typical work of redemption, how much more we may expect it here! Illustrated in the birth of Isaac after a symbolical manner, it certainly is eminently applicable, where He is introduced into human nature of whom Isaac was but the type. If it be objected that on this principle the supernaturalism of origin ought to have been made absolute through eliminating the maternity of Mary, as well as the paternity of Joseph, the answer is that the former could not be dispensed with, if the real connection of Jesus with our human nature was to be preserved and Docetism to be avoided. That this third point of view is not stressed in the narrative may be due to the prominence it later receives in the account of the baptism of Jesus.

THREE:
REVELATION CONNECTED
WITH JOHN THE BAPTIST

It is customary to designate John the Baptist 'the fore-runner' of Christ. The word occurs in Heb. 6.20, although without reference to John, and in a sense in which it could not apply to him. Apart from the word, the idea that John, through his historic activity, prepared the way for the work of Jesus finds clear expression in Lk. 1.17, 76, even though here by 'the Lord' proximately Jehovah were to be understood.

This whole idea of a divinely-arranged connection is spurned by many modern writers. It is attempted to separate John as much as possible from Jesus. Contrary to the Gospel representation, it is assumed that the two represented separate religious movements, which continued to run parallel for a considerable time. The testimony of the Gospels excluding this is exscinded as follows. The Fourth Gospel, which even more strongly than the others, and with a degree of pointedness, affirms the subserviency of John to Jesus, is declared unhistorical in this respect as in most others. The view has been formulated by Baldensperger (*The Prologue of the Fourth Gospel*, 1898) that the large space devoted to John in John chapters 1–3 is due to the apologetic purpose of convincing the Baptist-sect of the writer's day out of the mouth of their own master, that their place was within the Christian Church, even as John had said: 'I am not the Christ.' The stories of the Nativity in Luke which bring Jesus and John together from the earliest possible point through the relationship and intercourse of their families are held to be of a legendary character, and hence untrustworthy in the matter at issue. The pericope extract exclusive to Matthew [3.13–15], according to which John recognized in Jesus, as soon as the latter came to him, the Greater One, which, if not implying momentary revelation, would have to rest on previous acquaintance and recognition, is refused credence, partly because not found in Luke, partly because believed to be, within the first Gospel itself, irreconcilable with the doubting enquiry sent by John to Jesus whether He was 'the One to Come', or were they to wait for another? [11.1–3]. Mark, it is claimed, has in all these respects the older and correct tradition, which understood the first contact between Jesus and John to have taken place, when the latter had begun his preaching, and Jesus came to him as one among the many desiring to be baptized.

Others go even farther than this in eliminating from the record of the earliest preaching of John the reference to the Greater One as a reference to a Christ in general, interpreting it on the basis of the Christ-less eschatological programme, wherein Jehovah Himself appears in a supreme theophany. This would cut the connection not only between John and Jesus personally, but doctrinally between John and the Messianic hope. On such a supposition the impulse which, according to many writers, Jesus is believed to have at least received from the solemn occasion leading subsequently to His regarding Himself as the Messiah, is the only personal contact remaining.

The extreme step in this process of detaching John from Jesus is taken, where the spirit and content of the preaching of both are made of a conflicting nature. What John expected, it is held, bore strongly political features, and was for its coming dependent on the use of force. If this were according to facts, one might confidently say that John, instead of being the fore-runner, was in reality the fore-antagonist of the Saviour.

MATTHEW 11.2–19

The only apparent basis for these constructions being found in the passage Matt. 11.2–19, it seems best to define John's position relative to Jesus' work from the statements of Jesus' discourse contained in this passage. This is all the safer, since the unfavourable light in which John's enquiry makes him appear would not be in keeping with the Baptist's reputation in the early Church, and consequently must have had a solid ground in the tradition. The situation and the content of the enquiry are well known. Our interest attaches to Jesus' discourse to the multitude after the messengers had returned to their sender, from vs. 7 onward. In the thrice-repeated question, 'What went ye out to see?', Jesus corrects, first, two erroneous, next an inadequate opinion about John, evidently formed in part under the influence of John's inquiry. The first error is stated and rectified in vs. 7: the Baptist's apparent doubt was not caused by fickleness on his part: he was not a reed shaken with the wind. The second misconception is stated and corrected in vs. 8: the vacillation was not due to the discomfort of John's prison-life: he was not accustomed to the soft raiment worn in

King's houses. The third answer to the question recognizes that there was basal truth, only not full truth, in the people's classification of the Baptist as a prophet. He was a prophet, only more than one.

Then Jesus proceeds to define in what this 'more than a prophet' consists. First of all he is a way-preparing messenger sent before the face of the Lord, something that only in a metaphorical sense could be said of the previous prophets: they wrote of Jesus, John is one of whom it was written of old. So far as this is the case he belongs half-way to the fulfilment-era. The culmination of Old Testament prophecy is in him, and this position entitles him to be called 'greatest of them born of women'. As a messenger he comes immediately before the reality: all the prophets and the law prophesied (dealt with something future); John is Elias who was to come shortly before the coming of the day of Jehovah [*Mal.* 4.5]. Beginning with his days the Kingdom of heaven suffers violence, and the violent take it by force. Whatever the precise meaning of these figures in vs. 12 may be, it is clear, at any rate, that they imply the nearness, or even the presence of the Kingdom through the Baptist's own work. Through him the Kingdom had passed out of the sphere of pure futurity belonging to it under the Old Testament; it had become something actual engaging the thoughts and swaying the emotions of men. To have effected this was the great act of John, that which made him 'more than a prophet'.

And yet our Lord intimates that there is a qualification to this: John himself could not be classified with the new dispensation come in through the work of Jesus: 'He that is lesser (or least) in the Kingdom of Heaven is greater than he' [vs. 11]. This statement does not mean that John was not what we call 'saved', nor could it possibly mean that John would be excluded from the eschatological kingdom, against which compare Matthew 8.11. The true interpretation is that the Baptist would not partake of the privileges of the already coming Kingdom of which others partook through their association with Jesus. He continued to lead his life apart, on the basis of the Old Testament.

This also affords the explanation of John's somewhat impatient enquiry in regard to the Messianic authentication of Jesus. In it the Old Testament once more, as it were, voices its impatience about the tarrying of the Messiah. But as there, so here, the impatience centred on one particular point, the slowness of God's procedure in destroying the wicked. John had been specifically appointed to proclaim the judgment-aspect of the coming crisis. Hence a certain disappointment at the procedure of Jesus. Thus interpreted the enquiry not only does not imply previous non-acquaintance between the two; on the contrary it proves that John had taken note of Jesus, and that there had been intercommunication; else such a message could not have been sent. Vs. 6 also proves previous recognition and appraisal up to a point, only with a certain continuance of the Old Testament perspective. Thus the peculiarity of the answer returned to John, with its exclusive emphasis on the beneficent aspects of Jesus' work, is explained. These are not named merely as credentials, but equally much as characterizations. It was not Jesus' task for the present to judge, at least not in that way. The judgment would come at a subsequent stage. After all, Jesus had not lost sight of John's question. He answered it in the most delicate, yet forceful, way. As the subsequent discourse reveals, His heart was full of appreciation of the greatness of John, and, as the Fourth Gospel proves, full of love for his person on account of the generosity of John's self-effacement in the service of the Messiah [3.30; 5.35].

John's appurtenance to the Old Testament is further borne out by Jesus' parable in regard to the question of fasting [Mk. 2.18–22]. It is appropriate for John's disciples to fast, because they have not arrived at that wedding feast of joy at which Jesus' disciples are guests.

JOHN THE BAPTIST AND ELIJAH

Perhaps John's entire external mode of appearance and life are connected with his place within the Old Testament. He was a life-long Nazarite. His desert-surroundings were significant, as of old connected with the preparation for repentance [Hos. 2.14, 15; Isa. 40.1–4]. He was a reproduction of Elijah, that great prophet of repentance [Matt. 11.14; 17.10–13]. In the first passage the words 'if ye will receive it' indicate that some doubted the character of John as fore-runner Elijah, and also that Jesus accepted it. But there was a difference, perhaps, between the conception that Jesus attached to the reappearance of Elijah and that of the Jews. The latter seem to have expected a literal resurrection of Elijah. Thus we can explain the statement of John about his not being Elijah [John 1.21]. He disclaimed being Elijah in that realistic Jewish sense, but would not have denied being so in the symbolic sense affirmed by Jesus, as little as he would have disclaimed that the prophecies of Isaiah and Malachi were being fulfilled in him.

Perhaps the text of the Septuagint furnishes evidence for the antiquity of the Jewish belief concerning the actual return of the prophet, for in Mal. 4.5 it renders 'Elijah the Tishbite', whereas the original has 'Elijah the prophet'. The origin of the belief lay in the manner of

Elijah's ascent to heaven. The Evangelist Luke seems to recognize the symbolic significance of these externals about John, when he speaks of 'the day of his showing unto Israel' [1.80].

We thus see that John's fore-running of Jesus was to all intents a fore-running of the entire Old Testament with reference to the Christ. And this applied not by any means to externals only; the real substance of the Old Testament was recapitulated in John. If we distinguish the two elements of law and prophecy, both were plainly summed up in the message: 'Repent, for the Kingdom of Heaven is at hand.' But the connection between the two is not that of the mere addition of two unrelated things; the conjunction 'for' indicates that the motive for repentance lies in the near approach of the Kingdom, because the latter means to John, first of all, judgment. Compare the fan in the hand, the axe at the root.

JOHN THE BAPTIST'S TESTIMONY TO JESUS

In the testimony of the Baptist to Jesus as the Messiah we must distinguish two stages, the one recorded chiefly by the Synoptics, the other by the Fourth Gospel. Between the two lies the baptism of Jesus by John. The characteristic features of the first stage are the emphasis on the judgment and on the judging function of the Coming One who, however, is not explicitly named the Messiah. The figures used to describe his superiority are such, that no one less than God, and yet some one different from Jehovah pure and simple, must be thought of [*Matt.* 3.3, 11, 12; *Mk.* 1.3, 7; *Lk.* 3.4, 16, 17]. The 'fire' specified as the one of the two elements in which the Coming One will baptize is undoubtedly the fire of judgment, not, therefore, a synonym, but the opposite of the Holy Spirit [cp. *Matt.* 3.10–12; *Lk.* 3.16, 17]; Mark omits reference to the 'fire', and names only the Holy Spirit [1.8]. If the Holy Spirit stands for the salvation-element, the fact results that John speaks of the judging and saving aspects of the advent as coinciding, a feature in which likewise he reproduces the Old Testament standpoint. The phraseology of this earlier stage of the preaching is largely derived from Mal. 4, that in which the Evangelists speak of it from Isa. 40.

JOHN'S BAPTISM

The baptism of John in general and the baptism of Jesus by John in particular should not be separated. At that time and later there were many circles in which baptismal rites were practised, but these were all subject to repetition, whereas John's baptism was once for all [cp. *Matt.* 28.19; *Acts* 19.3; *Heb.* 6.2]. Its precedents and analogies will have to be sought in the Old Testament, not so much in the ceremonial lustrations of the Law, for these also required repetition, but rather, on the one hand in the washings preparatory to the making of the Old Covenant [*Ex.* 19.10, 14] and on the other in the great outpouring of water which the prophets announce will precede the eschatological era [*Isa.* 1.16; 4.4; *Mic.* 7.19; *Ezek.* 36.25–33; *Zech.* 13.1]. It ought to be noticed, that water appears in prophecy as a quickening, fructifying element, besides being the instrument of cleansing [*Isa.* 35.7; 41.18; 44.3ff.; *Zech.* 14.8]. It has been attempted to explain John's baptism from these Old Testament antecedents, but these were in part prophetic, in part typical, so that for fulfilment or repetition specific supernatural injunction was required. John could not simply proceed on the basis of the Old Testament in such a matter, and this is recognized on all sides [*John* 1.25, 33; *Matt.* 21.25].

Least of all can we consider John's baptism as a simple imitation of the so-called proselyte-baptism of Judaism. This was not at first a particularly outstanding rite, such as would have invited imitation on the part of John. It meant simply the application of the general Levitical law of cleansing to a proselyte, who, after having been circumcised, was still, owing to his previous contact with Gentiles, unclean, and so needed washing. And John scarcely went so far as to declare all those coming to him unclean pagans, to whom the principle of proselytism ought to be applied. Between Christian baptism and John's there did actually exist a close connection, as will be presently shown.

The true import of John's baptism must be inferred, partly from the descriptions given in the Gospels, partly from the general situation. Mark and Luke tell us that it was a 'baptism of repentance unto forgiveness of sins'. Matthew says that he baptized 'unto repentance', and that the people were baptized of him 'confessing their sins'. According to the one statement (Matthew) confession of sin was the accompaniment of the act, according to the other (Mark and Luke) forgiveness of sin was the goal, but in this no real contradiction exists. It might appear contradictory, when Matthew makes the confession precede and the repentance follow the baptism; here the solution will lie in distinguishing between a more external acknowledgment of sin and a deepened, intensified repentance [*Matt.* 3.6, 11]. It is somewhat uncertain how the Marcan and Lucan phrase 'baptism of repentance' is to be understood. The construction allows of its being a general characterization of the baptism as something having to do with repentance in one way or another. A better view is to take the genitive as a genitive of purpose: baptism intended to produce repentance, which makes it agree with Matt. 3.11. If repentance was the expected result of the act, it is clear that the rite cannot have been a mere piece of symbolism, but must have constituted a true sacrament, intended to convey some form of grace. And with this also agrees John's urging the people 'to bring forth fruit worthy of repentance'.

Weiss has suggested that the 'unto forgiveness' of Mark and Luke must be prospective: with a view to future forgiveness, that is, in the judgment. Grammatically the phrase 'unto forgiveness' might, no doubt, mean this, but it yields an over-pregnant sense. The Old Testament already is full of the forgiveness of sin, and John's work as the summing up of the Old Testament in itself could not have been entirely without it. The objection is made, however, that John pointedly contrasts what his baptism conveys, as 'water', with the reality of grace to be bestowed by the Spirit-baptism of the Coming One. But the Spirit covers more than forgiveness and, although the Baptist might, for the purpose of comparison, and, hyperbolically speaking, have put all the emptiness on the one side and all the fulness on the other side, this should not be literally understood, any more than when Paul and Hebrews seem to void the Old Testament of all grace. What John means is simply: compared with what the Christ brings, my work is as water compared to the Spirit; it does not follow from this that in the sphere of types itself it had no other function than typifying.

Another question arising is of an opposite nature, namely, how, if John's baptism be accorded real forgiveness of sin, it can be further distinguished from Christian baptism. On this question the post-Reformation Church has been divided. The Romanists, tending in their doctrine of the sacrament toward making the entire Old Dispensation purely typical, included in this opinion the baptism of John; the Protestant theology, both Lutheran and Reformed, with few exceptions, in reaction to the Romanist standpoint went to the opposite extreme and maintained that the baptism of John was fully identical with the Christian sacrament. Both positions are untenable: we shall have to say that John's baptism, together with all the Old Testament rites, had real grace connected with it, but only the Old Testament measure and quality of grace. What it had not was the Spirit in the specific Christian conception; for the bestowal of that, and its connection with baptism, are dependent on the Pentecostal outpouring of the Spirit. Consequently the baptism administered in the time between by the disciples of Jesus must be classified with the baptism of John,

317

as a continuation thereof, and not as an anticipation of Christian baptism.

How did John's baptism symbolize? Some take the view that the symbolism lay in the immersion signifying the doing away with the old life of sin and the emersion as the entrance upon a new state of righteousness. But, if this were correct, it would separate John's baptism entirely from all Old Testament precedents, for in the Old Testament symbolism of immersion is unknown. Even the washings of the entire body in certain instances of the ritual still remain washings; the immersion from a symbolic point of view is purely incidental. And on the other hand the spiritual things named, repentance and forgiveness of sin, point in the direction of cleansing. To this must be added that, through the medium of the water, there is a symbolic reference to the quickening by the Spirit (cp. *John* 3.5, 'born of water and the Spirit'].

Finally, for an adequate conception of John's baptism it ought to be viewed against the eschatological background of the prevailing expectation of his time. The atmosphere was surcharged with the thought of the end. John's baptism was specifically prospective to the fast-coming judgment and a seal of preparation for acquittal in this. The idea of baptism as a seal in this eschatological sense is something that has passed over to Christian baptism [cp. *Eph.* 1.13; 1 *Pet.* 3.21].

THE BAPTISM OF JESUS BY JOHN

Now, coming to the consideration of Jesus' baptism by John in particular, the main thing to remember is that we may not arbitrarily cut this loose from the import of the baptism in general. It were foolish to say that John administered two baptisms, one for the people and one for Jesus alone, and that these two had nothing in common with each other. Still, it is possible to go so far in the opposite direction as to deny the sinlessness of Jesus. And that is forbidden not on doctrinal grounds merely; the dialogue between John and Jesus recorded in Matt. 3.13–15 historically excludes it. Besides, the revelation connected with the baptism proves that the latter was something quite unique by which it differed in principle from the rite performed on the average Israelite. The suggestion of Weiss that this unique element be sought in the symbolism of Jesus' emerging from the life of privacy and entering upon a life of public service cannot be accepted, because it rests on the idea of submersion, and moreover would cut the bond between Jesus' baptism and that of the others, to whom such an entrance on public service did not apply.

The passage Matt. 3.13–15, when carefully scanned, gives us the solution of this problem, as to how Jesus' baptism could fit into the general scheme of John's ministry, and yet remain free of those elements in the latter relating to sinfulness and repentance. The dialogue with John brings out the following facts:

(*a*) John recognizes the rank and character of Jesus as putting Him beyond the need of his baptism; 'John forbade Him', vs. 14;

(*b*) this conviction of John is based on the Messianic position of Jesus; the words 'I have need to be baptized of Thee' cannot mean that Jesus should apply to John a water-baptism, thus merely reversing the roles; after John had just announced that the Greater One would baptize with the Holy Spirit, his confession of need of baptism by Jesus can refer to nothing else but that, and this involves the sinlessness of Jesus personally considered;

(*c*) John's protest, as well as the ground on which he bases it, are endorsed by Jesus when He insists, saying, 'Suffer it to be so now'; the term 'suffer' implies the absence of such subjective necessity as John had denied; it must be allowed for objective reasons;

(*d*) this objective necessity is something that operates, not for ever and under all circumstances, but just for the present situation, with a prospect half-opened, of future removal of the necessity;

(*e*) the reason for the present necessity consists, according to Jesus, in this, that 'thus it behoves us to fulfil all righteousness'; 'to fulfil all righteousness' is not here identical with the stereotyped formula in which the doctrine of vicarious atonement has so aptly expressed the principle of Christ's substitution for us in the keeping of the law. It should be taken in a less technical, popular sense; 'righteousness' is that which at any time, through the law or otherwise, is from Jehovah asked of Israel; in the present case this consisted in submission to the baptism of John, for this was not a matter of individual choice, but a national duty; both on Jesus and John ('us') this piece of righteousness had been imposed, and Jesus declares it a matter of duty to observe it;

(*f*) if, then, what is not incumbent on Jesus Himself in a personal capacity none the less appears a divinely imposed duty for Him because of his appurtenance to the people of Israel, there is no better formula for expressing this, than that He undergoes the baptism in virtue of his identification with Israel.

Adding to this that it is a temporary experience, we find ourselves as near as could be expected under the circumstances to an expression of the vicarious relation of Jesus to the people of God. And it is but one step beyond this, if, taking into account the general scope of

John's baptism, we should say that Jesus' identification with the people in their baptism had the proximate end of securing for them vicariously what the sacrament aimed at, the forgiveness of sin. Even with regard to repentance we may reason analogously; for if Jesus bore sin vicariously, and received forgiveness vicariously, then there can be no objection on principle to saying that He repented for the people vicariously. All these things are, however, hinted at here in a more or less enigmatic statement. The full exposition, which will at the same time furnish a full confirmation of the correctness of our exegesis, can be obtained only in the later discussion of John 1.29, 36.[1]

THE DESCENT OF THE SPIRIT ON JESUS

The baptism of Jesus was accompanied by two events of supreme importance – the descent of the Spirit and the announcement from heaven concerning Jesus' Sonship and Messiahship. Since the latter has been more fully discussed elsewhere,[2] we here confine ourselves to the observation, that the record does not lend itself to the theory of the baptism having been the occasion for the awakening of Jesus' Messianic consciousness. In Matthew the statement is purely objective: 'This is my beloved Son', which indicates that at least according to this Evangelist the assurance in the voice was not for Jesus alone. Nor can the varying forms of description used ('Lo, a voice from heaven' . . 'there came a voice from heaven' . . . 'a voice came from heaven') prove that the writers think of something perceptible to Jesus only, the less so, since the coming up out of the water, and the opening of heaven, to which the hearing of the voice is parallel, do not give in any way the impression of a visionary setting. Matthew's 'He saw' is certainly not meant of visionary perception, and Luke's 'in bodily shape like a dove' speaks against the subjectivity of the optical phenomenon. From John 1.34 we learn that the occurrence had to be perceptible to John, as well as to Jesus, since the former had to bear record concerning it. We may also compare the terms in which Peter speaks about the analogous phenomena at the transfiguration [2 *Pet.* 1.17, 18]. Evidently the voice had a sacramental significance for Jesus, and, if for no other than this reason alone, had to be objective.

In a sacrament, however, as a rule something real is conveyed, besides the assurance given. And so here the voice was followed by the descent of the Spirit. There are according to the New Testament three epochal occasions when an operation of the Spirit in connection

[1] See pp. 324–6.
[2] See pp. 348, 363ff.

with Jesus took place. The first of these has already been touched upon in connection with the virgin-birth. The second is this event at the baptism. The third happened in the resurrection of our Lord, and falls under the head of apostolic teaching. Here we are concerned with defining as closely as possible the necessity and nature of the second impartation. From the time of its occurrence may be inferred that it has its specific bearing upon the public ministry of Jesus, just as the first had upon the origin and constitution of His human nature and the third endowment is related to the heavenly ministry of the Lord. It made Him 'spiritual' [*Rom.* 1.4; 1 *Cor.* 15.45].

Jesus did not, of course, receive the Spirit as the agent of sanctification, for that would presuppose sinfulness, nor is there anywhere a trace of such function in the Gospels. But He could and did receive the Spirit as a pledge of the Father's approval of His mind and purpose expressed in submitting to the baptism, and of the effect God would give to it, when accomplished. In this there is an analogy to what the sealing with the Spirit means in baptism to every Christian; only in Jesus' case it was prospective.

Furthermore our Lord needed the Spirit as a real equipment of His human nature for the execution of His Messianic task. Jesus ascribed all His power and grace, the gracious words, the saving acts, to the possession of the Spirit [*Matt.* 12.28; *Lk.* 4.18; *Acts* 10.36–38]. And, through qualifying Him in this manner for achieving His Messianic task, the Spirit laid the foundation for the great Pentecostal bestowal of the Spirit afterwards, for this gift was dependent on the finished work. This explains the statement of the Baptist in John 1.33: '(God) said unto me, Upon whom thou shalt see the Spirit descending, and remaining upon Him, the same is He which baptizeth with the Holy Spirit.' It is perhaps due to this thought, that the preposition here used is *epi* with the accusative, an unusual construction with a verb of rest; it seems to denote the intent of the Spirit permanently to remain directed to and identified with the Saviour. Matthew, Mark and Luke have *eis*, which may either mean the approach of the Spirit towards Jesus or the entrance of the Spirit into Him.

The difference between this spiritual endowment of Jesus and that received by the prophets of old ought to be carefully noted. In the Fourth Gospel it is explicitly stated that God gave the Spirit to Jesus, and that, because it was a case of giving, no measure could be applied to the gift [3.34]; likewise it is emphasized that the Spirit descending abode upon Him [1.33]. The same thought, that of the totality and undividedness of the gift may be found in the description of Luke to the effect, that 'the Holy Spirit descended in a bodily form as a dove upon Him' [3.22]. Whilst in Matthew and Mark the phrase 'like a dove' may be understood as an adverbial qualification of the verb 'descending', serving to denote the slow deliberate movement of the Spirit in His coming upon Jesus, the version of Luke leaves no doubt as to the objective form of appearance assumed by the Spirit on this occasion. The Spirit resembled a dove, not merely was His motion like that of a dove. But even the other construction, if followed in Matthew and Mark, would not be without its own significance, for what descends deliberately intends to come to rest and abide.

In this, no less than in the totality of what descended, there was a difference from the ordinary prophetic bestowal of the Spirit. The prophets had visitations of the Spirit; the Spirit's impact upon them was abrupt, not continuous; in the case of Jesus His entire life was equably in every word and act directed by the Spirit. For the rest, why the figure of a dove should have been chosen for the Spirit's appearance, rather than that of some manifestation of light cannot be determined with certainty. The Old Testament nowhere compares the Spirit to a dove. It does represent the Spirit as hovering, brooding over the waters of chaos, in order to produce life out of the primeval matter. This might be found suggestive of the thought, that the work of the Messiah constituted a second creation, bound together with the first through this function of the Spirit in connection with it.

THE POST-BAPTISMAL TESTIMONY OF THE BAPTIST TO JESUS

There still remains to be discussed the post-baptismal testimony of John to Jesus. This is found in the Fourth Gospel. All the discourse of the Baptist here recorded revolves around Jesus and culminates in a triad of supreme declarations concerning Him. Foregoing to exegete all the statements, we confine ourselves to these outstanding deliverances, only adding the passage, disputed as to spokesmanship, at the close of chapter 3.

[1] *John 1.15, 30*

The first of the three declarations occurs in John 1.15, 30. It distinguishes in the Messiah's career two stages: the stage in which He comes after the Baptist, that is to say, succeeds the latter in his public ministry; the stage in which He nevertheless preceded John in the latter's appearance upon the scene; this can refer only to the Messiah's activity under the Old Testament. The A.V. renders here 'is preferred before me', understanding it of rank, but between the two clauses of chronological import this seems unnatural. Perhaps what has led to this rendering was the feeling that, in case the second clause applied to time, no proper distinction could be maintained between it and the third clause, 'for He was before me', because this likewise again speaks in terms of time. It had been overlooked, however, that though the second and third clauses sound very much alike in English, there is an important difference between them in the Greek: the middle clause reads, *emprosthen mou gegonen*, the final clause reads, *hoti protos mou en*. Both the prepositions and the verbs are different: *emprosthen* with the perfect of the verb expresses precedence in the sphere of becoming or appearing upon the scene, *protos* with the imperfect of the verb signifies absolute anteriority as to mode of existence; it relates to the eternal existence of the Lord, usually called his pre-existence [cp. *John* 1.1, 18]. On this view the conjunction *hoti* linking together clauses two and three is naturally explained: in Christ's eternal existence before time lies the possibility of His appearance and activity under the Old Testament. There is, therefore, no repetition between clauses two and three.

It has been observed that, even in this statement that marks the farthest advance in the Baptist's Christology, there is no loss of touch with the Old Testament. In Malachi, a prophetic book from which, as we have seen, so much of John's imagery is taken, we find in chapter 3 vs. 1 the distinction of the three stages in the eschatological advent, as it were, in preformation: first we have 'I send my messenger and he shall prepare the way before me'; this messenger was (in the fulfilment) John the Baptist; it covers, therefore, the public ministry of Jesus preceded by John's; in regard to it John could say: 'after me comes a man.' But in the same passage of Malachi, the Lord, before whom the messenger goes to prepare His way, is in the immediate sequel called 'the Messenger of the *Berith*, whom ye desire'; this refers to the figure otherwise called 'the Angel of Jehovah'. Of the Angel of ehovah it was known that at various points He had appeared and interposed in Old Testament history; this contains, therefore, in principle the second affirmation of John, 'came [or "became"] before me'. But in the prophet there is also an intimation of the third clause: 'He was before me', because 'the Lord whom ye seek', and who is come to His temple, is through apposition identified with the Angel of the *Berith*, at least, if 'even the Angel of the *Berith*', and not 'and the Angel of the *Berith*' be the correct rendering. In the latter case the epiphany of two persons would be foretold as occurring simultaneously, that of 'the Lord' and that of 'the Angel of the *Berith*'. Still, even so, one would be justified in finding here an intimation of the close relationship between Jehovah's advent and Jesus' advent, something fitting well into the general tenor of the Baptist's preaching from the beginning. The Old Testament already had made the Angel and Jehovah almost indistinguishable on certain occasions. If the one coming after John as to time of ministry was actually like both Jehovah and the Angel, then John could truly declare 'He was before me', in the most absolute sense.

[2] *John 1.29, 36*

The second outstanding piece of testimony from the Baptist's mouth is that found in John 1.29, 36: 'Behold the Lamb of God which takes away [or "takes upon Himself"] the sin [sing.] of the world', or in the abbreviated form of the second quotation: 'Behold the Lamb of God.' This enunciates a doctrine not made particularly prominent in the Fourth Gospel, viz. that of the vicarious sin-bearing of Christ. There is on this account all the more ground for trusting its authenticity. To explain the utterance as faithfully reflecting the historic occasion on which it was made, we need only place it in the light of the great event with its accompaniments that had immediately preceded, the baptism of Jesus, provided always that there had actually occurred at the baptism what Matt. 3.14, 15 relates, discussed by us above. If that meant a vicarious interpretation of Jesus' baptism, formulated in a dialogue between John and Jesus Himself, then certainly John, with the event that had just occurred vividly before his eyes, could hardly have spoken of it otherwise than is here done. It is the Baptist's commentary on his own and also on Jesus' act. Still John did not write this piece of commentary freely out of his own mind; he had here, no less than in the case of the second utterance, the guidance of the Old Testament to rely upon.

Two precedents for the figure of the lamb have been found: that of the sacrificial lamb, and the representation as a lamb of the Servant of Jehovah in Isa. 53. Some writers posit an alternative, thinking that John must have had in mind either the one or the other. But, perhaps, even for Isaiah the combination already existed; far more easily could it enter the mind of John, who must have been familiar with both the prophecy and the ritual. It must be admitted, however, that in the prophecy the lamb does not at the outset appear with ritual associations. Its primary use is to depict the innocence, meekness, and willingness to render vicarious service for the people through suffering and death. The features of innocence and meekness are inherent in the character of the lamb generically, but they are with special emphasis suggested here, because, the people having been described as a wayward, wandering flock, the very quality of a lamb sets the servant in contrast with this sinful condition.

But it immediately appears that these traits of innocence and meekness are not intended for the general purpose of idealizing the character of the Servant, but for the specific purpose of showing Him both fitted and willing to bear the sin for others. This is the transition between vs. 6 and vs. 7 in the prophecy: because innocent He can bear sin of others, because meek He is willing to do so. And also his appurtenance (with a distinction) to the flock serves its purpose here: being of the flock He can suffer for the flock. The vicariousness of His suffering unto death is described in the most explicit of terms in vss. 5 and 6. So far, however, there is no need of thinking of sacrifice, for vicariousness is not *ipso facto* sacrificial. In vs. 10 it becomes different; here the word *asham*, 'trespass-offering', is explicitly named as summing up in itself the entire preceding statement: 'when thou shalt make [or: He shall make] his soul a trespass-offering for sin', etc. That the trespass-offering is chosen from among the various kinds of sacrifice is probably not accidental; it was that kind of sacrifice in which the ideas of debt and restitution were inherent, so that the thought emerges of the Servant not merely atoning for the offences but also making good the obligation which, positively considered, was owed to God.

Now we must remember how in Isaiah the figure of the Servant only gradually detaches itself from the people of Israel, taken collectively, so that the exegetical dispute has arisen, whether He is meant for a separate person, or merely for an idealization of the people. This situation John must have found strikingly reproduced in the event of the baptism of Jesus. Jesus had come to him, acknowledging that personally He had nothing to confess. He had implied that it was different with His people, for whom a baptism of repentance unto forgiveness of sin had been ordained by God. He had further expressed the necessity of taking this baptism upon Himself on account of identification with the people. All this, dramatically enacted in the baptism itself, rose up for John as the precise fulfilment of the situation envisioned by the prophet Isaiah. How entirely the two concepts of 'the lamb' and that of 'removing sin' had grown together for John may be seen from the fact, that in the second utterance of the statement, vs. 36, the participial clause is omitted; it stood in no need of repetition; 'the Lamb' is *ipso facto* 'the sin-bearer'. The relative clause is simply epexegetical.

As to the meaning of the participle *airon* there is a dispute, some giving it the sense of 'removing', others that of 'taking upon oneself', both of which senses it may express in the Greek. The English Versions choose the former, 'which takes away' (R.V. in the margin: 'bears the sin'). But, if the words really express the situation John had just been witnessing, then the other rendering will have to be preferred. What Jesus had done in the baptism was not yet the actual removal of sin, but only as yet the taking of the sin upon Himself. To the other task his whole life was to be devoted. In Isaiah also we partly see the Servant depicted in assuming the sin of Israel, although here much of the real bearing enters into the description. The phrase 'Lamb of God' is the exact duplicate of the phrase 'Servant of Jehovah'. It means the lamb performing this task of sin-bearing as belonging to and in the service of Jehovah.

Finally, the difference ought to be noted between the range covered by the act according to the Prophet and according to the Baptist. In Isaiah it is the sin of Israel, here it is the sin of the world. There is some doubt, however, here as in other passages of the Gospel, whether 'world' may not have to be taken qualitatively rather than quantitatively. Still, in Isaiah already the note of universalism is not entirely absent [cp. 52.15].

[3] *John 1.34*

The third great post-baptismal declaration of John recorded in the Fourth Gospel is found in 1.34; 'And I myself have seen and have borne witness, that this is the Son of God.' In this the Baptist reflects upon his fidelity in observing and answering by witness the signal set for him by God in the descent of the Spirit upon Jesus. The close junction of 'seen' and 'borne witness' describes the immediacy of the carrying out of the command: I no sooner saw than I witnessed. The pronoun of the subject is expressed, 'I myself', to indicate, on the one hand, that this was eye-witness testimony, on the other, that it was official testimony. The range of the title 'Son of God' has been considered elsewhere.[1] That it cannot be lower in its import than the same title throughout the Gospel follows from the position that it has as the culminating piece of this first stage of witnessing, when compared with the statement of the author of the Gospel [20.31]. According to this statement the things recorded of Jesus were written to create belief in the divine Sonship of the Saviour. With this in view a series of episodes and discourses had been put in order. Obviously the John-the-Baptist section forms the first in this series, and therein lies the reason why it issues into the testimony about the Sonship under discussion.

[1] Cp. G. Vos, *The Self-Disclosure of Jesus*, pp. 140–227 (1926 ed.); pp. 141–226 (1953 ed.).

That it carried high meaning also appears from the first of the three declarations, in which nothing less than the pre-existence of the Messiah had been affirmed already.

John 3.27–36

In addition to these three supreme utterances there remains still the section 3.27–36 to be considered. This pericope falls into two pieces [vss. 27–30 and 31–36]. As to the former, here John the Baptist is by common consent represented by the Evangelist as the speaker. The occasion was the report brought to the Baptist by his disciples of the greater popularity of Jesus than that enjoyed by their Master. They do not take exception to Jesus' higher status as such, but only to His becoming the rival of John in the latter's own field through baptizing. This was correct as to the statement of fact, at least partially so [cp. 4.2]. Jesus exposes the absurdity of supposing the possibility of rivalry between Himself and John, thus vindicating the latter. Jesus stands so incomparably higher than all messengers of God that it could occur to John as little to conceive jealousy against Him, as the friend of the bridegroom (the presider at the wedding festivities) could do so with regard to the bridegroom. His work is to efface himself, and therein to find his supreme joy; cp. 'my joy' [vs. 29]. Notice that this figure of 'the bridegroom' reminds of Jehovah's relation to Israel.

From John 3.31 onward it is uncertain whether the Baptist remains the speaker, or the Evangelist here takes occasion to insert some reflections of his own on the theme touched upon by the Baptist. Something may be said in favour of each of these views. There seem to enter into the discourse certain characteristic thoughts of Jesus and the Evangelist, who would, of course, in writing the Gospel remember what Jesus had said on various occasions. Such elements are: the descent of Christ from the supernal world, the experiential character of His knowledge of the things of heaven, His identification with God, so that to hear Him is to seal the veracity of God, His all-comprehensive authority in the sphere of revelation, the function of faith as mediating eternal life. Especially with the preceding Nicodemus-discourse there are striking points of contact in regard to some of these matters.

Over against this must be set the weighty consideration, that vss. 31–36 are really needed to round off the argument of the Baptist on the absurdity of endeavouring to rival Jesus. The official impossibility of this had been shown in the preceding, but therein did not yet lie the highest reason for excluding such a state of mind. Of course, it remains possible that the Evangelist, perceiving the preliminariness and one-sidedness of the Baptist's argumentation, proceeded out of his own fuller knowledge to round it off with this discourse upon the transcendent nature and origin (not merely office) of Jesus. If he has actually done so, he has done so with consummate skill, seizing upon several important points of contact in the foregoing with what he wished to say. But these same points of contact can just as well be made to prove that we are here still in the circle of thought of the Baptist. Hence the choice is difficult. It will be noticed that after vs. 30 no pronoun of the first person, which might help us to identify the speaker occurs, and this slightly favours attribution of the words to the Evangelist.

We here content ourselves with briefly enumerating these points of contact with the historical situation that gave rise to the entire discourse. 'He that comes from above' [vs. 31] reminds of vs. 27; the contrast to this is worked out in three statements: 'he that is of the earth' (earthly origin of John), 'is earthly' (earthly mode of existence of John), 'and he speaks of the earth' (earthly mode of revelation-speech). Over against these three must be placed the reiterated 'is above all' which therefore requires to be unfolded for its full understanding in the three directions of the opposite; the absoluteness of Christ's revelation is guaranteed by its experiential character, 'what He has seen and heard' [vs. 32, first half]; the tragical element of the situation is brought out in the remainder of this verse, 'no man receives his witness'; this is the tragedy-note in John's peculiar self-effacing attitude, which makes Jesus' loving appreciation of his work all the more touching; at the same time the statement 'no man receives' involves a correction of the plaint of the disciples of John, 'all come to Him' [vs. 26].

It might seem an exaggeration, in view of the facts recorded in the Gospel itself in chapter 1, to say 'no man receives his witness'; but how the latter is meant, vs. 33 explains: no one has received his testimony in that absolute, comprehensive sense that belongs to receiving the testimony of God; 'for He whom God has sent speaks the words of God' [vs. 34]; in this and the explanation of motive that is added to it the speaker seems to return to the reasoning from the official point of view observed in vss. 27–30; 'for God gives not the Spirit by measure'; the correct interpretation of this has been above explained; it means, 'when there is a giving of the Spirit in the literal sense of giving the entire Spirit involved, there can be no measure to this' (notice the joining of the negation to the verb and the omission of the indirect object, making of it a general proposition); vs. 35, 'the Father loves the Son and has given all things into his hands' reminds most vividly of the voice from heaven at the baptism and the declaration of the election of Jesus to the Messianic office, which, as such, includes the committal of all things to the Son; finally vs. 36 draws from the foregoing objective characterization of Jesus and His office the practical consequence, that faith in Him is followed by eternal life, whilst unbelief with reference to Him results in exclusion from life and permanent abiding under the wrath of God. Here we seem to come closest to the teaching of Jesus and of the Evangelist in the Fourth Gospel. Notice how eternal life is placed in the present, and so is the wrath of God, for the wrath abides; both 'shall not see life' and 'abides on him' are to be understood eschatologically: the vision of life belonging to that final point, and the removal of the wrath at that point are denied.

FOUR:
REVELATION IN THE
PROBATION OF JESUS

THE TEMPTATION IN THE WILDERNESS

What we usually call 'the temptation of Jesus' at first seems to lie like an erratic block in the forefield of his public ministry. On closer examination we discover it to be indispensably connected with both what precedes and what follows. Because this connection is not truly appreciated, doubt has arisen in regard to the historicity and objectivity of what offers itself as a real event. On the mythological principle of interpreting the Gospel history it has been declared an embodiment in story form of the idea, that a personal encounter between the Messiah and Satan is essential to the eschatological drama. Because this had to happen, according to theory, it must have happened to Jesus, if so be He was the real Messiah.

On this view Jesus Himself had nothing whatever to do with the conception or shaping of the account; mythology furnished the framework, whilst the concrete features were borrowed from Old Testament history. Not so far goes the parabolic theory in detaching the story from the actualities of the life of Jesus. Jesus according to this theory told the account to the disciples, not meaning it to be taken by them in a factual sense, but simply as a parable through which He endeavoured to convey to them an impression of the many tempting solicitations that beset Him during his career. The disciples misunderstood this intent and changed it into the account of a fact of single concrete occurrence. On this view Jesus had at least something to do with the production of the story.

Over against both these views we may, in order to uphold the historicity of the event as a single definite occurrence, place the testimony of Matt. 12.29. Here Jesus distinguishes between the entering into the strong man's house and binding him, on the one hand, and the spoiling of the strong man's goods, on the other. The former is something that secures the possibility of doing something, the latter is

330

the following up of that possibility in acts. The context makes clear what the spoiling of goods consists in: it refers to the casting out of demons. Consequently the binding of the strong man, as something lying back of this, must be understood of something done to him whose property the demons are. According to uniform New Testament teaching the demons are subjects of Satan. Now Jesus here uses parabolic language but this cannot in the least alter the fact that behind the parable thus framed there must lie a concrete situation. Although our Lord does not say in so many words, 'I had to pass through a temptation before I could cast out demons', nevertheless something quite definite must be referred to by Him, something that we can even, up to a certain point, locate in time, because it must have fallen before the first casting out of demons, and these acts marked the very beginning of His ministry.

Moreover a diluted interpretation of the parable such as in modern expositions is often met with, to the effect that a man must first conquer evil within himself, before venturing to attack it on the outside, does not fit well into the terms of the figure. The entering into the house of a strong man does not naturally describe the falling into temptation; it depicts something more active and deliberate. Those who refuse, on account of the parabolic nature of the speech, to bring it into connection with the very realistic, though mysterious, narrative of the temptation, are bound by their refusal to attempt some other explanation, if possible less modern-sounding than the one referred to above. And especially the parabolic view constitutes a serious danger to belief in the sinlessness of Jesus, because it implies that on repeated occasions He had to fight a moral battle out within Himself, before He could proceed to reap the fruits of the victory.

The same parable, however, which vouches for the historicity of the event, likewise vouches for its objectivity. Much confusion of thought is created here by a failure to distinguish between the objectivity and corporealness of such a transaction. The second involves the first, but this cannot be reversed: an encounter between persons, especially in the supersensual world, can be perfectly objective without necessarily entering into the sphere of the corporeally perceptible. To what extent there was corporeal perceptibility in the event can only be inferred from the terms of its description, and not *a priori* decided from this parable. But objectivity is doubtless involved, because of the consequences; the casting out of demons appearing objective, the cause is naturally supposed to lie within the same sphere. And, all modern tortuous constructions notwithstanding, there can be no doubt that Jesus regarded the demons as actually existing supernatural beings, who could be spoken to and give answer, and exercised a wide sphere of baneful power. The reduction of all this to the rubric of superstition or psychological derangement is certainly not in accordance with the mind of the Evangelists. Any one who desires to dissociate Jesus from all these and other supernatural phenomena, must do so on the basis of *a priori* theological or philosophical premises, or because of the assumed identity of the recorded facts with phenomena in the sphere of paganism.

The passage in Matt. 12 yields still another item of information concerning the temptation of Jesus. His claim in the dispute with the Pharisees is that the casting out of demons is accomplished by the Spirit of God. The mention of the Spirit is here induced by the mention of Beelzebub, that is, Satan, in the charge of the Pharisees. But there is still another reason for the introduction of the Spirit here. In the accounts of the temptation we find the Spirit of God prominently referred to. Jesus was led up of the Spirit into the wilderness to be tempted of the Devil (Matthew): the Spirit drives Him into the wilderness, apparently for the same purpose (Mark); Jesus, being full of the Holy Spirit, was led of the Spirit into the wilderness, being forty days tempted of the Devil (Luke).

From these statements we learn two things: first, that the Spirit leading Him into the temptation was the Holy Spirit in His Messianic aspect. The close sequence between the accounts of the baptism and that of the temptation puts this beyond all doubt. No sooner has Jesus received the Messianic Spirit than the latter begins to function in that capacity by leading or driving Him into the temptation. The same Spirit who did this at the beginning afterwards enabled Him to cast out the demons. It was the execution of a definite programme in its very first beginning.

In the second place, something like this, done under the auspices of the Spirit, was a transaction behind which stood God Himself. For this reason it is useful to remind ourselves by our terminology, that, while this was on the one hand an act of Satan, it was on the other hand likewise the carrying out of a positive Messianic purpose of God. We can express this best by naming it from the point of view of Satan a 'temptation', from the point of view of the higher purpose of God a 'probation' of Jesus. And as regards Jesus, this eliminates every idea of the sole purpose of the event being a demonstration of His sinlessness. What had behind it a divine purpose cannot have been a mere experience to Jesus, something into which He was drawn unconsciously to Himself and through which He went unaware of its design. Of such an operation of the Spirit upon the Saviour, which would have made of Him a mere unwilling, unresponsive object of propulsion, there is nowhere any trace in the Gospels, and certainly Mark's 'drives Him into the wilderness' is not meant by the Evangelist so to be understood, but only stresses the powerful action of the Spirit, to which Jesus responded with equal energy.

THE LORD'S TEMPTATION AND OUR OWN

Our failure to gauge correctly the significance of the event springs to no small extent from the inclination and habit of finding in it an analogy primarily to our own temptations. This being so we take it too negatively, and do not sufficiently place it in a class by itself. In our case temptation chiefly raises the question of how we shall pass through it and issue from it without loss. In Jesus' case, while this consideration was not, of course, absent, the higher concern was not avoidance of loss, but the procuring of positive gain. And in order to see this we must compare it to the one previous occasion in Biblical history, when a procedure with an equally double-sided purpose had taken place, namely, the temptation of Adam related in Genesis, chapter 3.

Nor is this purely a theological construction on our part; Luke at least seems to have something of this kind in mind, when first carrying back the genealogy (in distinction from Matthew) to Adam, and then immediately subjoining to it this account of the probation of the Second Adam. It should be remembered, however, that with the analogy there existed a difference between the two cases. Adam began with a clean slate, as it were; nothing had to be undone, whilst in the case of Jesus all the record of intervening sin had to be wiped out, before the positive action for the procuring of eternal life could set in.

The clearest philosophy of this difference is given us by Paul in Rom. 5 [cp. especially vs. 15]. This connection of the probation of Jesus with the atoning removal of pre-existing sin will likewise make plain to us that the temptation had to carry in itself for Jesus an element of suffering and humiliation on our behalf, and not merely the exertion of a strenuous will for obedience. Here again there is a difference between Jesus' temptation and ours. To be tempted involves no special humiliation for us, because we are antecedently humiliated by the presence of sin in our hearts to which the solicitation merely has to address itself, which was quite different in the case of Jesus.

All that has been said does not take away the fact that there is an analogy between our temptations and that of Jesus. As is well known

333

the Epistle to the Hebrews lays stress on this in the New Testament. 'Tempted alike, [but] without sin', that is to say, without sin resulting from the temptation in His case, which but too infrequently can be said of us. Still, the author of Hebrews has not particularly in mind the temptation at the beginning of Jesus' ministry, but rather that connected with the passion at the close [Heb. 5.7–9].

We are now prepared to define more precisely in which way the probation underlay the subsequent execution of Jesus' redemptive work. Thus far we have only found that deliverance from demons is traced back to it. But we must further ask: on what principle? The principle is that of an anticipation of the fruits of Jesus' work based on the partial anticipation in principle of the work itself. The casting out of demons was part of the spoil from the battle of His life, and yet it was done when the work was scarcely begun. In the Fourth Gospel this idea of anticipated fruition, both on Jesus' and on the disciples' part occurs not seldom, but here the same idea is found in the Synoptics. One might say, it is true that, after all, the casting out of demons represents but a small portion of our Lord's saving work, too small indeed to suspend such a weighty construction on it. But perhaps He judged of that somewhat differently from what the modern mind is inclined to do. At any rate He has connected nothing less than the coming in of the Kingdom of God with this part of His ministry [Matt. 12.28; Lk. 11.20], and in all three of the Synoptics the antithesis between Satan's and God's kingdom is sharply brought out; where the former goes, the latter *ipso facto* rushes in [cp. vs. 30 in Matthew with vs. 23 in Luke].

THE SPECIFIC FORM ASSUMED BY OUR LORD'S TEMPTATION

We must now, in the next place, enquire what specific form the temptation or the probation assumed. Two possibilities suggest themselves: Jesus could be tempted in a matter not particularly belonging to his Messianic office, so that the sinful act held up before Him could have served as a temptation to any man standing under the ethical law. Or the suggestion made to Him could have been in some way connected with his Messianic calling, causing the sin, if committed, to be specifically Messianic sin.

The first two temptations plainly attach themselves to Jesus' Messianic status, being introduced by 'if thou be the Son of God'. In the third temptation this is not explicitly stated, but the obvious reason is that to mention in one and the same breath our Lord's divine Sonship and a matter of idolatry seemed out of place. The temptations, therefore, are Messianic. And yet the answers given by Jesus apparently proceed from the common human standpoint: 'man shall not live by bread alone'; 'thou shalt not tempt the Lord thy God'; 'thou shalt worship the Lord thy God and Him alone shalt thou serve'. Here no Messiahship whatsoever is referred to.

In this contrapointedness between temptation and answer lies the key to a correct understanding of what at bottom was taking place in. this crisis. It will be noticed that Jesus, while not directly affirming his Messianic position, does not deny, nay, by indirection rather acknowledges it. It could have been easy for Him to bring the whole transaction to an end by saying: I am not the Son of God. The problem, however, resolves itself into this: how can Messiahship and submission to the ethical obligations of common human conduct go together? For in the abstract, Messiahship might be supposed to be exempt from certain restrictions imposed upon ordinary man. As a Messiah in the abstract, Jesus would have committed no sin, if, when hungering, He had turned stones into bread. He could have assumed a sovereign attitude towards nature, instead of submitting to its limitations. If He insists upon conducting Himself like a man, dependent for his support on God, He must mean that his Messiahship, while quite real, is nevertheless passing through a certain phase to which these creaturely limitations, attended by suffering, inseparably belong.

He existed as Messiah in a state of humiliation. After that had been passed through, a state of exaltation would follow, in which these various things now offered to Him as temptations would become perfectly normal and allowable. What was not inherently sinful became so in His case, because of the law of humiliation and service under which His life had for the present been put. The animus of the temptation, from Satan's point of view, consisted in the attempt to move Him out of this spirit and attitude of service and humiliation, so as to yield to the natural desire for His Messianic glory without an interval of suffering. And this preliminary phase of Messiahship, which Satan suggests He should overleap, coincided in general with the condition and experience of a suffering man under God. Hence while Satan counsels Him to act like a super-man, in principle like God, our Saviour, with His repeated stress on what a man is obligated to, repudiates such self-exaltation. It is highly significant in this connection, that the words wherewith Jesus repels the tempter are taken from the Torah, the Book of the Law (Deuteronomy), as though by thus placing Himself under the Law Jesus wished to remind Satan of the real matter at issue, the question of humiliation versus the assertion of the prerogatives belonging to a state of glory.

THE LORD'S TEMPTATIONS INTERPRETED

The above is a somewhat different interpretation of this crisis in the life of Jesus from that which may be met with in the stereotyped 'Lives of Jesus', or in the average moralizing versions of the Gospel stories. The theory ordinarily met with will have it that Jesus in these temptations repudiated the Jewish corruption and prostitution of the Messianic hope along the three lines of its principal perversion. In the first temptation, it is held, He spurned the idea of selfish exploitation of the Messiahship for the incumbent's own ends or needs. The Messiah must not use His supernatural power for stilling His own hunger. His Messianic procedure must be altruistic through and through. In the second temptation Jesus waved aside the diversion of the Messiahship for selfish ambition, to be served by the assumption of the role of a wonder-working Messiah. And in the third temptation He was led to reject once for all the political, nationalistic associations of the idea, which, like the preceding two, made an appeal to the thirst for glory. We shall presently see that this view is not in accord with the replies Jesus made to the suggestions of the tempter. He, therefore, at any rate, did not so construe Satan's design.

It is fortunate that in interpreting the individual temptations, we have available the answers of our Lord, enabling us to work our way back to the inner design of the temptation, for we may safely assume that He meant to answer the tempter to the point. The meaning of the answer supplies the meaning of the Satanic suggestion. And besides this, since the words of the answers were taken from Scripture, and we may again safely assume that Jesus seized upon the real meaning and intent of the Scripture-passages, we can infer from a correct contextual exegesis of these what their point is, what consequently the point of Jesus' answer was, and what, behind the latter, the point in Satan's suggestion was.

DEUTERONOMY 8.3

In answering the first temptation our Lord quoted from Deut. 8.3: 'Man shall not live by bread alone, but by every word that proceeds out of the mouth of God.' In the context of these words Jehovah reminds the Israelites that, through feeding them supernaturally on manna, He meant to teach them the lesson of the ability of God to supply nourishment without the natural processes. There is no contrast here between spiritual food supplied by the Word of God and bodily food supplied in a physical way; in fact the experience of the Israelites would have been a poor method for teaching them that. Moreover in the discourse of Deuteronomy there is not the slightest point of contact for such an exegesis. The true meaning Jesus applies to Himself in essentially the same way which it applied to the Israelites. He had been brought by the Spirit into this situation, where God expected Him to hunger. Notice the occurrence of the words 'to prove', and 'to humble' in the context in Deuteronomy. And the probation consisted in placing before Him the necessity of exercising implicit trust in God as the One able to sustain His life notwithstanding the protracted fast. The 'word proceeding from the mouth of God' refers to the miracle-working word of omnipotence, the mere word requiring no natural means.

The best comprehensive term available for the state of mind revealed by Jesus is the word 'faith'. Only we should remember what this so richly endowed term involved of content on the present occasion. For Jesus here to exercise faith went much further than to practise the heroism of an endurance which will keep itself underneath the suffering. This forms part of the conception, indeed the Greek word *hypomone*, for 'patience', a species of faith, has been modelled upon it. But in the experience of Jesus, as in common Christian experience, the thing needed above all is the inner spirit of submission to God. The question was not in the first place what He should bear, pathologically considered, but how He should bear it. He had to work His way through this painful experience after an ideal fashion from a religious point of view.

And, once more, in this inward spiritual attitude the emphasis did not rest on the negative side only, it lay equally on the positive side. The temptation-suffering had to be borne with full appreciation, with full positive responsiveness to the plan of God. When Satan suggested that He should turn the stones into bread, he was endeavouring to move Jesus out of this faith with reference to His humiliation into an attitude of independent sovereignty, such as properly belonged to His exalted state only. Finally it should be noticed that what became a temptation was not the suffering of hunger only, but the danger of starvation, as also the quotation from Deuteronomy reads: 'Man shall not live by bread only.' Hence Mark and Matthew relate that angels came and ministered to Him.

DEUTERONOMY 6.16

In viewing the second temptation we again take our departure from the answer given by Jesus. This was taken from Deut. 6.16, where Moses says to the Israelites: 'Ye shall not tempt Jehovah your God, as ye tempted Him in Massah.' The event itself is described in Ex. 17, and again referred to in Deut. 9.22; 33.8. To tempt Jehovah has the meaning of 'proving God', that is, of seeking to ascertain by experiment whether His power to lead them to Canaan could be relied upon. It was a proving springing from doubt or outright unbelief. What happened at Massah figured in later times as the typical example of the sin of unbelief [Psa. 95.8; Heb. 3 and 4]. Our Lord plainly implies that casting Himself down from the height of the temple, trusting that angels would intercept His fall, would not in principle differ from the conduct of these murmuring Hebrews in the wilderness.

At first sight this seems incomprehensible, because such an exhibition on the part of Jesus might be construed as diametrically opposite to the state of mind actuating the Israelites at Massah. It certainly required a degree of trust to perform the act commanded by Satan. And yet, while a momentary abandon to faith, the venture would have been inspired by the shrinking from a protracted life of faith. In the sequel our Lord would have been led on in His ministry, not by an ever-renewed forth-putting of the same act of trust that God would preserve Him, but by the remembrance of this one supreme experiment, which rendered further trust superfluous. It would have involved an impious experimenting with the dependability of God. Afterwards His sense of safety would have depended, not on the promise of God, but on the demonstration solicited by Himself. The answer, therefore, here also addressed itself in the most direct manner to what was the springing-point of the temptation: 'Thou shalt not make experiments with Jehovah, thy God.' This second temptation ranges itself by the side of the first, in that in the latter, safety from starvation, in the former, protection from outside danger were at issue.

DEUTERONOMY 6.13
The third temptation differs from the preceding ones in two respects. First, it suggests an open act of sin, whereas up to this point the sinfulness of the act was skilfully disguised, and represented as lying within the sphere of what the Messiah could legitimately do. Here the act counselled is an act of Satan-worship, sinful per se. And secondly, Satan now for the first time introduces the element of self-interest, having previously confined himself to the role of a disinterested spectator, counselling Jesus for the latter's own good. In both these respects the third temptation moves on a lower plane of subtlety than the preceding two. It remains a mystery, how Satan, after the two preceding repulses, could entertain any serious hope of success in this

instance. And yet if, psychologically speaking, the attempt appears absurd, it must be acknowledged that the third temptation was a more fundamental one in that it uncovered the ultimate issue around which things had been revolving from the outset. The question at stake was, whether God should be God, or Satan should be God, and correspondingly, whether the Messiah should be God's or Satan's Messiah. For this is the deeper background which Satan's conditional 'if' and his consequent promise about the gift of the glory of the kingdoms reveals to us. The two acts would not have been single, isolated acts of sin. They would have involved a transfer of allegiance on Jesus' part from God to Satan. Hence our Lord's summary dismissal of the tempter: 'Get thee hence [or 'behind me'], Satan.' The appeal is made to Deut. 6.13 where all idolatry is on principle forbidden.

Although Satan in this third attempt, by coming out into the open and counselling something so flagrantly sinful, acted with desperately bad judgment, there are nevertheless some things to be taken into account, to render his conduct up to a certain point intelligible, if not intelligent. These are as follows:

(a) Satan seems to have counted on the effect of the suddenness of the assault; in the two preceding cases he had, as it were, submitted the case to Jesus for deliberate consideration; here he shows Him the object of attraction and fascination in a moment of time;

(b) he appeals to Jesus' deep-seated instinct for obedience and service as evinced in the foregoing answers. This seems an attempt to betray Him into that form of religious subjectiveness, wherein it makes no longer much difference who or what the object of service is, provided there be scope for the unfettered assertion of the religious instinct. This, of course, gives rise to a pseudo-religion, in which the processes are governed by man and not by God. Religion is not worship or service in the abstract; it is worship and service of the true God, and according to His revelation specifically.

In the light of this the quotation from Deuteronomy, 'the Lord thy God, and Him alone', obtains a deepened meaning. Pagan religion at bottom always emancipates itself from this objective bond. In reality to call it 'religion', or to speak of 'religions', in the plural, is a misnomer. That 'false religions' exist at all is due solely to the fact that subjectively the need for religion is innate in the human soul.

TEMPTABILITY AND PECCABILITY

Our view taken of the temptation, while by no means solving all the mysteries of the event, nevertheless is adapted to throw some light on an obscure subject. Two problems meet here. The one is the problem of the temptability of Jesus. The other is the problem of His peccability. How could He be tempted? we first enquire; and then, the temptation being given, how could He sin? It is clear that the first problem in a sense supersedes the second. If a person is liable to being tempted by something, this would seem to involve an imperfection. The absolute goodness would be immunity to sin, such as God always possesses, and the saints in heaven have finally arrived at. As a matter of fact temptation has found entrance both in the First and in the Second Adam. And yet its entrance alone did not imply the presence of sin.

The solution lies in this, that the course of action made to appeal to them was not a course of action inherently sinful, but in the abstract innocent and allowable, and which became productive of sin only owing to the positive prohibition under which God had placed the act. Through the abstract innocence of the act it could enter the mind of man and become an object of desire or undecided contemplation, so long as the divine prohibition was not called to remembrance and defied. If 'temptability' merely means openness of mind to an, in itself, innocent act, the difficulty might perhaps seem to be removed by this. But it might be objected with considerable force that this touches the psychological approach to temptation only, and lies in reality this side of the actual temptation itself. The temptation would begin only when the clear-cut alternative presented itself before the choosing mind – which shall it be, the taking of the thing in its innocence? or the rejection of it because forbidden by God?

And here the problem returns in all its acuteness: how could the preference of the taking to the obeying of the divine will be contemplated for a moment by the mind of a sinless person? For we must remember that the inclination of a sinless being is always towards God, and away from disobedience because of its love of God. What can we psychologically conceive able to overcome and reverse that? It is a problem that meets us already in the case of our first parents. But it presents a more difficult aspect yet in the case of Jesus. For Jesus differed from Adam in some respects, which make the counter-balancing factors for the repudiation of sin to be much more formidable, and in so far, the solvability of the problem to appear more impossible.

Jesus was not only innocent like Adam, He was possessed of and guided by the Spirit in all its fulness, and still further, if we accept the later teaching of the New Testament, His human nature was owned by the Person of the Son of God. To put the question under such circumstances seems to determine beforehand the negative answer, that He could not be tempted nor sin. The double mystery, therefore, that as to the temptability, and that as to the peccability of the Saviour, here appears as one in its root, and we simply must confess our inability to throw light upon it.

At the same time we should not let ourselves be taken in by the facile solution, which says: Jesus had a true human nature, and therefore, of course, He could be tempted and sin. This may have a certain relative value, because of the divine nature we *a priori* absolutely know, that it can be neither tempted nor sin. In that abstract, metaphysical impossibility the human nature of Jesus did not share. But the abstract, metaphysical possibility yields only an abstract, metaphysical contingency of being tempted and sinning. What is sought, where the problem is raised, is something different from that, namely, the psychological, ethical, religious conceivability of the entrance of real temptation and sin. With an appeal to Jesus' human nature as such nothing whatever is gained. To disillusion ourselves in regard to that, it suffices to remember that Jesus in His exalted state, and also the saints in heaven, possess a human nature, and yet are not thereby made capable of sinning.

The most current modern interpretation of the event meets with far greater difficulties in upholding the sinlessness of Jesus, than the one outlined above. The reason is that the Judaistic perversion of the Messianic idea, in the allurement of which is placed on this view the essence of the temptation, was not in itself an innocent thing. If Jesus felt the allurement exercised by it, and had to wage a battle against it, this seems to involve that He had to resist the seduction towards something wrong exerting power within Himself. A suggestion was injected into His soul, which was evil *per se*. It has been observed, however, that the same can not be evaded so far as the hypothetical part of the third temptation is concerned. But it was not the hypothesis here that made the appeal to Jesus. What was intended to appeal to Him was the rule over the kingdoms, and this again is not *ipso facto* sinful; on the contrary, it is something explicitly promised to the Messiah [cp. *Psa.* 2.8; 9; *Rev.* 11.15].

Still another objection to the popular view is that the replies of Jesus to Satan, if interpreted according to their true Old Testament import, do not contain a fitting refutation of the Satanic suggestion as the modern view understands them. That man shall not live by bread alone has nothing to do with the question of exploiting Messianic resources for selfish purposes. The bid for popular applause has nothing to do intrinsically with the prohibition of tempting God. Only in the third temptation does the quotation from the Old Testament fit better into the proposal of Satan.

The plan of temptation followed by Satan evinces, though not equal subtlety in all its parts, nevertheless a certain profundity of insight into the issues at stake, and a certain strategic eagerness to conquer Jesus, not at some subordinate point, but at the central, pivotal position, on which the successful outcome of the plan of redemption depended. Satan knew very well that this pivotal point lay in Jesus' absolute and resolute adherence to the principle of humiliation and suffering as the only road to victory and glory. It gave him, no doubt, a sinister satisfaction to attempt to overthrow the work of God and Christ at its very centre. Any kind of sin would have disqualified Jesus for His Messianic task, but the sin suggested here would have been a sin against the very heart and essence of the task.

FIVE:
THE REVELATION OF
JESUS' PUBLIC MINISTRY

[A] THE VARIOUS ASPECTS OF CHRIST'S
REVEALING FUNCTION

In thinking of the revelation mediated by Jesus we are in the habit of
confining ourselves to His walk and work on earth. This is not an
adequate conception, because it leaves out of account that Jesus existed
before He was born (pre-existence), and continued to exist after He
had been removed from earth (post-existence), and that both of these
states, by which his earthly life was surrounded, stood in close relation
to the large scheme of divine revelation as a whole.

Jesus' function while revealing God during His earthly life partook
of a peculiar adjustment to other organs and epochs of revelation,
through which certain limitations were imposed upon it, limitations
that did not belong to the two surrounding states. During His earthly
life He became One among many, a link, as it were, in the chain of
revealing organs. He was not intended, nor intended Himself, to
communicate the whole revealable volume of divine truth, so as to make
either what preceded or what followed dispensable. He did His part
of the whole, presupposing what the Old Testament had done before,
and reckoning with what the subsequent organs of New Testament
disclosure of truth concerning the work enacted by Him would do
after. In this sense He would be called both a Prophet and an Apostle.
Only, in remembering this, it is necessary to add that the limitations
under which Jesus put and kept Himself in this respect were of the
objective, and not of the subjective kind. They were the result not of
any inadequacy of knowledge, but of the enclosure of His function
within a scheme extending in both directions towards Him and away
from Him. Although He possessed the fulness of the divine truth
within Himself, and could have let it shine out through His subjectivity,
yet He forebore doing this, adjusting Himself to the process of which

M

He was the acme and centre, a process requiring both preparation and following up.

It will be seen that, thus defined, the idea of limitation of content, inherent in our Lord's earthly work, has nothing to do with the limitations which the theory of Kenosis assumes to have existed in Him. The latter are considered as subjective in nature arising from our Lord's having laid aside, or having divested Himself of the use of, such transcendent attributes as omniscience and omnipotence, so that in consequence His teaching was not free from mistakes, nor His power equal to omnipotence. In our opinion no change had taken place in the Deity, and the human nature did not fall in any sense short of the requirements the work of revelation made upon it. The limitations in what He was sent to do left the completeness and perfection of what He could have done in their full integrity.

FOUR DIVISIONS OF REVELATION BY CHRIST

Jesus' revelation-functioning during the Old Testament and after His ascension did not, however, complete the entire revealing task performed by Him, apart from his public ministry. For all this belongs to the sphere of redemption, and by the side of it we must place His mediation of the knowledge of God in nature. All that is disclosed of God to the mind of man through nature comes by Him. And we must not conceive of this as something purely preliminary, ceasing as soon as his activity in the Old Testament began or His incarnation took place. It is being continued now and will be continued for ever, interlinked with all that of redemptive disclosure is superimposed upon it.

Enumerating them in order, we obtain four divisions of revelation ministered in by Christ:

(a) that in Natural, or, otherwise called, General Revelation, extending from the creation of the world forward indefinitely;

(b) that under the economy of the Old Testament, extending from the entrance of sin and redemption till the incarnation;

(c) the disclosure of God made during His public ministry on earth, extending from the nativity until His resurrection and ascension;

(d) the revelation mediated by Him through His chosen servants, extending from the ascension until the death of the last inspired witness, speaking under the infallible guidance of the Holy Spirit.

We find these four functions spoken of severally in the Prologue of the Fourth Gospel. It is usually understood that the Evangelist here subsumes them under the name *Logos* given to Christ. *Logos* means

344

both reason and word, owing to the fine Hellenic perception, that the two processes of thinking and speaking are intimately related, thinking being a sort of inward speech, speaking a sort of outward thought. The *Logos* is, therefore, the outward Revealer of the inward mind of God. Some speculative theologians think that the idea does not relate to the process of speech *ad extra* at all, but describes the inward mode of existence of the Deity, on the principle that the Second Person of the Trinity is, as it were, the reverse, turned-round-side, of the First. Leaving this to one side, and confining ourselves to the sphere of revelation to the world, the question arises whether the name relates to any part of revelation exclusively, or whether it comprehensively relates to every component part of the process.

The tendency was at one time to keep the term *Logos* within the range of nature-revelation in contrast to the redemptive disclosure of God. Such a view would rule out from it not merely the redemptive revelation of the New Testament, but likewise that of the Old Testament. It would not have been as *Logos* that the Son of God appeared to Israel or to the Church after the incarnation. All His revealing work consisted from the creation onward, and through all time, in mediating the natural knowledge of God; that is, so far as the name *Logos* is concerned, though, of course, under other designations, He was recognized as performing the task of redemptive Revealer.

This view is not a plausible one, because the very point of the Prologue seems to be to link the revelations in nature and in redemption together. But this last point is also lost to view where, as Zahn would interpret the Evangelist, the name *Logos* is entirely associated with the incarnate, redemptive revelation mediated by Jesus on earth. According to this writer Jesus did not become the *Logos* or Word as such until the incarnation. Especially the statement in vs. 14 causes great difficulty on this interpretation.

Among those who hold that there is reference to both nature and redemptive revelation there is still a further difference as to whether the Evangelist makes special reference to the Old Testament as a separate stage or not. This touches the exegesis of vs. 11, viz., whether 'his own' there means men in general, 'his own' in virtue of creation, or means the nation of Israel. In the former case the rejection of the incarnate Redeemer on a large scale by the world is referred to, in the latter case the rejection of the incarnate Redeemer by the people of Israel.

A careful exegesis of the Prologue leads to the conclusion that the following stages are part of the *Logos*-work of which John is speaking:

345

(*a*) first the mediation to mankind of the knowledge of God conveyed through nature; this is a function which by no means ceased when the *Logos* became flesh, but is going on alongside of His incarnate, redemptive activity from the beginning onward till the end, as long as there shall be a world to need it;

(*b*) in the second place there is the redemptive revelation given to the Old Testament people of God; this had reference to redemption although it was mediated by the as yet un-incarnate Christ, so that as to the state in which the *Logos* mediated it there was as yet no difference between what He had been from the beginning of the world and what He was then;

(*c*) in the third place the *Logos*-function reached its climax, when the Word became flesh, and in this incarnate state, never to be laid aside again, issued the full interpretation of the redemptive work of God, either during His own earthly career in the state of humiliation, or during His exalted state, possessed since the resurrection and now brought to bear upon the redemptive revelation from heaven.

JESUS' REVEALING WORK IN THE GOSPELS

We here address ourselves particularly to the last-mentioned stage of Jesus' revealing work, that performed on earth and described and recorded in the Gospels. However, the mode of this is by no means uniform. In order to have a right understanding of it, we must draw certain distinctions, and not lose ourselves in the generality that Jesus was the Revealer of God on earth. The Gospels know and speak of two aspects or manners in which this took place. On the one hand Jesus disclosed God through what He was; His nature, His character were God-revealing; ultimately this involves and postulates His being divine in His nature, His being God. On the other hand Jesus also revealed God through the speech He brought from God, through the words He spake.

It goes without saying that these two modes were not sharply separated one from the other. The character-revelation never was entirely a mute one, unaccompanied by words; on the other hand the speech-revelation was in no small part a disclosure of character, first of the Speaker, and next of One duplicated. It is, therefore, not so much the absence or the presence of the thought of word-revelation, but rather the prominence of the thought of character-duplication in one of the sources that distinguishes the two aspects.

In the Fourth Gospel we find this thought in unique prominence. In the Synoptics it occasionally occurs, but what we mostly find there is the idea of revelation through direct speech concerning God. Matt. 11.27 furnishes an example within the Synoptics of the idea of God-disclosure by means of God-likeness, and for this very reason and its rareness in the Synoptics it has been called 'The Johannine *logion*'. Certain peculiarities follow in the wake of each of the two aspects distinguished. In John, because the idea in the foreground is that of Person-disclosure, the object of the revelation appears pointedly personal: it is God, or the Father, whom Jesus reveals rather than a thing connected with God. In the Synoptics, on the other hand, objectively represented things, such as the Kingdom of God, righteousness, etc., are more in evidence, although of course, these appear at no point detached from God in such a way as would make them religiously indifferent, after the well-known modern fashion.

Further, in John, because of this object-concentration of the revealed content in God, great stress is laid upon the pre-existence in Heaven through which Jesus was pre-eminently qualified for showing what He had to show, namely God, for in Heaven the main object of His vision was precisely God [cp. 1.51; 3.2; 5.30; 8.38]. Besides the pre-existence, the idea of an uninterrupted coexistence, as a source of revelation-knowledge during even the earthly life, is expressed in some of such passages.

Still further, the Johannine revelation concept carries in itself a strong soteric element. Revelation is not merely the prerequisite of salvation, as might more easily appear from the Synoptics; precisely because it confronts one directly with God in Christ it produces a transforming, cleansing effect through its own inherent action [8.32; 15.3]. The personally concentrated form in which the attributes and potencies of God are represented as incarnate in Jesus, fits in with this trend of thought. He is 'the life', 'the light', 'the truth' in Person.

Over against this complex of peculiarities in John we find in the Synoptics repeated references to the Spirit as the proximate source of the revelation conveyed by Jesus. The Fourth Gospel likewise mentions the Spirit, but not with such prominence in the same connection. The Baptist, while not recording the baptism directly, speaks of it as qualifying Jesus for conferring the Spirit upon others [1.33], but that is not quite the same as revealing through the Spirit. The emphasis on the divine nature has taken away the need of referring to this. Once, we find the characterization of the words of Jesus as 'Spirit and life' [6.63]. On the whole, the Spirit figures in John as a future gift, who will come after the departure of Jesus, and in that season will also act as the medium of revelation from Jesus to the disciples [16.13].

347

[B] THE QUESTION OF DEVELOPMENT[1]

Having now reached the point where the public ministry of our Lord opens up to our investigation, we are brought face to face with the question, whether there is observable within this teaching a development. In order to ensure clearness we must at the outset distinguish between subjective development in the mind of Jesus, His knowledge of and insight into the truth having grown as He progressed in His ministry, and objective development, the presentation of facts and teachings having been subject to progress from season to season.

Speaking in the abstract, no *a priori* objection can be raised even against the subjective kind of development. Jesus had a true human nature, and human nature as such is subject to development, which, however, is not equivalent to saying that it cannot exist under any conditions without development. The idea of evolution has taken such hold of the modern mind, and become so fascinating, that in many cases the existence of the gradual acquisition of knowledge by the mind of Jesus is simply assumed without enquiring into the concrete evidence. As a matter of fact evidence for this assumption does not exist, so long as the faultless nature of the content of the teaching is maintained. There is no point in the life of our Lord at which the inflow of a new substance or principle of thought can be traced. A breach between foregoing and following is nowhere perceptible. The incidents near Caesarea-Philippi have sometimes been seized upon to bear out such a construction, but, as afterwards will be pointed out, there was here no evidence of advance in enlightenment in the mind of Jesus, nor even an injection of something totally new into the minds of the disciples. The point of the episode is not that a confession took place of something wholly unknown before.

Still, progress in objective teaching there was, if not particularly here, yet at other points. The necessity for this would rise from the capability of apprehension in the disciples, which was less at the beginning than afterwards, and from the unfolding of the situation of the public ministry of our Lord, in which the opposition of His enemies was one of the chief determining factors, humanly speaking.

Our position, therefore, is: subjective development is allowable, but not actually proven; objective development in the teaching is necessary, and capable of being pointed out. However, to prevent misunder-

[1] Cp. G. Vos *The Self-Disclosure of Jesus* (1926) (edited and re-written by J. G. Vos 1954).

standing, we must add to this a somewhat more precise statement. Suppose subjective development were actually discovered, we could not grant that such development might be of every imaginable kind. We must distinguish progress from error to truth, and again progress from partial to more comprehensive and adequate apprehension of the truth. The former would be irreconcilable with the faultlessness of Jesus' teaching, the latter might be in perfect consonance with it.

Now, in consulting the modern discussions of the life and teaching of Jesus, we find that, as a matter of fact, the occasions where a progress of subjective insight into the truth is ascribed to Him are precisely of this kind, that He is assumed to have advanced from error to elimination of error. And this is not confined to matters of relatively smaller importance, such as questions of history and criticism, for these things are deemed nowadays often so trivial as to have lain entirely beyond the need of correction, and Jesus is easily allowed to have shared in such things the common opinions of His time and never to have developed away from them in His entire life. The points singled out, in regard to which the error-eliminating development is by preference affirmed, are rather the cardinal and most weighty subjects of His teaching. We are asked to believe that our Lord, about such matters as the Kingdom of God, His Messiahship, and the necessity or significance of His death, held not only different but contrary convictions at various points. The advocates of this belief frequently do not take pains to base it on evidence; it is simply taken for granted after the most facile manner.

It needs no pointing out that where this is done, both the presence of the divine nature in the Person of Jesus and the infallibility of His human nature have been in principle abandoned. He has become a teacher like every eminent teacher. A prophet He hardly can on such a supposition be called, for with the prophetic office infallibility was generally associated, and this opinion was doubtless shared by Jesus Himself. The consciousness of Messiahship could not possibly have lived in such an atmosphere, for, if even the Baptist was greater than every prophet, how much more Jesus, in His revelation-consciousness, must have considered Himself the summit of stability and reliability as to absolutely representing God always.

All that has been said above relates to the public ministry of Jesus only, for this alone is the section of Jesus' life which the record enables us to observe. As to His preceding private life there must have been psychical and ethico-religious development. The information we have on this is exceedingly scanty. It is confined to the statements in

Lk. 2.49–52. All the rest remains withdrawn in secrecy, and it would require a great deal of critico-historical self-confidence to construct on so small a basis what has been not infrequently called 'a biography of Jesus', or in a somewhat more modest language 'a life of Jesus'.

[C] THE METHOD OF JESUS' TEACHING

The question of allowable development leads on directly to that of the method of teaching. For it is obvious that in the point of method, more than anywhere else, a degree of variableness and adjustability to the development of the situation is to be observed. That the method of Jesus' teaching bore a specific character is certain, but the peculiarity can be more easily observed by putting the question in the negative: by the absence of which features was the method employed most clearly recognizable?

The features absent are systematizing, doctrinal-cohesive presentation of truth. This can be best realized by comparing the teaching of Paul, which while in no wise unduly theological, comes much nearer to doctrinal organization than does that of our Lord. The Jewish teaching of Jesus' time possessed likewise more of a systematic character than His. This was imparted unto it by the strict lines of the system of the Law within which it moved, but it was, from a theological point of view, shallow, and contained more flagrant inconsistencies than Paul's teaching has ever been charged with. In the whole range of Jesus' teaching there is practically nothing that approaches a definition of any subject, not even in regard to the Kingdom of God, which Paul a couple of times comes near to defining.

Now that which makes up for and corresponds to the absence of this abstract element is the concrete, imaginative way of handling principles for illustration's sake. The philologists say that all language has this concrete, physical background, so that there is really no spiritual thing or process that did not originally find expression through a material analogue. We cannot name or discuss the simplest thing but we speak in figures. Only we no longer realize it. The language, through oblivion of its own ancestry, has gradually raised itself to the plane of the spiritual world. But conscious employ of figurative modes of expression is something different, because it is intentional. It compares things in the visible, natural sphere to things in the invisible, spiritual. Of this consciously-comparative way of speaking there are several forms, to distinguish which is the business of rhetoric. Without binding ourselves to technical classification we here simply describe the use made of these various forms in our Lord's discourse. The generic name, under which these forms are usually classified in the Gospel exposition is that of 'parables'. It is better, however, to restrict this name to a species of the genus.

SIMILITUDES

The simplest forms of the whole group are what we call, or some books call, the simile and the metaphor. These are at one in comparing a single thing or person to a thing or person in a different sphere. But they differ in that the simile makes the comparison explicit, whereas the metaphor, by naming the thing to be compared outright with the name of the comparing figure, keeps it implicit. 'Herod is like a fox' would be a simile; 'go and tell that fox' is a metaphor. Such likenings of single things to single are rare in the Gospels. The parabolic comparison has this for its peculiarity, that it likens not single things one to the other, but some relation between certain items to some relation between other items. The figure is: as A is related to B, so C is related to D. From the fig tree we, no less than the disciples, can learn her parable: when the branches become tender (A), summer is nigh (B); even so when the eschatological premonitions occur (C), the end of the world is approaching (D). Care must be taken not to find (A) likened to (C), nor (B) likened to (D). Comparisons of this kind belong to the class of parables in the more restricted sense. For the sake of distinguishing them, however, we shall call them similitudes, because they call attention to the similarity between ever-recurring processes or sequences in nature and sequences in the redemptive world.

PARABLES PROPER

The second group in the circle of parables we designate by the name of parables proper, because to this class of comparative representations the name of 'parable' has become more popularly attached. These differ from the similitudes, in so far as they are clothed in the form of a story, the introductory formula being expressible by 'once upon a time', 'a sower went out to sow'. Although the process is here no less than in the similitude-group an ever-recurring process, yet for rhetorical effect it is pictured as a single event. The narrative-character thus imparted renders these parables-proper like unto fiction-stories designated as 'fables' in ancient literature. The difference lies in this, that the pagan fables introduce as their personages animals. Animals play next to no role in our Lord's parables, most of these being taken from the vegetable kingdom, but cp. Matt. 23.37; Lk. 13.34. Furthermore, the animals used for the furnishing of the pagan fable act unnaturally, from the animal point of view; having been put there in the place of men they are bound to forget their own nature, and must play out the role to the end. And from this again results the feature that the speaking and acting animals adopt a serio-comical behaviour. This last-mentioned feature is entirely absent from Jesus' parabolic teaching as from His teaching in general, for irony, which can here and there be detected, should not be confounded with comedy.

SPECIALIZATION-PARABLES

The third group of so-called parables may be called specialization-parables. Their use rests on the employment of the specialization-principle in our Lord's teaching in a wider sphere, outside of the strictly so-called parabolic material. By the specialization-method of teaching we understand that a lesson or principle, instead of being abstractly described, is placed before us in a single instance of its working. Thus the internal character of righteousness and sin is vividly illustrated in the Sermon on the Mount by specialization of the various cases of adultery, murder, etc. A little later on, the injunction as to what is to be taken on the propaganda-journey and what is to be left behind serves a similar purpose [Matthew 10]. Now this specialization-method can, instead of being introduced straightforwardly, just as well be presented in the parable form, and then results the specialization-parable. A clear instance of this is the parable of the Pharisee and the publican. Here not one process is taken out of the sphere of nature and another out of the spiritual sphere; both transactions belong to the same spiritual sphere, and by typifying the way in which the thing ought not to be done, and ought to be done, the lesson is carried home to the mind. These specialization-parables have this in common with the parable-proper group, that they likewise borrow the form of fiction: 'Once upon a time a Pharisee and a publican went up', etc.

THE 'ALLEGORICAL' METHOD

The question has been raised, whether Jesus, besides these parabolic forms of teaching, also employed what is called the 'allegorical' method. For practical purposes we may call an allegory a story in which not one central point of comparison is intended to be brought out, but in which around this one point there is intentionally and ingeniously woven a web of detail-comparisons in the two processes placed side by side. We cannot *a priori* exclude the employment of this method; in the Old Testament there are striking examples of it; use had been made of it in the ancient Stoic philosophy; further in the Alexandrian-Jewish Philonic speculation; then in the medieval theology, and up to most modern times in all sorts of curious twists of mysticizing. In all these successive streams of allegory the ostensible purpose has been to foist a group of ideas upon an underground of thought by nature foreign to it. The tradition became so luxuriant that even in Romanist circles the further employment of it had to be barred by setting up the rule: *Theologia parabolica non est argumentativa.*[1] For the loose elaboration of ideas it might be useful, but not for strict theological reasoning.

But, if all parabolical reasoning in the reproduction of our Lord's teaching is to be avoided, it becomes very questionable whether enough material of an unparabolic nature will remain to determine the main strands of His teaching by it at all. Protection, therefore, should not be sought in a surrender of all the parables to theological non-use, but in a careful safeguarding of the rules under which the use of this kind of the material can be safely conducted. One great rule has been framed for this purpose in modern times. It consists in insisting that in every parable there shall be recognized only one point of central comparison, and that all the further correspondences that may by ingenious exegesis be woven around this shall be deemed to lie outside the proper scope of the parable, and not entitled to authority from the intent of the framer, being from His point of view purely accidental. B. Weiss has in his commentaries on the Gospels most rigidly insisted upon this rule. Julicher has in his classic work on the parables gone one step further, in that he makes the presence of allegorical elements an infallible test of the spuriousness of the parts in which they occur, and thus is led to remove considerable material from the text as originally strange to Jesus.

This 'puristic' position is not in accord with the general tenor of Jesus' teaching. So far as we can observe, the question of rhetorical form possessed no independent interest for Him; if the form shines through its excellence, this is due not to conscious intent, but simply to the innate beauty of the vision of truth and of all things in Jesus' mind. Moreover, we have examples in the Gospels where the purity of form is sacrificed to the exigency of inculcating some principle of truth that could only through allegorical pressure be worked into the framework of the parabolic setting: Mk. 2.19, 20 and Matt. 22.2–14 [cp. *Lk.* 14.16–24]. On the other hand there are cases where the alle-

[1] That is, parabolic theology is not to be used in argument.

353

gorical possibilities of a parable are intentionally destroyed, not because of rhetorical objection to them, but for the sole reason that they detract from the singleness of purpose pursued in the parable. This is plainly observable in the parables of the unrighteous judge, of the unrighteous steward and of the wise and foolish virgins.

Of course, rhetorically considered, the allegory stands lower than the parable, because it is difficult to shape the account of happenings along two parallel lines belonging to two different spheres in such a way that the items in one series shall naturally correspond to those in the other series. An allegory always partakes of a certain unnaturalness; its composition requires a prolonged fashioning and arranging of the material except in the case where there exists a sort of pre-established harmony between the two lines of occurrence, the one having been shaped in the mind of the Creator of the two spheres with special analogy to the other, as in the case of the operation of fatherhood in the parable of the prodigal. Compare Ezekiel 17 for the inevitable unnaturalness in the ordinary allegory. Our Lord's parabolic teaching bears all the signs of unpremeditation and instantaneousness of utterance.

THE PHILOSOPHY OF THE PARABOLIC TEACHING

We next enquire into the philosophy of the parabolic teaching. One of the purposes it served was doubtless to render the truth more vivid through putting it in concrete form. Still, this is nowhere stated in so many words by Jesus. We must infer it from the general use to which such a form of representation was put by others at that time, for example, by the Jewish teachers.

Another purpose which can be observed in the working is the employment of the parable to intercept prejudice. Whilst the abstract formulation of some principle apt to create offence would as a rule have set the prejudice in motion before the subject could be dispassionately considered, the bringing of it forward in parabolized form invests it with a degree of innocency, so as to induce the mind to assent within the terms of the figure, an assent which it cannot easily withdraw when the equivalence of the lesson outside and inside the parable is reflected upon.

Still a third purpose of parabolic speech, and this is something far more strange to the modern mind, is that spoken of by Jesus in Matt. 13.13–16; Mk. 4.11, 12; Lk. 8.10. According to this statement the aim of parabolic teaching is to veil the truth, lest it should become clear and yield benefit to those unworthy of its reception. The difference between 'because they seeing, see not' (Matthew) and 'that seeing they may see, and not perceive', 'that seeing they might not see' (Mark, Luke) ought to be noticed.

Besides the rhetorical point of view, we can study the philosophy of the parables also from a theological point of view. It would be wrong to assume that the parables which Jesus spoke were nothing more than homiletical inventions, not based on any deeper principle or law. It would be more correct to call them spiritual discoveries, because they are based on a certain parallelism between the two strata of creation, the natural and the spiritual (redemptive) one, because the universe has been thus constructed. On the principle of 'spiritual law in the natural world', the nature-things and processes reflect as in a mirror the supernature-things, and it was not necessary for Jesus to invent illustrations. All He had to do was to call attention to what had been lying hidden, more or less, since the time of creation. This seems to be the meaning of Matthew's quotation from Psa. 78.2 [*Matt.* 13.35].

The marvellous acquaintance of Jesus' mind with the entire compass of natural and economic life, observable in His parables, may be explained from this, that He had been the divine Mediator in bringing this world with all its furnishings into being, and again was the divine Mediator for producing and establishing the order of redemption.

This fact underlies as a broad substratum all the parables in the Synoptics. In John this mode of teaching recedes somewhat into the background. Examples of parables in John are: 3.8; 11.9, 10; 12.24; 13.10; 16.21. But it is precisely in John that the theological principle of the duplex structure and stratification of the universe is explicitly enunciated. The great contrasts governing the teaching here, both of Jesus and of the Evangelist, are expressed in the terms 'earth' (opp. 'heaven'); the 'world' (opp. 'not this world'); 'the earthly things' (opp. 'the heavenly things'); 'the things beneath' (opp. 'the things above'). Between these fundamental contrasts the relation prevails that in order of thought and pre-eminence the heavenly things precede. They form the original, the opposites are the copies. Practically speaking, the higher sphere is that whither all religious tending and striving must be directed. Hence the 'supernaturalism' of Jesus' Gospel and of His Person, as determining that of the Gospel, finds most pointed expression in John. One might call it the anti-evolutionistic document in the Scriptures, *par excellence*, so far as ethics and religion are concerned [8.23].

'TRUE' AND 'TRUTH' IN THE FOURTH GOSPEL
The difference between the higher things and the lower things is not

Platonically conceived, as though there were more reality of being in the former than in the latter. Both are equally real. The difference comes in through an appraisal of quality. The technical term in John to mark the contrast is that of *aletheia*, 'truth'. The things in the supernal world possess the quality of 'true things'. It should be carefully noted that 'true' in such a connection does not have the ordinary sense of 'exact agreement with reality', for 'truth' thus understood is something located in the human mind subjectively, since in the mind alone such a thing as 'agreement' can exist. The true things in this specific Johannine acceptance have the truth inherent in themselves as an objective characteristic. They are true intrinsically. The intrinsic truth residing in them is just the specific character they bear as part of the supernal heavenly sphere.

The usage is found both in the discourses of Jesus and in the reflections upon them by the Evangelist. The *Logos* is 'the true light', that embodiment of the quality of light of which all other lights in the world are but copies and derivatives [1.9]. On the same principle Jesus calls Himself 'the true bread', 'the true vine' [6.32, 33; 15.1]. The adjective that is used in such statements is not the ordinary form *alethes*, but the stronger form *alethinos*. One might say that the entire supernal sphere is made up of 'alethinities'. The objectivity of the concept becomes most apparent by observing that this heavenly truth is, as it were, condensed, incorporated in the heavenly *Logos*: He is the truth, not, of course, because He is veracious and reliable, but simply, because He has the reality of heaven in Himself. Almost a definition of the idea in this sense is found in connection with 'the true bread' [6.32, 33]: 'My Father gives you the true bread from heaven, for the bread of God is He which comes down from heaven and gives life unto the world.' Even to God Himself can the predicate *alethinos* be applied [17.3]. He is the only God having the reality of the essential Godhead in Himself.

Besides this peculiar meaning of truth, there is found in John's Gospel also the ordinary sense of the word 'veracious' [3.33]. As an Old Testament coloured usage, there occurs further the equivalence of 'true' to 'morally good' [3.20, 21], where 'doing evil' and 'doing the truth' appear as opposites.

There are certain passages in the Gospel usually misunderstood, because of ignorance or non-regard of the peculiar notion of 'truth' commented upon. In 1.17: 'The Law was given through Moses; grace and truth came by Jesus Christ', the wrong inference may be easily drawn, that the Law contained not the truth. The meaning simply is, that it did not yet bring that full disclosure of the heavenly reality in Christ, which is 'the truth'. It contained the shadows and types, not as yet the antitypical revelation. 'Not-true' here is not the equivalent of 'false', as though a Gnostic idea came to the surface, an interpretation plainly excluded by the phrase 'through Moses' (not 'by Moses'). The giving of the Law by God through the mediation of Moses is presupposed. In the other member of the statement, 'came by Jesus Christ', the preposition 'by' is used.

In 4.23 the worship of the Father 'in Spirit and truth' bears no immediate reference to the sincerity pertaining to worship, for that, Jesus would probably not have denied to the Jewish or the Samaritan worship. It relates to the worship no longer bound by typical forms as to place and time and ceremony. In the place of these will come a worship directly corresponding in an unshadowy form to the heavenly original of God, who is Spirit. When the Jewish worship in Jerusalem and the Samaritan worship are, in this one respect of typical locality, placed on a line, this does not intend to place them on a line in all other respects, for Jesus says to the woman: 'Ye worship ye know not what: we [including Himself with the Jews] know what we worship: for salvation is from the Jews.'

Again in 14.6: 'I am the way and the truth and the life', truth has the same sense of heavenly reality. The question was as to the way to heaven. Jesus answers Thomas by saying that He Himself is the way. The two following concepts, 'the truth' and 'the life' explain the first; Jesus is the way to heaven, because in Him the heavenly substance is present, and more specifically, because the heavenly life is present. Therefore, in the contact with Him lies the solution of the problem raised by Thomas: 'No one comes unto the Father, but by me.'

Outside of the Fourth Gospel this peculiar connotation of 'the true substances' occurs mainly in the typological system of the Epistle to the Hebrews; compare 8.2, 'a minister of the true tabernacle'. In the Gospels, the only occurrence of it outside of John is in Luke 16.11, 'who will commit to your trust the true (riches)?'

[D] JESUS' ATTITUDE TOWARD THE SCRIPTURES OF THE OLD TESTAMENT

It is extremely important to obtain from Jesus' own, inside point of view a definite understanding of His attitude and relation to the Old

Testament. The emphasis should not lie in the first place on the testimony He bore to the truthfulness and value of the Scriptures then in existence. This is of great apologetic value, but it is not something in which Jesus stood alone. Every orthodox person, Jewish or Christian, shared that with Him. In His treatment of the Bible Jesus was the most orthodox of the orthodox. The ascription to Him of a laxer or freer attitude in this matter rests, as we shall presently show, on a lack of discrimination. What is sometimes half-contemptuously called a 'Bible-religion' was characteristic of His piety. But there was something in His consciousness about the Scriptures that was specifically His own, something which not even Paul nor any other New Testament teacher or organ of revelation could have shared with Him. Jesus, besides deriving much material from the Old Testament, and besides being aware that all His teaching was in strict conformity to the Old Testament, held a conviction that went far beyond this, and in regard to which it would be preposterous for any Christian to say that he could apply the same thing to himself.

What we mean is this, that Jesus regarded the whole Old Testament movement as a divinely directed and inspired movement, as having arrived at its goal in Himself, so that He Himself in His historic appearance and work being taken away, the Old Testament would lose its purpose and significance. This none other could say. He was the confirmation and consummation of the Old Testament in His own Person, and this yielded the one substratum of His interpretation of Himself in the world of religion. At the same time it is proof of the realistic view He took of the Old Testament religion. Neither that, nor His own religion, was a religion of nature pure and simple; it was a religion of factual redemptive interpositions on the basis of a previous, but obscured, natural knowledge of God. To interpret the central religion of Jesus as a species of religious love for nature may be Rousseau-esque or Renan-esque; it is neither Old-Testament-like nor Jesus-like.

A 'RELIGION OF THE BOOK'

To what extent our Lord's religion was a 'religion of the Book,' i.e., of the contents of a Book and of the language of a Book, can be shown in more than one way:

(*a*) His discourse is full of words, phrases, forms of expression, derived from the Scriptures. These are frequently not formal enough to call them intentional quotations; nevertheless their Biblical origin lies on the surface. An instance is the description of the unbelieving people as 'a wicked and adulterous generation' [*Matt.* 12.39; 16.4]. Numerous also are the conscious quotations. About these there are two peculiarities . . . they emerge with frequency where our Lord's teaching is recognized as moving on its highest levels; the higher it soars, the nearer it comes to the world of thought and the speech of the Old Testament. The beatitudes in the Sermon on the Mount furnish examples. Compare with the individual beatitudes: Psalm 17.15; 25.13; 37.9; 73.1, and many Psalter passages that turn the conception of poverty into a religious sense [cp. *Isa.* 57.15; 61.3]. The other peculiarity of the conscious quotations lies in this, that our Lord makes use of them in the supreme crises of His life. Psa. 42.6, 11; 43.5, He quotes in Gethsemane; from the cross He prays in the words of Psalm 22.1; 31.5;

(*b*) Jesus treats the Scriptures as a 'rule of faith and practice'. His gravest charge against the Pharisaic tradition-mongering is that for the sake of tradition it neglects the commandment of God. To the Sadducees He declares that their denial of the resurrection springs from not knowing the Scriptures. In His Sabbath-controversy with the Pharisees He appeals to the divine declaration in Hosea, 'I desire mercy, and not sacrifice'. His principle that marriage should be indissoluble, He bases on the Genesis record of how it was at the beginning;

(*c*) Jesus authenticates His own Messianic character and work by pointing out in them the fulfilment of Old Testament prophecy [*Mk.* 9.12; 12.10; 14.21, 27, 49; *Lk.* 4.17–19; 22.37; 24.25–27; *John* 3.14; 5.46].

In some of these passages the word *dei*, 'must', is made use of. Proximately this 'must' relates to the necessity of Scripture-fulfilment, although, of course, Scripture being the expression of the mind and purpose of God, the necessity is in its last analysis derivable from the latter. In this respect Jesus does not essentially differ from those whose treatment of prophecy is often stigmatized as literalistic and mechanical. He did not scorn appeal to the letter, where it was strikingly effective. At the same time, however, the Old Testament was to Him an organic expression of the truth and will of God. The great circumstances of the progressive development of revelation He took into account in measuring the applicability of rules of Scripture; His method for keeping the new situation in touch with ancient revelation was not the allegorical method. His hermeneutics were simple and straightforward. The danger of allegorizing His words lies at the present day among the ranks of those who, having inwardly departed from the Gospel teaching, nevertheless desire to make use of the prestige of His name for supporting their quite differently oriented notions. The percentage of 'liberal' sermons committing this sin of allegorizing is far greater than that of those who seek to give the truth greater effectiveness by means of allegorizing hermeneutics. A mistake committed for the sake of the Gospel is less flagrant than one perpetrated in the propagation of error, but, of course, it is still a mistake.

Finally it will be observed that in all His numerous appeals to Scripture our Lord proved the protagonist of those who make of the Scriptures an open book, a book for the people. As a matter of fact, in His life-time the tendency to make of it a book for the learned chiefly was already at work owing to the inherent trend of legalism and traditionalism; our Lord did not consider the common people as those 'who know not the Law' [John 7.49];

(d) While in all the above groups of cases our Lord's attitude towards the Old Testament can be determined indirectly, through observing the use He makes of it, there is a more direct way through noting His explicit deliverances on the character and provenience of Holy Scripture. In the parable of Dives and Lazarus He implies that Moses and the Prophets bear as plainly and incontrovertibly the signature of the supernatural on their faces as one risen from the dead or come back from Hades would (Lk. 16.29–31]. According to John 5.37–39 the Jews are blamed for not finding eternal life in the Scriptures, for the reason that they do not read them from the point of view of their fulfilment in Him. John 10.35 affirms in so many words that the Scripture cannot be broken. The underlying supposition of all arguing from Scripture as, in common with others, our Lord practised it, consists in this, that the Word of God has received from Him the quality of unbreakableness: not to believe involves an attempt to break something that God has declared sure;

(e) Exceedingly eloquent is, in this connection, that His opponents, who were over-eager to collect data for His heterodoxy, never made an attempt to cast suspicion on His attitude toward Scripture.

CERTAIN CRITICAL CLAIMS DISPROVED

The data just given, though obviously decisive, have nevertheless been called in question in view of certain statements in the Fourth Gospel which are interpreted as evidence of the semi-Gnosticizing character of this document. It is scarcely necessary to argue with those who bring this charge because they themselves do not believe that the statements appealed to are authentic statements of Jesus, the Fourth Gospel being in their opinion a late unhistorical product. Still, for those who place belief in the Gospel, the passages concerned may be briefly touched upon.

From the Prologue 1.17 is quoted. The charge of the falsehood of the Old Testament can be discovered here only through overlooking the peculiar meaning of 'truth' previously commented upon. The same applies to the alleged denial of the truth of the Jerusalem worship; this lacks the truth, not because it is false, but because it is typical, in still being bound to one definite place. Also the statement in 10.8, in which Jesus declares all that came before Him to have been thieves and robbers, has been interpreted in the Gnostic sense that a huge system of falsehood underlay the Old Testament. In all probability Jesus here refers to the leaders of the nation opposing Him, or to the false Messianic claimants that had preceded Him.

Another ground for denying Jesus' acceptance of the authority of the Old Testament is found in the utterances in which He declares certain institutions of the Old Dispensation abrogated, or at least capable of perfection. The questioning about fasting raised between His disciples and those of the Pharisees and of the Baptist can scarcely be brought under this head, because fasting was not prescribed by the Old Testament, except for the Day of Atonement, and what Jesus was questioned about evidently had reference to a much wider practice. Still, it is noteworthy that in His double parable about the old garment and the new wine Jesus puts the entire question on a wider basis, so as to make of it a question of suitability of forms of religion in general, when the Old is compared with the New (*Mk.* 2.21, 22]. The passage Mk. 7.14-19, in regard to what things defile man, shifts the rule from the outward to the inward, and thereby virtually abrogates the Mosaic regulations for ceremonial cleanness, as is possibly meant by the phrase 'purging all meats'. Our Lord further speaks of a fulfilment of the Passover in the Kingdom of God [*Lk.* 22.16].

The saying of the Sermon on the Mount, that He came 'to fulfil' may also be quoted in this connection, but in regard to it, all depends on the sense given the verb 'to fulfil', discussed below. It will be observed that in none of the instances quoted does Jesus criticize the Old Testament mode of life as though having been wrong for its own time, but only supersedes it as unsuitable for the incoming era. And the main point to observe is that He nowhere criticizes the abrogated modes of life on the ground of their not having been instituted by God. Yet this might have been expected, had it been the real ground of His setting these things aside, for He was most unsparing in His rejection of the traditional accretions of the Law, which He characterized as plants not planted by God [*Matt.* 15.13]. The supposition throughout is that God Himself, through Moses, gave these rules of life. They share with every part of the Old Testament in the quality of divine provenience.

Still, it did not follow that, because God had through revelation given a law, it therefore had to remain in force *in perpetuum*. The only question was who had the proper authority in this matter of regulating anew the mode of life in the theocracy, and plainly here the Messianic authority of Jesus Himself was taken by Him into consideration. Therein lies the reason why, even in the Sermon on the Mount, He modifies some of the ethical and social rules of life by His emphatic 'I say unto you'. The question is a question of the 'I', who speaks thus.

And still further we should notice that in this general programme of change and development Jesus never loses sight of the continuity that ought to exist in Revelation. The old is not ruthlessly sacrificed to the new, purely on account of the latter's newness. The idea is always that the old had the seeds of the new in itself. For this reason also a revolutionary discarding of the Old Testament is out of the question. The clearest proof for the maintenance of this identity between the two dispensations is in John 2.19–21. Here Jesus declares that the temple to be destroyed by the Jews will be raised up again in His raised body. As the former was a symbol of the Old, so the latter is the vital centre of the New, but the identity persists.

The statement from the Sermon on the Mount that Jesus came not to destroy but to fulfil must likewise be interpreted on the principle of continuity. This is so, no matter whether 'to fulfil' be given the sense of 'rendering more complete' or whether it be understood to mean 'to carry into practice'. It has been claimed that the former is required here, because of 'fulfilling' being the opposite to 'destroying', which it could be only in case it signified rendering more perfect. The rejoinder is that destroying can be a true opposite to putting into practice, in other words that disobeying can be a true equivalent to destroying, namely, in cases where the disobeyer sets himself up as an example in virtue of his position of leadership. That this usage is quite conceivable appears from Gal. 2.18, where the same word *kataluein* is applied to Peter, not because he had failed to perfect the law, but because he had set a bad example in not consistently observing it. The term 'to fulfil' would, when used of the prophets, naturally have the meaning of carrying into reality, and no one would think of making it signify 'to improve'; in fact the whole idea of improving the Prophets lies wholly outside the mind of Jesus.

Now in regard to the meaning of 'to fulfil' in Matt. 5.17-18, the Law cannot be separated here from the Prophets, for it will be noticed that we are not dealing in this verse with an instance of the common phrase, 'the Law and the Prophets', covering the entire Old Testament. If that were the meaning one could at least render 'to improve' the Old Testament. But this is impossible on account of the disjunctive 'or' between 'the Law' and 'the Prophets'. Strictly translated the sentence reads: 'Think not that I came to destroy either the Law or the Prophets; I came to fulfil both the Law and the Prophets.' Thus read, the words leave no room for the idea of improving upon the Law.

The self-consciousness of Jesus is placed in a strong light by His attitude towards so large a part of the Old Testament institutions. As has been shown, He ascribed the entire content of the Scriptures to revelation from God. And yet, in the face of this, He does not hesitate to reconstruct the practice of religion on a comprehensive scale. He could do so out of the consciousness of co-equal authority with God in the sphere both of revelation and of reorganizing the religion of Israel. In connection with this we must keep in mind that what He came to usher in was the eschatological state, in regard to which as Messiah He had full jurisdiction. Interesting further is the fact of His not arguing about the matter, but settling it with supreme authority. Paul had to labour and argue from the Old Testament itself to surmount the law-structure of the Old Testament. Jesus speaks as One who is sovereign in the sphere of truth, because He is King in the realm of realities to which the truth belongs.

[E] JESUS' DOCTRINE OF GOD

The question is frequently put, whether Jesus brought a new doctrine concerning God. Did He preach a God different from the God of the Old Testament? If so, then He also brought a new religion, for the one without the other is unthinkable. Much confusion of thought on this point is due to lack of proper distinction. Jesus was a true Revealer, and, since all revelation from a Scriptural point of view ultimately has God for its object, it was inevitable that Jesus should have made some contributions to the doctrine concerning God. So taken, the affirmation of the newness of his 'theology' is quite debatable.

Unfortunately the idea, where met with, in but too many cases bears a quite different complexion. The newness of teaching ascribed to Him in this field is not a newness of enlargement or additional clarifying of content, but a newness of rejection and correction of what had prevailed before. The Old Testament, we are told, contained quite faulty ideas about the nature of God. Especially the notions there found in regard to the ethical nature of God lie still in conflict with belief in Jehovah's absolute power, and autocratic caprice, nay, even with the husks of physical representations concerning His nature. It is clear that such a renewal of the doctrine of God cannot be credited to Jesus by any one believing in the reality and consistency of revelation.

But it is also clear that this opinion has not been formed by interrogating Jesus Himself in regard to the Old Testament doctrine of God, but that it is the result of a comparative study of the Old Testament doctrine and teaching of Jesus. It follows a procedure that may eventually lead to the correction of Jesus' own views in the matter. While to the science of comparative religion such a method cannot be forbidden, it is not the method of Biblical Theology. What we are concerned about is how the teaching of the Scriptures on the divine nature appeared to Jesus. We must endeavour to look at this subject, as at other subjects, from within His mind. Nor can we consider every utterance of Jesus involving criticism of current ideas about God as tantamount to a criticism of the Old Testament doctrine of the nature of Jehovah. The Old Testament and Judaism are not to be identified. The latter our Lord not seldom found fault with; that He did so with the former remains to be proved.

There is sufficient proof for the very opposite. This follows from the absence of any instance of criticism on this point. It follows further from His belief in the divine origination of the Old Testament, for if the Scriptures are from God, and yet contain an inadequate view of God, it is God Himself who has in them misrepresented Himself. This is evidence from silence and indirection, but positive statements are not lacking. When asked by the scribe as to the supreme commandment in the Law, and summing up its purport from Deut. 6.4, 5, Jesus quotes not only this summary of the perfect religion, but prefaces it, as is done in Deuteronomy by the description of God: 'Hear, O Israel: Jehovah our God is one Jehovah' (or, according to another rendering of the Hebrew: 'Jehovah is our God, Jehovah is One'). The connection of thought implies that the idea of Jehovah here enunciated is adequate for basing on it the ideal religion expressed in the commandments [Matt. 22.37–38; Mk. 12.29–30; Lk. 10.27].

In arguing with the Sadducees Jesus recognized the God of Abraham, Isaac and Jacob as His God (Lk. 20.37]. The argument is not chronological, as if hinging on the fact that still in Moses' time God called Himself the God of these patriarchs, which would further imply that at that point in history the patriarchs were still living, as to their souls at least. So understood the argument would not settle the point at issue between Jesus and the Sadducees, proving only that up to the time of Moses the patriarchs still possessed immortality of soul. The argument rests on the pregnant meaning of the phrase, 'the God of'. This avowal of Jehovah with reference to a person establishes a bond of such intimate communion that it becomes impossible to Him, as it were beneath his honour, to surrender such a person to death, even so far as the body is concerned, from which fact again follows the resurrection of all those of whom God calls Himself their God. So Jesus Himself explains this meaning in verse 38: 'For He is not a God of the dead, but of the living, for all live unto Him.' God is so constituted in His nature that of those religiously attached to Him eternal life and ultimate resurrection of the body can be confidently expected.

It has been asserted that Jesus, in thus identifying His idea of God with that of the Old Testament naïvely seized upon that in the Old Testament which was congenial to Himself, brushing all the rest aside as of no particular importance. That He should have unconsciously done so can, of course, neither be proved nor disproved, since it touches a process in His sub-conscious mind. On the other hand, that He should have held such a discriminating opinion with clear consciousness of what it involved is incredible because of His emphatic acceptance of the entire Old Testament as the Word of God. Jesus could not have retained His obvious reverence for the Scriptures, had He felt the necessity of rejecting a large part of their teaching, and that on such a central topic as the nature of God.

JESUS' TEACHING ON THE DIVINE FATHERHOOD

In the centre of our Lord's doctrine of God is usually placed His teaching on the divine Fatherhood. This is quite correct, seeing the important place and space it as a matter of fact occupies. It is necessary, however, at the outset to warn against certain misconceptions and mistaken corollaries that have fastened themselves upon this fact, largely relative to the absolute originality with which Jesus is supposed to have conceived the idea. As to the question of originality, we must not lose sight of the Old Testament, nor entirely of the circle of thought in Judaism. In both the idea was known, although, of course, in the one differently coloured from that in the other. The Old Testament predicates Fatherhood of Jehovah in the following passages:

Ex. 4.22; Deut. 1.31; 8.5; 32.6; Isa. 1.2; 63.16; Jer. 3.19; Hos. 11.1; Mal. 1.6. But over against this claim of continuity it is urged that the connection is purely formal, because Jesus combined with the name a totally different idea from that in the Old Testament. The points of difference stressed are three in number.

(a) Firstly, in the Old Testament, we are told, the Fatherhood describes the action of Jehovah only. He treats Israel as a father a son; it does not describe God's nature as paternal love in its inwardness.

(b) Secondly, the idea is in the Old Testament limited in its range, being applied to Israel only, and that in a collective capacity, not individually to the single Israelites,

(c) Thirdly, in the Old Testament the Fatherhood, or love of God, is placed by the side of other attributes, such as are not only different from but some of them directly contrary to His love, whereas in the teaching of Jesus the Fatherhood of love appears as the sole make-up of the divine character, all the other attributes being derivable and actually derived from it: God here is nothing but love.

These three contentions may be briefly answered as follows:

(a) The first rests on the correct observation, that in the Old Testament the description of God proceeds from the outward to the inward, whereas in the New Testament the opposite movement is to some extent observable. This is due to the general movement of the revelation-process. But the Old Testament does not confine itself to externals in its delineation of the divine character. Such a passage as Ex. 34.6, 7 is as near to character-description as anything in the New Testament. And on the other hand, there is much in the teaching of Jesus describing character, including love, which is concretely expressed, illustrated by action. So abstract a statement as 'God is love' comes as late as the Epistles of John. Jesus speaks of the idea largely in parables.

(b) The absolute extension of the range of God's Fatherhood to all individuals, and that in virtue of creation, rests on a mistaken interpretation of Jesus' thought. The Fatherhood of God and the sonship correlated with it are redemptive ideas. The best proof for this lies in their occasional eschatological application, for eschatology is simply the crowning of redemption [cp. *Matt.* 5.9; 13.43; *Lk.* 20.36]. That it belongs to the members of the Kingdom of God may also be inferred from the regular addition of the possessive pronouns 'your' and 'their', to the word 'Father' [cp. especially *Matt.* 6.32]. Where these are absent, and the simple article is used, 'the Father' is the correlate to Jesus, 'the Son' specifically, and not to the children of God in general [*Matt.* 11.27; 28.19; *Mark.* 12.32].

True, in the Fourth Gospel 'the Father' not seldom occurs with reference to the disciples, but throughout this Gospel the idea is prominent that Jesus introduces the disciples into his own relation (religiously considered) with God, so that, properly paraphrased, this Johannine 'the Father' means: 'He who is My Father, and through Me now also yours.' And in the Fourth Gospel an explicit denial of the sonship of the Jewish enemies of Jesus occurs [8.42]. The restriction of the idea of sonship carries with it that of the idea of Fatherhood.

It has been contended that God is never said to become Father, whilst of men it is said that they become the children of God, but this is not strictly true, because to God paternal acts, such as the impartation of life and adoption into sonship, are predicated which imply His becoming Father to believers in a very real sense. The question whether the love of God with reference to all men is affirmed in Jesus' teaching is an altogether different question. If it be answered in the affirmative, it will be necessary to distinguish clearly between the general love and the paternal love, the latter being reserved for the members of the Kingdom. In the Old Testament both the Fatherhood and the love are confined to the chosen people. Sometimes Ex. 4.22 is appealed to as implying the sonship of other nations, because Israel is called God's 'first-born son', which is supposed to signify that the others, though not 'first-born', are yet real sons of the second rank. But this is extracting altogether too much from a figure. The sonship of the others would have no particular bearing on the demand made upon Pharaoh. The simple meaning is that Israel is as precious to Jehovah as a first-born is to his father.

The places in the teaching of Jesus where a divine Fatherhood without reference to Kingdom-membership is found, do not on closer examination bear out this idea. In Matt. 5.45 Jesus enforces the command to love one's enemies with the reminder that God makes His sun to rise on the evil and good, and His rain to fall on the just and unjust alike. The argument, however, is not based on the idea that God is a Father to the good and the evil, and the just and the unjust alike, but on the principle that He is Father to the disciples, who therefore must copy their Father's character in showing goodness or kindness, irrespective of moral or religious excellence, to their fellow-men; the Fatherhood is introduced for the sole purpose of binding the disciples to reproduction of the divine character. Hence also the saying does not read: 'their Father', but 'your Father' sends sunshine and rain. Matt. 6.26 in the same manner speaks of the goodness of God

367

towards the birds of heaven, and He is in that connection called 'your heavenly Father'; in this case also not to describe God's relation to the birds as one of Fatherhood, but simply as one of perfect goodness and kindness, from which fact then the disciples may gather all the stronger assurance of His provision for them, because they are more than just birds in their relation to God, namely, His children; here again note the pronoun 'your'.

The parable of the prodigal illustrates, not the procedure of God to utter aliens, but to publicans and sinners who had wandered out of the sphere of redemptive sonship, which did not detract from God's cherishing His Fatherhood towards them. On the other hand, in the case of the Syro-Phoenician woman, who showed through her great faith that she possessed the spiritual qualifications, our Lord nevertheless insists upon the prior privileges of Israel by speaking of the crumbs that fall from the master's table. The indiscriminate extension of the idea from the redemptive sphere to the sphere of natural religion in its sinful state, while seemingly offering the advantage of an appeal of emotional strength to a wider range, at the same time loses much of the content stored up in the idea. One may say to all men that they are children of God, but in doing so one tells them less than what the idea conveys on the other view.

If in the foregoing respect the idea does not depart in principle from the Old Testament lines, remaining restricted as before to the people of God, nevertheless the range is greatly enlarged, because the range of the people of God is also greatly extended. From before being national it now becomes ethico-religious. And with this inevitably goes another change towards individualization. In the Old Testament it is not the individual, but the nation that is named 'the son of God'; by Jesus every disciple is so named. Still, even for this the basis was not altogether lacking in the Old Testament. The Messiah sustains a relation to Jehovah that is altogether individually conceived at the first, though its further purport relates to the people [cp. *Psa.* 2.7]. In Psa. 89.26 He is even represented as crying unto Jehovah, 'My Father', a unique instance in the Old Testament, since all the other invocations of God with the Father-name are instances of prayer by the congregations [*Isa.* 64.8]. In Hos. 1-3 there occurs a plural, 'the children of God' [1.10; cp. 11.1, 'I called my son out of Egypt']. In 'the children of Israel' no stress should be laid on the plural, because 'children of Israel' was the common name for the nation.

It should be remembered that the Fatherhood of God has not merely had its range enlarged, but that it was the very idea of fatherhood being more profoundly and individualistically understood, which has itself been the means for bringing this about. Herein lies precisely the difference between the practical utilization of the kingship idea and the fatherhood idea. The latter serves for the address in prayer, which is mostly individual, whereas in the kingship-address the recognition of sovereignty prevails. With absolute sharpness, however, this distinction between the two cannot be drawn, for the simple reason that to the antique Biblical consciousness the notion of fatherhood has a strong element of authority in it, and, on the other hand, the idea of kingship is more closely wedded to that of benevolence than we would feel, who are apt to cry out against a 'paternal government'. In the parable the king provides a banquet; for the authority of the father Mal. 1.6 may be compared. Still further we should remember that the individualistic background of the Messiahship would also inevitably work to the same effect in individualizing the Fatherhood for believers, since the New Testament, particularly the Fourth Gospel, is familiar with the thought of the assimilation in status of the Messiah's followers with Himself.

JESUS' STRESS ON THE DIVINE MAJESTY AND GREATNESS
Next to the benevolent side of God, expressed in His Fatherhood and love, the transcendental aspect of the divine nature is strongly recognized in the teaching of our Lord. By this we understand the divine majesty and greatness, usually summed up in the name of the incommunicable attributes. This side may not receive the same stress as the other, for the reason that the Deistic tendencies of Judaism could be relied upon to provide for this even more than was necessary. Nevertheless as an indispensable element in religion it appears in full vigour. Jesus upholds even in the closest approach to God the necessity of remembering that He is God. If calling God Father, the one praying must do so with the prefix 'heavenly' before it. Also the very first petition following this in the Lord's prayer, 'Hallowed be thy name', embodies the same idea.

It is necessary to keep these two elements of the love of God and of His heavenly majesty jointly in mind, in order to avoid onesidedness; they must likewise be conceived as interacting. God's majesty and greatness impart a specific character to the divine love. Love from and towards man are different from the same feeling as exercised between God and man. Much modern sentiment that is called religion has in effect ceased to be such, because it is brought down to the level of interhuman friendly and benevolent relations in which at the best the one party may be more influential than the other. Religion is something different from goodwill towards God.

Another interaction between the two aspects of the divine nature consists in this, that the consciousness of the greatness and omnipotence of God alone can make the benevolent aspect a source of help and salvation for man. The over-emphasis thrown on the divine love, to the exclusion of almost every other thing, has sometimes resulted in the practical exclusion of all soteric dependence on God. A God assuring us of the extension towards us of all the fulness of His love, and yet leaving us uninformed or unconvinced, or even sceptical in principle concerning the so-called transcendental or metaphysical side of His nature, would not be to us more than a human father or mother in some extremity, that is to say, He would not be from the standpoint of our need a God at all.

THE RETRIBUTIVE RIGHTEOUSNESS OF GOD

Besides the Fatherhood and the transcendent majesty of God there is still a third aspect of the divine nature to be considered. This is what we may call the retributive righteousness. It is by no means a negligible element in the divine character. Those who, dealing with the conception Jesus framed or had of God, leave it out of account, work with very inadequate material. This would not have to be the case, if, as some allege, it could be regarded as a deduction from the love of God in the consciouness of Jesus. But not only is there no evidence to that effect; the nature of the two conceptions is such as to render deduction from the one to the other, in either direction, inconceivable. To be sure, as regards the benevolent side of the retribution, this could be derived from the love of God for the disciples, and on that ground even included in the effects of the divine Fatherhood. The doctrine of reward within the Kingdom rests on that principle, as we shall soon see.

It is quite different with the penal side of the principle of retribution. Had Jesus only spoken of temporary punishment, and implied a limit to the state assigned in the judgment to the wicked, in that case also penal retribution, being interpreted on the basis of discipline, might be considered an outflow of God's Father-love. But the opposite is true; what Jesus teaches on this subject lies altogether in the other direction; it is not for the vindicatory punishment, but for the chastisement-punishment that one has to look for explicit evidence among His words. Eternal punishment cannot be a manifestation of love; far less, of course, can it be the expression of love towards those who suffer it. There is no escape from the acknowledgment of this fact,

370

except by assuming that the doctrine in question did not belong to Jesus' original, heart-rooted conviction, being at bottom only a lingering remnant of the Judaistic past, in which for many ages this bitter root of retribution had been nourished. This again is contrary to the facts viewed without prejudice. Of a perfunctory use of the idea in question there is nowhere any trace. On the contrary, the most solemn words, carrying upon their face the evidence of profound personal conviction, are used in dealing with this subject [*Matt.* 18.6; *Mk.* 9.42; *Lk.* 17.2]; especially the words about the traitor Judas are here to be noted [*Matt.* 26.24; *Mk.* 14.21].

We shall simply have to posit two principles here in Jesus' doctrine of God, neither of which permits of reduction to the other. A dualism, however, in the strict philosophical sense, this cannot be called. For that, it would be necessary to prove that love logically excludes righteousness and *vice versa*. The signature of the divine inner life as Jesus portrays it, is not one of abstract uniformity, but one of great richness and multiformity, allowing of more than one motive force.

It must be acknowledged that, taking all in all, there is a preponderance in bulk and emphasis on the side of the divine love. Nevertheless this phenomenon also should be historically explained and not be abused for reducing everything in Jesus' message to the one preaching up of love. The historical reason is not difficult to discover. In Judaism the principle of the divine love had become eclipsed, and the opposite principle of retribution exalted at its expense. God had become lowered to a commercial level of one who exploits man on the basis of *quid pro quo*. Over against this it was necessary to maintain the balancing doctrine that God takes a personal, affectionate interest in man, so as to make religion a matter of love; of God's giving of Himself to man, no less than of the keeping of man strictly to account. Jesus thus brought forward that side of the divine character which was suffering eclipse in the consciousness of the age to which He was addressing Himself. It would be a poor application of this method were we to condense the entire gospel to love and nothing else. Since at the present time the atmosphere is surcharged with the vague idea of an indiscriminate love, and all punitive retribution held at a discount, it is not following the example of Jesus to speak of nothing but the divine love to the obscuring of all the rest. We must put the stress where the decadence of the religion of our times has failed to put it, yet always so as to keep from discarding the other side. Thus alone can the mind of Jesus be faithfully reproduced.

[F] JESUS' TEACHING ON THE KINGDOM OF GOD[1]

[I] The Formal Questions

THE KINGDOM IN THE OLD TESTAMENT

According to the Synoptics the first message of Jesus at the opening of His public ministry concerned 'the Kingdom of God'. It was a message used before Him by John the Baptist, into whose perspective it especially fitted. The 'repent ye', preceding it, points to the judgment by which the coming Kingdom is to be introduced. Consequently the message is to all intents an eschatological message, and the Kingdom of which it speaks an eschatological state of affairs. As to the formal phrase, this is used already by the Baptist as something familiar to his hearers. It is not, however, a phrase of Old Testament coinage. While the idea occurs in the Old Testament, the finished phrase is not there as yet. Probably it is of Jewish provenience; exactly how old it is we cannot tell.

Though prominent in the Synoptics, the phrase is almost absent from John's Gospel. Aside from 18.36, where the reference is to the Kingdom of Jesus, rather than to the Kingdom of God, John 3.3, 5 is the only place where it occurs. This phenomenon is due to the Christological structure of the Gospel which resolves the content of what Jesus brings into the constituents of His Person, such as 'life', 'light', 'truth', 'grace'. The most prominent of these is 'life'. In the one passage of its occurrence the equivalence of life and Kingdom lies on the surface, because the figure of entrance into the Kingdom is made equivalent to the idea of entrance into 'life', which is 'birth'. The same equivalence also meets us in Mk. 10.17. This becomes explainable there, because the life is more unequivocally represented as the eschatological state of life, whereas in John it is rather two-sided. Another equivalent appears in Lk. 4.19, 43, 'the acceptable year of Jehovah', that is, the year of Jubilee, where, unlike to Matthew and Mark, 'the Kingdom of God' is not named as the first theme of preaching.

In the Old Testament the thing later called the Kingdom of God relates, as to substance, to two distinct conceptions. It designates the rule of God established through creation and extending through providence over the universe. This is not a specifically redemptive Kingdom

[1] Cp. G. Vos, *The Teaching of Jesus Concerning the Kingdom of God and the Church* (New York, 1903).

idea [cp. *Psa.* 103.19]. Besides this, however, there is a specifically-redemptive Kingdom, usually called 'the theocracy'. The first explicit reference to the redemptive Kingdom appears at the time of the exodus, Ex. 19.6, where Jehovah promises the people that, if obeying His law, they shall be made to Him 'a Kingdom of priests'. This relates to the proximate future, when the law shall have been promulgated. It speaks of a present Kingdom from the Old Testament point of view. Still, the Old Testament likewise speaks of the Kingdom as a futurity. It may seem strange that what one has, one should still look forward to, and that not as a matter of relative improvement, but as a matter of absolutely new creation. The explanation of this apparent contradiction must be sought along three lines.

(*a*) First, we must remind ourselves of the prevailingly abstract meaning which in the Old Testament the several words for 'kingdom' possess. Through substituting 'kingship' and then remembering that kingship means the performance of great acts of salvation for a people in which a relation of leadership is established, we can more easily understand how there may be a future aspect to the Kingdom of Jehovah: He will in an unprecedented sense make Himself the Saviour of and Ruler of Israel. Thus Saul and David attained to the kingship. Still, this might have led no farther than speaking of a re-enforcement of the Kingdom, had not in course of time the content of the eschatological hope become wedded to the future great self-assertion of Jehovah. A new Kingdom-appearance that had such associations amounted practically to a new Kingdom.

(*b*) Secondly, there were times in the history of Israel when the theocratic Kingdom, while never actually abrogated, was nevertheless to such an extent in eclipse, that a bringing in of the Kingdom of God *de novo* could properly be spoken of. The period of the captivity furnishes an example for this. Here again the hope of return never remained a hope of a return to conditions of the past pure and simple, but drew to itself the hope of the realization of the whole world to come, eschatologically conceived; hence not a return of the Kingdom, but the arrival of the same was felt to be the fitting manner of description.

(*c*) Thirdly, Messianic prophecy led to a similar way of speaking. The expected Messianic King is to be the perfect, ideal representative of Jehovah, who is the ultimate King at all times. But when Jehovah, in His kingship, will be perfectly and ideally represented by His Vice-regent, the Messianic King, and the latter will at the same time bring to realization the entire eschatological hope, then the representation of the Kingdom of God coming first in the future loses the strangeness that otherwise might have gone with it.

Jesus attaches Himself to this eschatological Old Testament manner of speech. The Kingdom of which He announces the nearness is that Kingdom which lay in the future in the Old Testament perspective. At His time the Jewish theocracy was still in existence, but He is so eschatologically oriented as never to refer to that as 'the Kingdom of God'. Even Matt. 8.12 and 21.43 need not be understood that way. Of this – from the Old Testament standpoint – future Kingdom He speaks at first as a unit without distinction as to parts or stages. But in the unfolding of His ministry, the Old Testament future thing resolves itself into two distinct phases or stages. He is in process of making the Old Testament futurity present, but in another sense it still remains future, even from His present point of view. Consequently the phenomenon of the Old Testament repeats itself: there are two Kingdoms, the one present, the other future, but both these have been obtained through the redivision of the one as yet undivided Old Testament eschatological Kingdom.

Such is the relation of the Kingdom-teaching of Jesus to the Old Testament. There is not quite the same resemblance between it and the contemporaneous Jewish ideas on the subject. In Judaism the Kingdom-idea had not been able to keep itself free from the faults that had invaded the Jewish religion generally. Judaism was a religion of law. So the Kingdom came to mean a more perfect enforcement of the legalistic principle than could be attained in the present state. Still, a difference in principle this could not make; the Kingdom, even in its future consummation, was bound to appear less new than it did to Jesus, who filled its content with concrete acts of unprecedented grace. Besides, the Kingdom remained to the Jews in its essence particularistic. Proselytism did not do away with the fact that pagans, in order to partake of its benefits, would previously have to become Jews through circumcision. The Kingdom-hope of the Jews was also politically-nationalistically coloured, whereas in the teaching of Jesus its tendency was in the direction of universalism. Finally, there was a considerable mixture of sensualism in the Jewish eschatology. Here the discrimination is more difficult to make. It mainly consists in this, that what to the Jews was a species of literal sensualism, was to Jesus an exemplification of His parabolic frame of mind, which makes the heavenly enjoyments, while retaining their full realism, yet processes of a higher, spiritualized world, in which even the body will have its place and part.

374

THE KINGDOM IN THE GOSPELS

The word *basileia*, used in the Gospels for 'Kingdom', either with 'God' or with 'Heaven' as its accompanying genitive, is capable of two renderings. In its abstract usage it denotes the sway, the exercise of royal rule. Side by side with this goes the concrete sense of whatsoever things go towards the making up of an organization called a kingdom. More particularly the things entering concretely into the making up of a kingdom are of three kinds. One can speak of a certain extent of territory as a kingdom; or, a body of subjects can be called by that name; or again, a complex of rights, benefits and treasures can be so designated. Now the question arises: When speaking of the Kingdom of God, did Jesus mean the phrase to be taken abstractly or concretely? Did He mean the sway of God, or did He mean the concrete embodiment of that sway, or its precipitate in resulting realities?

It is natural in seeking to answer this question, first of all to consult the Old Testament usage. The Old Testament, where the Kingdom-idea is referred to Jehovah, knows only the abstract sense, with the sole exception of Ex. 19.6, above commented upon. While the word *mamlakhah* is predominatingly concrete, and in that sense not seldom used of pagan kingdoms, yet there is no case on record of its application in the same way to the Kingdom of God (except in the Exodus passage). The two other words, *malkhuth* and *melukhah*, are mostly abstract, and in that sense freely applied to the Kingdom of Jehovah.

To judge from Jesus' closeness of touch with the Old Testament we may *a priori* be disposed to assume that to Him likewise the abstract idea of 'kingship' would furnish the starting-point. Still, the instances where this usage is beyond all question are far from numerous. On the principle of opposites we can gather this meaning from the passage Matt. 12.25, 26, where the kingdom of Satan appears to mean his authority, his rule, although the words 'city or house' might seem to point in the other direction. 'The coming of the Son of man in his *basileia*' predicted in Matt. 16.28 also seems to require the abstract understanding. Perhaps the small representation of the abstract meaning may be due to the fact of its latent presence in quite a number of cases, where we cannot tell whether it or the concrete sense is intended.

There is a group of sayings in which the phrase 'Kingdom of God' is joined to predicates of 'coming', 'appearing', 'being near', and similar terms of approach, and, although in such connections the concrete meaning is by no means excluded, yet on the whole the abstract sense seems the more suitable one. Side by side with this group, however,

N

there is an even larger one in which the figures used require the concrete conception in order to visualize them. Thus we find the phrases 'to call into', 'to enter into', 'to receive', 'to inherit', 'to be cast out from' the Kingdom of God, and others like these. The background of such language is local, and therefore concrete. Nor is it difficult to explain this transition from the preponderatingly Old Testament abstract employment of the term to the prevailingly concrete one in the mouth of Jesus. The shifting of the centre of gravity from law to grace has naturally brought this about. As soon as we fill our religious imagination with the palpable realities of redemption, these join themselves together to form the structure of a concrete organization or *milieu* of life; the Kingdom of God becomes incarnate. This was what happened to Jesus through His preaching of the gospel of grace, and we shall afterwards find it confirmed in His condensation of the Kingdom-idea into that of the Church.

Alongside of the phrase 'Kingdom of God' we find in the Gospel according to Matthew the companion phrase 'Kingdom of Heaven'. Outside of Matthew, except John 3.3, 5 in a rather uncertain variant reading, the Matthaean phrase nowhere appears. It is not however the exclusive name of the Kingdom in Matthew, for 'Kingdom of God' is likewise found [6.33; 12.28; 19.24; 21.31]. Resembling the expression 'Kingdom of Heaven', the term 'Father in Heaven' is also peculiar to Matthew, with the single exception of Mark 10.25. Luke employs once the analogous designation, 'the Father from Heaven' [11.2]. Among the passages where Matthew uses 'the Kingdom of God' there is only one [12.28] where the context supplies an explanation for the usage. In the other cases it is impossible to discern the reason for the divergence. Still further peculiar to Matthew is the use of 'the King-dom' without any genitival determination. This sounds almost like our modern colloquial manner of speaking of 'the Kingdom'. Finally, observe that in the remainder of the New Testament the expression 'Kingdom of God' is used exclusively; for example, in Romans, 1 Corinthians, Galatians, 1 and 2 Thessalonians, 2 Timothy.

'THE KINGDOM OF HEAVEN'

The question arises what this – to us somewhat mysterious – term 'Kingdom of Heaven' signifies. The genitive has been explained as a genitive of origin or quality, to mark the Kingdom off from earthly kingdoms. But this was so obvious in itself as to need no special affirmation in the absence of some definite historical occasion suggesting a special reminder. B. Weiss has assumed that this was actually the case, because, through the destruction of Jerusalem the expectation, hitherto cherished, that the centre of the coming Kingdom would be in Palestine, had become untenable, and the inference drawn that henceforth the centre would have to be located in heaven. This theory is not plausible; it cuts every connection between Jesus and this name. It would not have been self-evident that, Jerusalem being destroyed, it could no longer play any role in eschatological developments. The Jews for a long time after the fall of the city – and for that matter even today – counted on the rebuilding of the holy city, and in all likelihood Matthew, provided he did indeed cherish this attachment for an earthly centre of the Kingdom in Zion, would have reconciled the historical facts with his eschatological hope after the same manner. The theory also leaves unexplained the lack of uniformity in Matthew's use of 'Kingdom of Heaven' in preference to 'Kingdom of God'.

By far the best explanation of the phrase is that suggested by Schurer *et al.* On this view it attaches itself to the Jewish custom of using the word 'Heaven', together with other substitute terms, in place of the name of God, because the latter had in its various forms become an object of increasing avoidance. 'Heaven' thus simply meant 'God' by a roundabout manner of speaking. Traces of such usage may be found in other connections in the New Testament; the prodigal says to his earthly father, 'I have sinned against heaven, and in thy sight'; here 'heaven', in parallelism with the natural father, can only mean God. The question Jesus propounded to His critics: 'The baptism of John, was it from heaven or from men?' is to be explained on the same principle.

The adoption of this view, however, does not necessarily involve the conclusion that Jesus used 'Heaven' for 'God' from the same superstitious motive as had brought the custom into vogue among the Jews. Their scrupulosity was deistic in principle; the same feeling that induced them to keep God from degrading contact with the creation was here applied even to the name of God. Nevertheless there was in this Jewish avoidance an element of praiseworthy religious devotion; the proper estimate of God's exaltation above the world found expression in it. While this feeling in its commendable motive was shared by Jesus, it did not operate in His case to the point of eliminating the other names of God. In fact His plain aversion to the Jewish deism, and His desire to emphasize the close communion between God and man led in the opposite direction.

Even to the Jews, perhaps, 'Heaven' was not quite a mere substitute for 'God', but has its peculiar associations. One of these was the

N*

association of the supernatural; to say 'God has done a thing', and to say 'Heaven has done a thing' could have between them a perceptible shade of difference. God does all things, but what Heaven does is done supernaturally. 'The Father in Heaven' also can carry the same association [*Matt.* 16.17].

If 'Heaven' be taken in this way as a substitute for the name of God, it will be seen that in the phrase 'Kingdom of Heaven' it does not directly qualify the Kingdom. It means the Kingdom of Him who can be called 'Heaven'. Still, so far as 'Heaven' has any specific connotations, such as majesty, supernaturalness, perfection, these will unavoidably go to colour the conception also of the Kingdom belonging to this God.

MODERN THEORIES OF 'THE KINGDOM'

It has been stated above that, in the hands of Jesus, that which was from the Old Testament, and even John the Baptist's, point of view an undivided unit, unfolded itself into two phases or stages, distinguished as the present and the eschatological Kingdom. The view long prevailing, and still prevailing, is that Jesus through the labours of His ministry began to realize the Kingdom on earth, that this was a gradual process, that the labour on the Kingdom, to which His followers devoted themselves after Him, and which is still continued by us, is actual Kingdom-producing labour, and that this will go on through the ages of history up to the point set by God for the termination of this world-order, at which point through a catastrophe of world-transforming character the eschatological Kingdom-state will be introduced.

Those who favour the pre-millenarian construction of prophecy and history insert between these two stages a third intermediate one. With this, however, we are not at present concerned. Confining ourselves to the present gradual, and the future catastrophic realization of the Kingdom, we note that in recent times the former of these two has been denied to Jesus as an integral element of His thought. For convenience' sake we may call the advocates of this view the ultra-eschatologists. The difference between their construction and the older belief does not concern the eschatological issue of the Kingdom-process. In regard to this the two views are in agreement. But in regard to what this was to be preceded by in the opinion of Jesus there is difference.

The ultra-eschatologists deny the existence in Jesus' mind of the whole idea of a preliminary, gradual Kingdom. They reconstrue his expectations after this fashion: His own work was to Him not essentially different from that of John the Baptist, being of a purely pre-liminary character. It was not His task to set up the Kingdom; this implies denial of His Messianic consciousness. It was exclusively the work of God; at the appointed moment, all at once, and in its entire compass the Kingdom would appear and with it the end of this present world and the beginning of the other, eternal order of affairs. Jesus expected that this would happen during the course of His earthly life, or, should His death intervene, at least during the life-time of that generation.

This modern view has some extremely serious implications. It does away with the infallibility of Jesus, because things have not come to pass in accordance with the programme outlines; it shifts the emphasis in His teaching from the present-spiritual to the external-eschatological, making the former no more than a means to the latter, which alone deserved to His mind the name of 'the Kingdom'. It would have tended, had it really existed in His mind, towards minimizing the importance of present-world morality. Finally, it is apt to engender doubt as to His mental equilibrium, seeing that a man so absorbed by these radical other-worldly, fantastic speculations, could not have possessed a well-balanced psychical temper; He becomes a subject for psychiatric investigation.

In all the points where the theory registers denials we must part ways with it. On the other hand, in regard to the points in which it and we agree, we cannot deny it a certain credit, because it has revived interest in the matter of specific eschatology as an absolutely necessary thing. One sometimes meets with a type of Christian perspective which imagines that, by the steady advance of Christian processes of reformation and regeneration, supernaturally carried on, this world can be in course of time brought to a point of ideal perfection, so as to need no further crisis. A certain aversion to the supernatural as such frequently contributes toward the denial of that condensed supernaturalism called eschatology.

Over against this it is ever necessary to remind ourselves that abrupt eschatology is inherent in the Christian scheme. It was prepared under the auspices of this, born under them, and must in the end stand or fall with the acceptance or denial of them. This is generic eschatology. A simple consideration of the factors in the case suffices to show how indispensable it is. Even if by persistent application of the gradual processes in the most intensive missionary propaganda, it were possible to convert every individual in the world, this would not provide for the conversion of the generations passed away in the course of history, and which none of our means of grace can reach. And, even discounting this, the conversion of all individuals would not make of them perfectly sinless individuals, except one were to take refuge in the doctrine of perfectionism. The sum total of men, therefore, living at any time would, in order to form part of a perfect world, stand in need of a marvellous soteric and ethical transformation, such as would rightly deserve the name of eschatology. But even this would not exhaust the factors necessary for the establishment of a perfect order of affairs, because the present physical state of the world with its numerous abnormalities, including human physical weaknesses and defects, would render the continuance of such a state of perfection impossible. Thus there would be created as a further element in generic eschatology the need of a transformation of the physical universe, including the resurrection of the body.

Because this status of the question is so inadequately realized, the delusion has sprung up that what is needed to provide for all these elementary redemptive changes is pre-millenarianism. But pre-millenarianism is only a species of eschatological construction, and not the genus. To say we must have this species of the thing or we have nothing, is a disturbance of all the normal proportions in this matter. It is making illegitimate use of one special scheme, so as to obscure feeling for the generic scheme, which has by far the more ancient credentials, and into which every pre-millenarian scheme will have to be fitted in order to deserve the name of being Christian. Still, as a matter of fact, the pre-millenarian scheme has rendered service through reminding people of the need of a series of supernatural interpositions to carry the world to its ultimate destination. The trouble is that, if certain types of post-millenialism leave too little room for eschatology, pre-millenarian schemes bring in too much.

While we cannot expect the gradual development of the spiritual Kingdom to pass over automatically into the final state, there is nevertheless a fixed connection between the stage the former shall have reached at a certain point (known only to God), and the sudden supervention of the latter. The best confirmation of this principle is taught in the parable of the imperceptibly growing seed. The wheat grows up gradually, while the man sleeps and rises night and day, and he knows not how. But when the fruit is brought forth, immediately he puts in the sickle, because the harvest is come [Mk. 4.26-29]. The condition of ripeness in the grain determines the arrival of the harvest, but the grain cannot harvest itself; for that the interposition of the sickle is required [cp. also Matt. 13.39-41; 47-50]. It will be observed that this feature is not allegorically forced upon the parable, but is inherent in its very structure.

THE TWO-SIDED CONCEPTION OF THE KINGDOM

We must next examine the evidence from the words of Jesus for the view that His conception of the Kingdom was, or perhaps came to be, two-sided, containing first the idea of a present, inwardly-spiritual development, and secondly, that of a catastrophic ending-up. It is denied by no one, not even the ultra-eschatologists, that both these ideas are present, side by side, in the Gospels. No argument is needed to prove that. It is alleged, however, that the instances where the idea of the not-yet-eschatological existence appears, present later modifications of the original, purely eschatological idea as voiced by Jesus. The belief had been at first, both to Him and His first followers, that the Kingdom, in its full eschatological manifestation, was at hand. When the arrival of this tarried, and yet the words of Jesus could not be disavowed, a compromise was made to this effect, that the Kingdom had indeed come, and was present, only it had come and was present in the form of the Church. Thus the idea of a Church-Kingdom entered into the Gospels. It does not reflect in any sense the thought of Jesus, but only the later transformation of it, which the course of historic development had made it necessary to resort to. It will be observed, however, when we come to survey the material, that some of the sayings have the mark of authenticity so clearly written on their face as to allow of no such secondary origin.

Since there is agreement in regard to the authenticity of the eschatological conception, it is unnecessary to discuss passages. The most superficial inspection of the following will suffice: Matt. 8.11; 13.43; Mk. 14.25; Lk. 13.28, 29; 22.16. Especially with reference to his own future state of glory Jesus uses the term 'Kingdom' in this consummation-sense [*Matt.* 19.12; 20.21; *Lk.* 23.42]. Indeed the terms employed are obviously synonymous with other unequivocally eschatological terms, such as 'the coming *aeon*' [*Matt.* 12.32; 19.28; *Mk.* 10.30; *Lk.* 18.30]. And what ought to be noticed particularly is that in several of these sayings, not some such phrase as 'the consummation of the Kingdom', but the simple affirmation of the coming of the Kingdom is employed. This tends to show that in the usage of Jesus the Kingdom meant at first the final Kingdom, and the coming of that the real coming.

In examining the evidence for the other aspect two points should be kept in mind: (*a*) Is the Kingdom spoken of a present one to the time of the speaker? (*b*) Is it referred to as consisting in internal-spiritual realities? We rapidly run over the passages. Matt. 12.28 corresponding to Lk. 11.20; here Jesus affirms that the driving out of the demons by the Spirit signifies the coming of the Kingdom. The underlying principle is that in the world of spirits there is no neutral territory; where the demons depart, the divine Spirit enters. The statement cannot be robbed of its force by making 'come' mean 'come nigh'; nor should it, on the other hand, be forced to mean 'has come by surprise', for, while such is the connotation of the verb *phthanein* in the older Greek, it need not be in the later period. The passage, therefore, teaches a present Kingdom realized through the expulsion of demons, but casts no further light on the character of the Kingdom-state thus called into being.

The next passage examined is Lk. 17.21: 'The Kingdom of God is *entos* you.' The preposition *entos* here used has two meanings: it can signify 'in the midst of', but also 'within'. The passage is usually rendered with the latter meaning of the preposition. This would yield both the present existence and the spiritual make-up of the Kingdom. The objection has been raised that our Lord could not have said to the Pharisees that the Kingdom was within them, and further that the question put to Jesus as to the 'when' of the Kingdom would on such a view not have received any answer. Neither of these two arguments is conclusive. 'Within you' need not exactly mean within the persons addressed; the pronoun in such a way of speaking can be enclitic; the sense then would be equivalent to 'within people'. As to the second objection, we find that Jesus not seldom shifts a question from one sphere to another. Here He might properly have done so in order to intimate that not the 'when' but the 'where' is the all-important issue. In favour of 'within you' the following may be urged: Luke, for 'in the midst of' has always another expression, namely, the prepositional phrase *en meso*. Our passage would be the only one in Luke where *entos* were employed for that purpose. On the other hand, where the idea of 'interiority' is to be stressed *entos* appears, not only with Luke but likewise in the Septuagint. The passages quoted to support the meaning 'in the midst of' are all taken from the older Greek, not from the Hellenistic period. We are, therefore, warranted in giving the preposition *entos* here a peculiar colouring of inwardness.

Thirdly we look at the parallel passages Matt. 11.13; Lk. 16.16. Here Jesus declares that since the days of John the Kingdom suffers violence and is taken forcibly by violent men. Whatever the precise meaning of this parabolic saying may be, it certainly describes the actuality of the Kingdom since the days of John. In the Lucan parallel the same idea is expressed by representing the Kingdom as 'preached', that is as the object of an evangel. An evangel usually has reference to a present thing, and here must have so all the more, because of its opposite, 'the Law and the Prophets are until John'. The prophesying and typifying has given way to the proclamation of the fulfilment. Further, of a similar import is Matt. 11.11; Lk. 7.28. Our Lord, by denying that John himself is within the Kingdom, implies that such a being within was at that time a possibility; it was only John's peculiar position that kept him out.

In the fourth place we may appeal to the Kingdom parables [*Matt.* 13, *Mk.* 4, *Lk.* 8]. Here both the present reality and the spiritual nature of the Kingdom are plainly described. The ultra-eschatologists deny the force of this evidence, because here particularly they discover the hand of the traditional revisers, who brought the Church under the wing of the Kingdom. Their claim is that not so much in the parables themselves, but rather in the interpretations added, these de-eschatologizing features are in evidence. Or, where it is difficult to remove all traces of the idea of a present existence, they endeavour to change the subject of the comparisons, proposing to read: 'the preaching of the gospel is like, etc.' But the implications of presence are not confined to the interpretation of certain parables; they are scattered through the entire group, and as to changing the introductory formulas, this is forbidden by the highly idiomatic character of the latter in certain cases [cp. *Mk.* 4.11; *Lk.* 13.18].

Another method of neutralizing the evidence is more of an exegetical nature; it is proposed to reduce the presence of the Kingdom affirmed by Jesus to the presence of the premonitory signs or first slight beginnings; and in some of the parables, that have been immemorially quoted in proof of the present-Kingdom doctrine, the entire purport of the parable is changed, its point being sought in the contrast between the small first indications of something extraordinary approaching, and the tremendous mass at the end. But with this interpretation a certain degree of gradualness is in principle conceded, and the parables, especially those taken from the vegetable sphere, appear ill-adapted to describe the explosive character of the terminal events. Finally in Lk. 18.17 a clear distinction would seem to be drawn between the 'receiving of the Kingdom as a little child' and the 'entering into the Kingdom'. These two figures appear as exactly suited for describing the two distinct aspects in the Kingdom-movement, the gradual and spiritual on one hand, and the conclusive one on the other hand.

In the sixth place, Matt. 6.33 puts side by side the seeking after the Kingdom and the obtaining of such earthly things as food and raiment, which will be added unto the Kingdom (not unto the seeking after the Kingdom). According to Lk. 4.18–21 the contents of the 'acceptable year of Jehovah' are being realized through the activity of Jesus: 'this day is the Scripture fulfilled in your ears.' Further, Matt. 9.15; Mk. 2.19 represents the joy of the Kingdom-season as to such an extent present that it renders fasting inappropriate for the disciples. Finally, according to Matt. 13.16; Lk. 10.23, Jesus, turning to the disciples, pronounces them blessed for seeing and hearing those things which many prophets and kings had desired to witness but not attained unto.

For the sake of clearer distinction a brief formula of the difference between these two aspects of the Kingdom may be framed. The difference is as follows:

(a) The present Kingdom comes gradually, the final Kingdom catastrophically;

(b) the present Kingdom comes largely in the internal, invisible sphere, the final Kingdom in the form of a world-wide visible manifestation;

(c) the present Kingdom up to the eschatological point remains subject to imperfections; the final Kingdom will be without all imperfections, and this applies as well to what had remained imperfect in the spiritual processes of which the present Kingdom consisted, as to the new elements which the final Kingdom adds.

The stress on the present-spiritual Kingdom idea has exposed the concept to considerable misinterpretation, along the line of naturalizing the process of its coming. Especially the parables taken from the vegetable realm have tempted to this. But the point in these is not the naturalness of the development; it is only the gradualness, and gradual- ness and supernaturalness are not mutually exclusive. The first phase of the Kingdom-forming movement is just as supernatural as are the events at the end of the world, only they are not as conspicuously so. It is an offshoot of this misunderstanding, when the Kingdom-complex is too much restricted to ethical thoughts and processes. The Ritschlian School has made of the Kingdom almost exclusively an association of men interacting on the principle of love. This is not wrong in itself, but as a definition of the Kingdom it is utterly misleading, because it virtually dereligionizes the idea, and moreover shifts the realization of the Kingdom almost entirely from the work of God to the activity of man. Man brings in the Kingdom according to this view. According to Jesus' conception the opposite is true, to such an extent in fact that our Lord hardly ever represents Himself as the Realizer of the Kingdom.

Both these faults, as they hang together, can only be corrected together through explaining that the specifically religious belongs just as much to the Kingdom-circle as the ethical. Forgiveness of sin, communion with God, divine sonship, eternal life, these and other things are as truly ingredients of the Kingdom as the activities of men along the line of what is now, with a semi-Christian connotation, called 'service'.

[2] The Essence of the Kingdom

After having discussed the formal questions we now find ourselves face to face with the problem: What reasons induced our Lord to call the new order of things that He came to announce and to introduce by the name 'the Kingdom of God'? Other names were in themselves conceivable, so far as the religious substance was concerned. We cannot explain the use from the Old Testament, for there the formal name does not occur. Nor does current usage in our Lord's time on the principle of accommodation help us out, for to the Jew 'the Kingdom of God' was not then the most favoured phrase for designating the content of the eschatological hope. Other names, such as 'the coming world', 'the coming age' were preferred, possibly because to the deistically inclined consciousness of Judaism they less focused the concept on God and left more room for thinking of what it would mean for Israel.

And right here we discover the true meaning of our Lord's preference for the name. It sprang from His theocentric frame of mind, which is but another way of saying that it is a religious conception through and through. The intent with which it was used by our Lord was precisely the opposite to that half-conscious feeling that it somehow affords an opportunity to remain within the circle of religion and yet have less of the obsession of God in religion. To Jesus it meant: 'of God the Kingdom'; to not a few at the present day it apparently means: 'the Kingdom (of God)'. And to Jesus it was far less an ideal, and far more of an actuality, than it is felt to be by the modern mind. 'The Kingdom of God' is not His destiny nor His abstract right to rule – His sovereignty – it is the actual realization of His sway. In this sense, and in this sense only, can it 'come'; God possesses His sovereignty from the beginning, and that cannot 'come'. The proposal to bring the name nearer to the general understanding by substituting 'the sovereignty of God' leads on the wrong track, because sovereignty is only *de jure*, and not always *de facto*, and also because sovereignty, being an abstract

385

conception, could not mark the distinction between the abstract and the concrete Kingdom.

'Of God the Kingdom', then, means the actual exercise of the divine supremacy in the interest of the divine glory. Passages like Matt. 6.10, 33; Mk. 12.34 bear out this central idea [cp. also 1 Cor. 15.28].

This divine supremacy constituting the ideal state of religion branches out in several directions. At first, so long as the thing is considered in the abstract, it can be compared to a bundle of rays of light and action proceeding from and held together by the hand of God. But this is only provisional; the goal is that all these exercises of divine supremacy shall find their unitary organization in one royal establishment. The three principal spheres in which the divine supremacy works toward this end are the sphere of power, the sphere of righteousness and the sphere of blessedness. These will be briefly discussed in succession.

DIVINE SUPREMACY IN THE SPHERE OF POWER

The power element is already prominent in the Old Testament idea of the Kingdom of Jehovah. In the Gospels we meet it at the close of the Lord's Prayer, where 'power' is the first specification of what the Kingdom consists in: 'Thine is the Kingdom, [even] the power. . . .' Though this closing doxology is not found in Luke, and is absent from some good manuscripts also in Matthew, nevertheless it remains a valuable witness to what was associated with the Kingdom-idea in the minds of those using this very ancient prayer. According to Matt. 12.28, the casting out of demons is an exhibition of divine Kingdom-power (cp. Luke. 'the finger of God'), no less indeed than an assertion of Messianic sovereignty. The miracles in general likewise find their explanation from this point of view. Besides being credentials of Jesus, and beneficent actions of His grace, they are chiefly 'signs of the times', that is, signs of the arrival or nearness of the Kingdom, just as the symptoms of the sky are to the wise signs of the weather of the morrow. They are both symbolic of spiritual transactions and prophetic of things pertaining to the eschatological Kingdom. Mark 2.9 points to the present time, but on the whole the miracles rather point forward to the crisis at the end.

The Kingdom-making power is associated with the Spirit; of the qualification of Jesus by the Spirit for His words and works, mention has been made already. The direct connection of the Spirit with effects in the ethico-religious sphere is not frequently touched upon in the Gospel teaching [cp. Lk. 11.13]. It was reserved for Paul to work out

386

this part of Christian doctrine after the actual outpouring of the Spirit. To Jesus the Spirit is the Author of revelation and of miracles, and remains this even in the Fourth Gospel where He is promised as the substitute of the departed Jesus. The position of Jesus in the development of pneumatology as between the Old Testament and Paul can be broadly defined as follows: In the Old Testament the Spirit is the Spirit of the theocratic charismata, who qualifies prophets, priests and kings for their office, but is not communicable from one to the other. Of this charismatic Spirit Jesus has received the fulness, and, having the fulness, dispenses of it to His followers, first partially and by means of promise, then in greater fulness by way of fulfilment at Pentecost.

Now since the Spirit He dispenses is not only His own as an external possession, but, having become through the resurrection thoroughly incorporated into His exalted nature, He gives, when He gives it, of His own, and the union effected between Him and the Spirit and through the Spirit and believers, acquires the character of an organic mystical union, so that to be in the Spirit is to be in Christ. And the further result is that, the entire Christian life being to Paul a life of communion with Christ, it also becomes necessarily a life lived in and inspired by the Spirit in all its strata and activities.

Another approach to this experience of a wholly Spirit-filled life lies through the conception of the eschatological state as the state in which the Spirit is the pervasive element and characteristic force. And since the earthly life is a real anticipation of the eschatological state, first-fruits and earnest and seal of the same, then the equableness of Spirit-endowment and Spirit-influence pertaining to the one naturally comes to pertain to the other also.

FAITH AS RELATED TO THE KINGDOM'S POWER

To the Kingdom as power answers faith as the correlate of this power. The correlation is not complete, since faith bears a distinct relation to the divine grace, no less than to the divine power. In the Gospels, that of John excepted, faith mostly emerges in the miracle contexts, and should therefore be studied in close dependence on what the miracles are. It is, as it were, the subjectivity corresponding to the objective fact of the miracle. The question to ask therefore, is what peculiarity inheres in the miracles, which makes them draw to themselves the functioning of faith. Two points come under consideration here.

First, the miracles are beneficent, saving acts, which has the result of making them an exhibition of the divine grace and evoking in the recipients the mental state of trust. This, however, important though it be, should not receive the main stress. The miracles are beneficent, but this is an aspect they have in common with other aspects of the work of God. What is unique to the miracle is the assertion of absolutely divine supernatural power. The efficient cause of the miracle is something that man can contribute nothing to, because it is wholly dependent on the putting forth of the direct supernatural energy of God. Hence it is emphasized that the miracles are done by 'a word'; that is the word of omnipotent power, the mere word [*Matt.* 8.8, 16]. The relation of faith to the omnipotence of God is strikingly illustrated in the episode, Mk. 9.17–24. Jesus here remonstrates with the suggestion of the father, 'if thou canst do anything', with the reply, 'what! if thou canst!', thereby declaring that, since it is a question of divine omnipotence, all mention of adequacy of power ought to be eliminated from the outset. Before God there exists no 'if thou canst'.

In this dependence on the omnipotence and grace of God lies the religious rationale of faith. Faith is the practical (not purely reasoning) recognition on the part of a man that the saving work of the Kingdom is exclusively a divine work. Faith is not to be considered under the aspect of a magical compulsion, far less of an *ex-parte* human contribution to the accomplishment of the result, for if the latter were the case, faith would carry within itself an inner antinomy, being on the one hand a recognition that God alone must work, on the other hand an urge to fulfil at least a preliminary condition. We are told that Jesus could do no miracles where faith was absent, that a mere sign from heaven as such He could not give, and yet at the same time we are told that the miracles were to act as stimulators of faith. The solution lies in a distinction between two kinds of unbelief. Where the absence of faith amounted to deep-seated distrust of the divine method of saving, the mere doing of miracles could not have acted as an inducement of faith. It might have convinced of the presence of a supernatural power, but would have related the latter neither to God nor to Jesus, but to some demonic agency [*Matt.* 12.24]. In such a case, Jesus would do no miracle, because no true full-orbed faith would have resulted. Where it was a mere question of the absence of evidence, there the miracle could play its proper part to stimulate faith. What Jesus affirms of the demon cases is equally true of the miracle of salvation in general [*Matt.* 19.26]. Such things are possible to God and to God only. Faith, being the work of God, is something to be prayed for by Jesus on behalf of one in danger of losing it [*Lk.* 22.31, 32; *Mk.* 9.24].

In the principle that faith is a work of God, the other fact is given of its not being the mere arbitrary choice of man who simply wills or refuses to exercise it. It has behind it a motivation. Nor can it be explained as the upwelling of an irrational mystical urge, such as would need no rational motive. Faith presupposes knowledge, because it needs a mental complex, person or thing, to be occupied about. Therefore, the whole modern idea of preaching Jesus, but preaching Him without a creed, is not only theologically, not merely Scripturally, but psychologically impossible in itself. In fact knowledge is so interwoven with faith that the question arises, whether it be sufficient to call it a prerequisite, and not rather an ingredient of faith.

The very names by means of which Jesus would have to be presented to people are nuclei of creed and doctrine. If it were possible to eliminate this, the message would turn to pure magic, but even the magic requires some name-sound and cannot be wholly described as preaching without a creed. The vogue which this programme has acquired is to some extent due to the unfortunate, and altogether undeserved, flavour clinging to the term 'creed', as though this necessarily meant a minutely worked out theological structure of belief. That is not meant, but belief there must be before faith can begin to function, and belief includes knowledge [*Matt.* 8.10; *Lk.* 7.9]. This knowledge may have been gathered gradually, almost imperceptibly, from countless impressions received during a briefer or longer period of time, but epistemologically it does not differ from any other kind of mental act however acquired. To be sure, mere knowledge is not equivalent to full-orbed faith, it must develop into trust, before it is entitled to that name.

How closely faith is connected with the cognition-complex of the soul can best be gathered from our Lord's statements on the causes of unbelief. So far as these are not due to mere absence of informative knowledge, they can be reduced to the one case of 'being offended'. The Greek for this term is *skandalizesthai*. The *skandalon* is the chip of wood that holds the bait in a trap and causes the animal to be caught. Metaphorically speaking and with reference to faith, the offence is a temptation to unbelief. The peculiar feature of this representation is that Jesus has placed the 'offence' in Himself. There is something in His Person and claims and activity and ideals that becomes to his opponents an occasion for unbelief. The reason for this is that in all these respects He is diametrically opposite to what the Jews expected their Messiah to be and to do. They had their own preconceptions and ideal preferences about the Messiahship, and about the coming era of which this formed the centre. But these preconceptions and preferences were by no means so detached from their internal state of mind as to be innocent. The offence, therefore, was in the last analysis engendered by their nature, and thus the unbelief to which it gave rise was an outcome of their corrupt state of heart.

The psychology of the action of faith receives light from the verbal constructions used for describing it. The verb is *pisteuein*, the adjective is *pistos*, but in the Gospels this occurs only in the negative form of *apistos*: the positive has the passive sense of 'believed in', 'reliable'. *Oligopistos* means 'short of faith', not in the sense of lacking volume, but rather in the sense of not reaching far enough to attain the end. Of the prepositions used, *en* seems to be the least informing, since neither to the modern mind, nor to the Greek mind, either classical or Hellenistic, is it an indigenous, intelligible construction. Perhaps it derived from the Hebrew preposition *beth*, which had its own idiomatic local associations. The preposition *eis* is construed, of course, with the accusative; its meaning may be that of mental projection, 'towards' the object of faith, or that of local entrance into the object, 'to exercise faith into Christ'. The latter would be a more Johannine and Pauline than a Synoptical idea. *Epi* has two constructions, one with the dative, and one with the accusative; the former expresses the idea of believing 'on the ground of' (a connotation given by some also to *en*), the faith rising, as it were, out of the evidence; the latter resembles closely the construction with *eis*, except that the projection of the believing mind upwards towards the object of faith enters as a peculiar shade of colouring.

'FAITH' AS USED IN JOHN

The Johannine teaching on faith has certain sharply outstanding peculiarities which may here be briefly enumerated:

(a) Faith is throughout related to Jesus, co-ordinately with God, on account of the idea of Jesus' being the duplicate of God. In the Synoptics Jesus is not mentioned as the personal object of faith, except in Matt. 18.6; Mk. 9.42 (with somewhat uncertain text). The wrong inference that Jesus did not consider Himself the object of faith, or as a factor in salvation, has been drawn from this, but the inadequacy of the argument is clear from the fact that with reference to God also there is only one such explicit passage [Mk. 11.22], so that in point of statistics there is no difference. In John 14.1 (where the imperative rendering is to be preferred) the implication seems to be that the disciples, who through the tragic experience of the passion might be in danger of losing their faith in Christ, should, as it were, recover it through vigorously asserted faith in the Father. It is of course psychologically inconceivable that those who had been healed by Jesus should not have developed an attitude of trust towards Him.

(b) Faith is more a continuous, habitual relation between Jesus and the believer; in the Synoptics it appears mostly as a momentary act in those upon whom the miracles are wrought. Even here, however, attention is called by Jesus to the fact that what faith has done once it will do again; 'thy faith hath made thee whole'. In the storm Jesus remonstrates with the disciples for not having considered His presence with them a guarantee of continuous safety. Also the figure of 'shortness' of faith points to the nascent idea of faith as a habit, afterwards so fully worked out by Paul. Thus faith begins to cover the entire religious life as its indispensable basis.

(c) Faith, as by anticipation, lays hold of the glorified Jesus; it works in the present with the same effects as it will work in the future: Jesus *is* the bread of life; the cleansing of sins is given *now*.

(d) There is a most intimate association between faith and knowledge. This does not rest on any philosophical, particularly Gnostic, concept of the process of salvation. The knowledge is a practical knowledge of acquaintance and intimacy, more of the Shemitic than of the Hellenic type, as it is said of the sheep that they are known by the shepherd and know the shepherd's voice. Besides believing and knowing there is still a third term descriptive of close and intense religious occupation, namely, 'to behold', literally 'to gaze upon' (*theorein*). Interesting is the application of these several terms to the several subjects and objects of the act. In regard to Jesus' relation to the Father the verb 'to believe' is never found, the relation evidently being too direct and intimate for that. The Father 'knows the Son' and the Son 'knows the Father'. Of the relation between Christ and the disciple, all three – 'to believe', 'to know', and of the Holy Spirit, 'to behold' and 'to know' Him, not to believe on Him, are found.

(e) The doctrine as to the connection between unbelief and its source is more clearly set forth in John than in the Synoptics. Unbelief is shown to spring from a radically wrong attitude of man's nature towards God, for which even the name 'hatred' is not shunned. Unbelief is called 'the sin', not, as is sometimes imagined, as if under the regime of the gospel all other sins were discounted, and a totally new record begun in which only faith and unbelief would henceforth be decisive factors. Underlying the phrase 'the sin' is rather the recognition that in unbelief the deep inherent character of sin as a turning against God reveals itself.

(*f*) As to the sources of faith, these are described in four ways:
(*a*) faith is the result of a course of conduct; those believe who do the truth and walk in the truth, etc.;
(*b*) going farther back, it is the result of right spiritual perception wrought by God; they believe who have learned it or heard it from the Father;
(*c*) going still farther back, faith is the outcome of a state of being, described as being in the truth;
(*d*) finally, going back to the ultimate source: believers are those, who on the principle of sovereign election, have been given by the Father to the Son, or drawn to the Son by the Father.

These various terms are so strong as to have given rise to the charge that the Gospel is infected with Gnosticism, a heresy which distinguished between those who are not capable of salvation, on the one hand, and such as are not in need of salvation, on the other hand. But the Gospel has behind it a full and strong recognition of the Old Testament, from which an antecedent attitude towards the truth as determinative of the subsequent attitude towards Jesus can be explained.

DIVINE SUPREMACY IN THE SPHERE OF RIGHTEOUSNESS
The second line along which the supremacy of God in the Kingdom is worked out by Jesus is that of righteousness. Before all else it is necessary to fix sharply the Biblical concept of 'righteousness', common to both the Old Testament and the New Testament. Now, notwithstanding all our acquaintance with the Bible, we are hindered from correctly apprehending this by the common-parlance use the word has developed on the basis of legal tradition. Right is, according to the latter, what is equitable. The concept is framed on the mutual delimitation of rights between man and man; God does not enter into it, except indirectly as the guardian or champion for what ought to prevail inter-humanly.

At bottom this conception is, of course, a pagan one. According to Scripture 'righteousness' is that which agrees with and pleases God, and exists for His sake, and can only be adjudicated by Him. He is first of all, and above all, the interested Person. Without reckoning with Him in the three relations named there can be no actual existence of righteousness. There might be good or evil intrinsically considered as to results, but to speak of righteousness would under such circumstances have no meaning. And this God-referred righteousness is by no means a small department of religious life. Ethically considered, it covers all converse with God; to be righteous acquires the meaning of possessing and practising the true religion: righteousness is equivalent to piety. Our Lord's teaching on righteousness partakes throughout of this general character. Righteousness is from God as its source, it exists for God as its end, and it is subject to God as the ultimate Justifier.

This Scriptural idea of righteousness, however, stands in the closest connection with the Scriptural idea of the Kingdom of God. In the American political system there is no such intimate union between kingship and judgeship; the law-giving and executive functions are assigned to separate organs in the body politic. To the ancient (Shemitic) consciousness the King is *ipso facto* the Lawgiver and the Executor of the law [cp. *Psa.* 72; *Isa.* 33.22]. Far more also than we can imagine, the King is the centre of political life, for whose sake the state and the subjects exist. Modern individualism was not known. If we subtract from the words of Louis XIV their proud flippancy, the statement, '*L'état, c'est moi*' would most nearly express the idea. This is not from our point of view good politics. But in religion it is not only allowable; it is the only principle on which a truly religious relation can be built, and revelation has made use of this monarchial and King-centred state of affairs to build up its doctrine of the Kingdom of God in the sphere of righteousness.

We must now trace the presence of these ideas in the teaching of our Lord on the subject. This will be most conveniently done by defining the close identity and association affirmed by Him as between the Kingdom and righteousness, because in this way the theocentric character of His idea of righteousness will soon appear to be naught else in substance than His theocentric conception of the Kingdom.

This is observable along three lines:

(a) first the Kingdom (Kingship) of God is identified with righteousness. They are concurrent, or mutually in-existent, because the doing of righteousness amounts to the practical recognition and furtherance of His Kingship. The best example of this is in the sequence of the two petitions of our Lord's prayer: 'thy Kingdom come' and 'thy will be done'. Here in all probability both 'coming' and 'being done' are, in harmony with Western exegesis, to be understood eschatologically.

(b) In the second place, righteousness appears as a consequent to the Kingdom, one of the many gifts which the new reign of God freely bestows upon its members. The Old Testament had already held this new kind of righteousness in prospect. Jeremiah promises that Jehovah will write His Law upon the hearts of the people, and Ezekiel predicts that Jehovah will make them to walk in His statutes. That according to Jesus' conception the participants of this righteousness sustain a receptive attitude towards it appears from Matt. 5.6. It would, of course, be very easy, but none the less anachronistic, to import into this line of teaching all the Pauline ideas, according to which righteousness is the one great central gift in the life of the Christian, that on which everything else is based. As a matter of fact the parable of the Pharisee and the publican invites one to do this: the publican went home justified and not the Pharisee, because the former professed n ot to possess any subjective righteousness, and the Pharisee was rejected because of his consciousness of possessing much. As a matter of fact the principle of the Pauline doctrine and that of Jesus thus appear identical. The difference lies in two things: Jesus treats the entire gift as an undifferentiated unit, whereas Paul has learned to distinguish between the objective righteousness which becomes ours through imputation and the subjective kind which becomes ours through the inworking of the Spirit. But at bottom both are one as the gift of God, and according to Paul the latter comes as the fruit of the former. The second thing in which a difference is perceptible concerns the terminology. What Paul calls justification, Jesus calls entrance into the Kingdom or becoming a son of God. Righteousness is with Paul largely objective status, with Jesus largely subjective condition.

(c) In the third place the sequence between the two is reversed, righteousness coming first and the Kingdom as the ensuing reward. This is, of course, to be understood of the eschatological Kingdom, which is in such sayings promised as a recompense for the practice of righteousness in this life. It comes in appearance nearest to the Judaistic position, and has been consequently criticized not seldom as a remnant in our Lord's religion of the self-righteousness of Judaism. One need not wonder at this, when observing that in Matt. 6.5, 6, a reward is set even upon the proper observance of prayer. It has been attempted to remove words of this kind as non-cognate to the general religious mentality of Jesus. This affords no relief because the idea appears interwoven with so much of our Lord's practical exhortations, all labour in the Kingdom being represented as a labour behind the plough and in the vineyard, so that the matter, considered as a flaw, would vitiate a large strand in Jesus' teaching.

In order to reach clearness on the question we must first disabuse ourselves of the modern idea, as though every thought of reward in ethical relations were unworthy of the sacredness of ethics. This is an opinion ultimately based on the philosophy of the autonomy or deification of ethics, and behind that on the principle of unmotived free will. Man is not such an autonomous being that he can afford to scorn a reward from God, provided the idea of meritoriousness be kept absent from it. If that were man's normal ethical attitude, then man would be in ethics like unto God. Of Jesus Himself it is said that the idea of reward attracted and sustained Him and determined the result of His work [*Heb.* 12.2].

An important further consideration is, whether the reward promised is in principle of a lower, less noble nature than the conduct on which it is suspended. This is actually the case in Judaism, but the contrary is true of Jesus' teaching. Compare the conjoined clauses in the beatitudes. It is also of importance to note, whether the attraction of the peripheral reward operates to the exclusion of the supreme reward in the possession and enjoyment of God Himself, in which respect again the beatitudes may be consulted. Judaism put the doctrine of reward on a commercial (and therefore self-righteous) basis. It was a matter of man paying so much and getting back a proper equivalent. This principle of *quid pro quo* is destructive of the religious relation. Moreover it was applied equally to both rewards and retributive punishment. Of this there is no trace in the teaching of Jesus. He treats the idea of punishment of sin as something inseparable from the ethical nature of God, but does not affirm anywhere that God, by force of the same principle, must reward the practice of what is good. On the contrary, the servants who have done all that was required of them are still unprofitable servants (which is a different thing from saying that they are useless servants). The thought is that having served God to the full they are not inherently entitled to any reward; and, because the reward is not of necessity, neither can it be of exact equivalence: those that have worked a short time receive the same wages as those who have laboured long. On the basis of economic equity this would be disastrous, but on the basis of righteousness sovereignly applied it serves to bring out that important principle.

OUR LORD'S CRITIQUE OF JEWISH ETHICS

This is the place to insert a brief survey of our Lord's critique of Jewish ethics, which occupies considerable space in the Gospels. The Jewish ethic suffered from two fundamental defects: its tendency towards Deism and its infection by self-centredness. From these two main defects resulted the following serious faults:

(*a*) Externalism: the law was not obeyed with the idea of the supervision of God in mind; the service of the Law had taken the place of the service of the living God [*Gal.* 2.18–21].

(*b*) The breaking up of the Law from a well-organized state to a state of utter disorganization; great principles were not distinguished and in the light of these the minor questions judged; on the contrary, every single commandment was reduced to a level of casuistry. Over against this Jesus knows of the greater and the lesser commandment, of the things that ought to be done, and other things not to be left undone.

(c) From the same source sprang the negativism that so largely characterized the Judaistic law-practice. The main concern was not to attain the positive end of the Law, but rather to avoid negatively the disasters feared from non-observance; the system degenerated into a system of avoidance.

(d) The self-righteousness so severely castigated by Jesus grew on the same root, for where God is not recognized as the Inlooker into the moral process, it becomes relatively easy to believe that the essence of the Law has been kept, whereas in reality only the surface, that which falls under man's observation, has been skimmed.

(e) Last of all, from this delusive sense of performance springs the fault of hypocrisy, meaning by this here the objective kind of hypocrisy, discord between the heart and the outward life, which can, however, exist without conscious knowledge of the same on the hypocrite's part, which latter we call subjective hypocrisy.

REPENTANCE

Connected with our Lord's teaching on the righteousness of the Kingdom is His teaching on repentance. Just as His teaching on faith is the correlative of the power-aspect of the Kingdom, so that on repentance corresponds to the righteousness-aspect of the same. Hence the preaching began with the demand jointly for repentance and faith in the gospel. In this there is a perpetual witness to the constancy of the assumption of sin as the background of the offer of the gospel. The necessity for repentance as essential to participation in the Kingdom is not, however, of a meritorious significance. The man cast out from the feast on account of not having a wedding-garment, was excluded because his condition was not appropriate to the feast, not because he had not deserved the feast, for all the guests were taken from the highways and hedges [Matt. 22.11–13].

The state of mind described by what is theologically called repentance can be best ascertained from the Greek words found for it in the Gospels, although the possibility must be always reckoned with that the terms may have become stereotyped terms not any longer connoting consciously the original associations. These terms are the following:

(a) *metamelesthai* (impersonal) literally 'after-sorrow'. It denotes the emotional element of regret for a past act or course of action. Because of its emotional associations it has sometimes been thought to describe repentance as a superficial experience. This is incorrect; the experience can be superficial, but likewise can be profound, and when profound, can be taken *in bonum sensum*, as what Paul calls the 'sorrow after God', or *in malum sensum*, as when Judas is said to have 'repented himself'. In the bad sense it describes what is named 'remorse', literally the 'backbiting' of the soul upon herself; the noun to this is *metameleia*.

(b) *metanoein*, a change or rather reversal of *nous*; *nous* does not narrowly signify the mind, but the entire conscious life, will and affections included. In this word the preposition *meta* does not have, as in the preceding term, the temporal sense of 'after', but the metaphorical sense of 'round about'. The noun corresponding to this is *metanoia*. The terms are always used of saving repentance, that which is elsewhere called 'a repentance not to be repented of' [2 *Cor.* 7.10].

(c) *epistrephesthai*, 'to turn one's self about'. This describes not, as the two preceding terms do, an inner state of mind reflecting upon its past, or an inner change of mind turned into its opposite, but the turning of the will towards a new, opposite goal. It corresponds, strictly speaking, rather to 'conversion' than to repentance.

The specific character of Biblical repentance, as distinguished from experiences so named in paganism, lies first of all in the comprehensiveness of the turn of mind. It is 'after-sorrow', or reversal of consciousness, or redirection of the life upon an opposite goal, with regard to the whole content of the ethico-religious life. To the non-Christian mind repentance took place from one act to another, or from one course of action to another only. The cause of this difference is found in the lack on the pagan side of a comprehensive conception of sin. Where 'sin' in its comprehensive sense is not known, there real repentance cannot develop, even as a conception.

Secondly, and as a necessary result of the foregoing, the demand for repentance is addressed to all men. The disciples are not exempt from the clause 'if ye being evil' at a late point of their association with Jesus [*Lk.* 11.13]. Repentance must be preached among all nations [*Lk.* 24.47]. That Jesus sometimes seems to establish a difference between some to whom He feels called to preach and the greater number of those who need no repentance, and calls the latter in such a connection 'righteous' is to be understood from the standpoint of the estimate such people are apt self-righteously to put upon themselves [*Mk.* 2.17].

Even more specific than this is the God-centred character of the experience. Its point of departure, that from which the repentance takes place, is always something considered in its relation to God. The idea is religious, not world-ethical. The technical term for this state rendering repentance necessary is 'being lost', i.e. missing in one's normal relation to God. Those in need of repentance are like lost sheep, lost coins; the sin of the prodigal consists at bottom in this, that he has left the father's house. In the same way God is the central object on whom the repenting consciousness is focused; it is the offence offered to Him that stands in the foreground of the sorrow experienced.

Finally, the new direction of life which the repentance brings about finds its explanation in the absolute and exclusive subjection of the whole life with all its desires and purposes to God. In this connection there are found in the Gospels many apparently extreme sayings in regard to giving up all human interests and ties even of the most sacred nature, nay, of life itself, for the sake of a single-minded devotion to God. Such statements are not to be understood purely paradoxically. However, they are qualified in their range of obligation by Jesus Himself. Our Lord says: If thy hand, thy foot, thine eye offend thee, cut it off, pluck it out; it is only when these natural things become occasions for failing in the whole-souled devotion to God, that their absolute renouncement is demanded. From this, however, it follows that an abstract rule of universal surrender of such things cannot be laid down. It is the inner pseudo-religious attachment to something outside of God that must be given up in the interest of the true religion. And, on the other side, the facile excuse should not be too frequently urged that outward surrender is in no case needed, for in some situations this external renunciation may be the very thing needed to bring about the internal detachment of the soul which the Kingdom requires from all other things.

DIVINE SUPREMACY IN THE SPHERE OF BLESSEDNESS

In the third place, the Kingdom of God is the supremacy of God in the sphere of blessedness. The connection between God's kingship and blessedness is partly of a generally eschatological character, partly of a specific kingdom-eschatological character. It is inherent in the eschatological conception of things that the final, perfect order of things shall also be the order of things productive of the supreme state of happiness. From the point of view of the kingship it ought to be remembered that in the Orient the royal office had attached to it the regular belief and expectation that it existed for conferring blessedness upon the subjects of the realm. The thought of blessedness involved can be indiscriminately derived from the Fatherhood and from the Kingship of God; even the entire Kingdom can in this way be explained as a gift to the disciples from the divine Fatherhood (*Lk.* 12.32]. On account of the blessedness involved the Kingdom appears under the figure of a treasure or a precious pearl, in each case it being explicitly stated that the finder sold all he had in order to possess himself of the coveted object, which means, of course, that it was more precious than all other values combined.

The blessedness conferred by and with the Kingdom can be classified under the heads of a negative and of a positive blessedness. There are three principal ideas, that of salvation, that of sonship, and that of life. The idea of salvation is from the nature of the case both negative and positive, with the emphasis oscillating from the one side to the other. The idea of life is positive, and so is that of sonship.

KINGDOM AND CHURCH

The one subject remaining concerns the organization of the Kingdom into the form of the Church. The one clear case of development in our Lord's objective teaching on the Kingdom subject is to be found here. The two points on which the Caesarea-Philippi epoch shows an addition and an advancement are the providing of the Kingdom with an outward organism, and the endowment of it with a new dynamic of the Spirit. At all times there have been those who depreciated the Church in favour of the Kingdom. The reasons for such an attitude are varying. Sometimes 'anti-sectarianism' comes into play, and the ignoble sound of the word alone works havoc with verities of the gospel teaching. At other times it is pre-millenarianism, which desires to put off the Kingdom state to the ultimate temporal dispensation and consequently feels interested in keeping Kingdom and Church apart. On the other side undue identification of the Kingdom with the Church in every respect indiscriminately is insisted upon, as in Romanism where the Church visible draws under its power and jurisdiction every phase of life, such as science, art and others.

Sometimes theologians endeavour to make a distinction in this matter between the so-called visible and invisible Church, identifying the latter with the Kingdom, whilst excluding the former from it. And sometimes the exclusion goes farther, when to the Church only the character of a means to an end is conceded, whilst the Kingdom is regarded as the *summum bonum* and end in itself. The above-mentioned motive of anti-sectarianism is apt to ally itself with such an attitude, for disrespect is more easily entertained and cultivated where means rather than ends are in view.

A close study of the pericope Matt. 16.18–20 will show what value, if any, is to be allowed to these varying positions. We notice, first, that the Church and the Kingdom of God do not appear here as separate institutions. The figure of which our Lord avails Himself for speaking of the Church and speaking of the Kingdom closely unites the two. On Peter, confessing His Christhood and divine Sonship, He promises to build up the Church in the near future. This is the structure in building, vs. 18. In vs. 19, however, still using the same figure of building, He promises to Peter the keys of administration in this structure when completed. Undoubtedly then, the Church and the Kingdom are in principle one, and all such distinctions as are above enumerated break down before the simple logic of this unavoidable exegesis. So much is certain at least, that the Church is included in the Kingdom, and that it were foolish to seek to escape the reproach of the former in order to gain the imaginary distinction of the latter. And this does not merely render part of the Church Kingdom-territory, for example, the invisible Church; it will have to be extended likewise to the visible Church, for only with regard to that can 'keys' of administration and the functions of binding and loosing be spoken of.

It will be noticed that Jesus speaks of 'His Church'. The idea is not that hitherto no Church has existed. 'His Church' should be understood in contrast to the Old Testament Church organization which had now come to an end to make place for the Messiah's Church. This is the inner connection between the Church doctrine enunciated and the prediction of His suffering and death interwoven with it. In His rejection the Old Testament Church abrogated itself. The future is spoken of, because the new dynamic could not enter into the Church until after His exaltation.

This dynamic seems to be referred to in the statement about 'the gates of Hades' in vs. 18, at least on one interpretation of this figure, according to which Hades is depicted as a citadel from which a host of warriors stream forth, the corresponding picture to be supplied being that of the citadel of the Kingdom from which a power will issue overcoming the power of death. The underlying idea would be that Jesus through His resurrection will so fill His Church with unconquerable life, infusing it into her by the Spirit, that death will be wholly conquered by the Church [Rev. 1.18]. The other exegesis attaches itself to a proverbial use made of 'the gates of Hades' to describe figuratively the strongest structure conceivable, since from these gates no one has ever succeeded in escaping. Applied to the Church the figure would then mean that she is the strongest structure in existence, and would be simply a pendant to the characterization of Peter as a rock. The former view is to be preferred in a context where so many novel and weighty ideas emerge.

Besides this description of the Church in the figure of a building there are other sayings of our Lord which are sometimes quoted to establish a close connection between the Church and the Kingdom. Jesus speaks in several statements, belonging to this closing period of His life on earth, not only of a coming of Himself, but also of a very near coming of the Kingdom. The language is such that it could be readily applied, both as to nearness and forcibleness, to the eschatological coming of the Kingdom. The implication would then have to be that He did not anticipate a protracted existence of the Church in this world, but looked forward both to His own coming and to that of the consummate Kingdom as shortly to supervene. This, of course, would carry with it His fallibility in regard to this central topic of the eschatological hope. On the other hand, there are several sayings, especially in the closing discourses of the Fourth Gospel, in which a coming of Himself in invisible form, intended for the disciples, is referred to in semi-eschatological language. If there could be such an anticipated coming of Himself, distinct evidently from the eschatological coming, which is by no means eliminated from the Fourth Gospel teaching, then there can be no objection on principle to applying this same idea to the Kingdom-Church.

In conclusion we should observe that the Matthew pericope, as little as any other New Testament passage, gives countenance to the idea of the Church as a mere instrument of propaganda or an institute of missions, or whatever goal to which she may stand in a vital relation. The Church is all these things in part, but no one can truthfully say that these objectives are exhaustive of the purpose of existence of the Church. The conception of a thing as a mere instrument for endlessly reiterated self-reproduction is a hopeless conception in itself, for why should one exist to make others or an organism of others in perpetuation or extension of what exists at the present time, if this process is to have no fixed end? This whole view is a virtual denial of the eschatological setting of Biblical religion. The Church was born in and stands in the sign of consummation and rest as well as of motion. She consists not of mere doing, but likewise of fruition, and this fruition pertains not exclusively to the future; it is the most blessed part of the present life. And the best proof for the Church as an end in itself lies in the inclusion of the Church in the eschatological world, for that world is not the world of things aimed at, but of things attained unto.

INDEX
SUBJECTS & NAMES

O*

teaching of, use of metaphor in, 351
teaching of, use of parables in, 351, 352
teaching of, use of simile in, 351
JOHN THE BAPTIST,
appurtenance of to O.T. dispensation, 314–316
Jesus' teaching concerning, 312–314
messianic expectations of, 313–314
post-baptismal testimony of to Jesus, 322ff.
relation of to Jesus' work, 312ff.
revelation connected with, 331–332
testimony of to Jesus as the Messiah, 315
JOSEPHUS,
comment of on character of Mosaic constitution, 126
use of term 'theocracy' by, 125
Judaism, critical theory concerning origin of, 210
Judaizers, error of in interpreting patriarchal period on basis of the Mosaic, 78, 79
Julicher, on allegorical elements in parables, 353

KEIL,
view of concerning sacrifices, 163, 164
on meaning of *nabhi*, 191
Kernel-revelation, theory of, 214, 215
Kingdom-producing movement in Israel, connection of prophetism with, 186, 187
KINGDOM OF GOD,
and Kingdom of Heaven, 376
anti-eschatological views of not Biblical, 378–380
as reward, difference between Jesus' teaching and that of Judaism, 394, 395
association with righteousness in Jesus' teaching, 303ff.
cannot pass gradually from historical to eschatological stage, 380, 381
distinction between present and future aspects of, in Jesus' teaching, 383, 384
element of blessedness in conception of, 398, 399
element of power in conception of, 386ff.

element of righteousness in conception of, 392ff.
essence of in Jesus' teaching, 385ff.
evidence for historical and eschatological stages of in Jesus' teaching, 381, 382
faith as correlate of power in connection with, 387, 388
how distinguished from sovereignty of God, 385, 386
Jesus' teaching on, 372ff.
naturalizing misinterpretation of present-spiritual aspect of, 384, 385
objection to certain post-millennial views of, 380
objection to pre-millenarian view of, 380
objections to ultra – eschatologists' view of Jesus' teaching on, 378, 379
occurrence of phrase in the Gospels, 372
O.T. antecedents of conception, 372–374
present and eschatological stages of in Jesus' teaching, 378
pre-millenarian view of, 380
probable origin of phrase, 372
reality and character of present aspect of, in Jesus' teaching, 381ff.
relation between Jesus' and Paul's teaching concerning, 393, 394
relation of to Church, 399ff.
service rendered by pre-millenarian view of, 380
spirituality of present aspect of, in Jesus' teaching, 381ff.
theocentric view of in Jesus' teaching, 385, 386
ultra-eschatologists' view of Jesus' teaching on, 378–380
KINGDOM OF HEAVEN,
opinion of B. Weiss concerning, 376
probable explanation of phrase, 377, 378
significance of term, 376ff.
view of Schurer concerning phrase, 377
KOENIG,
denial that the Spirit is source of revelation in O.T., 219

Smend, statement concerning
prophets' attitude to sacrificial
cult, 210
SMITH, ROBERTSON,
on etymology of 'Jehovah', 117
on meaning of 'Jehovah', 118
on origin of Passover, 121
SOCIAL SIN OF ISRAEL,
condemned by the prophets, 273ff.
not condemned on basically
humanitarian grounds, 274–276
Sons of God, meaning of in Gen. 6;
48, 49
Soul-matter, animistic theory of as
explanation of laws of uncleanness, 178–180
Sovereignty of God, how distinguished from Kingdom of God,
385, 386
Space, God's relation to, 243
SPENCER,
on ceremonial law, 143
on religious condition of Israel in
Egypt, 111
SPIRIT,
descent of the on Jesus following
baptism by John, 320ff.
distinctive character of Jesus'
endowment with the, 321, 322
Spiritual law in the natural world,
355
STADE,
on etymology of 'Jehovah', 117
on historicity of patriarchs, 66, 67
on origin of monotheism, 209
Supernaturalism in mode of fulfilment
of promises to the patriarchs, 80
81
Symbols, how related to types, 144,
145

TABERNACLE,
symbolical and typical significance
of, 148ff.
typical significance of, 154, 155
Teaching of Jesus, see Jesus, teaching of
Temptability of Jesus, 339ff.
TEMPTATION,
principle of, symbolized by serpent
in Eden, 33
of Jesus, 333
See also Probation of Jesus
of Jesus, analogy of to our temptations, 333, 334

of Jesus, strategic eagerness of
Satan shown in, 342
of Jesus, strategy of Satan in the
third, 339
Ten Commandments, see Decalogue
Tent, dwelling of God, 148, 149
TERTULLIAN, 26
opinion of concerning visionary
state, 225
Testimony from heaven of Jesus'
Sonship and Messiahship, 320, 321
Theocracy, meaning of, 124–126
THEOLOGY,
based on revelation, 3
definition of, 3
division into four departments, 4
exegetical, 4ff.
exegetical, divisions of, 4, 5
natural, best system of not produced
in heathenism but under Christian
influences, 20
not 'Science of Religion', 3
Theophanies, localized within land of
promise, 70
Theophany, altars built at places of, 70
Time, relation of God to, 243, 244
Tongues, division of at Babel, 59, 60
Totemism, theory of as explanation of
laws of uncleanness, 174, 175
Tower of Babel, purpose of, 59
TREE OF KNOWLEDGE OF GOOD
AND EVIL,
interpretation of as stressing choice,
30
mythical interpretation of, 29
objections to mythical interpretation of, 30
Satans' false interpretation of, 32, 33
significance of, 27, 28
traditional interpretation of, 30, 31
why forbidden to Adam and Eve, 32
TREE OF LIFE,
meaning of, 27, 28
to be enjoyed by man after success-
fully undergoing probation, 28
Tribal particularism in worship of
gods, not monotheism but
monolatry, 62
Truth, special meaning of in certain
Gospel passages, 356, 357
TYPES,
historical, in O. T., 147, 148
how related to symbols, 144ff.
Typology, system of, 144ff.

INDEX
SCRIPTURE REFERENCES